# Capital Punishment
## in the
## United States

# CAPITAL PUNISHMENT IN THE UNITED STATES

*A Documentary History*

Edited by BRYAN VILA
and CYNTHIA MORRIS

Primary Documents in American History and Contemporary Issues

GREENWOOD PRESS
Westport, Connecticut • London

**Library of Congress Cataloging-in-Publication Data**

Capital punishment in the United States : a documentary history /
  edited by Bryan Vila and Cynthia Morris.
      p.      cm.—(Primary documents in American history and
  contemporary issues, ISSN 1069–5605)
    Includes bibliographical references and index.
    ISBN 0–313–29942–0 (alk. paper)
      1. Capital punishment—United States—History—Sources.
  2. Capital punishment—Law and legislation—United States—History.
  3. Capital punishment—Moral and ethical aspects—United States.
  4. United States—Politics and government.   5. United States—
  History—Sources.   I. Vila, Bryan, 1947–  .  II. Morris, Cynthia,
  1961–  .  III. Series: Primary documents in American history and
  contemporary issues series.
  HV8699.U5C3   1997
  364.66'0973—DC21        96–51137

British Library Cataloguing in Publication Data is available.

Library of Congress Catalog Card Number: 96–51137
ISBN: 0–313–29942–0
ISSN: 1069–5605

First published in 1997

Greenwood Press, 88 Post Road West, Westport, CT 06881
An imprint of Greenwood Publishing Group, Inc.

Printed in the United States of America

∞™

The paper used in this book complies with the
Permanent Paper Standard issued by the National
Information Standards Organization (Z39.48–1984).

10 9 8 7 6 5 4 3 2 1

## Copyright Acknowledgments

The editors and publisher gratefully acknowledge permission to reprint material from the following sources:

DOCUMENT 28: "Gas Kills Convict Almost Instantly." *Associated Press*, February 8, 1924. Reprinted by permission.

DOCUMENT 30: Eugene Lyons, *The Life and Death of Sacco and Vanzetti* (New York: International Publishers, 1927 [New York: Da Capo Press, 1970]): 169–171. Reprinted by permission of International Publishers.

DOCUMENT 31: Lewis E. Lawes, *Life and Death in Sing Sing* (Garden City, N.Y.: Doubleday, Doran, 1928), 155–157. Reprinted by permission.

DOCUMENTS 33, 38, 40, 49, 61, 75, 84, 94, 107: George Gallup, *The Gallup Poll: Public Opinion 1935–71*, Vol. One, 45, 85; Vol. Two, 1117, 1187–1188, 1518; Vol. Three, 2016. Random House, 1972. *Gallup Opinion Index* 1976, 24; *Gallup Opinion Index* 1985, 4–5; *The Gallup Poll: Public Opinion 1988*, 250–251; *The Gallup Poll: Public Opinion 1991*, 128, 129–130; *The Gallup Poll: Public Opinion 1994*, 148, 149. Copyright © 1937, 1938, 1953, 1957, 1966, 1976, 1985, 1988, 1991, and 1994 by Scholarly Resources Inc. Reprinted by permission of Scholarly Resources Inc.

DOCUMENTS 39, 43, 55, 56, 68: "Eisenhower Is Denounced to 5,000 in Union Sq. Rally," June 20, 1953 (excerpt); "Six Justices Agree: President Says Couple Increased 'Chances of Atomic War,'" by Luther A. Huston, June 20, 1953 (excerpt); "Caryl Chessman Executed; Denies His Guilt to the End," by Lawrence E. Davies, May 3, 1960 (excerpt); "States on Move: Half of Legislatures Considering Bills on Capital Offenses," by Jerry M. Flint, March 11, 1973 (excerpt); and "Death Penalty Opponents Embittered by Execution," May 26, 1979; "President Asks Law to Restore Death Penalty: Gives Drug Plan," by Warren Weaver, Jr., March 11, 1973 (excerpt). Copyright © 1953, 1960, 1973, 1979 by The New York Times Company. Reprinted by permission.

DOCUMENT 42: Excerpts from *The Death Penalty*, by Thorsten Sellin. Copyright © 1959 by The American Law Institute. Reprinted with permission.

DOCUMENT 46: Gerald H. Gottlieb, "Testing the Death Penalty," *Southern California Law Review* 34 (1961): 268–281. Reprinted with the permission of the *Southern California Law Review*.

DOCUMENT 48: "ACLU's New Stand on the Death Penalty." *Civil Liberties* 227 (June 1965). From the Records of the American Civil Liberties Union, Seeley G. Mudd Manuscript Library, Department of Rare Books and Special Collections, Princeton University Library. Reprinted courtesy of the American Civil Liberties Union.

DOCUMENT 51: "Documents for Proceeding in Federal Habeas Corpus in a Capital Case in Which Execution Is Imminent." New York: National Association for the Advancement of Colored People (NAACP) Legal Defense and Educational Fund, Inc., 1971. Excerpts reprinted by permission of Anthony G. Amsterdam.

DOCUMENT 57: Marvin E. Wolfgang and Marc Riedel, "Race, Judicial Discretion, and the Death Penalty." *The Annals of the American Academy of Political and Social Science* 407 (May 1973): 129–130. Reprinted with permission.

DOCUMENT 58: Excerpts from *Capital Punishment: The Inevitability of Caprice and Mistake*, Second Edition, Augmented by Charles L. Black, Jr. Copyright © 1981, 1974 by W. W. Norton & Company, Inc. Copyright © 1977, 1978 by Charles L. Black, Jr. Reprinted by permission of W. W. Norton & Company, Inc.

DOCUMENT 59: Ernest van den Haag, *Punishing Criminals*. New York: Basic Books, 1975 [Lanham, Md.: University Press of America, 1991], 208–210, 212–213, 219–220, 221. Reprinted with permission from the author.

DOCUMENT 60: Isaac Ehrlich, ''The Deterrent Effect of Capital Punishment: A Question of Life and Death.'' *American Economic Review* LXV, no. 3 (June 1975): 398, 415–417. Reprinted by permission of the American Economic Association and the author.

DOCUMENT 65: Lawrence R. Klein, Brian Forst, and Victor Filatov, ''The Deterrent Effect of Capital Punishment: An Assessment of the Estimates.'' In Alfred Blumstein, Jacqueline Cohen, and Daniel Nagin, eds., *Deterrence and Incapacitation: Estimating the Effects of Criminal Sanctions on Crime Rates* (Washington, D.C.: National Research Council, National Academy of Sciences, 1978), pp. 357–359. Reprinted with permission from *Deterrence and Incapacitation*. Copyright 1978 by the National Academy of Sciences. Courtesy of the National Academy Press, Washington, D.C.

Isaac Ehrlich (in cooperation with Randall Mark). Excerpts from ''Fear of Deterrence: A Critical Evaluation of the 'Report of the Panel on Research on Deterrent and Incapacitative Effects.' '' *Journal of Legal Studies* VI, no. 2 (June 1977): 293–316. Copyright 1977 by the University of Chicago. Reprinted by permission of the *Journal of Law & Economics*, The University of Chicago, and the authors.

Alfred Blumstein, Jacqueline Cohen, and Daniel Nagin, eds., *Deterrence and Incapacitation: Estimating the Effects of Criminal Sanctions on Crime Rates* (Washington, D.C.: National Research Council, National Academy of Sciences, 1978), 61–62. Reprinted with permission from *Deterrence and Incapacitation*. Copyright 1978 by the National Academy of Sciences. Courtesy of the National Academy Press, Washington, D.C.

DOCUMENT 67: Walter Berns, *For Capital Punishment: Crime and the Morality of the Death Penalty*, 172–173. New York: Basic Books, 1979. Reprinted with permission of the author.

DOCUMENT 71: Fred Barbash, ''Justice Powell Urges End to Death Sentence Delaying.'' *Washington Post* (10 May 1983): A2. Copyright © 1983 The Washington Post. Reprinted with permission.

DOCUMENT 73: Ernest van den Haag and John P. Conrad, *The Death Penalty: A Debate* (New York: Plenum Press, 1983), 293–294, 296, 298–300. Reprinted by permission of Plenum Press and Ernest van den Haag.

DOCUMENT 74: David C. Baldus, Charles Pulaski, and George Woodworth, ''Comparative Review of Death Sentences: An Empirical Study of the Georgia Experience.''*Journal of Criminal Law and Criminology* 74 (1983): 706–710. Reprinted with permission of the authors.

DOCUMENT 77: Anthony Amsterdam, ''In Favorem Mortis: The Supreme Court and Capital Punishment,'' *Human Rights* 14, no. 1 (Winter 1987): 14–16, 57–58. Copyright © 1987 by the American Bar Association. Reprinted by permission from the American Bar Association and the author.

DOCUMENT 80: Victor L. Streib, *Death Penalty for Juveniles* (Bloomington: Indiana University Press, 1987): 71, 189. Reprinted by permission.

DOCUMENT 81: Excerpts from *Death Is Different: Studies in the Morality, Law, and Politics of Capital Punishment*, by Hugo Adam Bedau. Copyright © 1987 by Hugo Adam Bedau. Reprinted with the permission of Northeastern University Press, Boston.

DOCUMENT 82: Hugo Adam Bedau and Michael L. Radelet, ''Miscarriages of Justice in Potentially Capital Cases,'' *Stanford Law Review* 40, no. 21 (November 1987): 78–81, 83–86. Reprinted by permission of the authors.

DOCUMENT 83: Stephen J. Markman and Paul G. Cassell, ''Protecting the Innocent: A Response to the Bedau-Radelet Study,'' *Stanford Law Review* 41, no. 1 (November 1988): 121–

*To our parents,*
James and Patricia Vila and
Herbert and Anita Morris

# Contents

## PART II: THE ABOLITION MOVEMENT GAINS GROUND, 1800–1917

## PART IV: CAPITAL PUNISHMENT IN THE COURTS, 1960–1976

# Series Foreword

This series is designed to meet the research needs of students, scholars, and other interested readers by making available in one volume the key primary documents on a given historical event or contemporary issue. Documents include speeches, debates and letters, congressional testimony, Supreme Court and lower court decisions, government reports, biographical accounts, position papers, statutes, and news stories.

The purpose of the series is twofold: (1) to provide substantive and background material on an event or issue through the text of pivotal primary documents that shaped policy or law, raised controversy, or influenced the course of events; and (2) to trace the controversial aspects of the event or issue through documents that represent a variety of viewpoints. Documents for each volume have been selected by a recognized specialist in that subject with the advice of a board of other subject specialists, school librarians, and teachers.

To place the subject in historical perspective, the volume editor has prepared an introductory overview and a chronology of events. Documents are organized either chronologically or topically. The documents are full text or, if unusually long, have been excerpted by the volume editor. To facilitate understanding, each document is accompanied by an explanatory introduction. Suggestions for further reading follow the document or the chapter.

It is the hope of Greenwood Press that this series will enable students and other readers to use primary documents more easily in their research, to exercise critical thinking skills by examining the key documents in American history and public policy, and to critique the variety of viewpoints represented by this selection of documents.

# Preface

We initially undertook the somewhat daunting task of editing this book for two reasons: First, we saw a need for an objective volume that presented both sides of the highly charged capital punishment debate in a nonadversarial way; and second, we wanted to explore the historical and ecological framework in which this centuries-old debate has unfolded. Understanding how various and often seemingly unrelated social, economic, and political factors have impacted public attitudes, legislation, and judicial decisions pertaining to capital punishment adds an important level to our understanding of their significance. Viewing capital punishment within this larger framework also may be particularly useful to those interested in predicting—or helping to guide—the future of capital punishment in the United States.

Interestingly, as we researched and edited this volume, we each found our individual viewpoints on capital punishment repeatedly challenged, and ultimately refined. By actively seeking documents pertaining to both sides of the capital punishment controversy, we were obliged to give equal time and attention to views other than our own. This turned out to be an extremely valuable endeavor—in fact, sometimes it was the documents we disagreed with most that helped us to better define our own views. We hope this volume will help the reader do the same.

Reading the complete, first-hand accounts of various scholars, activists, judges, lawmakers, and others was especially interesting—and often much more powerful than second-hand accounts or brief excerpts ever could be. Although space limitations typically prevented us from reproducing more than a small portion from each of these fascinating documents, we urge anyone who is interested in exploring the issues surrounding capital punishment in greater depth to seek out and read these materials.

How did we select the documents included in this volume from among the thousands of things that have been written on capital punishment? We used several criteria. First, we wanted the documents to be representative historically, and therefore we attempted to include items from as many different time periods as possible, beginning with the first colonial settlements in the "New World." We also wanted to cover as many different issues as possible within the capital punishment debate, and therefore we selected what was either the first or what we believed was the "definitive" article pertaining to a particular issue, rather than including several articles that each covered the same issue. Sometimes, documents were selected because they and their authors were (or are) particularly noteworthy or influential. We included articles pertaining to several highly-publicized executions—such as Sacco and Vanzetti, the Rosenbergs, Caryl Chessman, Gary Gilmore, Robert Alton Harris—because such executions often were pivotal in the history of capital punishment or brought new issues in the debate to public attention. We also attempted to include as many of the major Supreme Court decisions pertaining to capital punishment as possible, as these decisions chronicle the changing status of capital punishment in the United States.

Of course, due to space limitations, this volume contains only a small fraction of the wide range of books, articles, cases, and other documents pertaining to the capital punishment controversy. It is our hope that those interested in further reading on this subject—or in obtaining the complete text of documents from which excerpts were taken—will make use of the select bibliography at the end of this book, which lists all the materials that we found useful in editing this volume.

As the many citations throughout the book and the bibliography indicate, our volume is indebted to the previous research and writings of many scholars and authors. We would like to express our deep appreciation to them, as well as to our advisory board members—Hugo Adam Bedau, Gilbert Geis, Raymond Paternoster, Mark Tushnet, and Ernest van den Haag—whose comments and suggestions have been invaluable in editing this book. In addition, we thank the extremely helpful and knowledgeable staff of the University of California, Irvine, Library—particularly the Document Delivery Service and the Interlibrary Loan staff, who kept up (and put up) with our numerous requests. We also would like to express our appreciation to poet Tom Disch, who provided us with background on his poem *Capital Punishment* (see Document 108); to Professor James Vorenberg, who provided us with background on the President's Commission Report (Document 50); to Professor Floyd Feeney, who assisted us with background information on the late John P. Conrad; to Michael D'Amelio at the New York University School of Law and Nancy Young at Princeton University's Seeley G. Mudd Manuscript Library, who both went out of their way to track down important historical documents for us; and to Emily Birch, acquisitions editor for Greenwood Press, whose friendly guidance has been greatly appreciated during this past year. As always, the support from both of our families has been a great comfort.

# Introduction

## A LONG HISTORY OF CONTROVERSY

Capital punishment is a highly controversial and emotional subject about which most people seem to have strong opinions. The debate is by no means new—there are conflicting references to capital punishment dating back to the Bible (see Document 1). Nearly two millennia later, we're still arguing the issue and perhaps are no closer to resolving it.

In the United States, controversy over capital punishment began in colonial times when, against the wishes of the English Crown, some settlements enacted only a few capital laws (Document 3). Soon after the War for Independence and the adoption of the Constitution, America's death penalty debate began in earnest. Armed with the right to free speech afforded by the new democracy, and infused with a "revolutionary spirit" as well as the philosophies of the European Enlightenment, some Americans began to question whether government should have the power to end a life—even the life of a convicted criminal.

Tracing the evolution of the capital punishment debate from this period forward—and in the original words of many of its most eloquent and vociferous participants—has proven to be a fascinating experience. Perhaps more revealing than the changes that have occurred is the fact that many of the issues and arguments of the debate appear to have changed so little over time.

## RELIGIOUS ARGUMENTS

The earliest arguments both for and against capital punishment were taken directly from the Bible. Early colonial settlements such as the Massachusetts Bay Colony, for example, relied on scriptural justification for their capital laws (Document 2). And in their execution sermons, Puritan ministers drew heavily from the Bible—particularly the "eye for an eye" Mosaic code of the Old Testament—as they admonished the condemned and explained why they must be put to death for their "sins" (Documents 4 and 7). However, as opposition to the death penalty grew, those opposed to capital punishment also found support for their views in the Bible—typically in the "turn the other cheek" doctrine of the New Testament.

The religious argumentation that was a hallmark of the early death penalty debate, particularly during the colonial era and again during the religious revival of the 1840s, is by no means a dead issue. Religious arguments continue to be part of the pro- and anti-capital punishment rhetoric to this day. And, like moral arguments, which we discuss next, they tend to remain fairly static over time, perhaps because they are based on people's deep-rooted beliefs and values rather than on empirical research, constitutional law, or practical issues.

## MORAL ARGUMENTS

Objectively speaking, plausible moral arguments can be made both for and against capital punishment. Long a key element of the debate, moral arguments also have tended to remain fairly static over the years, and often have been used in conjunction with religious arguments. Two moral arguments have remained particularly important throughout the death penalty debate: retribution and the sanctity of life.

Those favoring the death penalty often argue that society must express moral outrage at—and condemnation of—heinous crimes such as murder. The Rev. George Barrel Cheever (Document 19), for example, argued, "There ought to be such a penalty, high, awful, distinctive, to mark this crime [murder] in its *retribution*, as it stands in its *guilt*, paramount to every other. The conscience of society should be educated in the view of such a penalty; if it were not, or when it is not, poor and cheap indeed is the estimate placed upon the sacredness of human life." More than one hundred years later, conservative scholar Ernest van den Haag (Document 59) also argued, "When murder no longer forfeits the murderer's life . . . respect for life itself is diminished, as the price for taking it is. Life becomes cheaper as we become kinder to those who wantonly take it." And in writing the majority opinion upholding new guided discretion death penalty statutes in 1976 (Document 62), Supreme Court Justice Stewart noted that "In part, capital punishment is an expression of society's moral outrage at particularly offensive conduct. This function may be unappealing to many, but it is essential in an ordered society that asks its citizens to rely on legal processes rather than self-help to vindicate their wrongs."

Conversely, abolitionists often argue that rather than upholding the sanctity of life, the death penalty violates it. This was the contention of Thomas Upham (Document 17), a nineteenth-century Congregationalist minister and professor of moral and mental philosophy at Bowdoin College. Similarly, legislator and editor John O'Sullivan (Document 18) argued in 1841 that "No more impressive lesson could be taught by society . . . than to respect the life of man even in the person of the very wretch who has himself forgot to respect it in the person of the victim he did not spare." In the modern era, virtually the same arguments still are being made by abolitionists. For example, lawyer Gerald Gottlieb (Document 46) contended in 1961 that "This act by the state [execution] tends to cheapen the very values that refer to humanity itself, to lower the opinion of humanity regarding itself and to diminish its standards of decency, of conscience and of culture."

## DETERRENCE

Proponents of capital punishment typically consider deterrence to be one of its fundamental goals. The execution sermons of the early colonies were full of warnings against following in the footsteps of the condemned, and executions were public events designed to instill fear and reverence for the law in the people of the community. As Rev. Nathan Strong (Document 5) explained in 1777, "One reason why it is necessary the unhappy person should thus die, is that others may be fortified against temptation by the spectacle of horror, and the bitter consequences of transgression."

However, many early opponents of the death penalty believed that executions aggravated rather than deterred crime. As evidence, they pointed to the public disorder, rioting—and even murder—that sometimes accompanied public executions, and were significant factors in the decision to shift to private executions in the 1830s. "[F]ear of the gallows does not restrain from murder," said Louisiana legislator Edward Livingston in 1825 (Document 14). "We have seen a deliberate murder committed in the very crowd assembled to enjoy the spectacle of a murderer's death; and do we still talk of its force as an example?" Influential editor Horace Greeley (Document 22) noted in 1850 that capital punishment "tends to weaken and destroy the natural horror of bloodshed." And in a 1924 debate, famous abolitionist lawyer Clarence Darrow (Document 29) stated, "We teach people to kill, and the State is the one that teaches them."

These same issues have been the subject of even greater attention and controversy in the modern era, as scientific studies have attempted to determine whether capital punishment acts as a deterrent to murder and/or whether it has a "brutalizing" effect on society. But despite numerous studies conducted by many different researchers—including Thorsten Sellin (Document 42), who in research beginning in 1959 found no deterrent effect; Isaac Ehrlich (Document 60), who in 1975 found evidence to the contrary; William J. Bowers (Document 85), who in 1988 reported findings of a brutalization effect; and William C. Bailey (Document 92), who in 1990 found neither brutalization nor deterrent effects—at present there still are no definite and conclusive answers to either question. Therefore it is likely that research—and controversy—on this important issue is likely to continue for years to come.

## INCAPACITATION

As noted criminologist James Q. Wilson has pointed out, "Whatever else may be said about the death penalty, it is certain that it incapacitates" (1985:178). Indeed, prior to the development of an extensive prison system, execution may have been considered the only sure way to prevent offenders from repeating their crimes. However, when long-term incarceration became a plausible alternative to capital punishment in the late eighteenth and early nineteenth century, the incapacitation argument began to heat up.

Abolitionists typically argue that the death penalty is no longer necessary because life imprisonment will incapacitate equally well. For example, in 1850, Horace Greeley (Document 22) pointed out that execution might still be necessary in the western territories, but not in the New England states. "Here," he said, "are prison-cells wherefrom escape is impossible; and if there be any fear of [the convict] assaulting his keeper or others, that may be most effectively prevented." In 1961, abolitionist lawyer Gerald Gottlieb questioned the constitutionality of the death penalty on several grounds, including its function given the availability of life imprisonment (see Document 46). And in 1990, researcher Julian H. Wright, Jr. (Document 90) pointed out that life-without-parole not only offers protection through incapacitation but also "is a swifter and surer penalty in most cases than the death penalty."

However, retentionists argue that a "life" sentence does not always mean that a convicted murderer will remain in prison for the rest of his or her life, nor does it prevent convicted murderers from killing again inside the prison walls. As Frank Carrington put it, "Why don't we just give murderers a life sentence and keep them inside forever so they can't harm the innocent in our society? Because, first of all, they can and do harm other prisoners, and guards, . . . but additionally, because there is for all intents and purposes no such thing as a 'life sentence' in American prisons" (Carrington 1978:105). Therefore, he and other retentionists tend to believe that the only way to truly incapacitate murderers is to execute them.

## IRREVOCABILITY

Unlike most other penalties, the death penalty is irrevocable. Therefore, the danger of executing an innocent person is a concern shared by both abolitionists and retentionists.

This issue received heightened attention early in the twentieth century as a result of the controversy surrounding the 1927 execution of Nicola Sacco and Bartolomeo Vanzetti (Document 30), who proclaimed their innocence to the end, and whom many people believed. In 1957 and 1960, respectively, the executions of Julius and Ethel Rosenberg (Document 39) and Caryl Chessman (Document 43) also focused public attention on the possibility of executing the innocent. More recently, the cases of *Coleman v. Thompson* (1991, Document 95) and *Herrera v. Collins* (1993, Document 101) have brought the issue back into the spotlight.

Also fueling the modern debate is a 1987 study in which Hugo Adam Bedau and Michael Radelet identified 350 people who had been wrongly convicted in capital (or potentially capital) cases in the United States between 1900 and 1985—23 of whom were actually put to death (Document 82). But while abolitionists such as Bedau and Radelet argue that even this relatively small number of wrongful executions makes the risk of imposing the death penalty on an innocent person unacceptable, many retentionists see things differently. As Ernest van den Haag (Document 73) argued in 1983, "such miscarriages of justice do not warrant abolition of the death penalty. Unless the moral drawbacks of an activity or practice, which include the possible death of innocent bystanders, outweigh the moral advantages, which include the innocent lives that might be saved by it, the activity is warranted" (226).

## ARBITRARINESS AND DISCRIMINATION

Although historical evidence reveals a long tradition of discriminatory application of the death penalty—and indeed several abolitionists throughout America's early history noted that the death penalty appeared to be imposed more frequently on the poor and minorities—

discrimination did not become a major issue in the capital punishment debate until the second half of the twentieth century. It was then that the civil rights movement of the 1960s focused increased public attention and research on the subject. Results of the research proved disturbing. For example, in 1973, social scientists Marvin E. Wolfgang and Marc Riedel (Document 57) reported that "Among 1,265 cases in which the race of the defendant and the sentence are known, nearly seven times as many blacks were sentenced to death as were whites." And in a series of studies conducted during the 1980s, law professor David C. Baldus and his colleagues found that defendants charged with killing whites were 4.3 times as likely to receive a death sentence as those charged with killing blacks, and that black defendants were 1.1 times as likely to receive a death sentence as other defendants (Document 79).

In addition to contending that the death penalty is disproportionately imposed upon the poor and minorities, many abolitionists also claim that juror discretion in death sentencing is likely to produce arbitrary and capricious death sentences—a claim that resulted in a successful Eighth Amendment challenge to existing death penalty statutes in the 1972 case of *Furman v. Georgia* (Document 54). However, while new guided-discretion statutes enacted since *Furman* were intended to resolve this problem, many abolitionists argue that death sentences still are being meted out arbitrarily by juries.

Retentionists, on the other hand, typically claim that if there *is* discrimination in capital sentencing, it is not the fault of the penalty, but rather its application. Ernest van den Haag (Document 59) explains that "Penalties themselves are not inherently discriminatory; distribution, the process which selects the persons who suffer the penalty, can be. . . . The defect to be corrected is in the courts." Similarly, Frank Carrington argues that "if a penalty is so arbitrarily applied as to make it unconstitutional, the answer is not, as the abolitionists suggest, to do away with it altogether, but to refine our standards so that the penalty is not applied in an arbitrary manner" (Carrington 1978:116).

## CONSTITUTIONAL ARGUMENTS

The constitutional arguments for and against the death penalty are numerous. Those sentenced to death have challenged the constitutionality of their sentences with regard to the prescribed mode of execution, the sentencing procedures used by the court and jury, and the application of the penalty to their particular crime or personal situation.

Important as these arguments are, perhaps the most significant arguments in recent years are those that challenge the constitutionality of the death penalty itself, rather than the constitutionality of individual sentences. Abolitionists claim that although the death penalty was considered an acceptable practice by the framers of the Constitution, in the modern era it constitutes the type of cruel and unusual punishment forbidden by the Eighth Amendment. As lawyer Gerald Gottlieb explained when he first raised the issue in 1961, "The sentence of death violates the Eighth Amendment to the United States Constitution if the sentence and its execution are repugnant to the evolving standards of decency that mark the progress of our maturing society" (see Document 46). In denouncing the death penalty for the first time in 1965 (Document 48), the American Civil Liberties Union pointed out, "The fact that capital punishment has been acceptable in the past is no reason for its continuation. The rack and the screw; drawing and quartering; flogging—all have been used and subsequently rejected as maturing and sensitizing notions of the essential commands of human decency demonstrated the barbarity of the practices."

Retentionists, however, argue that the majority of Americans support the death penalty and death penalty legislation, and therefore it is not generally considered unacceptable under modern standards of decency. Indeed, the Supreme Court in the 1976 case of *Gregg v. Georgia* (see Document 62) upheld the constitutionality of capital punishment, stating that "The most marked indication of society's endorsement of the death penalty for murder is the legislative response to *Furman*. The legislatures of at least 35 States have enacted new statutes that provide for the death penalty for at least some crimes that result in the death of another person." And Ernest van den Haag notes, "What is the use of having a Constitution if we follow 'evolving standards,' invented, decided upon, and imposed by judges, instead of following the constitutional amendments that we have committed ourselves to follow until and unless they are amended further?" (1983:181).

## PRACTICAL ISSUES

In recent years, as prisoners' habeas corpus appeals have deluged the courts and stalled capital cases for years, practical issues have become increasingly important in the death penalty debate.

Abolitionists argue that the death penalty cases clog our courts with lengthy trials and appeals that—while essential to ensuring the defendant's rights—are more expensive than life imprisonment without parole. Such factors have led Richard Dieter (see Document 100), director of the Death Penalty Information Center, to comment, "the secondary smoke surrounding the death penalty is getting noticed and may eventually prove its downfall. . . . Like the health costs related to cigarettes which we all pay through insurance premiums and taxes, the death penalty is just becoming too expensive even for those who endorse it" (1994: 82–83).

However, retentionists, while not disputing the enormous costs of the modern death penalty, do not see abolition as the answer. Instead, they are seeking ways to reduce the time and costs involved by limiting the number of habeas appeals allowed, and putting strict time limits on them.

In fact, as we were writing this book, Congress and President Clinton hurriedly enacted an "Effective Death Penalty Act" designed to speed capital appeals through the courts. The Supreme Court showed equal haste in hearing a challenge to the new law (Document 112).

## THE APPROACH OF THIS VOLUME

The documents included in this volume chronicle what we believe are the most critical issues, events, and philosophical changes in the history of the ongoing capital punishment debate. In an effort to better illustrate the rich and varied nature of the debate, we have attempted to bring together many different types of documents—including book excerpts, scholarly articles, position statements, court rulings, congressional bills, newspaper accounts, and even poetry. We also have made every attempt to present both sides of the debate as completely and objectively as possible.

The volume opens with a chronology of important events in the history of capital punishment in the United States. Following are six parts, each of which includes an introduction that places the era to be discussed in historical and ecological context and gives an overview of the major events and trends in the capital punishment controversy. Each document also includes a brief introduction that explains its significance to the capital punishment debate.

Part I looks at early views on capital punishment from the colonial era to just after the War for Independence. Part II (1800–1917) covers a long period during which the abolitionist movement appeared to gain ground, despite interruption and setback by the Civil War. Part III (1918–1959) focuses on four decades in which war and economic depression typically overshadowed capital punishment issues. Part IV (1960–1976) reviews a period in which the capital punishment debate was waged primarily in the courts—leading to the demise of death penalty statutes enacted prior to 1972, and to the creation of new state and federal death penalty laws. Part V (1977–1989) covers an era in which the death penalty debate basically began anew, as the constitutionality of new death penalty laws was tested. Part VI (1990–   ) looks at the death penalty debate as it continues in the 1990s.

Finally, to aid the reader we include a glossary of legal terms used in the book, lists of federal and state capital offenses and U.S. executions from colonial times to 1995, selected U.S. Supreme Court cases, an extensive listing of capital punishment interest groups and related organizations, and a select bibliography of books, articles, court cases, and other documents that were especially useful to us in editing this volume.

## TWO IMPORTANT POINTS

Because we have made every effort to copy each document exactly as it appeared in original form, it's important to note that many of the documents in this book—particularly the older historical documents—contain misspellings and grammatical errors. In all but a few cases of potentially confusing spelling errors, we have chosen to present the documents as they were originally written, without detracting from them with numerous corrections and/or notations acknowledging the errors.

Furthermore, readers may notice that while one of our stated goals is to present both sides of the capital punishment debate as objectively as possible, more of the documents in this book favor the abolition of capital punishment than its retention. This imbalance does not reflect any intentional bias on our part, but rather is due to the fact that in researching the book, we found substantially more abolitionist than retentionist documents. We believe this most likely is because the death penalty has a long history of support in our culture and is in place in the majority of states, and therefore retentionists need expend less effort to maintain capital punishment than the abolitionists who seek to eliminate it.

Some retentionists, such as Ernest van den Haag, the John M. Olin Professor of Jurisprudence and Public Policy at Fordham University in New York, suggest that this imbalance also may arise from the fact that those most likely to be active in the capital punishment debate are the well educated and/or affluent, such as academics, judges, and lawyers, who also tend to be more insulated from the depredations of murderers and other criminals (van den Haag 1990:502–503).

Experience leads us to believe that Professor van den Haag's points may, at least for some people, be true. However, it also is possible that many well-educated and informed people reject capital punishment for other reasons, including moral and/or religious beliefs, or practical reasons associated with its expense and adverse effects on the legal system.

## A BRIEF REVIEW OF STATE AND FEDERAL CAPITAL PUNISHMENT LAWS AND THE COURT SYSTEM

Because this volume is intended for a wide range of readers with varying backgrounds, we conclude this introduction with the following brief overview of state and federal capital punishment laws and the U.S. court system.

### State and Federal Capital Punishment Laws

Historically, as we discuss in Part One, some of the early colonies had laws that made a wide range of crimes punishable by death. For example, the laws of the Massachusetts Bay Colony, while considerably more lenient than the capital laws of the Puritans' British homeland, included the following capital offenses: idolatry, witchcraft, blasphemy, murder, manslaughter, poisoning, bestiality, sodomy, adultery, man-stealing, false witness in capital cases, and conspiracy and rebellion (see Document 2). Over the years, capital reform has significantly diminished the types of crimes punishable by death. Today, twelve states and the District of Columbia do not have the death penalty. Thirty-eight states, the federal government, and the U.S. military retain capital punishment, primarily for the crime of aggravated murder, although some also consider offenses such as treason, sexual assaults on children, or aircraft piracy to be capital crimes (see Appendix A for a complete list of state and federal capital offenses).

### The Courts and Capital Punishment

The United States has two distinct yet overlapping court systems that deal with capital cases: the federal court system and the state court systems.

The federal system has three tiers: ninety-four district courts that conduct trials regarding violations of federal laws, twelve regional courts of appeal ("circuit courts") that review criminal and tax matters from the district courts in their geographical region, and the Supreme Court of the United States, which reviews lower court decisions and state and federal statutes to determine if they are in keeping with the intent of the Constitution.

Each state and territory has an independent court system that deals with violations of state law. Although the state court systems vary somewhat from one another, most have at least three levels of courts: original trial courts, intermediate-level appellate courts, and a state supreme court, which is the highest court of appeals within the state system.

A person who commits a murder that is punishable by death under a state's law is tried in that state's trial courts. Under current law, if he or she is found guilty and a death sentence is imposed, the case is automatically reviewed by a state appellate court. If the convicted murderer appeals the guilty verdict—or the imposition of the death sentence—the appellate court will examine the written transcript of lower court proceedings to assure that they were carried out fairly and in accordance with proper procedure and state law.

Federal courts become involved in capital cases when a federal capital statute (e.g., assassination of the president or a member of congress) is violated or when a person convicted and sentenced to die in a state court appeals to a federal court on the ground that the state conviction or sentence violated his or her constitutional rights.

Within the federal court system, the United States Supreme Court is the ultimate "court of last resort." In addition to its power of judicial review of congressional legislation and executive branch acts, the Supreme Court has jurisdiction over any case involving a substantial question regarding federal law. Therefore, it may review both federal appellate court decisions and state supreme court decisions that involve issues of federal law. With regard to the death penalty, this means that the Supreme Court often is asked to rule on cases in which the constitutionality of a particular state or federal death penalty law is in question, or in which the defendant claims that his or her constitutional rights were violated by the state or federal trial court via the trial and/or sentencing procedures leading to his or her death sentence, or by the appellate court on appeal. Such appeals are within the jurisdiction of the Supreme Court, even when state capital punishment laws or procedures are involved, because they deal with the application of the Bill of Rights to the states, which is a federal issue.[1]

Appeals to the Supreme Court request the Court to issue what is known as a *writ of certiorari*, or an order to the lower court to certify the court record and send it up to the higher court. The Supreme Court may either grant the request, which means it agrees to hear and rule on the case, or deny certiorari. If it denies certiorari, the lower court's decision stands.

## NOTE

1. However, this was not always the case. Initially, the Bill of Rights was intended primarily to protect citizens from abuses by the federal government, and therefore only a few of its clauses applied directly to the states. This changed

with the enactment, in 1868, of the Fourteenth Amendment, which contained due process language that was almost identical to the Fifth Amendment, except that it applied to the states. The amendment, which was primarily intended to ensure that the states did not violate the rights of African Americans freed from slavery as a result of the Civil War, was seldom applied during the years immediately following the war. But by the beginning of the twentieth century, the Supreme Court began to use the due process clause of the Fourteenth Amendment to apply many of the provisions of the Bill of Rights to the states. Under this view, if a clause of the Bill of Rights is "fundamental to the American scheme of justice," it is deemed to be incorporated in the Fourteenth Amendment and thus applied to limit the states in the same manner as it limits the federal government (Rotunda 1993:355–359).

# Significant Dates in the History of Capital Punishment

| | |
|---|---|
| 1641 | The Massachusetts Bay Colony establishes its Body of Liberties |
| 1682 | William Penn establishes a *Frame of Government* for the new colony of Pennsylvania |
| 1764 | Italy's Cesare Beccaria publishes his famous *Essay on Crimes and Punishment* |
| 1787 | Benjamin Rush presents *An Enquiry into the Effects of Public Punishments Upon Criminals and Upon Society* |
| 1790 | The world's first penitentiary is established in Pennsylvania |
| 1791 | The Bill of Rights is adopted |
| 1794 | William Bradford presents *An Enquiry How Far the Punishment of Death Is Necessary in Pennsylvania* to the Pennsylvania legislature |
| 1825 | Edward Livingston presents his proposal for a System of Penal Law for Louisiana |
| 1834 | First private execution in the United States is held in Pennsylvania |
| 1836 | Robert Rantoul presents his *Report on the Abolition of Capital Punishment* to the Massachusetts legislature |
| 1836 | Tobias Purrington presents his *Report on Capital Punishment Made to the Maine Legislature* |
| 1841 | John O'Sullivan delivers his *Report in Favor of the Abolition of the Punishment of Death by Law* |
| 1843 | Famous debate, "Ought Capital Punishment to Be Abolished?" is held between the Rev. George Barrel Cheever and abolitionist John O'Sullivan at the Broadway Tabernacle |
| 1844 | Charles Spear publishes his *Essays on the Punishment of Death* |
| 1845 | The Society for the Abolition of the Punishment of Death—the first national abolition society—is formed |

1845    Abolitionist Lydia Maria Child publishes her influential *Letters from New York*

1847    Michigan becomes the first state to abolish the death penalty

1868    The Fourteenth Amendment is ratified by the states

1879    *Wilkerson v. Utah*: The Supreme Court upholds execution by firing squad as constitutional

1890    *In re Kemmler*: The Supreme Court upholds execution by electric chair as constitutional

1910    *Weems v. U.S.*: The Supreme Court's first interpretation of the Eighth Amendment's "cruel and unusual" punishment clause

1924    First gas chamber execution

1924    Famous debate, *Is Capital Punishment a Wise Public Policy?* is held between Clarence Darrow and Alfred J. Talley

1927    The execution of Sacco and Vanzetti

1932    *Powell v. Alabama*: The Supreme Court overturns the death sentences of seven black youths on the ground that they were denied the right to effective counsel

1945    The execution of Private Eddie Slovik: First American since 1864 executed for desertion during wartime

1947    *Louisiana ex rel. Francis v. Resweber*: The Supreme Court deems that a second attempt at execution after a technical failure does not constitute cruel and unusual punishment

1947    *Patton v. Mississippi*: The Supreme Court sets a new precedent for the prohibition of racial discrimination by jury selection

1953    The execution of Julius and Ethel Rosenberg

1958    *Trop v. Dulles*: The Supreme Court declares that the Eighth Amendment "must draw its meaning from the evolving standards of decency that mark the progress of a maturing society"

1959    Thorsten Sellin publishes his study of *The Death Penalty*

1960    The execution of Caryl Chessman

1963    *Rudolph v. Alabama*: In a dissenting opinion to the Supreme Court's decision to deny certiorari, Justice Goldberg questions the constitutionality of the death penalty

1965    The American Civil Liberties Union takes a stand against the death penalty

1967    The "Last Aid Kit" is circulated to lawyers nationwide by abolitionist lawyers Anthony Amsterdam and Jack Himmelstein

1968    *Witherspoon v. Illinois*: The Supreme Court rules that the practice of excluding prospective jurors who have reservations about the death penalty from capital trials results in juries whose sentencing decisions could be considered biased and therefore unconstitutional

1971     *McGautha v. California* and *Crampton v. Ohio*: The Supreme Court rules that standardless juries and unitary trials are constitutional in death penalty cases

1972     *Furman v. Georgia*: The Supreme Court rules that the death penalty, as currently administered, is "cruel and unusual punishment in violation of the Eighth and Fourteenth Amendments," leading to the commutation of all death row prisoners' sentences

1975     Isaac Ehrlich publishes "The Deterrent Effect of Capital Punishment: A Question of Life and Death"

1976     *Gregg v. Georgia* and *Woodson v. North Carolina*: The Supreme Court upholds new guided discretion death penalty statutes in Georgia, Florida, and Texas, and deems new mandatory capital punishment statutes in North Carolina and Louisiana unconstitutional

1977     Gary Gilmore is executed

1977     *Coker v. Georgia*: The Supreme Court rules that the death penalty is an excessive punishment for rape

1978     *Lockett v. Ohio*: The Supreme Court rules that in a capital case, the jury must be allowed to consider the full spectrum of mitigating circumstances

1979     John Spenkelink is executed

1982     *Enmund v. Florida*: The Supreme Court rules that the death penalty is an excessive punishment for one whose role in a felony murder is minor

1982     *Eddings v. Oklahoma*: The Supreme Court rules that courts must consider a juvenile's youthfulness as a mitigating factor during capital sentencing

1983     Supreme Court Justice Powell urges an end to death sentence delays

1983     *Barefoot v. Estelle*: The Supreme Court upholds expedited federal review procedures in death penalty appeals and also upholds the prosecution's right to present psychiatric evidence regarding a defendant's future dangerousness during the penalty phase of a capital trial

1983     The initial "Baldus study" is published

1986     *Ford v. Wainwright*: The Supreme Court rules that execution of the insane is unconstitutional under the Eighth Amendment

1987     *Booth v. Maryland*: The Supreme Court rules victim impact statements inadmissible during a capital trial

1987     *McCleskey v. Kemp*: The Supreme Court rejects the claim that social science data established that the death penalty law in Georgia was unconstitutional because of racial discrimination

1988     *Thompson v. Oklahoma*: The Supreme Court rules unconstitutional the execution of an individual who was under sixteen at the time of his crime

1989    *Stanford v. Kentucky*: The Supreme Court rules that execution of individual who was sixteen or seventeen at the time of his crime is constitutional

1989    *Penry v. Lynaugh*: The Supreme Court rejects the claim that the Eighth Amendment prohibits the execution of the mentally retarded

1991    *Coleman v. Thompson*: The Supreme Court upholds a state procedural ruling rejecting a death penalty appeal filed three days after the deadline

1991    *Payne v. Tennessee*: The Supreme Court reverses its decision in *Booth,* *now* ruling victim impact evidence admissible in capital trials

1992    Robert Alton Harris is executed

1993    *Herrera v. Collins*: The Supreme Court rules that a claim of innocence based on newly discovered evidence is not grounds for federal habeas relief

1994    Supreme Court Justice Harry A. Blackmun renounces capital punishment in a dramatic dissent from the majority opinion in *Callins v. Collins*

1994    *Simmons v. South Carolina*: The Supreme Court rules that states must inform juries if a life-without-parole sentence is available as an alternative to the death penalty

1995    U.S. executions are at their highest level since 1957

1996    The *Antiterrorism and Effective Death Penalty Act of 1996* becomes law, substantially altering procedures for habeas appeals

1996    *Felkner v. Turpin*: The Supreme Court rules that at least one portion of the "Effective Death Penalty Act" is constitutional

# Capital Punishment
## in the
## United States

# Part I

# Early Views on Capital Punishment: Colonial Era to Independence

## MOTIVATION FOR EARLY EMIGRATION TO THE "NEW WORLD"

From the first colonial settlements until the War for Independence, numerous social, political, economic, demographic, philosophical, and ideological changes took place in North America that contributed to the colonists' revolt. Many of these changes also had an impact on American attitudes toward crime and punishment—including capital punishment.

To understand how these broad ecological changes eventually affected attitudes about capital punishment, it is important to look first at the historical setting in which the early American colonies were founded.

Beginning in the sixteenth century, Europe experienced an unprecedented period of innovation, growth, and expansion. Innovations in commerce, shipping, and the transmission of information enabled Europeans to conduct long-distance maritime trade on a large scale for the first time. At the same time, agricultural and industrial technology led to marked increases in productivity of food and other essential goods. As a result of these changes, the population grew rapidly, the cost of living rose, and people began to move away from farms to live and work in cities. This combination of factors increased the attractiveness of North America both as a new source of raw materials and as an outlet for excess population. For England in particular, emigration to North America also provided a solution to the problem of religious and political dissenters, who had become more prevalent as the result of the new rationalistic philosophies, religious foment, and social changes that occurred during this period.

## THE CAPITAL LAWS OF THE EARLY COLONIES

Not surprisingly, then, religious beliefs strongly influenced the social and political structure of the first permanent European holdings in eastern North America—including the capital laws. While the nature and number of offenses designated as capital crimes varied significantly from colony to colony, a theme common to most was their reliance on biblical scripture as justification for their designation as capital crimes.

The capital laws of the early colonies—which typically included such offenses as idolatry, adultery, bestiality, witchcraft, and blasphemy—often have been described as harsh. Indeed, many of the laws *were* harsh by today's standards, but they seem much less so when compared to those of their British homeland, which at the time had about fifty-five capital laws. Moreover, in some settlements such as the Massachusetts Bay Colony, where twelve offenses were capital in 1641, several of the laws seldom if ever were enforced.

The most lenient capital laws were in Pennsylvania and West Jersey, where William Penn's Quakers sought to establish utopian societies in which people controlled themselves out of an enlightened understanding of proper behavior rather than because of threats of social sanction (see Document 3). In the early years of these two colonies, murder and treason were the only capital crimes.

Conversely, some of the harshest capital codes were in the southern colonies. Entrepreneurial colonists such as planters in Virginia, Maryland, Georgia, and Carolina had to maintain a large cheap labor force. They relied on indentured workers and slaves to grow labor-intensive crops such as tobacco, sugar, and rice. To keep these populations under control, the Slave Codes enacted during the 1660s included a long list of behaviors that were considered crimes only if committed by blacks. Furthermore, slaves were subjected to numerous capital laws that did not apply to the free population (Paternoster 1991:8). As we shall see in later chapters, the desire to control African slaves in the southern colonies laid a legal and cultural foundation for harsher punishments of blacks in the South—a tradition that many scholars argue continues today.

## RAPID GROWTH, INCREASED DIVERSITY, AND BRITISH INTERVENTION LEAD TO INCREASED CAPITAL LAWS

During the eighteenth century, the colonies grew extremely rapidly. For example, in 1680, the population of Pennsylvania was only 4,000; within sixty years it had risen to 80,000 and still was growing rapidly. Overall, the population of the colonies was doubling every twenty-five years, prompting British economist Thomas Malthus to make his famous observation about the enormous potential for population growth in environments where resources are plentiful. High birth rates and lower mortality accounted for much of this growth in the colonies' population, but the majority continued to come from immigration.

Equally important, the nature of the immigrants coming to the colonies changed remarkably between 1700 and 1775. Although there had been substantial differences between the early settlements, each individual colony had tended to be quite homogenous. However, instead of middle- and working-class English, the new immigrants were paupers and convicts, Scottish, Irish, and German refugees, and slaves from Africa.

As the colonies grew and became more heterogeneous, common beliefs and culture that once had provided a strong foundation for informal control of people's behavior through socialization and social pressure were challenged. Partly in response to these new challenges, capital punishment laws typically were expanded. Given the absence of a prison system—what few jails existed were used almost exclusively to detain prisoners for short periods of time until they could be tried—stricter capital laws may have been perceived as the only solution to increased difficulties in maintaining public order and increased fears resulting from greater social and cultural diversity.

However, England also was partly responsible for the increase in capital laws in the colonies. While the English Crown largely had ignored the new settlements at first, allowing them great autonomy in creating their own societies, it never had been pleased with their lenient laws. Now, as the colonies grew in economic importance to England, the Crown attempted to reassert authority over them. Expanding its own capital laws until they numbered more than two hundred by the early nineteenth century, England also forced adoption of harsher penal codes in several of the colonies.

## INFLUENCE OF THE SCIENTIFIC REVOLUTION AND THE ENLIGHTENMENT

At the same time England was attempting to exert greater political influence over the colonies, other European influences—specifically the intellectual and philosophical shifts of the Scientific Revolution and of the Enlightenment—slowly were beginning to make their way to the colonies. Interestingly, these influences would help move the colonists further away from acceptance of British rule.

The Scientific Revolution of the seventeenth century was based on the notion of the superiority of reason as a guide to all knowledge and human concerns. One of the most prominent leaders of the revolution was Englishman John Locke (1632–1704), perhaps best known for his *Two Treatises on Government* (1689) and his *Essay Concerning Human Understanding* (1690).

The philosophies of Locke's *Treatises*—specifically his sanctioning of rebellion—helped inspire the colonists to revolt. But it was his *Essay*, in which Locke argued that all human knowledge and ideas were based on sensation and experience, that provided the impetus for numerous reforms in the American penal system—including education and other measures to prevent criminal misconduct as well as attempts to rehabilitate those convicted of crimes.

The writings of Locke and other philosophers of the Scientific Revolution, including Newton, Montesquieu, and Voltaire, spawned a subsequent philosophical movement in eighteenth-century Europe known as the Enlightenment, which was characterized by the notion of progress and a challenging of traditional Christian dogma.

During this period, Cesare Beccaria (1738–1794), the jurist son of an Italian marquis, argued that because suicide was a sin, no man had the authority to give another the right to kill him. Further, said Beccaria, the death penalty served as an example of barbarity, rather than a deterrent to it. As an alternative, he argued for proportional punishments designed to deter crime—such as a lifetime of imprisonment and servitude as punishment for murder. Such punishments, he said, not only served as a lasting—rather than fleeting—example to others, but were in some ways harsher than execution because of their duration, and thus served as a better deterrent.

Beccaria's book, *An Essay on Crimes and Punishments*, was published in Italy in 1764, at the height of the Enlightenment, and was a huge success throughout Europe. By 1773, an English translation of the book was available in New York; but due to preoccupation with the Revolutionary War, it wasn't until several years later that Beccaria's book had an impact in America. When it did, that impact was significant. Their independence won, Americans were eager for political reform as they shaped the new government and system of laws. And thus began the first real debate over capital punishment in the United States.

## THE EARLY ABOLITION MOVEMENT IN THE NEW REPUBLIC

Among the first Americans to be swayed by Beccaria's arguments was Thomas Jefferson (see Document 6). The draft bill submitted by Jefferson in 1779 to the Virginia Legislature that proposed substituting more proportionate sentences for previously capital offenses cited Beccaria three different times. But unlike Beccaria, Jefferson was not in favor of complete abolition of the death penalty. It was Benjamin Rush, a Philadelphia physician and signer of the Declaration of Independence, who launched the first major movement against capital punishment in the United States in 1787 with a widely read treatise denouncing the death penalty and advocating establishment of a "house of repentance" for convicted criminals. Three years later, the world's first penitentiary was established at the Walnut Street Jail in Philadelphia.

Rush's influence also helped to revive the Philadelphia Society for Relieving Distressed Prisoners, which had been organized in 1776, but was quickly overwhelmed by the revolution. Renamed the Philadelphia Society for Alleviating the Miseries of Public Prisons, it began its work anew in 1787 with a membership that included Rush, Caleb Lownes, Tench Coxe, Thomas Wistar, and other notables. Some of these reformers' descendants continue to carry on their prison reform work within the same organization, which was renamed the Pennsylvania Prison Society in 1933 (Sellin 1967:105).

By the end of the eighteenth century, convinced by Rush and others that solitary repentance was the key to reforming criminals, nearly every state legislature had adopted the idea of the penitentiary. Indeed, in 1791, the Board of Inspectors in Philadelphia proclaimed: "The prison is no longer a scene of debauchery, idleness, and profanity . . . but a school of reformation" (in Masur 1989:88).

No state, however, abolished capital punishment entirely. Only Pennsylvania, after adopting "degrees of murder" in 1794, eliminated the death penalty for all crimes except first degree murder. Premeditated (first degree) murder still would be punished by death, but now a jury also had the option of convicting a defendant of second degree (unpremeditated) homicide, which did not carry a mandatory death sentence (Tushnet 1994:21).

## DOCUMENT 1: The Bible and Capital Punishment

The death penalty debate is as old as the Bible—literally. The Bible contains numerous and often seemingly conflicting references to capital punishment—from the "eye for an eye" Mosaic code of the Old Testament (Document 1C) to the "turn the other cheek" Christian doctrine of the New Testament (Document 1D).

From colonial days to the present, biblical arguments have figured prominently in both sides of the capital punishment debate in the United States. Following are just a few of the most frequently quoted passages.

### A. GOD SPEAKING TO NOAH

Whoso sheddeth man's blood, by man shall his blood be shed: for in the image of God made he man.

*Source*: Genesis 9:6. All of these references are from the King James Version of the Bible (New York: World Publishing Company).

### B. THE SIXTH COMMANDMENT

Thou shalt not kill.

*Source*: Exodus 20:13.

### C. GOD SPEAKING TO MOSES

And he that killeth any man shall surely be put to death.

And he that killeth a beast shall make it good; beast for beast. And if a man cause a blemish in his neighbour; as he hath done, so shall it be done to him; Breach for breach, eye for eye, tooth for tooth: as he hath caused a blemish in a man, so shall it be done to him *again*.

And he that killeth a beast, he shall restore it: and he that killeth a man, he shall be put to death.

*Source*: Leviticus 24:17–21.

## D. JESUS SPEAKING TO THE MULTITUDES IN THE SERMON ON THE MOUNT

Ye have heard that it hath been said, An eye for an eye, and a tooth for a tooth:

But I say unto you, That ye resist not evil: but whosoever shall smite thee on thy right cheek, turn to him the other also.

*Source*: Matthew 5:38–39.

## E. THE EPISTLE OF THE APOSTLE PAUL TO THE ROMANS

Let every soul be subject unto the higher powers. For there is no power but of God: the powers that be are ordained of God.

Whosoever therefore resisteth the power, resisteth the ordinance of God: and they that resist shall receive to themselves damnation.

For rulers are not a terror to good works, but to the evil. Wilt thou then not be afraid of the power? do that which is good, and thou shalt have praise of the same:

For he is the minister of God to thee for good. But if thou do that which is evil, be afraid; for he beareth not the sword in vain: for he is the minister of God, a revenger to *execute* wrath upon him that doeth evil.

*Source*: Romans 13:1–4

## F. THE REVELATION OF ST. JOHN THE DIVINE

He that leadeth into captivity shall go into captivity: he that killeth with the sword must be killed with the sword. Here is the patience and the faith of the saints.

*Source*: Revelation 13:10.

## DOCUMENT 2: The Capital Laws of Massachusetts (1641)

The Bible not only is an early source of controversy over capital punishment, it also is the source of most of our nation's first death penalty laws.

The capital laws of the Massachusetts Puritans, for example, were strongly influenced by Mosaic Code of the Old Testament. In fact, all but the last of the twelve laws included in the Bay Colony's 1641 Body of Liberties were accompanied by the biblical reference or references from which they were derived.

While many of these laws seem particularly harsh, the code might be considered almost lenient, at least in terms of the number of capital crimes, when compared to the capital laws of the Puritans' British homeland. There, about fifty-five crimes—including burglary, robbery, and larceny—were punishable by death at the time (Hook and Kahn 1989:21; Mackey 1976:xii).

Furthermore, it appears that at least some of the twelve capital laws adopted by the Massachusetts Bay Colony may not have been strictly adhered to. As one historian put it, "[i]f some of the laws selected from the Bible for inclusion in the Massachusetts code proved to be impracticable, then they need not be enforced to the hilt. They could well remain on the statute books as reminders of the standard of conduct expected of Godly people" (Powers 1966:253).

## 94. *Capitall Laws*

### 1. [Idolatry]

Dut. 13. 6,10.
Dut. 17. 2,6.
Ex. 22. 20

If any man after legall conviction shall have or worship any other god, but the lord god, he shall be put to death.

P. 14.
S. 1.

### 2. [Witchcraft]

Ex. 22. 18.
Lev. 20. 27.
Dut. 18. 10.

If any man or woeman be a witch, (that is hath or consulteth with a familiar spirit,) They shall be put to death.

S. 2.

### 3. [Blasphemy]

Lev. 24. 15, 16.

If any man shall Blaspheme the name of god, the father, Sonne or Holie ghost, with direct, expresse, presumptuous or high handed blasphemie, or shall curse god in the like manner, he shall be put to death.

S. 3.

### 4. [Murder]

Ex. 21. 12.
Numb. 35. 13, 14, 30, 31.

If any person commit any wilfull murther, which is manslaughter, committed upon premeditated mallice, hatred, or Crueltie, not in a mans necessarie and just defence, nor by meere casualtie against his will, he shall be put to death.

S. 4.

## 5. [Manslaughter]

Numb. 25. 20, 21.
Lev. 24. 17.

If any person slayeth an other suddaienly in his anger or Crueltie of passion, he shall be put to death.

S. 5.

## 6. [Poisoning]

Ex. 21. 14.

If any person shall slay an other through guile, either by poysoning or other such divelish practice, he shall be put to death.

S. 6.

## 7. [Bestiality]

Lev. 20. 15, 16.

If any man or woeman shall lye with any beaste or bruite creature by Carnall Copulation, They shall surely be put to death. And the beast shall be slaine and buried and not eaten.

S. 7.

## 8. [Sodomy]

Lev. 20. 13.

If any man lyeth with mankinde as he lyeth with a woeman, both of them have committed abhomination, they both shall surely be put to death.

S. 8.

## 9. [Adultery]

Lev. 20. 19, and 18, 20.
Dut. 22. 23, 24.

If any person committeth Adultery with a maried or espoused wife, the Adulterer and Adulteresse shall surely be put to death.

S. 9.

## 10. [Man-stealing]

Ex. 21. 16.

If any man stealeth a man or mankinde, he shall surely be put to death.

S. 10.

## 11. [False Witness in Capital Cases]

Deut. 19. 16, 18, 19.

If any man rise up by false witnes, wittingly and of purpose to take away any mans life, he shall be put to death.

S. 11.

## 12. [Conspiracy and Rebellion]

If any man shall conspire and attempt any invasion, insurrection, or publique rebellion against our commonwealth, or shall indeavour to surprize any Towne or Townes, fort or forts therein, or shall treacherously and perfediouslie attempt the alteration and subversion of our frame of politie or Government fundamentallie, he shall be put to death.

S. 12.

*Source*: *The Body of Liberties*, 1641. In William H. Whitmore, *A Bibliographical Sketch of the Laws of the Massachusetts Colony from 1630 to 1686* (Boston: Rockwell and Churchill, 1890), 55.

---

## DOCUMENT 3: William Penn's *Frame of Government* (1682)

---

William Penn (1644–1718), best known as the founder of Pennsylvania, was an outspoken, lifelong advocate of religious and civil liberty.

Much to the dismay of his father, an admiral in the British navy who adhered to the Anglican faith, young William was influenced by the Puritan religion at an early age, and was expelled from Oxford for his nonconformist religious views.

Hoping to rid him of his Puritan sympathies, Penn's father sent him abroad. Young William traveled throughout Europe for several years, studied law for a year in England, and then went to Ireland in 1667 to manage his father's estates. It was there that he converted from Puritanism to the similarly despised Quaker faith, becoming a vigorous member of the Society of Friends.

When his father died in 1670, Penn inherited his fortune, his estates, and his position at court. In 1681, Penn became proprietor of Pennsylvania, which was given to him in lieu of repayment of an outstanding loan from his late father to King Charles II. Penn, who had been persecuted both in England and Ireland for his religious faith, took this opportunity to create an ideal Christian commonwealth—his "Holy Experiment."

Penn's *Frame of Government* for the new colony (also called the Great Act of 1682) was an unusually liberal document that provided for a governor, a council, and an assembly elected by freeholders. An accompanying series of laws provided for religious liberty, free elections, trial by jury, and a mild penal code in which murder and treason were the only crimes made punishable by death.

However, the English Crown, which was never pleased with Pennsylvania's criminal code, in 1718 forced Pennsylvania to adopt a much harsher penal code that included more than a dozen capital offenses (Bedau 1964:6; Filler 1952).

Following is an excerpt from Penn's introduction to the *Frame of Government*. Although it doesn't address the subject of capital punishment directly, it is important because it offers good insight into Penn's beliefs regarding the purpose and function of government and laws, including capital laws.

[T]here is hardly one Frame of Government in the World so ill designed by its first Founders, that in good Hands would not do well enough; and Story tells us, the best in ill ones can do nothing that is great or good; Witness the *Jewish* and *Roman* States. Governments, like Clocks, go from the Motion Men give them, and as Governments are made and moved by Men, so by them they are ruined too. Wherefore Governments rather depend upon Men, than Men upon Governments. Let Men be good, and the Government can't be bad; if it be ill, they will cure it. But if Men be bad, let the Government be never so good, they will endeavour to warp and spoil it to their Turn.

I know some say, Let us have good Laws, and no matter for the Men that execute them: But let them consider, That though good Laws do well, good Men do better: For good Laws may want good Men, and be abolished or evaded by ill Men; but good Men will never want good Laws, nor suffer ill ones. 'Tis true, good Laws have some Awe upon ill Ministers, but that is where they have not Power to escape or abolish them, and the People are generally wise and good: But a loose and depraved People (which is to the Question) love Laws and an Administration like themselves. That therefore, which makes a good Constitution, must keep it, *viz.* Men of Wisdom and Virtue, Qualities, that because they descend not with worldly Inheritances, must be carefully propagated by a virtuous Education of Youth; for which After-Ages will owe more to the Care and Prudence of Founders and the successive Magistracy, than to their Parents for their private Patrimonies.

THESE Considerations of the Weight of Government, and the nice and various Opinions about it, made it uneasy to me to think of Publishing the ensuing Frame and Conditional Laws, foreseeing, both the Censures they will meet with from Men of differing Humours and Engagements, and the Occasion they may give of Discourse beyond my Design.

BUT next to the Power of Necessity, (which is a Solicitor that will take no Denial) this induced me to a Complyance, that we have (with Reverence to GOD and good Conscience to Men) to the best of our Skill, contrived and composed the *FRAME and LAWS of this Government*, to the great End of all Government, *viz. To support Power in Reverence with the People, and to secure the People from the Abuse of Power*; that they may be free by their just Obedience, and the Magistrates Honourable for their just Administration: For Liberty without Obedience is Confusion, and Obedience without Liberty is Slavery. To carry this Evenness is partly owing to the Constitution, and partly to the Magistracy: Where either of these fail, Government will be subject to Convulsions; but where both are wanting, it must be totally subverted: Then where both meet, the Government is like to endure. Which I humbly pray and hope GOD will please to make the Lot of this of *Pensilvania*. Amen.

*Source*: William Penn, Preface to *The Frame of the Government of the Province of Pensilvania in America*, 1682 (Philadelphia: B. Franklin, 1740). [Early American Imprints (New York: Readex Microprint, 1985), 11–12.]

## DOCUMENT 4: New England Execution Sermon and Condemned's Response (1686)

Although many of those convicted of capital crimes in the early colonies actually received punishments less than death (Powers 1966: 275–286, 300–301), those who *were* executed were killed publicly and with great religious fanfare.

The Puritan ministers took advantage of these well-attended community events to deliver "execution sermons" in which they described the condemned's crimes in great detail, admonished him for his sins, urged him to repent, and warned the community at large of the dangers of following in his destructive path (Cohen 1988:148).

The sermons usually were given both on the Sunday before the execution and on the day of the hanging (Cohen 1988: 147). They often were printed in pamphlets—along with the confessions of the criminal and an account of his last words[1]—and sold to spectators on execution day (Masur 1989:26).

In addition to serving as a graphic reminder to the community of the wages of sin, execution sermons also typically contained a great deal of rhetoric to justify the execution. In seventeenth century New England, where capital crimes largely were defined by biblical scripture (see Document 2), arguments in support of capital punishment focused primarily on the "word of God." However, both judicial discretion and the deterrent value of capital punishment also were sometimes mentioned by Puritan ministers as justification for the death penalty (Cohen 1988:149–150).

Following are excerpts from an execution sermon by Increase Mather, one of the most prominent Puritan ministers of the day, and the "last words" of the condemned murderer, James Morgan.

**NOTE**
1. These confessions typically were "edited" for the prisoner by the attending minister (Masur 1989:33–34).

## A. INCREASE MATHER ADDRESSING THE CROWD

Propos. 3. The Murderer is to be put to death by the hand of Publick Justice. And this confirms the former Propositions concerning the greatness of this Sin. Men may not pardon or remit the Punishment of that Sin. Among the Jews there was no City of Refuge for a wicked or wilful man-slayer; and it is said in the 31 verse of this Chapter, You shall take no satisfaction for the life of a Murderer which is guilty of death, but he shall surely be put to death. This sin shall not be satisfyed for, with any other punishment, but the death of the Murderer. There are some Crimes, that other punishment less than Death may be accepted of, as a Compensation for the wrong done; either by some Mulct or Fine on their Estates, or some other Corporal Punishment less than death: but in case of Murder no Fine or Imprisonment, or Banishment, or corporal punishment less than death can be accepted: You shall take no satisfaction for the life of a murderer. And indeed Equity requires this: by the law of Retaliation, it is meet that men should be done unto, as they have done to others; and that as limb should go for limb, so Life for Life. But besides that, there are two Reasons mentioned in the Scripture, why the Murderer must be put to Death.

Reas. 1. That so the Land where the murder is committed may be purged from the guilt of Blood[.] For Murder is such a sin as does pollute the very Land where it is done; not only the person that has shed blood is polluted thereby, but the whole Land lies under Pollution until such time as Justice is done upon the Murderer. Thus in the 33. v. of this Chapter, this is given as the Reason why no Satisfaction might be taken for the life of a Murderer; so shall ye not pollute the land wherein you are; for blood it defileth the land, and the land cannot be cleansed of the blood that is shed therein, but by the blood of him that shed it. One Murder unpunished, may bring guilt & a curse upon the whole Land, that all the Inhabitants of the Land shall suffer for it; So that Mercy to a Murderer is Cruelty to a People. Therefore it is said concerning the Murderer, Thine eye shall not pity him but thou shall put away the guilt of innocent blood from Israel, that it may go well with thee. If the Murderer be not punished it may go ill with the Whole, all may fare the worse for it; if the sin be not duly punished, there is a partaking in the guilt of it.

Reas. 2. Because man is made in the Image of God. This reason is mentioned Gen. 9. 6. Whosoever sheddeth mans blood, by man (i. e. by some man in Authority, proceeding in an orderly way of Judicature, as the Hebrew Expositors do rightly interpret the words) shall his blood be shed, for in the Image of God made He him.

## B. INCREASE MATHER ADDRESSING THE CONDEMNED MAN

1. Consider what a sinner you have bin. The Sin which you are to die for, is as red as Scarlet; and many other sins, hath your wicked life been filled with. You have been a stranger to me, I never saw you, I never

heard of you, till you had committed the Murder for which you must dye this day; but I hear by others, that have known you, how wicked you have been, and you have your self confessed to the world, that you have been guilty of Drunkenness, guilty of Cursing & Swearing, guilty of Sabbath-breaking, guilty of Lying, guilty of secret Uncleanness; as Solomon said to Shimei, Thou knowest the wickedness which thine own heart is privy unto: so I say to you. And that which aggravates your Guiltiness not a little, is, That since you have been in Prison, you have done wickedly; you have made your self drunk several times since your Imprisonment; yea, and you have bin guilty of Lying since your Condemnation. It was said to a dying man, Dost not thou fear God, seeing thou art under Condemnation! Oh what a sinner have you bin! for since you have bin under Condemnation, you have not feared God. And how have you sinned against the Gospel? What Unbelief, what Impenitency have you bin guilty of!

Consider 2. What Misery you have brought upon your self, on your Body, that must dye an accursed death: you must hang between Heaven and Earth, as it were forsaken of both, and unworthy to be in either. And what Misery have you brought upon your poor Children! you have brought an everlasting Reproach upon them. How great will their Shame be, when it shall be said to them, that their Father was hang'd, not for his goodness, as many in the world have bin, but for his wickedness: not as a Martyr, but as a Malefactor, truly so! But that which is Ten Thousand Thousand times worse than all this, is, That you have (without Repentance) brought undoing Misery upon your poor yet precious Soul: not only Death on your Body, but a Second Death on your never-dying Soul. It is said in the Scripture, That Murderers shall have their part in the lake, which burns with fire and brimstone, which is the Second Death. Rev. 21, 8. O tremble at that!

## C. THE LAST EXPRESSIONS & SOLEMN WARNING OF JAMES MORGAN

I Pray God that I may be a Warning to you all, and that I may be the last that ever shall suffer after this manner. in the fear of God I warn you to have a care of taking the Lords Name in vain. Mind & have a care of that sin of Drunkenness, for that sin leads to all manner of sins and Wickedness: (mind & have a care of breaking the sixth Commandment, where it is said, Thou shalt do no Murder) for when a man is in Drink, he is ready to commit all manner of Sin, till he fill up the cup of the wrath of God, as I have done by committing that sin of Murder. I beg of God as I am a dying man, and to appear before the Lord within a few minutes, that you may take notice of what I say to you. Have a care of drunkenness, & ill Company, and mind all good Instruction, and don't turn your back upon the Word of God, as I have done. When I have bin at meeting, I have gone out of the meetinghouse to commit sin & to please the lust of my flesh. Don't make a mock at any poor object of pity, but bless God that he has not left you as he has justly done me to commit that horrid sin of Murder. Another thing that I have to say to you, is to have a care of that house where that wickedness was committed, & where I have bin partly ruind by. But here I am, and know not what will become of my poor soul which is within a few moments of eternity. I have murder d a poor man, who had but little time to repent, and I know not what is become of his poor soul; O that I may make use of this opportunity that I have! O that I may make improvement of this little little time, before I go hence and be no more. O let all mind what I am saying now I am going out of this world. O take warning by me, and beg of God to keep you from this sin which has bin my ruine. [His last words were] O Lord, receive my spirit, I come unto thee O Lord, I come unto thee O Lord: I come, I come, I come

*Source*: Increase Mather, *A Sermon Occasioned by the Execution of a Man Found Guilty of Murder* (Boston: R. P., 1687). In Sacvan Bercovitch, ed., *Execution Sermons* (New York: AMS Press, 1994), 11–12, 30–31, 35–36.

---

## DOCUMENT 5: *The Reasons and Design of Public Punishments* (Nathan Strong, 1777)

---

Nearly a century after Increase Mather's public condemnation of James Morgan (see Document 4), execution sermons that included justifications for the death penalty still were being given in the newly established republic.

Interestingly, however, the nature of the execution sermon was changing to reflect the new focus on government, the common good, and protection of liberty and property that occurred in the decades after the American Revolution (Cohen 1988:154, 156). Many sermons now included legal as well as religious justifications for the execution, as evidenced by the following execution sermon by Nathan Strong, pastor of the First Church of Hartford.

The melancholy spectacle which is soon to be exhibited, hath drawn together a vast concourse of people, who are doubtless influenced by various motives to be spectators of so awful a scene. Some by true seriousness, and many to gratify a vain curiosity. Curiosity is but a poor motive for collecting on such an occasion—the person who can go and look on death, merely to gratify an idle humour, is destitute both of humanity and piety.

Such awful exhibitions are designed that others may see and fear.— Go not to that place of horror with elevated spirits, and gay hearts, for death is there! justice and judgment are there! the power of government, displayed in its most awful form, is there.

One reason why it is necessary the unhappy person should thus die, is that others may be fortified against temptation by the spectacle of horror, and the bitter consequences of transgression. When you look thereon, learn the venerableness of the state and of civil government— the sacred nature of those laws made to protect liberty and property, and our obligations to obedience—learn that sin is punished by infamy, distress and death—that the man who injures his country, and will not be restrained by considerations of duty, justice and gratitude, must be cut off from the earth that others may be safe—remember that lesser sins, though they are not made capital by the laws of the State, lead directly towards the same untimely end.

*Source*: Nathan Strong, *The Reasons and Design of Public Punishments* (Hartford, Conn.: Eben. Watson, 1777). [Early American Imprints (New York: Readex Microprint, 1985), 17.]

---

## DOCUMENT 6: *A Bill for Proportioning Crimes and Punishments* (Thomas Jefferson, 1779)

By 1779, the first abolitionist rumblings with regard to capital punishment were just beginning to make their way to America from Europe.

The European debate over capital punishment had been instigated primarily by Cesare Beccaria (1738–1794), the jurist son of an Italian marquis, in his 1764 book *An Essay on Crimes and Punishments*. Beccaria argued that the death penalty served as an example of barbarity rather than a deterrent to it, because it sanctioned the taking of human life—the very act it was intended to deter.

As an alternative to capital punishment, Beccaria advocated proportional punishments designed to deter crime—such as a lifetime of imprisonment and servitude as punishment for murder. He argued that such punishments not only would serve as a lasting—rather than fleeting—example to others, but were in some ways harsher than execution because of their duration, and thus served as a more effective deterrent.

On the other side of the Atlantic, Thomas Jefferson (1743–1826) was among the first Americans to be influenced by Beccaria's philosophy of punishment. Although Jefferson was not in favor of the complete abolition of capital punishment, he appears to have been impressed by Beccaria's ideas on proportioning punishments to fit crimes.

Shortly before becoming Governor of Virginia in 1779, and some twenty-two years before he was inaugurated as President of the United States, Jefferson drafted *A Bill for Proportioning Crimes and Punishments in Cases Heretofore Capital* for submission to the Virginia legislature. In it, he cited Beccaria several times.

The bill proposed the elimination of the death penalty in Virginia for all crimes except murder and treason. For other crimes, such as manslaughter, rape, and robbery, Jefferson advocated specific penalties such as a number of years at hard labor, loss of land and goods, reparation, or a physical punishment based upon the crime committed.

However, while Beccaria's philosophies eventually would gain a wide following in America during the decades that followed, Jefferson's bill was slightly ahead of its time. It was not adopted, and the Virginia legislature did not reform its penal code until 1796.

Whereas it frequently happens that wicked and dissolute men resigning themselves to the dominion of inordinate passions, commit violations on the lives, liberties and property of others, and, the secure enjoyment of these having principally induced men to enter into society, government would be defective in it's principal purpose were it not to restrain such criminal acts, by inflicting due punishments on those who perpetrate them; but it appears at the same time equally deducible from the purposes of society that a member thereof, committing an inferior injury, does not wholly forfiet the protection of his fellow citizens, but, after suffering a punishment in proportion to his offence is entitled to their protection from all greater pain, so that it becomes a duty in the legislature to arrange in a proper scale the crimes which it may be necessary for them to repress, and to adjust thereto a corresponding gradation of punishments.

And whereas the reformation of offenders, tho' an object worthy the attention of the laws, is not effected at all by capital punishments, which exterminate instead of reforming, and should be the last melancholy resource against those whose existence is become inconsistent with the safety of their fellow citizens, which also weaken the state by cutting off so many who, if reformed, might be restored sound members to society, who, even under a course of correction, might be rendered useful in various labors for the public, and would be living and long continued spectacles to deter others from committing the like offences.

And forasmuch the experience of all ages and countries hath shewn that cruel and sanguinary laws defeat their own purpose by engaging the benevolence of mankind to withhold prosecutions, to smother testimony, or to listen to it with bias, when, if the punishment were only proportioned to the injury, men would feel it their inclination as well as their duty to see the laws observed.

For rendering crimes and punishments therefore more proportionate to each other: Be it enacted by the General assembly that no crime shall be henceforth punished by deprivation of life or limb except those hereinafter ordained to be so punished.

If a man do levy war against the Commonwealth or be adherent to the enemies of the commonwealth giving to them aid or comfort in the commonwealth, or elsewhere, and thereof be convicted of open deed, by the evidence of two sufficient witnesses, or his own voluntary confession, the said cases, and no others, shall be adjudged treasons which extend to the commonwealth, and the person so convicted shall suffer death by hanging, and shall forfiet his lands and goods to the Commonwealth.

If any person commit Petty treason, or a husband murder his wife, a parent his child, or a child his parent, he shall suffer death by hanging, and his body be delivered to Anatomists to be dissected.

Whosoever committeth murder by poisoning shall suffer death by poison.

Whosoever committeth murder by way of duel, shall suffer death by hanging; and if he were the challenger, his body, after death, shall be gibbetted. He who removeth it from the gibbet shall be guilty of a misdemeanor; and the officer shall see that it be replaced.

Whosoever shall commit murder in any other way shall suffer death by hanging.

*Source*: Thomas Jefferson, *A Bill for Proportioning Crimes and Punishments in Cases Heretofore Capital* (1779). In Julian P. Boyd, ed., *The Papers of Thomas Jefferson*, Vol. 2 (Princeton: Princeton University Press, 1950), 492–495 (footnotes omitted).

## DOCUMENT 7: The Execution of Hannah Ocuish (1786)

Despite early attempts toward penal reform that began in America shortly after the Revolution, many executions continued to take place under circumstances that would be considered appalling by today's standards.

The execution of twelve-year-old Hannah Ocuish, for example, is significant because of her extreme youth, apparent mental retardation, and numerous other mitigating factors that were taken into account at her trial but not considered sufficient to spare her life.

Hannah, whose mother was an alcoholic Pequot Indian and whose father was an unknown white man, was abandoned when she was quite young and eventually went from foster home to foster home.

Already well known for stealing and harassing people in her home town of Groton, Connecticut, Hannah was condemned for pummeling and strangling to death the six-year-old daughter of a well-to-do New London family who had tattled on her for stealing some strawberries a few weeks earlier. While there was no question that Hannah had committed the murder—in fact, she had confessed to it—her age, low I.Q., and disrupted family background made it questionable whether she could be held wholly accountable for her actions. However, the judge disagreed, saying, "the sparing of you on account of your age, would, as the law says, be of dangerous consequences to the public by holding up an idea, that children might commit such atrocious acts with impunity" (quoted in Streib 1987:75).

Indeed, Henry Channing, who delivered Hannah's execution sermon, took the opportunity to send a warning to the youngsters in the audience, along with the usual admonition of the condemned.

## My Young Friends.

To you the present scene speaks in striking language, teaching you the value of a parent's tender care.—Think not that crimes are peculiar to the *complexion* of the prisoner, and that ours is pure from these stains. Surely an idea so illiberal and contracted cannot find a place in the breast of a generous youth.—Know, my brothers, that *that* casket, notwithstanding its colour, contains an immortal soul, a Jewel of inestimable value; which, polished by divine grace, would shine in yonder world with a glorious lustre: while the Jewel in a brighter casket, being left in its natural state, would be *blackness and darkness forever*.

There behold, my young brethren, the fate of one, who, with a mind not below the common level, has been left unrestrained to the guidance of guilty passions and a corrupt heart.—Have you virtuous and affectionate parents who, with anxious concern, endeavour to instruct you in those principles which are necessary to secure you from infamy like this? Can you refuse them an unreserved obedience and the returns of grateful affection?—Can you wish to add one pang to those which a parent's heart has already felt on your account?—Think, O heart-rending thought! think what would be their feelings, if they whom their souls love should for their over-much wickedness be made, as this unhappy criminal, a public spectacle of infamy and guilt.—Could there be any sorrow like unto this sorrow?—Spare, O spare a parent's aching heart and let there be no cause to look forward to a scene which cannot be borne even in thought.

*Hear,* my brother, *the instruction of thy father, and forsake not the law of thy mother: for they shall be an ornament of grace unto thy head and chains about thy neck. Enter not into the path of the wicked, and go not in the way of evil men. Avoid it, pass not by it, turn from it, and pass away: for they sleep not except they have done mischief; and their sleep is taken away, unless they cause some to fall. For they eat the bread of wickedness and drink the wine of violence. But the path of the just is as the shining light, that shineth more and more unto the perfect day.* Early chuse this path of wisdom, and your own experience will prove that the *ways of wisdom are ways of pleasantness, and that all her paths are peace.* Great indeed will be your peace when a dying Parent shall pronounce you an obedient and affectionate child; and those lips which had not instructed you in vain, shall close with commending you in the quivering accents of death, to that Being in whom *the fatherless findeth mercy.* May he hear and be well pleased with this last effort of parental love: and repay your respectful obedience and sincere affection into your own bosoms. And may God in his infinite goodness, grant, that when you shall take the places of your fathers, you may never have cause to feel the unutterable pangs of that parent's heart, who has a *son that is a grief to his father, and bitterness to her that bare him.*

*Source:* Henry Channing, *God Admonishing His People of Their Duty as Parents and Masters,* second edition (New York: T. Green, 1786). [Early American Imprints (New York: Readex Microprint, 1985), 23–25.]

---

## DOCUMENT 8: *An Enquiry into the Effects of Public Punishments Upon Criminals and Upon Society* (Benjamin Rush, 1787)

---

While European philosophers of the Enlightenment such as Cesare Beccaria were responsible for planting the first seeds of abolitionist sentiment in America, it was a Philadelphia physician, Benjamin Rush (1745–1813), who is credited with launching the first major movement against capital punishment in the United States.

Rush, a signer of the Declaration of Independence, is perhaps best known for his work *An Enquiry into the Effects of Public Punishments Upon Criminals and Upon Society,* which he initially delivered as a speech at the home of Benjamin Franklin and subsequently published as a treatise.

Rush's treatise was prompted by the passage six months earlier of

Pennsylvania's Act of 1786. The act, known as the "wheelbarrow law," made many crimes that once were punishable by death, such as robbery, burglary, and sodomy, now punishable by a certain number of years at hard, public labor—typically in the streets of Philadelphia and neighboring towns.

The goal of the laws was to reform the criminal through hard work and public humiliation and to deter others from committing similar crimes. However, within a very short time, it became clear to Rush and many others that the new laws were falling far short of this goal and even might be contributing to the further corruption of the offenders they were meant to reform (Masur 1989:79).

In his treatise, which has been called "America's first reasoned argument stressing the impolicy and injustice of the death penalty for murder" (Schwed 1983:11), Rush denounced both the death penalty and the new laws, calling instead for the establishment of a "house of repentance," or penitentiary.

The treatise was widely publicized and highly controversial, earning Rush a strong following among advocates of abolition and prison reform. As a result, the Philadelphia Society for Alleviating the Miseries of Public Prisons was founded soon after, and in 1789, the wheelbarrow law was repealed. In 1790, the world's first penitentiary was established at the Walnut Street Jail in Philadelphia.

I have said nothing upon the manner of inflicting death as a punishment for crimes, because I consider it as an improper punishment for *any* crime. Even Murder itself is propagated by the punishment of death for murder. Of this we have a remarkable proof in Italy. The Duke of Tuscany, soon after the publication of the Marquis of Beccaria's excellent treatise upon this subject, abolished death as a punishment for murder. A gentleman, who resided five years at Pisa, informed me, that only five murders had been perpetrated in his dominions in twenty years. The same gentleman added, that after his residence in Tuscany, he spent three months in Rome, where death is still the punishment of murder, and where executions, according to Doctor Moore, are conducted with peculiar circumstances of public parade. During this short period, there were sixty murders committed in the precincts of that city. It is remarkable, the manners, principles, and religion, of the inhabitants of Tuscany and Rome, are exactly the same. The abolition of death alone, as a punishment for murder, produced this difference in the moral character of the two nations.

I suspect the attachment to death, as a punishment for murder, in the minds otherwise enlightened, upon the subject of capital punishments, arises from a false interpretation of a passage contained in the old testament, and that is, "he that sheds the blood of man, by man shall his blood be shed." This has been supposed to imply, that blood could only be expiated by blood. But I am disposed to believe, with a late commentator [Rev. William Turner] upon this text of scripture, that it is rather a *prediction*, than a *law*. The language of it is simply, that such will be the depravity and folly of man, that murder, in every age, shall beget murder. Laws, therefore, which inflict death for murder, are, in my opinion, as unchristian as those which justify or tolerate revenge; for the obligations of christianity upon individuals, to promote repentance, to forgive injuries, and to discharge the duties of universal benevolence, are equally binding upon states.

The power over human life, is the solitary prerogative of HIM who gave it. Human laws, therefore, rise in rebellion against this prerogative, when they transfer it to human hands.

If society can be secured from violence, by confining the murderer, so as to prevent a repetition of his crime, the end of extirpation will be answered. In confinement, he may be reformed—and if this should prove impracticable, he may be restrained for a term of years, that will probably be coeval with his life.

There was a time, when the punishment of captives with death or servitude, and the indiscriminate destruction of peaceable husbandmen, women and children, were thought to be essential to the success of war, and the safety of states. But experience has taught us, that this is not the case. And in proportion as humanity has triumphed over these maxims of false policy, wars have been less frequent and terrible, and nations have enjoyed longer intervals of internal tranquility. The virtues are all parts of a circle. Whatever is humane, is wise—whatever is wise, is just—and whatever is wise, just, and humane, will be found to be the true interest of states, whether criminals or foreign enemies are the objects of their legislation.

I have taken no notice of perpetual banishment, as a legal punishment, as I consider it the next in degree, in folly and cruelty, to the punishment of death. If the receptacle for criminals, which has been proposed, is erected in a *remote* part of the state, it will act with the same force upon the feelings of the human heart, as perpetual banishment. Exile, when perpetual, by destroying one of the most powerful principles of action in man, viz. the love of kindred, and country, deprives us of all the advantages, which might be derived from it, in the business of reformation. While certain passions are weakened, this noble passion is strengthened by age; hence, by preserving this passion alive, we furnish a principle, which, in time, may become an overmatch for those vicious habits, which separated criminals from their friends, and from society.

Notwithstanding this testimony against the punishment of death and perpetual banishment, I cannot help adding, that there is more mercy to the criminal, and less injury done to society, by both of them, than by *public* infamy and pain, without them. . . .

I shall conclude this enquiry by observing, that the same false religion and philosophy, which once kindled the fire on the altar of persecution, now doom the criminal to public ignominy and death. In proportion as the principles of philosophy and christianity are understood, they will agree in extinguishing the one, and destroying the other. If these principles continue to extend their influence upon government, as they have done for some years past, I cannot help entertaining a hope, that the time is not very distant, when the gallows, the pillory, the stocks, the whipping-post, and the wheel-barrow (the usual engines of public punishments) will be connected with the history of the rack, and the stake, as marks of the barbarity of ages and countries, and as melancholy proofs of the feeble operation of reason, and religion, upon the human mind.

*Source*: Benjamin Rush, *An Enquiry into the Effects of Public Punishments Upon Criminals and Upon Society* (Philadelphia: Joseph James, 1787). [New York: Readex Microprint, 1985, 15–18.]

## DOCUMENT 9: The Bill of Rights (1791)

When America's founding fathers drafted the Constitution, their main concern was to preserve the new democracy and protect against future tyranny by ensuring separation of power between the executive, legislative, and judicial branches of government.

However, soon after the Constitution was ratified by the states, its framers realized that by focusing so heavily on these objectives, they had neglected to provide written assurances to protect the rights of individual citizens against possible abuses by the new federal government. This, therefore, is the goal of the first ten amendments to the Constitution, also known as the Bill of Rights, adopted December 15, 1791.

Three of these amendments—along with the Fourteenth Amendment, added in 1868 (Document 23)—later would figure in numerous constitutional challenges to the death penalty: the Fifth Amendment (Document 9A), for its assurance that no person shall be compelled to testify against himself and also for its clause ensuring due process of law in a capital trial; the Sixth Amendment (Document 9B), for its promise of an impartial jury in all criminal prosecutions; and the Eighth Amendment (Document 9C), for its assurances against cruel and unusual punishments.

The Eighth Amendment has been particularly important in death penalty cases. Although capital punishment undoubtedly was in use and was not considered "cruel and unusual punishment" when this amendment was added to the Constitution in 1791, modern-day abolitionists have claimed that "evolving standards of decency" have rendered the death penalty unconstitutional.

## A. THE FIFTH AMENDMENT

No person shall be held to answer for a capital, or otherwise infamous crime, unless on a presentment or indictment of a grand jury, except in cases arising in the land or naval forces, or in the militia, when in actual service in time of war or public danger; nor shall any person be subject for the same offense to be twice put in jeopardy of life or limb; nor shall be compelled in any criminal case to be a witness against himself, nor be deprived of life, liberty, or property, without due process of law; nor shall private property be taken for public use, without just compensation.

## B. THE SIXTH AMENDMENT

In all criminal prosecutions, the accused shall enjoy the right to a speedy and public trial, by an impartial jury of the State and district wherein the crime shall have been committed, which district shall have been previously ascertained by law, and to be informed of the nature and cause of the accusation; to be confronted with the witnesses against him; to have compulsory process for obtaining witnesses in his favor, and to have the assistance of counsel for his defense.

## C. THE EIGHTH AMENDMENT

Excessive bail shall not be required, nor excessive fines imposed, nor cruel and unusual punishments inflicted.

*Source*: Constitution of the United States.

---

## DOCUMENT 10: *An Enquiry How Far the Punishment of Death Is Necessary in Pennsylvania* (William Bradford, 1793)

By 1793, the abolition and penal reform movement instigated by Benjamin Rush and his followers had gained considerable momentum in Pennsylvania.

The movement progressed even further when William Bradford, attorney general of Pennsylvania who later would become attorney general for the United States, investigated the possibility of reducing the number of capital crimes in the state. In his report, Bradford became one of the first to define the distinction between first- and second-degree murder and to argue for the abolition of capital punishment for all crimes except first-degree murder and treason. He also strongly supported early childhood education as a means of preventing later criminal behavior, and spoke favorably of the state's new prison system.

In 1794, due in large part to the continuous efforts of Bradford and Rush, the Pennsylvania legislature abolished the death penalty for all crimes except first-degree murder. New York in 1796 was the first state to follow Pennsylvania's example, retaining the death penalty only for murder and treason. Virginia, which in 1785 had rejected Thomas Jefferson's proposal to reduce its number of capital crimes, was among a number of other states that adopted similar reforms during the next two decades. And as they did so, each state—with the lofty goals of reforming criminals—began constructing its own prisons and penitentiaries (Mackey 1976:xvi–xvii; Masur 1989:86–87; Schwed 1983:11–12).

## On Capital Punishments

IT being established, That the only object of human punishments is the prevention of crimes, it necessarily follows, that when a criminal is put to death, it is not to revenge the wrongs of society, or of any individual—"it is not to recall past time and to undo what is already done:" but merely to prevent the offender from repeating the crime, and to deter others from its commission, by the terror of the punishment. If, therefore, these two objects can be obtained by any penalty short of death, to take away life, in such case, seems to be an authorised act of power. . . .

## Murder

Murder, in its highest degree, has generally been punished with death, and it is for deliberate assassination, if in any case, that this punishment will be justifiable and useful. Existence is the first blessing of Heaven, because all others depend upon it. Its protection is the great object of civil society and governments are bound to adopt every measure which is, in any degree, essential to its preservation. The life of the deliberate assassin can be of little worth to society, and it were better that ten such atrocious criminals should suffer the penalty of the present system, than that one worthy citizen should perish by its abolition. The crime imports extreme depravity and it admits of no reparation. . . .

But while I speak thus of deliberate assassination, there are other kinds of murder to which these observations do not apply: and in which, as the killing is in a great measure the result of *accident*, it is impossible the severity of the punishment can have any effect. The laws seem, in such cases, to punish the act more than the intention: and, because society has unfortunately lost one citizen, the executioner is suffered to deprive it of another.

In common understanding the crime of murder includes the circumstance of premeditation. In the laws of William Penn, the technical phrase *malice aforethought*, was avoided; and "wilful and *premeditated* murder" is the crime which was declared to be capital. Yet murder, in judicial construction, is a term so broad and comprehensive in its meaning as to embrace many acts of homicide, where the killing is neither wilful nor premeditated. "A. shooteth at the poultry of B. and, by *accident*, killeth a man; if his intention was to *steal* the poultry it will be murder: but if *done wantonly* it will be barely man-slaughter." Again, "A parker found a boy stealing wood in his masters ground: he bound him to his horse's tail and beat him. The horse took fright, run away and killed the boy. This was held to be murder." In the latter case there was no design to kill; in the former not the least intention to do any bodily harm.

I am sensible how delicate a step it is to break in upon the definition of crimes formed by the accumulated care of ages; but, when we consider how different, in their degree of guilt, these offences are from the horrid crime of deliberate assassination, it is difficult to suppress a wish, that some distinctions were made in favor of homicides which do not announce extreme depravity. . . .

## Conclusion

IT is from the ignorance, wretchedness or corrupted manners of a people that crimes proceed. In a country where these do not prevail moderate punishments, strictly enforced, will be a curb as effectual as the greatest severity.

A mitigation of punishment ought, therefore, to be accompanied, as far as possible, by a *diffusion of knowledge* and a *strict execution of the laws*. The former not only contributes to enlighten, but to meliorate the manners and improve the happiness of a people.

The celebrated *Beccaria* is of opinion, that no government has a right to punish its subjects unless it has previously taken care to instruct them in the knowledge of the laws and the duties of public and private life. The strong mind of *William Penn* grasped at both these objects, and provisions to secure them were interwoven with his system of punishments. The laws enjoined all parents and guardians to instruct the children under their care so as to enable them to write and read the scriptures by the time they attained to twelve years of age: and directed, that a copy of the laws (at that time few, simple and concise) should be used as a school book. Similar provisions were introduced into the laws of Connecticut, and the Select Men are directed to see that "none suffer so much barbarism in their families as to want such learning and instruction." The children were to be "taught the laws against capital offences," as those at Rome were accustomed to commit the twelve tables to memory. These were regulations in the pure spirit of a republic, which, considering the youth as the property of the state, does not permit a parent to bring up his children in ignorance and vice.

The policy of the Eastern states, in the establishment of public schools, aided by the convenient size and *incorporation* of their townships, deserves attention and imitation. It is, doubtless, in a great measure, owing to the diffusion of knowledge which these produce, that executions have been so rare in New England; and, for the same reason, they are comparatively few in Scotland. Early education prevents more crimes than the severity of the criminal code.

The constitution of Pennsylvania contemplates this great object and directs, That "Schools shall be established, by law, throughout this state." Although there are real difficulties which oppose themselves to the *perfect* execution of the plan, yet, the advantages of it are so manifest that an enlightened Legislator will, no doubt, cheerfully encounter, and, in the end, be able to surmount them.

*Secondly*—Laws which prescribe hard labor as a punishment should be strictly executed. The criminals ought, as far as possible, to be collected in one place, easily accessible to those who have the inspection of it. When they are together their management will be less expensive, more systematic and beneficial—Their treatment ought to be such as to make their confinement an *actual* punishment, and the rememberance of it a terror in future. The labor, in most cases, should be real *hard* labor—the food, though wholesome, should be *coarse*—the confinement sufficiently *long* to break down a disposition to vice—and the salutary rigor of *perfect solitude, invariably* inflicted on the greater offenders. Escapes should be industriously guarded against—pardons should be rarely, *very rarely*, granted, and the punishment of those who are guilty of a second offence should be sufficiently severe.

The reformation of offenders is declared to be one of the objects of the Legislature in reducing the punishment—But time, and, in some cases, *much time*, must be allowed for this. It is easy to counterfeit contrition; but it is impossible to have faith in the sudden conversion of an old offender.

On these hints I mean not to enlarge—but they point to objects of great importance, which may deserve attention whenever a further reform is attempted.

The conclusion to which we are led, by this enquiry, seems to be, that in all cases (except those of high treason and murder) the punishment of death may be safely abolished, and milder penalties advantageously introduced—Such a system of punishments, aided and enforced in the manner I have mentioned, will not only have an auspicious influence on the character, morals, and happiness of the people, but may hasten the period, when, in the progress of civilization, the punishment of death shall cease to be necessary; and the Legislature of Pennsylvania, putting the key-stone to the arch, may triumph in the *completion* of their benevolent work.

*Source*: William Bradford, *An Enquiry How Far the Punishment of Death Is Necessary in Pennsylvania* (Philadelphia: Dobson, 1793). [Early American Imprints (New York: Readex Microprint, 1985), 6–7, 35, 37–38, 43–46 (footnotes omitted).]

---

## DOCUMENT 11: *An Account of the Alteration and Present State of the Penal Laws of Pennsylvania* (Caleb Lownes, 1794)

Four years after the establishment of the first penitentiary at the Walnut Street Jail in Philadelphia (see Document 8), Caleb Lownes, one of the penitentiary's inspectors, wrote a progress report on the reformed prison titled *An Account of the Alteration and Present State of the Penal Laws in Pennsylvania.*

Lownes was a Quaker merchant who long had worked toward prison reform and the abolition of capital punishment. Like his contemporary Benjamin Rush, he believed that solitary confinement was the key to reforming the criminal mind. The theory was that removal of the often negative stimulation of the outside world would make the criminal better able to contemplate his actions and thus see the error of his ways (Masur 1989:81–82, 86).

In his report, Lownes appeared confident that the newly reformed prison was a great success—beneficial both to the prisoner and to the community. He reported that recidivism was low among pardoned offenders, crime was down on the city streets and highways outside of town, and when crimes were committed, juries no longer were reluctant to convict, as they often had been when punishments were considered too harsh. Hence, at least in Lownes' opinion, it seemed that Philadelphia was on the right track toward penal reform.

How little effect the former system of punishments had in preventing of crimes, is too well known to need any explanation at present. We are now to examine, whether any beneficial consequences have followed the alteration that has taken place in the treatment of the convicts.

It is not more than two years that the new regulations have had their full operation, although the law which authorised them, was passed some time before. But in that short time, the effects which have flowed from them, have been remarked with much satisfaction by the citizens at large, as well as by those whose situation offered superior opportunities for observing them. These effects proceed, either from a real reformation taking place in the minds of the prisoners, or from a terror of the consequences which they know will attend a second confinement.

During their continuance in prison, they learn many things which operate as a check upon the commission of new crimes. They learn the difficulty of evading justice; and that, as the laws are now mild, they will be strictly put in execution. They now see that juries are not unwilling to convict, and that pardons are not granted till they discover some appearances of amendment. The penalty, though not severe, is attended with many unpleasant circumstances, and many of them deem the constant return of the same labour and of coarse fare, as more intolerable, than a sharp, but momentary punishment. They know that a second conviction would consign them to the solitary cells and deprive them of the most distant hopes of pardon. These cells are an object of *real terror* to them all, and those who have experienced confinement in them, discover by their subsequent conduct, how strong an impression it has made on their minds. They know that mercy abused, will not be repeated, and neither change of name nor disguise, will enable them to escape the vigilant attention with which they are examined. These reflections, or reflections like these, have had their weight: for out of near 200 persons who at different times have been recommended to, and pardoned by the governor, only four have been returned: three from Philadelphia, re-convicted of larceny, and one from a neighouring county. As several of those, thus discharged, were old offenders, there was some reason to fear, that they would not long behave as honest citizens. But, if they have returned to their old courses, they have chosen to run the *risk* of being hanged in other states, rather than encounter the *certainty* of being confined in the penitentiary cells of this. We may therefore conclude, that the plan adopted has had a good effect on these; for it is a fact well known, that many of them were heretofore frequently at the bar of public justice, and had often received the punishment of their crimes under the former laws.

Our streets now meet with no interruption from those characters that formerly rendered it dangerous to walk out of an evening. Our roads in the vicinity of the city, so constantly infested with robbers, are seldom disturbed by those dangerous characters. The few instances that have occurred of the latter, last fall, were soon stopped. The perpetrators proved to be strangers, quartered near the city, on their way to the westward.

Our houses, stores, and vessels, so perpetually disturbed and robbed no longer experience those alarming evils. We lay down in peace—we sleep in security.

*Source*: Caleb Lownes, *An Account of the Alteration and Present State of the Penal Laws of Pennsylvania* (Lexington, Mass.: J. Bradford, 1794). [Early American Imprints (New York: Readex Microprint, 1985), 18–19.]

# Part II

---

# The Abolition Movement Gains Ground, 1800–1917

## ABOLITION AND PENAL REFORM

During the nineteenth century, the goals of abolitionists were intertwined with those of prison reformers in part because they tended to share a common view of humanity, but also because effective reform of prisoners provided for both groups an attractive alternative to execution.

In keeping with ideas that had grown out of the Enlightenment and the American Revolution, reformers held that less severe and more sure penalties which acknowledged the dignity of the individual and emphasized proportionate and minimal punishment would be more able to protect the public by deterring and reforming offenders. Central to this movement was the development of the penitentiary system. In contrast to prisons—which were characterized as schools for crime, debauchery, idleness, and profanity—penitentiaries were to be schools of reform that would encourage prisoners to develop morals, rectitude, and self-respect through prayer, reflection, and solitude.

However, early enthusiasm for the penitentiary as an alternative to capital punishment soon was dampened. By the turn of the century—thirteen years after Benjamin Rush launched the first major movement against capital punishment and ten years after the first penitentiary was opened—it was apparent that the expensive and overcrowded facilities were failing to reform criminals or prevent crime. While supporters argued that more time was all that was needed to improve the effectiveness of the penitentiary (see Document 12), this did not appear to be the case. In 1817, authorities in Philadelphia and Massachusetts reported that roughly a third of their current convicts had been released from the penitentiary system previously.

By 1822, after three decades of experimentation in the United States and elsewhere, many of the strongest proponents of the penitentiary system were forced to conclude that problems with design, over-crowding, management, and administration still were keeping most penitentiaries from living up to their promise (see Document 13). Un-willing to accept defeat, however, they continued to maintain that the problems were correctable and that rational attempts to reform offend-ers ultimately would prevail, unlike "barbarous and cruel" practices such as corporal and capital punishment.

During this early period of penal reform in America, Europeans such as English prison reformer John Howard (1726–1790) and English phi-losopher Jeremy Bentham (1748–1832) were especially influential.

Howard, whose book *The State of the Prisons in England and Wales; with Preliminary Observations; and an Account of some Foreign Pris-ons* had been published in England in 1777, has been called the "first man to make a comprehensive study of the institutional treatment of offenders, and, indeed, the first to make a detailed analysis of any social problem" (Howard 1958:164). Howard's observations and views on prison reform had an impact on many Americans during the nineteenth century, including Thomas Eddy (see Document 12), a Quaker mer-chant whose efforts on behalf of prison reform earned him the title "Howard of America" (Masur 1989:86).

Bentham—expanding on Beccaria's ideas on crime, punishment, and deterrence—argued that the goal of all laws should be to promote the greatest happiness for the greatest number of people. It followed, he said, that the main goal of punishment was to deter crime, which threatens the happiness of the majority. An individual's motivation to commit a crime would be most diminished, Bentham believed, if the severity of punishment matched the severity of the crime committed. Moreover, to be consistent with the goal of maximizing happiness, pun-ishment should be used only for warning, prevention, and rehabilita-tion—not retribution.

Never content to merely philosophize, much of Bentham's work was directed toward practical matters such as the design of prisons, gov-ernmental reform, and the writing of model legal codes that were sim-ple, coherent, and understandable. Perhaps in part because of his support for the emancipation of colonies and the extension of democ-racy and self-government into all fields, Bentham's writings struck a chord with many influential American readers. One of Bentham's cor-respondents in particular, American diplomat and politician Edward Livingston, developed a model system of penal law for Louisiana that, while not enacted, was very influential in the United States and abroad and had a significant impact on the nascent anti-gallows movement (Mackey 1976:xix; Schwed 1983:12).

## A SHIFT TO PRIVATE EXECUTIONS

Despite this new emphasis on milder punishments and reformation of criminals, many executions still took place during the early 1800s. However, by the 1830s a striking change began to occur in the way executions were carried out. In response to increasing concern that the public spectacle of execution served to inflame rather than deter the passions of potential criminals—and a series of riots at a time when many feared a crisis of public order—jurisdictions began turning to private rather than public executions in the 1830s and 1840s. Pennsylvania was the first state to do so, holding the first private execution (in a prison yard) in 1834; by 1845 every state in New England and the Mid-Atlantic region had abolished public executions (Masur 1989:94). These changes came at a time when wild growth, frequent mob violence (Lane 1979; Lane and Turner 1978; Weinbaum 1978), and the influx of foreign immigrants into urban areas was contributing to social disorder and increasing the fears of investors and merchants.

Roughly a quarter of a million immigrants arrived in the United States between 1790 and 1820, when partial immigration records began to be kept. As was the case for most of the next fifty years, the vast majority of the immigrants were from northern and central Europe. In the next twenty years, at least 152,000 immigrants arrived. The tempo of immigration increased rapidly in the twenty years after that, as another 630,000 immigrants were recorded. Although many of these immigrants joined the rapid westward expansion, others stayed in the port cities.

As evidence of this remarkable growth, in 1790 only two U.S. cities had populations over 25,000 (U.S. Bureau of Census 1975:11, 106): however, "[b]y 1820 New York had 124,000 inhabitants, Philadelphia 113,000, Baltimore 63,000, Boston 43,000, and New Orleans 27,000. In 1860 the respective figures were: New York, 1,080,000; Philadelphia 566,000; Baltimore 212,000; Boston 178,000; New Orleans 169,000. Chicago, which did not even exist until the 1830s, was by 1860 a great railroad center" (Cunliffe 1993:148).

Concerns about disorder associated with public executions also were supported by a new psychological theory of phrenology that captured the imagination of many Americans. Developed by two Austrian physicians, Johann Spurzheim and Franz Joseph Gall, phrenology was popularized in America by Scotland's George Combe, who used it to explain, in "scientific" terms, why public executions demoralized spectators. Phrenologists viewed the brain as the mind's organ, believing that different regions governed such behavioral dispositions as destructiveness and benevolence. They thought, for example, that people in whom the "destructive" brain region was overdeveloped and unrestrained by the "benevolent" region were especially prone to violent or criminal behaviors. The opposite was true of those whose benevolent regions were highly developed. Thus, according to Combe, "the view of public executions is insupportable to some individuals, and delightful to others" and, although the death penalty was intended to act as a deterrent, its effect on witnesses varied (Combe 1819:147–150).

At a time when fear of public disorder was so high that *any* public gathering could lead to a riot, phrenology provided a compelling argument that swayed many legislators to abolish public executions. The move away from public executions evoked mixed feelings among both proponents and opponents of capital punishment. On the one hand, more private and less spectacular executions were consistent with the norms and customs relating to privacy, gentility, and social order held by many reformers. Conversely, private executions could be interpreted as undemocratic and shameful acts that concealed the horrors of state-sponsored executions from public view (see Document 17). Furthermore, abolitionists may have feared that making executions more "comfortable" threatened to reduce anti-gallows public sentiment. Yet at the same time, private executions undermined the contention that hangings served as a deterrent to crime (Masur 1989:117).

## ANTI-GALLOWS SOCIETIES

Despite the shift from public to private executions, the anti-gallows movement that had emerged during the early nineteenth century became stronger than ever before during the 1830s and 1840s. The movement—which had led to the creation of numerous anti-gallows societies—was bolstered by the tides of religious revival, social reform, and romanticism that were sweeping the country. It also was aided by innovations in printing technology,[1] which enabled the widespread dissemination of reform ideas and also helped to unite opponents of the death penalty with other reformers (e.g., temperance, peace, women's rights), with whom they typically shared similar religious and philosophical beliefs. This was especially true of the anti-slavery movement—which also may have captured the attention of anti-gallows activists because of the disproportionate number of crimes for which blacks could be given the death penalty and the disproportionate imposition of the penalty on blacks.

While the influence of Enlightenment philosophers such as Beccaria and Bentham remained very important, it was moral and theological issues that often dominated the capital punishment debate during this period of romanticism and religious revival. Clergy from reform churches such as the Unitarian and Universalist sects denounced state-sanctioned killings on religious grounds. Meanwhile, powerful and influential leaders from more orthodox Calvinist sects such as the Presbyterians and Congregationalists, men such as the Reverend George Cheever (see Document 19), appealed to divine authority to argue the opposite. By the mid-1800s, public conflict over capital punishment reached fever pitch as essays for and against the death penalty were featured in newspapers, periodicals, and pamphlets.

By the mid-1800s, the anti-gallows societies had made major gains. The eloquent prodding of people like Robert Rantoul, Jr., in Massachusetts, Tobias Purrington in Maine, John L. O'Sullivan in New York, and Marvin H. Bovee in Wisconsin had convinced several states' legislatures to abolish the death penalty while many more reduced the number of capital crimes. When the Civil War began, neither burglary nor robbery were punishable by death in three-quarters of the states. However, at this time the campaign against capital punishment had ground to a halt because, like most reformers, abolitionists had come to see slavery as the greatest evil plaguing the land and their moral and political energies were absorbed by the Civil War (Schwed 1983:15). According to Mackey (1976:xxix), by 1857 only Universalist minister Charles Spear continued to devote most of his time to fighting the death penalty—and he soon was forced to become less active by financial pressures and ill health. While some viewed this as a failure for the anti-gallows movement, others, such as newspaper editor and poet Walt Whitman, viewed the progress that had been made as an important step toward what would be a long process of social evolution (Mackey 1976:xxviii).

## POST–CIVIL WAR

Abolitionist activity after the Civil War was sporadic and the results were mixed. According to Schwed, "the severe cruelties of the war rendered insignificant for many the executions of persons who were, after all, convicted murderers" (1983:15). This insensitivity probably was aggravated also by widespread postwar violence and traumatic reconstruction as well as by general social disorganization. The end of the war and the beginning of the industrial revolution were accompanied by massive waves of immigration—which poured ever larger proportions of people from eastern and southern Europe as well as Asia into America's industrializing cities.

In this environment, activists such as Marvin H. Bovee set their sights on the more modest goal of substituting discretionary for mandatory capital punishment in the belief that this would drastically curtail executions. They achieved their goal; by 1895 the death penalty no longer automatically followed a guilty verdict in twenty-one states. But they were wrong about the end result. Executions continued unabated (Mackey 1976:xxx).

The rapid social, economic, technological, and demographic changes of the late nineteenth century placed heavy strains on society. What only a hundred years before had been a relatively homogeneous group of colonies with a population of four million and an economy based mostly on agriculture and the export of raw materials had been transformed. More than sixty million people with diverse economic interests and cultural beliefs now competed in a largely unstructured free-for-all dominated by the interests of eastern banking, rail, and industrial monopolies. Regional, racial, and ethnic divisions were multiplied by increasing differences between occupational and class interests. These conflicts often were played out violently as strike breakers clashed with unionists, Klansmen terrorized blacks and recent immigrants, and thousands of people were lynched each decade by vigilantes (U.S. Bureau of the Census 1975:422).

## CONSTITUTIONAL ISSUES

Although abolitionists were relatively inactive during the post–Civil War upheaval, a number of constitutional issues that would have a major impact on capital punishment were developing around the Eighth Amendment and the newly-enacted Fourteenth Amendment, which was passed by Congress in 1868 (see Document 23). Although the latter promised equal protection for all Americans under the Bill of Rights and mandated that the states respect those rights and observe "due process" restrictions, little changed in many states for decades. A century later, however, the "due process" clause would become central to many legal challenges of capital sentencing procedures.

Another constitutional issue, the Eighth Amendment prohibition against cruel and unusual punishment, was developed in a series of cases between the late 1870s and 1910. In *Wilkerson v. Utah* (see Document 24), the Supreme Court held that execution by firing squad was neither unusual nor cruel. In *Kemmler* (see Document 25), it ruled that execution by electric chair, while "unusual" in the sense that it was novel, was not cruel and that the Eighth Amendment did not forbid technological changes. In *Weems v. U.S.* (see Document 27), shortly after the turn of the century, the Court set a new standard with regard to cruel and unusual punishment and for the first time overturned a statutory form of punishment. Although *Weems* itself was not a capital punishment case, it would affect many subsequent challenges to the death penalty.

## RESURGENT ABOLITIONIST ACTIVITIES

After the abuses and discord of the post–Civil War era, a progressive spirit began to take hold near the turn of the century. The antitrust movement mobilized support against monopolies. The Populist Party coalesced around the converging interests of farmers and industrial workers, then was swallowed up by the Democrats. And the anti-capital punishment movement revived, as hundreds of small campaigns and modest successes on the local level resulted in a substantial move toward abolition (Mackey 1976:xxxii). As the debate heated up—in marked contrast to the mid-1800s—arguments tended to focus much more strongly on issues of expediency and deterrence.

Retentionists included "guardians of society" such as judges, prosecuting attorneys, and police chiefs who argued that the death penalty was indispensable for preventing murder and that abolition would result in an increase in lynchings as people took matters into their own hands—especially when dealing with the large proportion of the population who were immigrants and blacks (Mackey 1976:xxxv). One Tennessee businessman, for example, argued in a letter to his governor that the death penalty was necessary because "a large Negro population" and "some whites" in his state were undeterred by the penitentiary, believing that they were better off there than on the outside (Galliher et al. 1992:557). Against sentiments such as these were arrayed a growing list of prominent political, business, government, and religious leaders, as well as journalists and writers, who argued that death sentences were not a deterrent to crime.

When America's entry into World War I fostered racism, nativism, suspicion, and fear that provided fertile soil for retentionist arguments, the abolition movement stalled out once again—as in the 1860s—a casualty of war (Mackey 1976:xxxvi).

## NOTE

1. The "penny press," made possible by the development of steam-driven and cylindrical presses, revolutionized the newspaper industry. At a cost of

one cent instead of the previous six, newspapers now were available and affordable for the general public, and they were sold daily on street corners. As a result, the number of daily papers in the United States more than doubled between 1830 and 1840 (Masur 1989:114).

## DOCUMENT 12: *An Account of the State Prison or Penitentiary House, in the City of New-York* (Thomas Eddy, 1801)

In New York, one of the strongest supporters of the prison reform movement was Thomas Eddy (1758–1827). Eddy, a Quaker of Irish descent, was a successful New York businessman who devoted himself primarily to philanthropic activities.

Influenced by the ideas of Cesare Beccaria, Charles-Louis Montesquieu, William Penn, and noted English prison reformer John Howard, Eddy was especially devoted to the cause of prison reform.

After visiting Philadelphia's new penitentiary at the renovated Walnut Street Jail in 1796, Eddy and his fellow activists were instrumental in obtaining legislative authorization for a similar penitentiary in New York—the Newgate Prison in Greenwich Village. Eddy acted for several years as an inspector and agent for the new penitentiary and helped supervise its operations.

However, soon after the turn of the century, it became apparent to many citizens in New York and elsewhere that the penitentiary system wasn't living up to its promise to reform criminals and prevent crime. In addition, the new penitentiaries already were becoming overcrowded, and costs were mounting (Masur 1989:88–89).

Eddy—who remained convinced that it was only a matter of time before society would begin to reap the benefits of the penitentiary—was concerned about the public's growing dissatisfaction with the new system, and he feared a call for the resurrection of the death penalty for many crimes.

In his 1801 report *An Account of the State Prison or Penitentiary House, in the City of New-York*, which included a detailed account of the prison itself, prison operations (including costs), and the treatment of prisoners and efforts to reform them, Eddy took the opportunity to address many of the criticisms against the penitentiary system, urging legislators and citizens to be patient and not to thwart the new reform effort in its infancy.

The work of reformation is slow, and must encounter many and strong prejudices, and the force of long-established opinions. It was prudent to listen to the voice of those who advised a forbearance of further change till experience had fully ascertained the advantages and defects of the new system. These will be gradually developed in the progress of the experiment; but many years are necessary to its completion. A slight acquaintance with the nature of man and the history of society is sufficient to convince the considerate and dispassionate observer, that the full effects of an institution of this kind cannot be felt, nor the trial of its wisdom and efficacy be fairly and satisfactorily made, until after a long and persevering attention to its management and operations.

It is to be lamented, that many good citizens, feeling a just abhorrence at crimes, consulting the suggestions of virtuous indignation, rather than the principles of justice, become impatient that the alteration of the penal code has not yet produced greater and more decided effects, and diminished the number of the guilty. They, sometimes, even express a regret at the change which has been wrought in our laws, and returning to a system of accumulated severity and terror, wish to see every offence against life and property punished with death; as if crimes would cease with the extermination of the criminal. But let such turn their eyes inward upon their own hearts, and analyze the source from whence such wishes arise. Let them consider the effects produced on society and manners by the rapid increase of wealth and luxury, natural population, and emigration, which consequently augment the number of crimes, whether the laws be mild or sanguinary. Let them consult reason, and the experience of the most enlightened nations, which prove beyond all contradiction, that crimes are most frequent where the laws are most rigourous; that punishments *mild* and *certain* more effectually prevent crimes than those which are sanguinary and severe. Let them at least examine, before they condemn, a system sanctioned by different legislatures, prudent and enlightened, and applauded by the wisest and best men in all civilized countries.

Source: Thomas Eddy, *An Account of the State Prison or Penitentiary House, in the City of New-York* (New York: Isaac Collins and Son, 1801), 15–16.

---

## DOCUMENT 13: *Report on the Penitentiary System in the United States* (1822)

Twenty-one years after Thomas Eddy argued that patience would prove the benefits of the penitentiary system (see Document 12), he and eight other members of a New York committee appointed to conduct a nationwide evaluation of the system concluded that the system had failed to fulfill the expectations of its founders and advocates.

In its lengthy report, the committee identified numerous defects in the system—including poor design of the prisons, failure to separate novice or nonviolent criminals from violent and hardened offenders, overcrowding, frequent pardons, inappropriate diet, lack of a school for juvenile offenders, absence of moral and religious instruction, the frequent change of superintendents and governors, and too much regard to revenue.

But despite these failures, the committee maintained that the penitentiary system still could be modified and improved to meet the expectations that originally had been set for it—to reform criminals and reduce crime. Toward this end, it provided a series of recommendations that addressed each of the above concerns. Central to the reform plan was a return to the notion that solitary confinement was key to reforming serious and violent offenders.

In defending the recommendation to retain and improve the faulty system, the committee asserted that "the Penitentiary System, as it now exists, in the United States, with all its defects, is preferable to the former systems of punishment in this country." Some of the committee's final arguments—in which it also stressed the importance of serving as a role model to other countries undergoing penal reform—are excerpted below.

We are fully aware, that great consideration is attached to the Penitentiary System in the United States, by the enlightened men in Europe, who are now combining their exertions to produce a radical reform in Penal Jurisprudence. Nor are improvements in the execution of Penal laws confined to England. The Report of the Prison Society of Paris, shews that much is doing in France, to combine punishment with reformation. In Ireland, the labours of the Dublin Association, for the improvement of prisons, are working salutary changes. In Switzerland, some useful reforms are taking place. In Russia, an Association for the same purpose has been created: the location is at St. Petersburgh, under the sanction of the Emperor Alexander, who, is giving force and authority to its proceedings, throughout his wide dominions. In Sweden, and Norway, information of the condition of all the jails is collecting under the patronage of the two governments, that the hand of correction may be successfully applied in the treatment of criminals after their sentence to public prisons. Let them not feel their prospects darkened—let not their efforts be weakened, by the partial failure of our own system. Not a fact remains on record—not a defect has been revealed, in the progress of thirty years, to convince us that it cannot be rendered all that it was ever expected to be. And the Committee do feel themselves bound to lay down the following broad positions:

*First.* That the Penitentiary System, as it now exists, in the United States, with all its defects, is preferable to the former systems of punishment in this country.

*Secondly.* That it is capable of being so improved, as to become the

most judicious and effective system of punishment ever known in ancient or modern times.

*Thirdly.* That where it has been properly administered, as it formerly
was in Pennsylvania and New-York, it has succeeded and answered the
expectations of its early friends.

*Fourthly.* That solitary confinement, by night and by day, combined
with other regulations suggested in this Report, will remedy all existing
evils.

*Fifthly.* That it is the duty of the different states of the Union to proceed, without delay, to its improvement and perfection.

*Lastly.* That corporal punishments and the infliction of death, would
not prove congenial to the moral sentiments and feelings of the American
people: and that the transportation of convicts, is visionary, impracticable, and would not prevent crimes and offences, even if it were adopted
in our penal statutes. The Committee hope and trust, that enlightened,
humane, and public spirited individuals, of the different States in the
Union, will feel the responsibility that rests upon this country in relation
to the System of which we have so fully spoken.

This is no common age in the annals of mankind. More is now doing
to ameliorate the condition and to promote the happiness of the human
race, than any period of society has accomplished. The errors and vices
of preceding centuries are in the way of correction. There is a unity of
thought, design, and action, among the most powerful empires of the
earth, that stands a moral phenomenon in the history of governments.
At length the spirit of Howard begins to walk abroad over the face of
Europe; at length his voice is heard from the dark abodes of the wretched
and forsaken of our species—from the peaceful vallies of Switzerland,
to the Kremlin of Moscow. Penal jurisprudence gathers around it the
regards of the jurists and the lawgiver, and commands the illustrations
of genius and reflection. Its importance to the welfare and safety of
nations is duly considered, and one improvement is rapidly succeeding
another. What do we then owe to ourselves—what do we owe to the
world as a nation? Are we to permit caprice and prejudice to govern us,
on a subject interesting to ourselves and interesting to mankind, or are
we to remember that a great experiment in civil policy, blended with the
dearest interests of humanity, should not be abandoned, until tested by
fidelity and candour? If a mild Criminal Code, can be fairly tried any
where, it can be tried in this country. Our institutions were established
on the will of the people. They were the offspring of enlightened views
and independent feelings. Education is more generally diffused here,
than elsewhere on the civilized globe. The civil relations of life are less
complex—there is less of poverty and less of oppression. The cry of
bread and the approach of general want, are never known: popular sentiment is disposed to mildness, and to the adoption of virtuous restraints.

If the Penitentiary System should be abandoned, in such a country, what would the legislators of Europe hereafter say? What, would those who must hereafter raise their voices in our own halls of legislation, say? A System founded on benevolent principles, was tried for thirty years under circumstances the most propitious: it terminated in failure and disappointment. Why should we again traverse the same ground of experiment to meet with the same calamitous results! The causes of its failure would not descend to an impartial posterity, with the story of its unfortunate termination. A lasting and unqualified condemnation would settle over its untimely grave. Devoutly do we trust that this train of prospective reflections will never exist in sober reality. Is an attempt to impose the Criminal laws of nations worthy of a free people? Is an attempt to wipe from the Penal codes of empires the shades of barbarism and cruelty by example, worthy of christian land? Are the interests of humanity and the elevation of our species, objects worthy of constant solicitude, among a people who have laid the deep foundations of the most rational and perfect constitution of government that the long career of six hundred centuries has produced? When popular states, in the vigor of virtue and enterprise, forget the glorious march of the human mind that has struck them into existence—when they forget their character in the scale of principalities and kingdoms, and the hopes of the bond and the free that are embosomed in their fortunes—when such states turn back and pursue the steps that lead to the dark policy of despotic governments, the prospects of progressive improvement among mankind are indeed forlorn and discouraging. There are principles and feelings in the American nation that will produce results more grateful and beneficent.

*Source*: Charles G. Haines, *Report on the Penitentiary System in the United States* (New York: Mahlon Day, 1822), 95–98 (footnotes omitted).

---

## DOCUMENT 14: Edward Livingston (1825)

Another prominent penal reformer of the early nineteenth century was Edward Livingston (1764–1836). Livingston, a New York lawyer and diplomat, graduated from the College of New Jersey (Princeton) in 1781. He was admitted to the bar in 1785, and soon after began practicing law in New York City.

A Jeffersonian Republican, Livingston served three terms in Congress (1795–1801) and then was appointed U.S. Attorney for New York and, simultaneously, mayor of New York.

   In 1804, following a bout with yellow fever during which one of his agents absconded with treasury bonds, leaving him heavily in debt to the federal government, Livingston moved to New Orleans to start his life and career anew. There, he speculated in real estate to help pay off his debts, and he rose to prominence once again in the legal profession.

   In 1820, Livingston was elected to the Louisiana legislature, and the following year he was commissioned to revise Louisiana's penal laws—a task that took him four years due to a fire that destroyed the first version of his work.

   When completed in 1825 and presented to the Louisiana legislature, Livingston's proposed System of Penal Law for Louisiana included a Code of Crimes and Punishments, Code of Procedure, Code of Evidence, Code of Reform and Prison Discipline, and Book of Definitions.

   The plan for penal reform—which included a house of detention, a penitentiary, a house of refuge and industry, and a school of reform—focused on the prevention of crime rather than on punishment. For example, in his Code of Crimes and Punishments, Livingston argued against capital punishment on the basis of its ineffectiveness as a deterrent to crime. Livingston was especially opposed to public executions, which he believed aggravated rather than deterred crime.

   Livingston's code was not adopted by Louisiana, but its publication and wide circulation brought Livingston national and international recognition and made a significant contribution to the budding anti-gallows movement in the United States (Mackey 1976:xix; Schwed 1983:12).

To apportion the punishment to the offence, does not mean to make the culprit suffer the same quantity of evil which he inflicted by his crime; that would be both impossible and unjust. It means, that the punishment should be such as to deter from the commission of the crime, but no greater. If, then, death has not this effect, why ought it to be applied? But that it has not this effect, is shown by reasoning and by fact. Why then will you continue to apply it? Pressed by this inquiry, we have the same eternal answer—murder deserves death. Out of this circle no reasoning can drive them. Sometimes, indeed, we are asked, are you sure that if we give up this punishment, your substitute will prove effectual? If you mean so effectual as to eradicate the crime, I answer, No! But I am as sure as experience and analogy, and reasoning united, can make me, that it will be more effectual. What is it we fear? Why do we hesitate? You know, you cannot deny, that the fear of the gallows does not restrain from murder. We have seen a deliberate murder committed in the very crowd assembled to enjoy the spectacle of a murderer's death; and do we still talk of its force as an example? In defiance of your menaced punishment, homicide stalks abroad and raises its bloody hand at noon-day in your crowded streets; and when arrested in its career, takes shelter under the example of your laws, and is protected by their very severity, from punishment. Try the efficacy of milder punishments; they have succeeded. Your own statutes, all those of every state in the union, prove that they have succeeded, in other offences; try the great experiment on this also. Be consistent; restore capital punishments in other crimes, or abolish it in this.

*Source*: Edward Livingston, "Introductory Report to the Code of Crimes and Punishments," 1825. In *The Complete Works of Edward Livingston on Criminal Jurisprudence*, Vol. 1. Originally published by The National Prison Association in 1873. [Montclair, N.J.: Patterson Smith, 1968, 214–215.]

## DOCUMENT 15: *Report on the Abolition of Capital Punishment* (Robert Rantoul, 1836)

In Massachusetts, one of the most ardent and eloquent abolitionists of the day was Robert Rantoul, Jr. (1805–1852).

Rantoul, a lawyer and Democratic statesman in conservative Massachusetts, was influenced early in his career by the writings of Cesare Beccaria, and by his father, who also had been a legislator and a pioneer in the movement to abolish capital punishment in Massachusetts.

Rantoul apparently was well aware that—like his chosen political affiliation—his support for the abolition of capital punishment and other unpopular reforms such as the temperance movement was detrimental to his political career (Hamilton 1854:8). Yet he remained firm and outspoken in his views, and he was elected a representative to the Massachusetts state legislature for four consecutive years beginning in 1835. It was as a member of this legislature's judiciary committee that he submitted what is perhaps his most famous and comprehensive report advocating the abolition of the death penalty.

Rantoul was appointed United States District Attorney for Massachusetts in 1845, a position he held until 1849, when he resigned. In 1851, his opposition to the extension of slavery led to his election to the U.S. Senate, filling the seat Daniel Webster gave up on being appointed Secretary of State. Later that year, Rantoul was elected to the federal House of Representatives.

Rantoul, who died of a sudden illness in 1852, continued to argue for the abolition of capital punishment throughout his life, both through his legislative career and as a member of the Massachusetts Society for the Abolition of Capital Punishment. Yet, while the efforts of Rantoul and others contributed to increased abolitionist sentiment in Massachusetts and other states, Massachusetts remained steadfast in its commitment to the gallows (Masur 1989:160).

Has society the right to take away life? . . .

Protection being the only object of society, it follows that we surrender to it, for the purpose of preserving our natural rights as nearly unimpaired as conflicting claims will in the nature of things admit, only so much liberty as it is necessary should be relinquished to that end. To give up more, by the division of a hair, would be to counteract so far the very endeavor we are making when we are forming the social compact to secure the full enjoyment of our natural rights. It needed not, therefore, the authority of Montesquieu, or of Beccaria, to give weight to the maxim, that every punishment which does not arise from absolute necessity; and even every act of authority of one man over another, for which there is not an absolute necessity, is tyrannical. The right to punish crimes is founded upon the necessity of defending the public liberty, and is coextensive only with that necessity. . . .

When we surrendered to society the smallest possible portion of our liberty, to enable us the better to retain the aggregate of rights which we did not surrender, did we concede our title to that life with which our Creator has endowed us? Is it to be conceived that we have consented to hold the tenure of our earthly existence at the discretion, or the caprice of a majority, whose erratic legislation no man can calculate beforehand? While our object was to preserve, as little impaired as might be possible, all our rights, which are all of them comprehended in the right to enjoy life, can we have agreed to forfeit that right to live while God shall spare our lives, which is the essential precedent condition of all our other rights? Property may be diminished, and afterwards increased. Liberty may be taken away for a time, and subsequently restored. The wound which is inflicted may be healed, and the wrong we have suffered may be atoned for; but there is no Promethean heat that can rekindle the lamp of life if once extinguished. Can it be, then, that while property, liberty, and personal security are guarded and hedged in on every side, by the strict provisions of our fundamental constitution, that life is unconditionally thrown into the common stock, not to be forfeited in a specific case, agreed upon beforehand at the organization of our society, but in all such cases as the popular voice may single out and make capital by law? Have we entered into any such compact?

The burthen of proof is wholly upon those who affirm that we have so agreed. Let it be shown that mankind in general, or the inhabitants of this Commonwealth in particular, have agreed to hold their lives as a conditional grant from the State. Let it be shown that any one individual, understanding the bargain, and being free to dissent from it, ever voluntarily placed himself in such a miserable vassalage. Let there, at least, be shown some reason for supposing that any sane man has of his own accord bartered away his original right in his own existence, that his government may tyrannize more heavily over him and his fellows, when all the purposes of good government may be amply secured at so much cheaper a purchase. In no instance can this preposterous sacrifice be implied. It must be shown by positive proof that it has been made, and until this is undeniably established, the right of life remains among those reserved rights which we have not yielded up to society. . . .

Not only has no man actually given up to society the right to put an end to his life, not only is no surrender of this right under a social compact ever to be implied, but no man can, under a social contract, or any other contract, give up this right to society, or to any constituent part of society, for this conclusive reason, that the right is not his to be conveyed. Has a man a right to commit suicide? Every Christian must answer, no. A man holds his life as a tenant at will,—not indeed of society, who did not and cannot give it, or renew it, and have therefore no right to take it away,—but of that Almighty Being whose gift life is, who sustains and continues it, to whom it belongs, and who alone has the right to reclaim his gift whenever it shall seem good in his sight. A man may not surrender up his life until he is called for. May he then make a contract with his neighbor that, in such or such a case, his neighbor shall kill him? Such a contract, if executed, would involve the one party in the guilt of suicide, and other in the guilt of murder. If a man may not say to his next neighbor, "when I have burned your house in the night time, or wrested your purse from you on the highway, or broken into your house in the night, with an iron crow, to take a morsel of meat for my starving child, do you seize me, shut me up a few weeks, and then bring me out and strangle me, and in like case, if your turn comes first, I will serve you in the same way," would such an agreement between ten neighbors be any more valid or justifiable? No. Nor if the number were a hundred instead of ten, who should form this infernal compact, nor if there should be six hundred thousand, or seven hundred thousand, or even fourteen millions, who should so agree, would this increase of the number of partners vary one hair's breadth the moral character of the transaction. If the execution of this contract be not still murder on the one side and suicide on the other, what precise number of persons must engage in it, in order that what was criminal before may become innocent, not to say virtuous,—and upon what hitherto unheard of principles of morality is an act of murder in an individual, or a small corporation, converted into an act of justice whenever another subscriber has joined the association for mutual sacrifice? It is a familiar fact in the history of mankind, that great corporations will do, and glory in, what the very individuals composing them would shrink from or blush at; but how does the division of responsibility transform vice into virtue, or diminish the amount of any given crime? The command, "Thou shalt not kill," applies to individual men as members of an association, quite as peremptorily as in their private capacity; and although men in a numerous company may keep one another in countenance in a gross misdeed, and may so mystify and confuse their several relations to it, as that each one may sin ignorantly, and therefore in the sight of the Searcher of Hearts be absolved from intentional guilt, still that it does not alter the true nature of the act must be obvious, as also that it is equally our duty to abstain from a social as from a personal crime, when once its criminality is clearly understood.

*Source*: Robert Rantoul, Jr., *Report on the Abolition of Capital Punishment* (From the Legislative Documents of 1836). In Luther Hamilton, ed., *Memoirs, Speeches and Writings of Robert Rantoul, Jr.* (Boston: John P. Jewett, 1854), 439–444.

---

## DOCUMENT 16: *Report on Capital Punishment Made to the Maine Legislature* (1836)

The same year Robert Rantoul was speaking out against capital punishment to the Massachusetts legislature, Tobias Purrington, a state senator from Brunswick, Maine, was making a similar plea to the Maine legislature.

The following year, Maine became the first state to declare what amounted to a moratorium on the death penalty. It did so without actually eliminating the death penalty—instead, the new law required that a prisoner's execution warrant could not be issued until at least one year after his sentencing date, and even then, it only could be issued if the governor specifically ordered it. As expected, the new law—enacted partly in response to a riot that had erupted during a public hanging—virtually put an end to executions in Maine (Mackey 1976:xxi-xxii; Schwed 1983:14).

But it wasn't until forty years later, in 1876, that capital punishment officially was abolished in Maine. Maine's death penalty subsequently was reinstated in 1883 and again abolished in 1887.

It is obvious to every mind, that hanging a man by the neck, burning him at the stake, strangulation in the prison, or decapitation, cannot reform him or restore any thing to the injured party. What has been said, it is believed, clearly proves that no absolute necessity, and consequently no right, exists for perpetuating a practice so revolting to the better feelings of men; and, could human testimony avail any thing in this case, that of the distinguished Franklin, Rush, and Bentham might be quoted against it, based upon reason, philosophy, and the dictates of humanity.

Reparation for the injury done is very justly an object of punishment, or rather the attainment of which justice demands. But, as it cannot, in the nature of things, always be made, it becomes a secondary consideration. Reformation of the criminal is the great object of punishments in general; and as we have hospitals for the cure of diseases of the body, so we should consider penitentiaries hospitals for the cure of moral diseases; and the detention of convicts in the latter should, as in the former, be till the malady is cured. Relapses may, and undoubtedly will, occur; but, in general, when the cure is effected, the convict may be safely restored to his friends and society. . . . But for the punishment of the crime of deliberate or wilful murder, perpetual confinement to hard labor in the State prison ought justly to be inflicted; but, even in these cases, moral instruction should be connected with the labor required; for, although the criminal may be guilty of crimes of great turpitude, we should not abandon a fellow-being to drag out a miserable existence without an effort to reclaim him; for, by this measure, all become benefitted who are in any way connected with him. Reclaim the convict, and you benefit him; he will become more obedient, and will sustain better the relations between himself and his keepers; he will become more industrious, and perform his work better, and hence more profitable to the State. While thus the dictates of humanity are complied with, the criminal will feel the punishment with greater severity, because he will have been made to see the nature of the crime for which he has been incarcerated in a prison, and the justice of which he will also perceive and voluntarily acknowledge, and even express his gratitude for the blessings of prison instruction. While the public exhibition of such facts will have a tendency to elevate public morals, they will have a much greater effect to deter men from the commission of crimes than the punishment of death can possibly have; and, when contrasted with the latter, your Committee do not hesitate which to prefer. Firm, but humane and kind, treatment will subdue that moroseness and obduracy of heart which cruelty and the halter, in prospect, could never effect. Imprisonment for life in the State prison, connected with labor and moral instruction, furnishes also a perpetual admonition to the wicked; whereas the infliction of death is short and transient, and its effects upon such minds are pernicious.

Source: Tobias Purrington, *Report on Capital Punishment Made to the Maine Legislature in 1836* (Washington, D.C.: Gideon, 1852), 19–21.

## DOCUMENT 17: *The Manual of Peace* (Thomas C. Upham, 1836)

By the mid-1830s—prompted both by the growing belief in the impressionability of the mind and increased concerns over the public rioting that often accompanied public executions—most states began to shift from public to private executions (Masur 1989:98–102).

One abolitionist who vehemently opposed this shift was Thomas Upham (1799–1872), a Congregationalist minister and professor of moral and mental philosophy at Bowdoin College from 1824 to 1867.

Upham believed that private executions had no place in a republican society, insisting—though he opposed capital punishment on the basis of the sanctity of human life—that: "If business of this nature is done at all, it must be done in the light of day."

In his widely-read book *The Manual of Peace*, Upham argued against both war and capital punishment, and advocated raising the standard of character in the community through education and moral training in order to enable the adoption of a milder criminal code.

While Upham's book was influential, he was wrong in his prediction that the American public would not accept the shift to private executions. The change went mostly unchallenged, even by abolitionists. As one capital punishment historian explained: "The opponents of capital punishment might have been expected at the time to challenge private executions, but they never did. Some of them condemned the elitist nature of private executions. Others argued that prison hangings repudiated the logic of a defense of the death penalty. But, generally, they believed that the elimination of public executions would lead to the total abolition of capital punishment" (Masur 1989:113).

As a general thing, persons of refined feeling and just sentiments are not disposed to be present; it is a sight, however criminal the victim may be, which they find to be strongly repugnant to something within them. And of those who are present, what do we find to be the conduct under circumstances, which we should naturally suppose would impress and affect the rudest minds? It is undeniable and perfectly notorious, that the great body of them exhibit, except at the very moment of the execution, the most surprising thoughtlessness and levity. The occasion is generally made one of great riot, noise, confusion, drunkenness, and every species of crime.—This is universally admitted to be the case. So much so that some of the United States have recently enacted, that executions shall not be public. A great anomaly this in a republican government! Our courts of justice must be open to the public; the deliberations of our legislatures must be public; not even a poor free-masonry society is to be tolerated, because its ceremonies are secret; but when life is to be taken, when a human being is to be smitten down like an ox, when a soul is to be violently hurled into eternity, the most solemn occasion that can be witnessed on earth, then the public must be excluded. But the American public will not long submit to this. If business of this nature is done at all, it must be done in the light of day; if the continuance of capital punishments depends upon their being inflicted in private, it may be regarded as certain, that they cannot long exist in this country. . . .

In conclusion we would remark, that the subject of crimes and punishments, has been but imperfectly understood. Men have too often measured the influence of punishment by the degree of suffering alone. They think the harder the blow, the more good is done; and that the good result will be precisely in proportion to its severity. This is too limited a method of estimating this matter. In estimating the influence and anticipated results of any proposed punishments, it is necessary to take a combined view, on the one hand, of the suffering; and on the other, of the character of the person, on whom it is inflicted. A light punishment will have more effect on a man of high character, than a severe one will have on a man of low and abandoned character. The great object of punishments, stated in a single sentence, is to secure a compliance with the wholesome laws of society. In order to secure this object perfectly, it is necessary not only to provide for inflicting suffering on offenders, but to make provision also for raising the standard of character through the community generally. The more you raise the standard of character in the community, the more you can lower the scale of penal enactments. . . . Let every effort, therefore, be made by the legislature and by private individuals to diffuse knowledge among the people. Men have long enough acted on the principle of trampling upon and destroying each other; let them reverse the maxims of their conduct, and seek to bind up the wounds of their fellow-men, and to save them. Here is a great work to be done; a work honorable as it is great; a work, which aims at the renovation of society, not by the inefficacious methods of the block, the gallows, and the guillotine; but by the nobler methods of moral culture; by purifying the fountain of good and evil in the youthful breast; by planting the seeds of knowledge and virtue, which shall afterwards spring up and incorporate the strength of their branches and the beauty of their flower and foliage in the mature life and action of the man.

*Source*: Thomas C. Upham, *The Manual of Peace* (New York: Leavitt, Lord, and Brunswick, Me.: Joseph Griffin, 1836), 234–235, 250–251.

**DOCUMENT 18:** *Report in Favor of the Abolition of the Punishment of Death by Law* **(John O'Sullivan, 1841)**

In 1841 New York, a young man named John O'Sullivan (1813–1895) was fast becoming one of the nation's best known opponents of the death penalty.

O'Sullivan, a Democratic member of the New York legislature and cofounder and editor of the popular *United States Magazine and Democratic Review*, was only twenty-eight when he delivered his *Report in Favor of the Abolition of the Punishment of Death by Law* to the legislature.

O'Sullivan's report opened with religious argumentation—a hallmark of many abolitionist arguments during that era of religious revival. However, practical issues also were addressed throughout the report, as O'Sullivan sought to prove that the death penalty was not an effective deterrent to crime and therefore not an effective or necessary punishment.

But despite significant and widespread abolitionist activities by O'Sullivan and others in New York during the nineteenth century, the state did not abolish the death penalty until 1965.[1] It was reinstated thirty years later, in 1995 (see Document 109).

**NOTE**
1. Although New York abolished the death penalty for most crimes in 1965, the death penalty was retained in cases involving the murder of an on-duty police officer, or of anyone by a prisoner under a life sentence.

The practice of capital punishment by society, for the purpose of exerting a moral influence on the minds of men to deter them from the crime of murder, is in truth a suicidal one—its direct tendency being clearly subversive of its own object. The Voice of God has issued the perpetual and universal mandate to the race of his creation, *"Thou shalt not kill!"* From the inmost depths of man's own nature, where reside all those instincts and sympathies that bid him revolt with horror from the thought of murder, the same Voice still forever repeats to him the high and holy law, *"Thou shalt not kill!"* It should be the policy of all social government to maintain and magnify, by every means in its power, this great idea of the inviolability of the life of man—of the sanctity of that unknown principle of vitality which, coursing to and fro through vein and artery, with the blood which the Noahic precept and the Mosaic law invested with so peculiar a sacredness, constitutes the basis of that strange union of spirit and matter, of soul and body, of which is composed this fearful and unfathomable mystery of our humanity. That blood should never be shed—that union should never be severed—whether by public or private hand, *"for in the image of God made He man!"* This sacro-sanctity of human life should never be violated. Though he should be crimsoned thrice over with the blood of the most deliberate and malignant crime, still in the murderer's own person should the holiness of this high principle be always recognised and respected. Fresh from his fratricide, the command of God was that upon him who should slay Cain, *"vengeance should be taken sevenfold."* No more impressive lesson could be taught by society, to reach the universal public mind and heart,—and to deepen and to strengthen there this universal sentiment which, far more than the terror of halters and scaffolds, is the shield that surrounds our daily path and our midnight sleep with safety,—than to respect the life of man even in the person of the very wretch who has himself forgot to respect it in the person of the victim he did not spare. Treat as a madman him who could be guilty of such a monstrous and stupendous outrage upon his own proper nature—and none but madmen will commit it. "Let the idea of crime, horrible crime," says Mr. Rantoul in his report to the Massachusetts Legislature, in February, 1836, "be indissolubly and universally associated with the voluntary and deliberate destruction of life under whatever pretext. Whoever strengthens this association in the public mind, does more to prevent murders than any punishment, with whatever aggravation of torture, can effect through fear. The denomination of Friends have always been educated in this idea, and among them murders are unknown. The strongest safeguard of life is its sanctity; and this sentiment every execution diminishes."

More would be done by this means to prevent the commission of murder, than by the decimation of a whole people to prevent it by terror.

*Source*: John L. O'Sullivan, *Report in Favor of the Abolition of the Punishment of Death by Law* (New York: J. & H. G. Langley, 1841). [New York: Arno Press, 1974, 89–90.]

## DOCUMENT 19: Rev. George Barrel Cheever (1843)

One of the strongest opponents of John O'Sullivan's efforts to abolish the death penalty in New York was George Barrel Cheever (1807–1890).

Cheever, a clergyman and ardent anti-slavery advocate, graduated from Bowdoin College in 1825 and from Andover Seminary in 1830. He began his career in Massachusetts, but eventually moved to New York, where he became pastor of the Allen Street Presbyterian Church in 1838.

Soon after arriving in New York, Cheever became embroiled in the state's growing capital punishment controversy. Cheever defended the death penalty on biblical grounds as staunchly as O'Sullivan opposed it in the name of the Bible. And, also in direct opposition to O'Sullivan's views, Cheever believed that the death penalty was an extremely effective deterrent to murder, and therefore a necessary punishment for practical as well as moral reasons.

In 1842, shortly after O'Sullivan presented his *Report in Favor of the Abolition of the Punishment of Death by Law*, Cheever published *Punishment by Death: Its Authority and Expediency* and dedicated it to the New York legislature.

In January and February of 1843, Cheever and O'Sullivan debated the issue "Ought Capital Punishment to Be Abolished?" on three evenings over a three-week period at the Broadway Tabernacle, a public meeting hall in New York City.

But rather than resolving any issues, the debate resulted in increased hostility between O'Sullivan and Cheever and their supporters that was played out in the local newspapers and in additional debates during the 1840s. It also led to increased tensions between Universalist and Unitarian ministers, who tended to oppose the death penalty, and Presbyterian and Congregationalist ministers, who continued to support it (Masur 1989:151–152).

## ENORMITY OF THE GUILT OF MURDER, AND NECESSITY OF A PENALTY THAT SHALL MAKE IT PARAMOUNT IN ITS RETRIBUTION, AS IT STANDS IN ITS GUILT.

There is no computing the enormity of the guilt of murder. It stands alone, and unapproached by any other crime in its atrocity. Its intrinsic enormity, and its dreadful consequences are such that we need not wonder at the language in which it is described and denounced by Jehovah, nor at the penalty of death affixed to it. It is right, it is benevolent, it is necessary, that such a crime should invariably, without any exception in any case whatever, be punished with the extremest penalty of which heaven has annexed the authority to human law. There ought to be such a penalty, high, awful, distinctive, to mark this crime in its *retribution*, as it stands in its *guilt*, paramount to every other. The conscience of society should be educated in the view of such a penalty; if it were not, or when it is not, poor and cheap indeed is the estimate placed upon the sacredness of human life.

The object of all punishment is benevolent, it is the well-being of the community. It is to prevent crime by supporting law. The penalty of the law must be an evil, which the man intending crime will balance against the good he proposes to himself by the crime. He must fear the evil more than he desires the good. Do you say that men commit crimes in passion, and that there is seldom this balancing of motives and considerations? I answer, this may possibly be true in regard to all minor penalties, and this is one strong argument for having in the case of murder so terrific, strong, overbearing a penalty, that it shall break down all other considerations, that it may stem the torrent of passion, that the criminal may hear a voice amidst the roar of the tempest of passion commanding him to refrain.

## INJUSTICE AND INHUMANITY OF THE ABOLITION OF THE PENALTY OF DEATH FOR MURDER.

I have shown that this penalty is necessary for the restraint of crime and the protection of society. I shall now show that the proposed abolition of it is unjust and inhuman in the last degree. It is a policy, the cruelty and barbarism of which is susceptible of a perfect demonstration. It introduces the element of inhumanity into the very education of society. Your jurisprudence is a most important part of your education for the community. It trains the common conscience. But in the abolition of this penalty, you occasion a general degradation of the moral sense; you teach that there is no difference between the guilt of murder, and that of mere forgery and stealing. You lessen men's estimate of the sacredness of human life, and you are unconsciously training men's passions for the cruelty of murder. You degrade the whole subject and science of morals; for this is at the foundation of it, involving all its principles. You give place and full swing to duelling, bloody riots, and private revenge. What you refuse as a government to do for the family and friends of the murdered man, and for the interests of the community, you may be sure the malignity of private revenge will not fail to accomplish. You take away the strong security of your police, and you expose the lives of your jail-keepers to imminent hazard.

## TWO THINGS INCONTROVERTIBLE; MEN'S LOVE OF LIFE, AND THEIR FEAR OF DEATH.

To have any ground of plausibility in your argument from expediency for abolishing the penalty of death for murder, you have to deny two things; first, that life is the most sacred and desirable of all possessions; and second, that death is the most terrible of all evils. Now on both these points the sense of mankind is undeniable. There may be deranged creatures, who deny both the desirableness of life, and the terribleness of death; just as there are hypochondriacs, who say that their heads are turned round upon their shoulders, so that they can only look behind them; and there may be inveterately hardened creatures, who have so drugged and stupified the moral sensibility with crime, that no consideration whatever will move them; but these exceptions no more weaken the power of the argument, than the fall of a solitary leaf in a great forest can prove the death of the whole foliage. You might as well bring forward one of your monsters of the menageries, your oxen with two heads, or your calves with five legs, to disprove by such a *lusus naturæ* the fact that oxen have but one head, and that calves are quadrupeds. You would be just as wise to take a petrified vegetable from the bottom of a swamp as an example of the qualities of the living vegetable world, as to take the heart of a Newgate criminal, to prove that death is not the greatest of all evils.

Now, life being the most sacred of all possessions, it is the natural judgment of mankind that you must guard it by the most terrible of all penalties. But if life be the most precious of all possessions, the human mind again declares that death is the most dreadful of all evils, and therefore consequently the most powerful of all penalties to restrain men from taking life. Until you have disproved these two things, you cannot advance one step in your argument. There is no room for you. You have to root out and destroy these two arguments of the human mind, that life is the most desirable and sacred of all possessions, and that Death is the King of Terrors. If you can do this, you can change the nature of mankind. But if not, then the conclusion is irresistible on the ground of expediency, that capital punishment is the most efficacious of all penalties to restrain men from the crime of murder, and consequently for the good of society ought to be practised.

*Source*: George B. Cheever, *Capital Punishment, The Argument of Rev. George B. Cheever in Reply to J. L. O'Sullivan, Esq.* (New York: Saxton and Miles, 1843), 42–43, 53–54, 76–78.

---

## DOCUMENT 20: *Essays on the Punishment of Death* (Charles Spear, 1844)

As Cheever and O'Sullivan waged their battle over the death penalty in New York, Charles Spear (1801–1863) campaigned tirelessly in support of legislative measures for the benefit and reformation of criminals in Boston.

Spear, a philanthropist and Universalist minister, was a regular visitor at the local prison; he often took discharged convicts to his home, where he let them stay until they found work.

Spear also served as secretary of the Massachusetts Society for the Abolition of Capital Punishment, which he helped to found in 1844. And in 1845 he launched a weekly anti-gallows newspaper titled *The Hangman*. A year later, the title of the paper was changed to *The Prisoner's Friend*, and in 1848 the weekly paper was transformed into a monthly newsletter, which endured until 1859.

Spear was strongly influenced by Thomas Upham (see Document 17), who during an 1842 meeting encouraged him to make the abolition of capital punishment his primary cause (Masur 1989:134). Upham's apparent influence—particularly with regard to the "inviolability of human life"—seems evident in Spear's widely successful 1844 book, *Essays on the Punishment of Death.*

We sincerely believe that the only doctrine that will ever secure to man his just rights, will be that of the Inviolability of Human Life. We must begin here. When this is once felt and understood, we may expect an end to tyranny and oppression throughout the world. Life is sacred. It belongs to Him who gave it. It is in the hands of its Author. The voice of God has sent forth his perpetual and universal mandate. 'THOU SHALT NOT KILL.' This voice speaks from the very depths of our natures, 'THOU SHALT NOT KILL!' That strange union of spirit and body which composes this fearful and unfathomable mystery of our humanity is not to be severed, neither by the hand of a human government, nor by the hand of the individual; *'for in the image of God made He man.'* And that image must not be marred. It must be respected, and tenderly treated, even in the murderer's own person, though he be crimsoned over with blood. . . .

Our Declaration of Rights says that 'all men are created equal; that they are endowed by their Creator with certain inalienable rights; that among these are life, liberty, and the pursuit of happiness.' But, is our right to life secured while the doctrine of the inviolability of human life is denied? It may be said that it was the great design of the framers of our constitution to secure this right. We freely admit that such was the object; but, then, we have inwoven in all our laws, civil and martial, the life-taking principle; thus, building up with the one hand, and throwing down with the other. It may be said, that, as members of the compact, we agree to give up a certain portion of our rights. Admitting this compact, we have shown . . . that man could not give the right of life to any being or government, for he has no right to take his own life; and, of course, cannot give it to another. We have shown,—and we wish the advocates of the present law would look at this point,—that, to be consistent, they must maintain suicide to be justifiable; an act which many of them think punishable with eternal death. . . .

Had Jesus been governed by human wisdom, he would have pronounced blessings upon the proud, the rich and the popular. His first labor was to abrogate forever the law of retaliation. 'It hath been said, thou shalt love thy neighbor and hate thine enemy, but I say unto you, love your enemies, bless them that curse you, do good to them that hate you.' But can we love another, and put him to death? How much love does the government feel when the unhappy culprit is forced from his cell to the place of execution? It is the spirit of retaliation. There is no feeling for the offender. One great object must, from necessity, be excluded; which is, the good of the unhappy culprit. Indeed, the great ends of punishment are entirely set aside. The community receive no reparation, nor would they if ten thousand lives were taken. The example, instead of being beneficial, brutalizes and hardens the heart. The law is wholly subversive of any good, and entirely contrary to the spirit of Christianity. . . .

We kill one man in order to reform or confirm the virtue of another. It is an entire perversion of all moral reasoning. History, observation, and experience all demonstrate that crimes increase with the severity of laws. Public executions tend to promote cruelty and a disregard for life.

*Source*: Charles Spear, *Essays on the Punishment of Death* (Boston: Charles Spear, 1844). [Littleton, Colo.: Fred B. Rothman, 1994, 26, 89, 176, 197 (footnotes omitted).]

## DOCUMENT 21: *Letters from New York* (Lydia Maria Child, 1845)

Lydia Maria (Francis) Child (1802–1880), a prolific Massachusetts writer known as one of the first and foremost anti-slavery advocates of the day, also was an opponent of the death penalty.

Prior to her marriage to David Lee Child, a Boston lawyer, in 1828, Child already had published two novels, *Hobomok* (1824) and *The Rebels* (1825); had founded a bimonthly magazine, *Juvenile Miscellany* (1826); and had run a private school in Watertown, Massachusetts (1825–1828).

Soon after her marriage, she and her husband joined the anti-slavery movement in Boston, and her writing turned to the anti-slavery cause. In 1833, Child published one of the first anti-slavery books, *An Appeal in Favor of That Class of Americans Called Africans*. The book was highly controversial, making Child as many enemies as converts to her way of thinking, and resulting in a significant drop in the sale of her other books.

Undaunted, Child continued her campaign against slavery. Eventually, she and her husband moved to New York, where she served as editor of a weekly abolitionist newspaper, the *National Anti-Slavery Standard*, from 1841 to 1849.

Child published *Letters from New York* (1845), an extremely popular compilation of her private correspondence that covered a wide range of subjects, including the following letter on capital punishment. According to one historian, "It is likely that one of her published letters, read by thousands, had a greater effect on public sentiment than the numerous resolutions passed by all the anti-gallows societies combined" (Masur 1989:122).

## LETTER XXXI.

November 19, 1842

To-day, I cannot write of beauty; for I am sad and troubled. Heart, head, and conscience, are all in battle-array against the savage customs of my time. By and by, the law of love, like oil upon the waters, will calm my surging sympathies, and make the current flow more calmly, though none the less deep or strong. But to-day do not ask me to love governor, sheriff or constable, or any man who defends capital punishment. I ought to do it; for genuine love enfolds even murderers with its blessing. By to-morrow, I think I can remember them without bitterness; but to-day, I cannot love them; on my soul, I cannot.

We were to have had an execution yesterday; but the wretched prisoner avoided it by suicide. The gallows had been erected for several hours, and with a cool refinement of cruelty, was hoisted before the window of the condemned; the hangman was all ready to cut the cord; marshals paced back and forth, smoking and whistling; spectators were waiting impatiently to see whether he would 'die game.' Printed circulars had been handed abroad to summon the number of witnesses required by law:—'You are respectfully invited to witness the execution of John C. Colt.' I trust some of them are preserved for museums. Specimens should be kept, as relics of a barbarous age, for succeeding generations to wonder at. They might be hung up in a frame; and the portrait of a New Zealand Chief, picking the bones of an enemy of his tribe, would be an appropriate pendant.

This bloody insult was thrust into the hands of *some* citizens, who carried hearts under their vests, and they threw it in tattered fragments to the dogs and swine, as more fitting witnesses than human beings. It was cheering to those who have faith in human progress, to see how many viewed the subject in this light. But as a general thing, the very spirit of murder was rife among the dense crowd, which thronged the place of execution. They were swelling with revenge, and eager for blood. One man came all the way from New Hampshire, on purpose to witness the entertainment; thereby showing himself a likely subject for the gallows, whoever he may be. *Women* deemed themselves not treated with becoming gallantry, because tickets of admittance were denied *them*; and I think it showed injudicious partiality; for many of them can be taught murder by as short a lesson as any man, and sustain it by arguments from Scripture, as ably as any theologian. However *they* were not admitted to this edifying exhibition in the great school of public morals; and had only the slim comfort of standing outside, in a keen November wind, to catch the first toll of the bell, which would announce that a human brother had been sent struggling into eternity by the hand of violence. But while the multitude stood with open watches, and strained ears to catch the sound, and the marshals smoked and whistled, and the hangman walked up and down, waiting for his prey, lo! word was brought that the criminal was found dead in his bed! He had asked one half hour alone to prepare his mind for departure; and at the end of that brief interval, he was found with a dagger thrust into his heart. The tidings were received with fierce mutterings of disappointed rage. The throng beyond the walls were furious to see him with their own eyes, to be sure that he was dead. But when the welcome news met *my* ear a tremendous load was taken from my heart. I had no chance to analyze right and wrong; for over all thought and feeling flowed impulsive joy that this 'Christian' community were cheated of a hanging. They who had assembled to commit legalized murder, in cold blood, with strange confusion of ideas, were unmindful of their own guilt, while they talked of his suicide as a crime equal to that for which he was condemned. I am willing to leave it between him and his God. For myself, I would rather have the burden of it on my own soul, than take the guilt of those who would have executed a fellow-creature. *He* was driven to a fearful extremity of agony and desperation. He was precisely in the situation of a man on board a burning ship, who being *compelled* to face death, jumps into the waves, as the least painful mode of the two. But they, who thus drove him 'to walk the plank,' made cool, deliberate preparations to take life, and with inventive cruelty sought to add every bitter drop that *could* be added to the dreadful cup of vengeance.

To me, human life seems so sacred a thing, that its violent termination always fills me with horror, whether perpetrated by an individual or a crowd; whether done contrary to law and custom, or according to law and custom. Why John C. Colt should be condemned to an ignominious death for an act of resentment altogether unpremeditated, while men, who deliberately, and with malice aforethought, go out to murder another for some insulting word, are judges and senators in the land, and favourite candidates for the President's chair, is more than I can comprehend. There is, to say the least, a strange inconsistency in our customs. . . .

In looking at Capital Punishment in its practical bearings on the operation of justice, an observing mind is at once struck with the extreme *uncertainty* attending it. The balance swings hither and thither, and settles, as it were, by chance. The strong instincts of the heart teach juries extreme reluctance to convict for capital offences. They will avail themselves of every loophole in the evidence, to avoid the bloody responsibility imposed upon them. In this way, undoubted criminals escape all punishment, until society becomes alarmed for its own safety, and insists that the next victim *shall* be sacrificed. It was the misfortune of John C. Colt, to be arrested at the time when the popular wave of indignation had been swelling higher and higher, in consequence of the impunity with which Robinson, White, and Jewell, had escaped. The wrath and jealousy which they had excited was visited upon him, and his chance for a merciful verdict was greatly diminished. The scale now turns the other way; and the next offender will probably receive very lenient treatment, though he should not have half so many extenuating circumstances in his favour.

Another thought which forces itself upon the mind in consideration of this subject is the danger of convicting the innocent. Murder is a crime which must of course be committed in secret, and therefore the proof must be mainly circumstantial. This kind of evidence is in its nature so precarious, that men have learned great timidity in trusting to it. In Scotland, it led to so many terrible mistakes, that they long ago refused to convict any man of a capital offence, upon circumstantial evidence....

Few know how numerous are the cases where it has subsequently been discovered that the innocent suffered instead of the guilty. Yet one such case in an age is surely enough to make legislators pause before they cast a vote against the abolition of Capital Punishment.

But many say, 'the Old Testament requires blood for blood.' So it requires that a woman should be put to death for adultery; and men for doing work on the Sabbath; and children for cursing their parents; and 'If an ox were to push with his horn, in time past, and it hath been testified to his owner, and he hath not kept him in, but that he hath killed a man or a woman, the ox shall be stoned, and his owner also shall be put to death.' The commands given to the Jews, in the old dispensation, do not form the basis of any legal code in Christendom. They *could* not form the basis of any civilized code. If one command is binding on our consciences, *all* are binding; for they all rest on the same authority. They who feel bound to advocate capital punishment for murder, on account of the law given to Moses, ought, for the same reason, to insist that children should be executed for striking or cursing their parents.

'It was said by them of *old* time, an eye for an eye, and a tooth for a tooth; but *I* say unto you, resist not evil.' If our 'eyes were lifted up,' we should see not Moses and Elias, but *Jesus only*.

Source: Lydia Maria (Francis) Child, Letters from New York, third edition (New York, C. S. Francis, 1845). [Freeport, N.Y.: Books for Libraries Press, 1970, 220–222, 226–227, 230.]

## DOCUMENT 22: "Death by Human Law" (Horace Greeley, 1850)

As founder and editor of the famous New York Tribune, Horace Greeley (1811–1872) was one of the nineteenth century's most influential opponents of both capital punishment and slavery.

An ardent protectionist and staunch conservative, Greeley was one of the leaders in the formation of the Republican party in the United States.

He also was a "self-made" man. Greeley's life began in poverty, and he left school at the age of fourteen to serve an apprenticeship at a Vermont newspaper. When the newspaper folded in 1830, he headed for New York to pursue a journalism career.

After a series of jobs, Greeley founded his first publication—a weekly literary and nonpartisan political journal called the New Yorker—in 1834. The magazine was always on the verge of bankruptcy, so to add to his income, Greeley wrote for the Daily Whig. He also edited two weekly campaign papers for the Whig party, the Jeffersonian in 1838 and the Log Cabin in 1840.

In 1841, Greeley founded the daily New York Tribune, a Whig-oriented "penny paper." Though the new publication got off to a slow and rocky start, by 1846 it was considered the best, and was the most popular, newspaper in New York City.

In his editorials—and through numerous public lecture tours, books, and pamphlets—Greeley opposed slavery and capital punishment, urged freedom of speech and of the mail for abolitionists, and supported the temperance movement, cooperative shops, and labor unions.

The following essay against capital punishment, which appeared in his 1850 book Hints Toward Reforms, originally was delivered by Greeley as a public lecture.

All speculation on the *right* of the community to take human life is preposterous. Self-preservation is the primal law; and if the death of any individual is necessary to the safety of the commonwealth, he must die. I doubt whether there is one theoretical denier of the right of society to take life who—if he saw a man forcing his way into the window of his family's sleeping apartment, and knew that the ruffian would, in order to rob securely, murder the mother and babes there lying in unconscious slumber—would hesitate to catch up a rifle and shoot the burglar dead on the spot. This would imply no malice toward the victim of his own evil designs—no desire to harm him—no wrath, even—but a simple choice that of two evils the greater should be averted by interposing the lesser. . . .

Man must live—Society must exist—the Right must maintain its ascendency—Cultivation and Food-producing must have scope, though robbers should die, the wrong should suffer, and weeds be exterminated in consequence. Whatever degree of severity and amount of destruction may at any time be necessary to maintain this rightful supremacy of good over evil stands justified by the constitution of the universe. It is not cruel but merciful; not wrathful and vindictive but benignant and humane. . . .

The principle is the same with regard to nations as individuals. A nation which should declare war and proceed to invade another's territory, burn its towns and slaughter its resisting people, because of past depredations on the property or outrages on the persons of some of the citizens of the former within the territory of the latter, would surely be guilty of a wanton and inexcusable resort to bloodshed. . . .

But a nation is invaded and its very existence threatened by some powerful neighbor—as that of Greece was by Xerxes, that of France by the Saracens, that of Russia by Napoleon. It is the plain duty of its people to resist with all their might, and roll back the tide of invasion across their frontiers. It is better for Humanity that thousands should die than that millions should be made slaves, and their children after them. But there is necessarily and properly no vengeful feeling on their part—no wish to harm an individual of the invading host—nothing but submission to the stern, sad necessity of sacrificing the invaders or themselves to the preservation of the most sacred Rights of Man. . . .

—And now to killing malefactors by sentence of law. Is it ever justifiable? I answer yes, *provided* Society can in no other way be secured against a repetition of the culprit's offence. In committing a murder, for instance, he has proved himself capable of committing more murders— perhaps many. The possibility of a thousand murders is developed in his one act of felonious homicide. Call his moral state depravity, insanity, or whatever you please, he is manifestly a ferocious, dangerous animal, who can not safely be permitted to go at large. Society must be secured against the reasonable probability of his killing others, and, where that can only be effected by taking his life, his life must be taken.

—But suppose him to be in New-England, New-York or Pennsylvania—arrested, secured and convicted—Society's rebel, outcast and prisoner of war—taken with arms in his hands. Here are prison-cells wherefrom escape is impossible; and if there be any fear of his assaulting his keeper or others, that may be most effectively prevented. Is it expedient or salutary to crush the life out of this helpless, abject, pitiable wretch?

I for one think it decidedly *is not*—that it is a sorrowful mistake and barbarity to do any such thing. In saying this, I do not assume to decide whether Hanging or Imprisonment for Life is the severer penalty. I should wish to understand clearly the moral state of the prisoner before I attempted to guess; and, even then, I know too little of the scenes of untried being which lie next beyond the confines of this mortal existence to say whether it were better for any penitent or hardened culprit to be hung next month or left in prison to die a natural death. What is best for that culprit I leave to God, who knows when is the fit time for him to die. My concern is with Society—the moral it teaches, the conduct it tacitly enjoins. And I feel that the choking to death of this culprit works harm, in these respects, namely:

1. *It teaches and sanctions Revenge. . . .*

2. *It tends to weaken and destroy the natural horror of bloodshed. . . .*

3. *It facilitates and often insures the escape of the guilty from any punishment by human law. . . .*

4. *It excites a pernicious sympathy for the convict. . . .*

—But I do not care to pile argument on argument, consideration on consideration, in opposition to the expediency, in this day and section, of putting men to death in cold blood by human law. It seems to me a most pernicious and brutalizing practice. Indeed, the recent enactments of our own, with most if not all of the Free States, whereby Executions are henceforth to take place in private, or in the presence of a few select witnesses only, seem clearly to admit the fact. They certainly imply that Executions are of no use as examples—that they rather tend to make criminals than to reform those already depraved. When I see any business or vocation sneaking and skulking in dark lanes and little by-streets which elude observation, I conclude that those who follow such business feel at least doubtful of its utility and beneficence. They may *argue* that it is 'a necessary evil,' but they can hardly put faith in their own logic. When I see the bright array of many-colored liquor-bottles, which formerly filled flauntingly the post of honor in every tip-top hotel, now hustled away into some side-room, and finally down into a dark basement, out of the sight and knowledge of all but those who especially seek them, I say exultingly, 'Good for so much! one more hoist, and they will be—where they should be—out of sight and reach altogether:'—so, when I see the Gallows, once the denizen of some swelling eminence, the cynosure of ten thousand eyes, 'the observed of all observers,' skulking and hiding itself from public view in jail-yards, shutting itself up in prisons, I say, 'You have taken the right road! Go ahead! One more drive, and your detested, rickety frame is out of the sight of civilized man for ever!'

Source: Horace Greeley, "Death by Human Law," 1850. In Philip English Mackey, ed., *Voices Against Death: American Opposition to Capital Punishment, 1787–1975* (New York: Burt Franklin, 1976), 112–119.

## DOCUMENT 23: The Fourteenth Amendment, Section 1 (1868)

One year after the Thirteenth Amendment abolished slavery in 1865, the Fourteenth Amendment was passed by Congress. The Amendment—ratified by the states in 1868—eventually was interpreted to mean that the Bill of Rights applied to all Americans, and that it was the duty of the states to ensure these rights.

At the time of its passage—a time when blacks typically were given harsher criminal penalties for crimes than were whites—it appeared that the Amendment would guarantee that all Americans would be subjected to similar criminal punishments, regardless of their race. As Jacob M. Howard, an influential member of the Michigan Senate's Joint Committee on Reconstruction, explained in 1866, the Fourteenth Amendment "prohibits the hanging of a black man for a crime for which the white man is not to be hanged" (Meltsner 1973:74).

However, although the states made a token effort to comply with the Amendment by taking criminal statutes that punished blacks more harshly than whites off their books, little actually changed in many states for decades. It wasn't until more than a century after its adoption that the Fourteenth Amendment—particularly its "due process" clause—became important in a number of legal challenges to existing capital sentencing procedures.

All persons born or naturalized in the United States, and subject to the jurisdiction thereof, are citizens of the United States and of the State wherein they reside. No State shall make or enforce any law which shall abridge the privileges or immunities of citizens of the United States; nor shall any State deprive any person of life, liberty, or property, without due process of law; nor deny to any person within its jurisdiction the equal protection of the laws.

Source: Constitution of the United States.

## DOCUMENT 24: *Wilkerson v. Utah* (1879)

Despite heavy abolitionist activity during the nineteenth century, only a few constitutional challenges to the death penalty were made during that era. Of these, most dealt with the constitutionality of the method of execution that had been prescribed by the legislature.

For example, in the 1879 case of *Wilkerson v. Utah*, the defendant claimed that execution by firing squad was a violation of his Eighth Amendment protection against cruel and unusual punishment.[1]

Utah law at the time provided that every person found guilty of murder would be put to death, but did not prescribe the method of execution to be carried out—leaving that determination up to the court.

Upon hearing the case, the Supreme Court unanimously upheld the lower court's sentence of execution by firing squad—determining that it was well within the authority of the court to prescribe that particular mode of execution. In the Court's opinion, delivered by Justice Clifford, it was noted that execution was the usual punishment for premeditated murder and that the death penalty had been carried out by firing squad in Utah for many years and therefore was not unconstitutional.

### NOTE

1. As Georgetown University Law Professor Mark Tushnet pointed out in electronic correspondence with the authors, Utah was still a territory in 1879 and therefore subject to the Eighth Amendment, which applied both to states and territories of the United States, but not to the more recently adopted Fourteenth Amendment, which applied only to the states.

Mr. Justice **Clifford** delivered the opinion of the court: . . .

Cruel and unusual punishments are forbidden by the Constitution, but the authorities referred to are quite sufficient to show that the punishment of shooting as a mode of executing the death penalty for the crime of murder in the first degree is not included in that category, within the meaning of the 8th Amendment. . . .

Difficulty would attend the effort to define with exactness the extent of the constitutional provision which provides that cruel and unusual punishment shall not be inflicted; but it is safe to affirm that punishments of torture . . . are forbidden by that amendment to the Constitution. . . .

Concede all that, and still it by no means follows that the sentence of the court in this case falls within that category, or that the Supreme Court of the Territory erred in affirming the judgment of the court of original jurisdiction. Antecedent to the enactment of the Code which went into operation March 4, 1876, the Statute of the Territory passed March 6,

1852, provided that when any person was convicted of any capital offense, he shall suffer death by being shot, hanged or beheaded, as the court may direct, subject to the qualification therein expressed, to the effect that the person condemned might have his option as to the manner of his execution, the meaning of which qualification, as construed, was that the option was limited to the modes prescribed by the statute, and that if it was not exercised, the direction must be given by the court passing the sentence.

Nothing of the kind is contained in the existing Code, and the Legislature in dropping the provision as to the option failed to enact any specific regulation as to the mode of executing the death penalty. Instead of that, the explicit enactment is that every person guilty of murder in the first degree shall suffer death, or upon the recommendation of the jury, may be imprisoned at hard labor in the penitentiary for life, at the discretion of the court.

Beyond all question, the first clause of the provision is applicable in this case, as the jury gave no such recommendation as that recited in the second clause, the record showing that the verdict was unconditional and absolute, from which it follows that the sentence that the prisoner shall suffer death is legally correct. . . .

Had the statute prescribed the mode of executing the sentence, it would have been the duty of the court to follow it, unless the punishment to be inflicted was cruel and unusual, within the meaning of the 8th Amendment to the Constitution, which is not pretended by the counsel of the prisoner. Statutory directions being given that the prisoner when duly convicted shall suffer death, without any statutory regulation specifically pointing out the mode of executing the command of the law, it must be that the duty is devolved upon the court authorized to pass the sentence to determine the mode of execution and to impose the sentence prescribed. . . .

Persons guilty of murder in the first degree "shall suffer death" are the words of the territorial statute; and when that provision is construed in connection with section 10 of the Code previously referred to, it is clear that it is made obligatory upon the court to prescribe the mode of executing the sentence of death which the Code imposes where the conviction is for murder in the first degree, subject, of course, to the constitutional prohibition, that cruel and unusual punishment shall not be inflicted.

*Source*: 25 *Law. Ed.* (1879), 346–348.

## DOCUMENT 25: *In re Kemmler* (1890)

In 1888, just six years after electricity was made available to the residents of New York City, the state authorized a new, "improved" method of administering the death penalty—the electric chair.

The new mode of execution was hailed as "the most humane and practical method known to modern science of carrying into effect the sentence of death in capital cases" in the 1888 "Report of the Commission to Investigate and Report the Most Humane and Practical Method of Carrying Into Effect the Sentence of Death in Capital Cases" (Zimring and Hawkins 1986:111).

In 1889 William (Willie) Kemmler was the first person sentenced to die in "the chair." Kemmler challenged the sentence on the ground that the new mode of execution violated his Eighth Amendment protection against cruel and unusual punishment.

The Supreme Court ruled against Kemmler and his Eighth Amendment claim. In so doing, it cited the findings of the New York commission's report and the opinion of the state supreme court, which stated, "We have read with much interest the evidence returned to the county judge, and we agree with him that the burden of the proof is not successfully borne by the relator. On the contrary, we think that the evidence is clearly in favor of the conclusion that it is within easy reach of electrical science at this day to so generate and apply to the person of the convict a current of electricity of such known and sufficient force as certainly to produce instantaneous, and therefore painless, death" (quoted in 136 U.S. 436, 433).

However, in Kemmler's case, death by electrocution was not instantaneous, as had been anticipated. After the current had been applied for seventeen seconds and then turned off, Kemmler was still alive. After an additional four seconds of electrical current, Kemmler was pronounced dead (Schwed 1983:22).

FULLER, C. J. [delivered the opinion of the Court]. . . .

Punishments are cruel when they involve torture or a lingering death; but the punishment of death is not cruel within the meaning of that word as used in the constitution. It implies there something inhuman and barbarous,—something more than the mere extinguishment of life. The courts of New York held that the mode adopted in this instance might be said to be unusual because it was new, but that it could not be assumed to be cruel in the light of that common knowledge which has stamped certain punishments as such; that it was for the legislature to say in what manner sentence of death should be executed; that this act was passed in the effort to devise a more humane method of reaching the result; that the courts were bound to presume that the legislature was possessed of the facts upon which it took action; and that by evidence taken *aliunde* the statute that presumption could not be overthrown. They went further, and expressed the opinion that upon the evidence the legislature had attained by the act the object had in view in its passage. The decision of the state courts sustaining the validity of the act under the state constitution is not re-examinable here, nor was that decision against any title, right, privilege, or immunity specially set up or claimed by the petitioner under the constitution of the United States.

*Source*: 10 S.Ct. (1890), 930–934.

## DOCUMENT 26: *Resist Not Evil* (Clarence Darrow, 1902)

The new century began with a strong resurgence of abolitionist activity that continued throughout the Progressive Era until the onset of World War I.

One of the most eloquent and persuasive abolitionists of this period was Clarence Darrow (1857–1938), a lawyer perhaps best known for defending John Scopes—a young Tennessee schoolteacher tried for teaching the Darwinian theory of evolution to his students—in 1925.

Born in Kinsman, Ohio, Darrow was admitted to the Ohio bar at the age of twenty-one and practiced there for nine years. He moved to Chicago in 1887, where he worked as the state's corporation counsel and then as an attorney for the Chicago & North Western Railway. During the Pullman Strike of 1894, Darrow—a champion of the labor union—resigned to devote himself to labor issues, serving as defense counsel in a number of high-profile labor cases.

Darrow, who also was active in politics, was elected to the Illinois legislature in 1902, the same year he published *Resist Not Evil*, in which he argued against war and all other forms of violence, including capital punishment.

Darrow later would become a criminal lawyer and serve as defense counsel in the famous Loeb-Leopold death penalty trial of 1924 (see Document 29) and as a founding member of the American League to Abolish Capital Punishment.

His other books on the subject of crime, deterrence and capital punishment include *Crime and Criminals* (1907), *An Eye for An Eye* (1914), and *Crime, Its Cause and Treatment* (1922).

All punishment and violence is largely mixed with the feeling of re-venge,—from the brutal father who strikes his helpless child, to the hangman who obeys the orders of the judge; with every man who lays violent unkind hands upon his fellow the prime feeling is that of hatred and revenge. Some human being has shed his neighbor's blood; the state must take his life. In no other way can the crime be wiped away. In some inconceivable manner it is believed that when this punishment follows, justice has been done. But by no method of reasoning can it be shown that the injustice of killing one man is retrieved by the execution of an-other, or that the forcible taking of property is made right by confining some human being in a pen. If the law knew some method to restore a life or make good a loss to the real victim, it might be urged that justice had been done. But if taking life, or blaspheming, or destroying the prop-erty of another be an injustice, as in our short vision it seems to be, then punishing him who is supposed to be guilty of the act, in no way makes just the act already done. To punish a human being simply because he has committed a wrongful act, without any thought of good to follow, is vengeance pure and simple, and more detestable and harmful than any casual isolated crime. . . .

Punishment brings positive evil. Any possible good that it may pro-duce is at the best problematical and wholly impossible to prove. From the first victim whom the state degrades with punishment, the evil and the hardship and suffering moves on to family and friends. In no theory of the law is compensation, or recompense, or making good, any part of punishment. If taking the life of the prisoner could bring to life the victim whom he killed there might be some apparent excuse for the punishment of death. If imprisoning in the penitentiary in any way retrieved a wrong or made up a loss, a prison might be tolerated, and some relation might be shown between punishment and crime. Even in cases where a fine is administered, in place of imprisonment, the fine does not go in any way to retrieve any loss, but goes to the state as pure punishment and nothing else. Everywhere in the theory and administration of punishment is the rule the same. The one purpose is to injure, to harm, to inflict suffering upon the individual whom society sets apart.

*Source*: Clarence S. Darrow, *Resist Not Evil* (Chicago: Charles H. Kerr, 1902), 56–57, 117–118.

## DOCUMENT 27: *Weems v. U.S.* (1910)

The case of *Weems v. U.S.*, though not a death penalty case, is significant to the history of capital punishment in the United States because it set a new standard for interpretation of the cruel and unusual punishment clause of the Eighth Amendment which later figured in numerous constitutional challenges to the death penalty.

Paul Weems, a cashier in the U.S. Coast Guard in the Philippine Islands, was convicted of falsifying a public record (a captain's cash book) in an apparent attempt to embezzle what amounted to a little over 600 pesos.

Although the islands, which had been ceded to the United States by Spain in 1898, now were subject to the rule of the U.S. Constitution, they still adhered to some of their old Spanish laws as well. As a result, Weems was sentenced to fifteen years of "cadena temporal" for his crime. The sentence required that he would work at "hard and painful labor," always chained, with "no assistance from friend or relative" for the duration of the sentence. Upon release, Weems also would be subject under the Philippine law to lifelong surveillance and a loss of all his civil rights as "accessory" punishments.

Upon hearing the case, the U.S. Supreme Court found this punishment to be excessively harsh and grossly disproportionate to the crime committed and therefore unconstitutional under the cruel and unusual clause of the Eighth Amendment. As one noted death penalty researcher explained, "*Weems v. United States* was the first Supreme Court interpretation of the 'cruel and unusual punishment' clause of the Eighth Amendment, the first case in which it reversed a conviction under that interpretation, and the first case in which the Court struck down a statutory mode of punishment as unconstitutional" (Bedau 1977:32).

## A. OPINION OF THE COURT

Mr. Justice **McKenna** delivered the opinion of the court: . . .

The punishment of *cadena temporal* is from twelve years and one day to twenty years . . . which "shall be served" in certain "penal institutions." And it is provided that "those sentenced to *cadena temporal* and *cadena perpetua* shall labor for the benefit of the state. They shall always carry a chain at the ankle, hanging from the wrists; they shall be employed at hard and painful labor, and shall receive no assistance whatsoever from without the institution."... There are besides certain accessory penalties imposed, which are defined to be (1) civil interdiction; (2) perpetual absolute disqualification; (3) subjection to surveillance during life. . . .

These provisions are attacked as infringing that provision of the Bill of Rights of the islands which forbids the infliction of cruel and unusual punishment. It must be confessed that they, and the sentence in this case, excite wonder in minds accustomed to a more considerate adaptation of punishment to the degree of crime. . . .

There are degrees of homicide that are not punished so severely, nor are the following crimes: misprision of treason, inciting rebellion, conspiracy to destroy the government by force, recruiting soldiers in the United States to fight against the United States, forgery of letters patent, forgery of bonds and other instruments for the purpose of defrauding the United States, robbery, larceny, and other crimes. Section 86 of the Penal Laws of the United States . . . provides that any person charged with the payment of any appropriation made by Congress, who shall pay to any clerk or other employee of the United States a sum less than that provided by law, and require a receipt for a sum greater than that paid to and received by him, shall be guilty of embezzlement, and shall be fined in double the amount so withheld, and imprisoned not more than two years. The offense described has similarity to the offense for which Weems was convicted, but the punishment provided for it is in great contrast to the penalties of *cadena temporal* and its "accesories." If we turn to the legislation of the Philippine Commission we find that instead of the penalties of *cadena temporal*, medium degree (fourteen years, eight months, and one day, to seventeen years and four months, with fine and "accesories"), to *cadena perpetua*, fixed by the Spanish Penal Code for the falsification of bank notes and other instruments authorized by the law of the kingdom, it is provided that the forgery of or counterfeiting the obligations or securities of the United States or of the Philippine Islands shall be punished by a fine of not more than 10,000 pesos and by imprisonment of not more than fifteen years. In other words, the highest punishment possible for a crime which may cause the loss of many thousand of dollars, and to prevent which the duty of the state should be as eager as to prevent the perversion of truth in a public document, is not greater than that which may be imposed for falsifying a single item of a public account. And this contrast shows more than different exercises of legislative judgment. It is greater than that. It condemns the sentence in this case as cruel and unusual. It exhibits a difference between unrestrained power and that which is exercised under the spirit of constitutional limitations formed to establish justice. The state thereby suffers nothing and loses no power. The purpose of punishment is fulfilled, crime is repressed by penalties of just, not tormenting, severity, its repetition is prevented, and hope is given for the reformation of the criminal. . . .

It follows from these views that, even if the minimum penalty of *cadena temporal* had been imposed, it would have been repugnant to the Bill of Rights. In other words, the fault is in the law; and, as we are pointed to no other under which a sentence can be imposed, the judgment must be reversed, with directions to dismiss the proceedings.

## B. DISSENTING OPINION

Mr. Justice **White**, dissenting: . . .

I can deduce no ground whatever which, to my mind, sustains the interpretation now given to the cruel and unusual punishment clause. On the contrary, in my opinion, the review which has been made demonstrates that the word "cruel," as used in the Amendment, forbids only the lawmaking power, in prescribing punishment for crime, and the courts in imposing punishment, from inflicting unnecessary bodily suffering through a resort to inhuman methods for causing bodily torture, like or which are the nature of the cruel methods of bodily torture which had been made use of prior to the Bill of Rights of 1689, and against the recurrence of which the word "cruel" was used in that instrument. . . .

In my opinion, the previous considerations also establish that the word "unusual" accomplished only three results: First, it primarily restrains the courts when acting under the authority of a general discretionary power to impose punishment, such as was possessed at common law, from inflicting lawful modes of punishment to so unusual a degree as to cause the punishment to be illegal, because to that degree it cannot be inflicted without express statutory authority; second, it restrains the courts in the exercise of the same discretion from inflicting a mode of punishment so unusual as to be impliedly not within its discretion, and to be consequently illegal in the absence of express statutory authority; and, third, as to both the foregoing, it operated to restrain the lawmaking power from endowing the judiciary with the right to exert an illegal discretion as to the kind and extent of punishment to be inflicted. . . .

True, the imprisonment is at hard and painful labor. But certainly the mere qualifications of painful in addition to hard cannot be the basis upon which it is now decided that the legislative discretion was abused, since to understand the meaning of the term requires a knowledge of the discipline prevailing in the prisons in the Philippine Islands. The division of hard labor into classes, one more irksome, and, it may be said, more painful than the other in the sense of severity, is well known. . . . I do not assume that the mere fact that a chain is to be carried by the prisoner causes the punishment to be repugnant to the Bill of Rights, since, while the chain may be irksome, it is evidently not intended to prevent the performance of the penalty of hard labor. Such a provision may well be part of the ordinary prison discipline, particularly in communities where the jails are insecure, and it may be a precaution applied, as it is commonly applied in this country, as a means of preventing the escape of prisoners; for instance, where the sentence imposed is to work on the roads or other work where escape might be likely. I am brought, then, to the conclusion that the accessory punishments are the basis of the ruling now made, that the legislative discretion was so abused as to cause it to be necessary to declare the law prescribing the punishment for crime invalid. But I can see no foundation for this ruling, as, to my mind, these accessory punishments, even under the assumption, for the sake of argument, that they amounted to an abuse of legislative discretion, are clearly separable from the main punishment,—imprisonment. Where a sentence is legal in one part and illegal in another, it is not open to controversy that the illegal, if separable, may be disregarded and the legal enforced. . . . But it is said here the illegality is not merely in the sentence, but in the law which authorizes the sentence. Grant the premise. The illegal is capable of separation from the legal in the law as well as in the sentence; and because this is a criminal case, it is none the less subject to the rule that where a statute is unconstitutional in part and in part not, the unconstitutional part, if separable, may be rejected and the constitutional part maintained.

*Source*: 30 S.Ct. (1910), 544–567.

# Part III

## War and Economic Depression Overshadow Capital Punishment, 1918–1959

### TUMULTUOUS CHANGE

Comparatively little public attention was paid to capital punishment during the tumultuous four decades from 1918 to 1959. Following World War I, the United States struggled to adapt to fundamental demographic change as it surged from economic boom to prolonged depression to global war to another depression, another war, and—finally—economic recovery and prosperity.

The reform movement in the United States declined during the second decade of the twentieth century as Americans were more occupied with external than domestic affairs. Although many had envisioned World War I as extending the ideals of progressivism to the world at large, the war itself actually deepened ethnic divisions, threatened civil liberties, and sapped the idealism of a generation (Wade 1993). While abolition of capital punishment remained on many reformers' agendas, it tended to rank well below priorities such as relief programs for the poor and unemployed, civil rights, and political reform. Oftentimes, as we discuss later, it appeared that only the occasional celebrity case kept capital punishment from receding entirely from public view.

An important consequence of the urban growth that had begun a decade earlier was felt in 1920 as, for the first time, more than 50 percent of Americans lived in urban areas. The consequences of this demographic shift increased over the next 40 years as rural population remained relatively constant while urban population more than doubled. Increasingly, young people were moving to the cities and immigrants were settling there rather than on rural farms as often had been the case in the nineteenth century. By 1960, only 30 percent of the population remained in rural areas.

Just as urban areas had disproportionately benefitted from the prosperity of the 1920s, they also were hardest hit by the economic depression that followed in the 1930s. As the Great Depression persisted, unlike previous economic depressions which had been relatively transient, overall unemployment hovered around 25 percent and urban unemployment sometimes was twice that. Even the middle class experienced prolonged hardship. "Farmers armed themselves to prevent the foreclosure of mortgages. Sporadic rioting in cities accompanied evictions. Illness related to stress multiplied, suicides soared" (Wade 1993:403). As the New Deal was forged in the 1930s during what Wade called "the most contentious [decade] since the controversy over slavery in the 1850s" (1993:404), reformers focused their energies on relief programs and politics rather than social reforms such as capital punishment. When war once again overtook the country in 1941, the issue receded almost entirely.

## ABOLITIONIST INFLUENCE DECLINES

During the period from 1918 to 1959, opponents of the death penalty such as Clarence Darrow and the wardens of Sing Sing and San Quentin fought an uphill battle against strong and consistent support for capital punishment. In the first Gallup Poll to query respondents about the death penalty in 1937, a strong majority of Americans supported the death penalty for murder. This was not to change until 1957, when half of the respondents said that they did not favor the death penalty for murder (see Documents 33, 38, and 40).

High profile cases, such as those involving the alleged anarchists Sacco and Vanzetti in the 1920s and convicted atomic spies Julius and Ethel Rosenberg thirty years later, occasionally brought the issue of capital punishment to the fore for a time. But day to day the practice faced only limited opposition. Over five thousand people were executed from 1918 to 1959, and most of them, like Army private Eddie Slovik (see Document 34), died without major debate or public fanfare.

## EXECUTIONS WANE

It is difficult to assess the effect of abolitionist activities during this period. On the one hand, as Zimring and Hawkins (1986:28) note, not a single state repealed death penalty legislation between 1917 and 1957. On the other, even though both the number and rate of homicides fluctuated considerably during the period, the number of executions per homicide declined quite steadily (Bowers 1984:54; Maguire and Pastore 1995:table 6.82; U.S. Bureau of Census 1975: 414). Clearly, the tendency to execute murderers in the United States as a whole was waning.

Regional differences in executions, however, remained strong. Almost two-thirds of all executions from the mid-1930s to the mid-1960s took place in ten states. The southern region alone accounted for more executions than all other regions of the country combined (Paternoster 1991:14; Schwed 1983:21; Zimring and Hawkins 1986:30). Nor were executions evenly distributed among racial and ethnic groups. On a per capita basis, roughly five times as many blacks as whites were executed. And, although only about 12 percent of the people executed had received the death sentence for rape, almost all of them were non-whites (Paternoster 1991:15).

## PREAMBLE TO CHANGE

A gradual resurgence of anti-death penalty activities during the late 1950s was bolstered by the work of French writer and Nobel Laureate Albert Camus, who attacked the death penalty with a passion, arguing that it was brutalizing and ineffective against what are mostly impulsive acts (Camus 1959:15–17). Although the public debate would not truly begin to heat up again until Thorsten Sellin's seminal research on deterrence and the death penalty was published in 1959 (see Document 42), case law regarding execution methods and procedures (Documents 28 and 35), the right of defendants to effective counsel (Document 32), racial discrimination (Document 36), and what constituted cruel and unusual punishment (Documents 28, 35, and 41), developed steadily from World War I until 1959.

## DOCUMENT 28: First Gas Chamber Execution (Gee Jon, 1924)

During the 1920s, another new form of execution, thought to be even more "humane" than electrocution, was introduced.

Execution by lethal gas was first adopted in Nevada. The so-called "Humane Death Bill"—which abolished other forms of execution in the state—was signed by the governor on March 28, 1921. Previously, the condemned in Nevada were given a choice between hanging and shooting.

Just as electrocution was challenged as a cruel and unusual mode of execution by Willie Kemmler in 1890 (see Document 25), execution by lethal gas soon was challenged on the same grounds upon appeal to the state supreme court. The petitioners, Gee Jon and Hughie Sing—convicted of the tong murder of Tom Quong Kee—were the first sentenced to die by lethal gas.

In denying the appeal, Justice Coleman (writing the opinion of the court) relied on the interpretation of the Eighth Amendment prohibition against cruel and unusual punishment set forth in the *Kemmler* case, stating that the court was "not prepared to say that the infliction of the death penalty by the administration of lethal gas would of itself subject the victim to either pain or torture" (Berkson 1975:29).

Hence, on February 8, 1924, Gee Jon became the first person put to death in the gas chamber.

CARSON CITY, Nev., Feb. 8 (Associated Press).—Lethal gas as a form of capital punishment was used for the first time here today when Gee Jon, a Chinaman, convicted of killing a rival tong man, was put to death.

Physicians and scientists who attended the execution were unanimous in pronouncing it a swift and painless method. Several of them said they thought it the most merciful form yet devised.

The official physicians, who watched at a window with newspaper men, were A. Huftaker, E. E. Hamer and Major D. A. Turner of the Army Medical Reserve Corps. The doctors asserted that the Chinaman lapsed into unconsciousness after his first breath of the vaporized acid. Death, they said, came virtually instantly, although the condemned man's head continued to move up and down for six minutes. This movement, they explained, was probably muscular reaction after death. The doctors agreed that the condemned man did not suffer.

The condemned prisoner was walked [f]orty yards into the prison yard. When he approached the death chamber, he walked steadily, although two guards held him by the arms. He was immediately strapped in the chair in the death house.

Gee Jon was in the chair when reporters arrived. Guards reported that he had wept a little as he was placed in the chair. The Captain of the guards said to him, "Brace up!" and after that he displayed no emotion.

When the gas was turned on he raised his head and looked around at the hissing sound of the liquid hydrocyanic acid being blown in from an adjoining compartment of the little building. Then his head fell forward. His expression remained placid during the six minutes that followed while his head moved.

During the execution, the witnesses could smell the gas, but it did not appear to have any harmful results or even bother any one. After the execution, the chemists ordered that thirty minutes elapse before the chamber was emptied of gas, but an hour passed before the physicians were permitted to enter.

It was charged that Gee Jon and another Chinese, now serving a life term, were sent from San Francisco by a Tong to "execute" Tom Quon Kee, member of a rival Tong. In the long legal fight to stave off the execution, two appeals were made to the Supreme Court of the United States on the ground that the lethal gas was an "unusual and inhuman" form of execution. The Supreme Court refused to hear the petitions.

*Source*: "Gas Kills Convict Almost Instantly," Associated Press, February 8, 1924. In *New York Times*, February 9, 1924, 15.

---

## DOCUMENT 29: *Is Capital Punishment a Wise Public Policy?* (Clarence Darrow and Alfred J. Talley, 1924)

During a time when public support for the death penalty appeared to be on the rise, Clarence Darrow (see Document 26) remained one of its most steadfast opponents.

Darrow gained nationwide attention for his views on the death penalty in 1924, when he served as defense counsel to Nathan Leopold and Richard Loeb, two wealthy Chicago youths who had kidnapped and murdered a fourteen-year-old schoolboy. Considered a remarkably persuasive lawyer, Darrow convinced the judge to give the convicted child-killers life sentences instead of the death penalty.

Darrow and other abolitionists saw the judge's decision as a promising sign during what had otherwise been difficult times for opponents of the death penalty, and they took the opportunity to increase their activities, which included the founding of the American League to Abolish Capital Punishment (Mackey 1976:xxxviii). But many people were angered by the Chicago court's decision, including Alfred J. Talley, a New York judge who publicly attacked Darrow's views on the death penalty shortly after the trial ended (Mackey 1976:167).

Darrow and Talley publicly debated the subject on September 23, 1924, at the Metropolitan Opera House in New York City. Following are excerpts from that famous debate, which asked the question, "Is Capital Punishment a Wise Public Policy?"

## A. ALFRED J. TALLEY

Those who would seek to take away from the State the power to impose capital punishment seek to despoil the symbol of justice. They would leave in her hands the scales that typify that in this country at least all are equal before the law and that these scales must never tip from one side to the other, loaded on either side with power or influence of the litigant that comes to the temple of justice. They would leave over her eyes the bandage that typifies that she must be no respecter of persons, but they would take from her hand the sword, without which the other symbols would be meaningless things. For if justice has not the right to enforce her edicts and her mandates, then her laws may be lost upon a senseless people. (Applause) . . .

I say it is the time for sensible men and women to come to a realization that there is one way to deal with the criminal and the malefactor, and that is with certainty and severity. There is no other way in which the integrity of the people of this country or the sanctity of the law may be observed. I am in favor of abolishing capital punishment when the murderers of the country abolish its necessity. (Applause)

## B. CLARENCE DARROW

We teach people to kill, and the State is the one that teaches them. (Applause) If a State wishes that its citizens respect human life, then the State should stop killing. It can be done in no other way, and it will perhaps not be fully done that way. There are infinite reasons for killing. There are infinite circumstances under which there are more or less deaths. It never did depend and never can depend on the severity of the punishment. . . .

There is just one thing in all this question. It is a question of how you feel, that is all. It is all inside of you. If you love the thought of somebody being killed, why, you are for it. If you hate the thought of somebody being killed, you are against it. (Applause) . . .

Now, why am I opposed to capital punishment? It is too horrible a thing for a State to undertake. We are told by my friend, "Oh, the killer does it; why shouldn't the State?" I would hate to live in a state that I didn't think was better than a murderer. (Applause)

But I told you the real reason. The people of the State kill a man because he killed someone else—that is all—without the slightest logic, without the slightest application to life, simply from anger, nothing else!

I am against it because I believe it is inhuman, because I believe that as the hearts of men have softened they have gradually gotten rid of brutal punishment, because I believe that it will only be a few years until it will be banished forever from [e]very civilized country—even New York—because I believe that it has no effect whatever to stop murder. (Applause) . . .

There isn't, I submit, a single admissable argument in favor of capital punishment. Nature loves life. We believe that life should be protectd and preserved. The thing that keeps one from killing is the emotion they have against it; and the greater the sanctity that the State pays to life, the greater the feeling of sanctity the individual has for life. (Applause)

There is nothing in the history of the world that ever cheapened human life like our great war; next to that, the indiscriminate killing of men by the States.

## C. ALFRED J. TALLEY

I hate the thought, despite what Mr. Darrow says, of anybody being killed. There is nothing inconsistent with those of us who believe that capital punishment is an essential, a necessary thing, in the maintenance of law and order in a sovereign State—there is nothing inconsistent with our abhorrence of killing. No man ever spoke on a public platform who had more of a horror in his heart against the one who would strike down life than I have. But the killing that I abhor is the killing of the victim of a wanton crime, that I think of first, and then it is time enough to think of the killing of the man who desecrated the law by taking a human life. (Applause)

*Source*: Clarence Darrow and Alfred J. Talley, *Is Capital Punishment a Wise Public Policy?* (New York: League for Public Discussion, 1924). [Chicago: Chicago Historical Bookworks, 1991, 22, 25, 31, 38–41.]

## DOCUMENT 30: The Execution of Sacco and Vanzetti (1927)

Three years later, another death penalty case made national—and international—headlines.

Nicola Sacco and Bartolomeo Vanzetti were Italian immigrants and self-proclaimed anarchists who were convicted and sentenced to death for the murders of two men during a payroll robbery at the South Braintree Shoe Company, just outside of Boston, on April 15, 1920.

During their unsuccessful seven-year struggle against their death sentences—during which time they consistently maintained their innocence—Sacco and Vanzetti gained a tremendous following—primarily among the working class—both in America and abroad. Many people believed that they were innocent victims of the frenzied "Red Scare" that followed World War I, making every foreigner suspect—especially those who maintained unpopular political views (Lyons 1927:36–42).

Indeed, much of the evidence in the case suggests that Sacco and Vanzetti may have been innocent (Radelet et al. 1992:98–99). Moreover, in 1925 Celestino Madeiros, a man condemned for another murder, said that he had been involved in the South Braintree robbery and that Sacco and Vanzetti "were not in said crime" (Lyons 1927:123), but his confession came too late to be of any help to Sacco and Vanzetti.

From August 3, 1927, when the Governor of Massachusetts announced his decision to affirm the death sentences, until August 23, 1927, when the executions took place, massive demonstrations protesting the decision were held all over the world. Following the lead of the workers, many intellectuals and artists—including scientists, philosophers, writers, and poets—also joined in the cause (Lyons 1927: 171).

Although the protests were unsuccessful, they did much to keep the abolitionist cause alive during the unreceptive climate of the 1920s and 1930s—and they led to a significant increase in membership in the newly formed American League to Abolish Capital Punishment (Mackey 1976:xxxix).

A hurricane of protest swept through the world after the decision of Governor Fuller to electrocute Sacco and Vanzetti was flashed to every corner of the earth. Resentment and dismay broke in furious floods. Workers poured into the streets of the world, demonstrating and pleading and threatening.

Such an international demonstration would have been utterly impossible a generation ago. Cables, radio, improved news-gathering facilities, the development of the press, made the events in Boston known to the rest of the globe almost instantaneously. Every meeting, every demonstration was intimately aware of similar meetings and demonstrations elsewhere. The protest thus attained a force and direction never before equaled. The workers did not feel isolated; they threw themselves into the fight conscious of the fellowship of millions of others of every color and nationality.

The protest for Sacco and Vanzetti in the seven days between August 3 and August 10 has never been surpassed—except in the twelve days which were to follow August 10. There are no words to compass its immensity. We can merely list at random meetings, parades, resolutions, strikes, in widely separated parts of the world, and multiply them a hundredfold to get some notion of the movement.

In the names of Sacco and Vanzetti, tens of thousands of workers in London gathered in Hyde Park and Trafalgar Square, day after day, singing the "Red Flag," and denouncing American capital. They set up a gruesome replica of the Massachusetts electric chair. Throngs watched a mock electrocution with a uniformed war veteran as victim. Infuriated crowds marched upon the American Embassy in Grosvenor Square. Thirty thousand Parisian workers came into the streets to follow a meek peasant woman, Vanzetti's sister Luigia, in a parade. There were demonstrations before the American consulates in Munich and Cherbourg, in far-off Morocco, in which police charged the demonstrators. Delegations bearing resolutions called upon American official representatives in Bucharest, Vienna, Berlin, Stockholm, Lisbon, Madrid, Ottawa; in Tokio and Cape Town. General strikes were called in cities of Argentina, Uruguay, Mexico. Strikes occurred in a score of cities in the United States. Throughout the vast territory of the Soviet Union hundreds of meetings took place. The national legislatures of Argentina and of Uruguay sent petitions to America.

Several hundred thousand men and women laid down their tools in New York to gather in a series of indoor meetings called by the socialists and a huge outdoor meeting on Union Square, arranged by the Sacco-Vanzetti Emergency Defense Committee, a united-front committee of communists, anarchists, I.W.W.'s, left-wing trade-unionists. Perhaps 25,000 gathered on the square under the heaviest police guard in the city's history, and at least 25,000 more filled the surrounding streets unable to get into the square. Chicago demonstrations were scattered by police tear-bombs and riot guns. Ten thousand silk workers struck in Paterson, New Jersey, and sporadic strikes of miners took place in Colorado and Pennsylvania. Men and women concentrated in Boston, paraded before the State House, were beaten and arrested—and paraded once more.

Besides these mass demonstrations there came from all over the world messages pleading or demanding that the electrocution be stopped; from labor leaders, government officials, literary men, famous journalists, scientists and philosophers. In the Dreyfus case the intellectual minority, under Zola, led the world protest, and mass demonstrations followed. In the Sacco-Vanzetti case, on the contrary, the workers' mass movement came first and remained first; the classless or bourgeois intelligentsia followed belatedly. The voices of George Bernard Shaw, H. G. Wells, Romain Rolland, John Galsworthy, Albert Einstein, Sinclair Lewis, of religious leaders and humanitarians, were raised in behalf of the two condemned Italian workers. But they were lost in the roar of working-class protest.

*Source*: Eugene Lyons, *The Life and Death of Sacco and Vanzetti* (New York: International Publishers, 1927). [New York: Da Capo Press, 1970, 169–171.]

## DOCUMENT 31: Sing Sing Warden Lewis E. Lawes (1928)

In 1928, one of the most prominent and active members of the American League to Abolish Capital Punishment was a man who supervised hundreds of executions in his role as a prison warden.

Lewis E. Lawes (1883–1947), who served as warden of New York's Sing Sing prison from 1920 to 1941, was not always an opponent of capital punishment. From the start of his career in prison work as a guard at New York's Clinton prison in 1905 until he was appointed warden of Sing Sing, Lawes was, in his own words, "a firm believer in the social necessity of capital punishment" (Lawes 1928:137).

However, soon after becoming warden of Sing Sing, Lawes began to question the efficacy of the death penalty as a deterrent to murder. Based on his research, he eventually concluded that the death penalty was a "positive failure as a deterrent" because "the causes of crime are economic and sociological with roots far deeper than mere punishment can hope to affect" (Lawes 1928:141).

During his tenure at Sing Sing, Lawes not only became a vehement opponent of the death penalty, but also introduced a number of reforms in prison administration. In addition, he wrote numerous books and articles on the subject of the death penalty and penal reform, including *Man's Judgment of Death* (1923), *Life and Death in Sing Sing* (1928), *Twenty Thousand Years in Sing Sing* (1932), *Cell 202 Sing Sing* (1935), *Invisible Stripes* (1938), and *Meet the Murderer* (1940).

Not only does capital punishment fail in its justification, but no punishment could be invented with so many inherent defects. It is an unequal punishment in the way it is applied to the rich and to the poor. The defendant of wealth and position never goes to the electric chair or to the gallows. Juries do not intentionally favour the rich, the law is theoretically impartial, but the defendant with ample means is able to have his case presented with every favourable aspect, while the poor defendant often has a lawyer assigned by the court. Sometimes such assignment is considered part of political patronage; usually the lawyer assigned has had no experience whatever in a capital case. Even after death, distinction prevails. Where there are relatives who can afford to do so, the body may be claimed and taken away. The law states that the unclaimed body shall be buried on prison ground and in quicklime.

It is a punishment, too, that falls most severely on the family of the defendant; for the murderer himself, his suffering is soon over. The wives, the mothers, the children are the ones who suffer. I yield to no one in acknowledging the duty we owe to the family of the murderer's victim, but I have very grave doubt whether society is right in inflicting this terrible burden on the innocent family of the murderer, believing, as I do, that the punishment serves no purpose other than to get rid of the murderer.

It is a punishment of absolute finality; there is no opportunity for the correction of mistakes. For that very reason, some juries will not inflict a punishment so irrevocable. I have known several men who have been very close to the chair, and who, afterward, were found to be innocent. Still other men have been commuted to life imprisonment in almost the last moments of their lives. If they deserved commutation, they did not deserve death, and yet they were within a few moments of it. Finally, it has so many legal safeguards that it is slow in operation and so arbitrary that it cannot be made to fit all of the varying degrees of even first-degree murder. By reason of all these defects, it remains a useless punishment too seldom applied by judge and jury to be a warning.

Capital punishment has never been and never can be anything but an uncertainty. It is a punishment for revenge, for retaliation, not for protection. We can have a punishment that is possible of application with both certainty and celerity, that presents an opportunity for individualization of treatment, and that is in accord with modern criminological methods. Can we not have the vision to see the possibilities of the future, the courage and faith to progress toward those possibilities?

Bulwer Lytton truly said: "Society has erected the gallows at the end of the lane instead of guide posts and direction boards at the beginning."

Source: Lewis E. Lawes, *Life and Death in Sing Sing* (Garden City, N.Y.: Doubleday, Doran, 1928), 155–157.

## DOCUMENT 32: *Powell v. Alabama* (1932)

In the landmark case of *Powell v. Alabama*, the Supreme Court over-turned the death sentences of seven black youths on the grounds that they had been denied the right to effective counsel, and the Court ordered a new trial.

The petitioners—who, along with two other black youths not rep-resented in this case, had become known as the "Scottsboro Boys"—allegedly had raped two white girls on a freight train traveling through Alabama following a fight with seven white youths who also were on the train (six of whom they reportedly threw off the train). A message about the incident had been sent ahead, and before the train reached Scottsboro a sheriff's posse arrested the defendants. They were greeted in Scottsboro by a large and apparently hostile crowd, and arraigned the same day (287 U.S. 45, 50–51).

The defendants—who all were poor, illiterate, and from other states—apparently weren't asked whether they had or were able to employ their own lawyers, whether they wanted to have counsel ap-pointed, or whether they had friends or relatives they could contact for assistance. In fact, no trial lawyer was specifically designated to rep-resent the defendants until the morning of the first of three separate one-day trials beginning six days after their indictment (287 U.S. 45, 52, 56). All seven defendants—each of whom pleaded not guilty—were convicted and sentenced to death.

Upon appeal the petitioners claimed, among other things, that they had been "denied the right of counsel, with the accustomed incidents of consultation and opportunity of preparation for trial" (287 U.S. 45, 50).

The Court—ruling for the first time on the issue of right to counsel—agreed, stating that "the right to counsel being conceded, a defendant should be afforded a fair opportunity to secure counsel of his own choice. Not only was that not done here, but such designation of coun-sel as was attempted was either so indefinite or so close upon the trial as to amount to a denial of effective and substantial aid in that regard" (287 U.S. 45, 53).

## A. OPINION OF THE COURT

MR. JUSTICE SUTHERLAND delivered the opinion of the Court. . . .
It has never been doubted by this court, or any other so far as we

know, that notice and hearing are preliminary steps essential to the passing of an enforceable judgment, and that they, together with a legally competent tribunal having jurisdiction of the case, constitute basic elements of the constitutional requirement of due process of law. . . .

What, then, does a hearing include? Historically and in practice, in our own country at least, it has always included the right to the aid of counsel when desired and provided by the party asserting the right. The right to be heard would be, in many cases, of little avail if it did not comprehend the right to be heard by counsel. Even the intelligent and educated layman has small and sometimes no skill in the science of law. If charged with crime, he is incapable, generally, of determining for himself whether the indictment is good or bad. He is unfamiliar with the rules of evidence. Left without the aid of counsel he may be put on trial without a proper charge, and convicted upon incompetent evidence, or evidence irrelevant to the issue or otherwise inadmissible. He lacks both the skill and knowledge adequately to prepare his defense, even though he have a perfect one. He requires the guiding hand of counsel at every step in the proceedings against him. Without it, though he be not guilty, he faces the danger of conviction because he does not know how to establish his innocence. If that be true of men of intelligence, how much more true is it of the ignorant and illiterate, or those of feeble intellect. If in any case, civil or criminal, a state or federal court were arbitrarily to refuse to hear a party by counsel, employed by and appearing for him, it reasonably may not be doubted that such a refusal would be a denial of a hearing, and, therefore, of due process in the constitutional sense. . . .

In the light of the facts outlined in the forepart of this opinion—the ignorance and illiteracy of the defendants, their youth, the circumstances of public hostility, the imprisonment and the close surveillance of the defendants by the military forces, the fact that their friends and families were all in other states and communication with them necessarily difficult, and above all that they stood in deadly peril of their lives—we think the failure of the trial court to give them reasonable time and opportunity to secure counsel was a clear denial of due process.

But passing that, and assuming their inability, even if opportunity had been given, to employ counsel, as the trial court evidently did assume, we are of opinion that, under the circumstances just stated, the necessity of counsel was so vital and imperative that the failure of the trial court to make an effective appointment of counsel was likewise a denial of due process within the meaning of the Fourteenth Amendment. Whether this would be so in other criminal prosecutions, or under other circumstances, we need not determine. All that it is necessary now to decide, as we do decide, is that in a capital case, where the defendant is unable to employ counsel, and is incapable adequately of making his own defense because of ignorance, feeble mindedness, illiteracy, or the like, it is the duty of the court, whether requested or not, to assign counsel for him as a necessary requisite of due process of law; and that duty is not discharged by an assignment at such a time or under such circumstances as to preclude the giving of effective aid in the preparation and trial of the case. To hold otherwise would be to ignore the fundamental postulate, already adverted to, "that there are certain immutable principles of justice which inhere in the very idea of free government which no member of the Union may disregard." . . .

The United States by statute and every state in the Union by express provision of law, or by the determination of its courts, make it the duty of the trial judge, where the accused is unable to employ counsel, to appoint counsel for him. In most states the rule applies broadly to all criminal prosecutions, in others it is limited to the more serious crimes, and in a very limited number, to capital cases. A rule adopted with such unanimous accord reflects, if it does not establish, the inherent right to have counsel appointed, at least in cases like the present, and lends convincing support to the conclusion we have reached as to the fundamental nature of that right.

## B. DISSENTING OPINION

MR. JUSTICE BUTLER, dissenting. [MR. JUSTICE MCREYNOLDS concurred in the opinion.]

The Court, putting aside—they are utterly without merit—all other claims that the constitutional rights of petitioners were infringed, grounds its opinion and judgment upon a single assertion of fact. It is that petitioners "were denied the right of counsel, with the accustomed incidents of consultation and opportunity of preparation for trial." If that is true, they were denied due process of law and entitled to have the judgments against them reversed.

But no such denial is shown by the record. . . .

When the first case was called for trial, defendants' attorneys had already prepared, and then submitted, a motion for change of venue together with supporting papers. They were ready to and did at once introduce testimony of witnesses to sustain that demand. They had procured and were ready to offer evidence to show that the defendants Roy Wright and Eugene Williams were under age. The record shows that the State's evidence was ample to warrant a conviction. And three defendants each, while asserting his own innocence, testified that he saw others accused commit the crime charged. When regard is had to these and other disclosures that may have been and probably were made by petitioners to Roddy and Moody before the trial, it would be difficult to think of anything that counsel erroneously did or omitted for their defense.

If there had been any lack of opportunity for preparation, trial counsel would have applied to the court for postponement. No such application was made. There was no suggestion, at the trial or in the motion for a new trial which they made, that Mr. Roddy or Mr. Moody was denied such opportunity or that they were not in fact fully prepared. The amended motion for new trial, by counsel who succeeded them, contains the first suggestion that defendants were denied counsel or opportunity to prepare for trial. But neither Mr. Roddy nor Mr. Moody has given any support to that claim. Their silence requires a finding that the claim is groundless, for if it had any merit they would be bound to support it. And no one has come to suggest any lack of zeal or good faith on their part.

*Source*: 287 U.S. 45 (1932), 68–76.

---

## DOCUMENT 33: Public Opinion and the Death Penalty (1937–1938)

During the 1930s, the number of executions was higher than in any other previous decade in American history: 1,676 executions took place, compared to an average of 1,148 per decade between 1880 and 1920, and 4,831 (total) prior to 1880 (Schneider and Smykla 1991:6–7). Of course, both the number of homicides and the population also were growing rapidly throughout this era.

Not surprisingly, support for the death penalty—as measured by the Gallup Poll—also was strong during the 1930s.

Following are reports from the two years during the 1930s that the Gallup Poll asked survey respondents questions about the death penalty.

## A. GALLUP POLL REPORT, JANUARY 3, 1937

JANUARY 3
CAPITAL PUNISHMENT
Interviewing Date 12/1–6/36
Survey #59                                              Question #3
  *Do you believe in the death penalty for murder?*
Yes                          61%
No                           39

*Asked of those who answered in the affirmative: Are you in favor of the death penalty for persons under 21?*

Yes                          46%

No                           54

## B. GALLUP POLL REPORT, JANUARY 16, 1938

### JANUARY 16
### CAPITAL PUNISHMENT

Interviewing Date 12/1–6/37

Survey #105                                                     Question #1a

*Do you favor or oppose capital punishment for murder?*[1]

Favor                        65%

Oppose                       35

Interviewing Date 12/1–6/37

Survey #105                                                     Question #1b

*Do you favor or oppose capital punishment for women convicted of murder?*

Favor                        58%

Oppose                       42

*Source*: George Gallup, *The Gallup Poll: Public Opinion 1935–71*, Volume One, 1935–1948 (New York: Random House, 1972), 45, 85. Copyright 1972 by Scholarly Resources Inc. Reprinted by permission of Scholarly Resources Inc.

**NOTE**

1. According to Robert M. Bohm, "American Death Penalty Opinion, 1936–1986: A Critical Examination of the Gallup Polls" (Bohm 1991a:116), the following figures from this 1972 report on the Gallup Poll are not accurate. Bohm says original Gallup Poll databases stored at the Roper Center for Public Opinion Research in Storrs, Connecticut, state that in the December 1937 poll, 61 percent favored capital punishment for murder, 33 percent were opposed to it, and 7 percent were undecided.

---

## DOCUMENT 34: *The Execution of Private Slovik* (1945)

---

On the morning of January 31, 1945, three months before the end of hostilities in Europe during World War II, on the outskirts of the mountain town of St. Marie aux Mines in eastern France, a man was marched outside a small house to an enclosed courtyard, bound to a post, and shot to death with M-1 rifles by twelve American soldiers in front of a general and forty-two witnesses (Huie 1954:121, 231, 236).

The man was not a Nazi war criminal, but a private in the United States Army, Eddie D. Slovik—the only American to be executed for desertion during wartime since 1864 (Huie 1954:8).

Slovik was by no means the only soldier to desert during World War II. In fact, about 40,000 soldiers were believed to have done so; and of these, 2,864 were tried by general courts-martial. Most of them received prison terms, although 49 death penalties also were approved. However, none of the other death sentences was carried out—the military typically commuted them and released deserters from prison shortly after war's end (Huie 1954:11–12).

Why, then, was Private Slovik executed? Army officials claimed it was to set an example in order to maintain future discipline or to serve as a lesson of the price that must be paid to win the war (see Documents 34A and 34C).

However, Slovik—who had served jail time for embezzlement and also had a long history of arrests for petty theft and breaking and entering prior to his military service—believed he had been singled out more for his criminal past than for what he had—or rather, hadn't—done. On the morning of his execution, he said, "They're not shooting me for deserting the United States Army—thousands of guys have done that. They're shooting me for the bread I stole when I was twelve years old" (quoted in Huie 1954:21). Indeed, a statement made by one of the reviewers of Slovik's case lends some credibility to this assumption (see Document 34B).

## A. COMMENT OF MAJOR FREDERICK J. BERTOLET IN REVIEWING THE ACTION OF THE COURT AND CONVENING AUTHORITY

[Private Slovik] has directly challenged the authority of the [United States], and future discipline depends upon a resolute reply to this challenge. If the death penalty is ever to be imposed for desertion it should be imposed in this case, not as a punitive measure nor as retribution, but to maintain that discipline upon which alone an army can succeed against the enemy.

## B. ENDORSEMENT OF BRIGADIER GENERAL E. C. McNEIL, ASSISTANT JUDGE ADVOCATE GENERAL

This is the first death sentence for desertion which has reached me for examination. It is probably the first of the kind in the American Army for over eighty years—there were none in World War I. In this case the extreme penalty of death appears warranted. This soldier had performed no front line duty. He did not intend to. He deserted from his group of fifteen when about to join the infantry company to which he had been assigned. His subsequent conduct shows a deliberate plan to secure trial and incarceration in a safe place. *The sentence adjudged was more severe than he had anticipated*, but the imposition of a less severe sentence would only have accomplished the accused's purpose of securing his incarceration and consequent freedom from the dangers which so many of our armed forces are required to face daily. *His unfavorable civilian record indicates that he is not a worthy subject of clemency.* [Italics Huie's.]

## C. MESSAGE OF LIEUTENANT COLONEL JAMES E. RUDDER TO HIS REGIMENT FOLLOWING THE EXECUTION OF PRIVATE SLOVIK (JANUARY 31, 1945)

MESSAGE
TO: Soldiers of the 109th Infantry
Today I had the most regrettable experience I have had since the war began. I saw a former soldier of the 109th Infantry, Private Eddie D. Slovik, shot to death by musketry by soldiers of this regiment. I pray that this man's death will be a lesson to each of us who have any doubt at any time about the price that we must pay to win this war. The person that is not willing to fight and die, if need be, for his country *has no right to life*. [Italics Huie's.]

According to record, this is the first time in eighty years of American history that any United States soldier has been shot to death by musketry for deserting his unit and his fellow man. There is only one reason for our being here and that is to eliminate the enemy that has brought the war about. There is only one way to eliminate the enemy and that is to close with him. Let's all get on with the job we were sent here to do in order that we may return home at the earliest possible moment.

JAMES E. RUDDER
Lt. Col., Infantry
Commanding

*Source*: William Bradford Huie, *The Execution of Private Slovik* (New York: Duell, Sloan and Pearce, 1954), 9, 117, 196–197.

---

## DOCUMENT 35: *Louisiana ex rel. Francis v. Resweber* (1947)

---

In 1947, a new issue arose in the death penalty debate: Does a second attempt at execution after a technical failure constitute cruel and unusual punishment?

The Supreme Court addressed this question in the case of *Louisiana ex rel. Francis v. Resweber*. Willie Francis had been sentenced to death for murder in 1945, at the age of fifteen. On May 3, 1946, he was placed in the electric chair. The executioner threw the switch, and Francis received a heavy jolt of electricity, but due to a technical malfunction in the state's portable electric chair, the jolt was not lethal. Francis was taken back to prison, and the execution was rescheduled to take place on May 9 (329 U.S. 459, 460–461).

Francis challenged the second execution attempt, claiming that having to undergo the psychological stress of preparing for execution not once, but twice, was akin to torture and therefore unconstitutional under the Eighth Amendment (329 U.S. 459, 464). Four of the justices agreed with Francis, characterizing the process as "death by installments" (see Document 35B).

However, the majority upheld the death sentence, explaining that the repeated attempt at execution could only be considered "cruel" if it was purposely inflicted by the state, rather than "an unforeseeable accident" (see Document 35A).

Francis was executed May 9, 1947.

## A. OPINION OF THE COURT

MR. JUSTICE REED announced the judgment of the Court in an opinion in which THE CHIEF JUSTICE, MR. JUSTICE BLACK and MR. JUSTICE JACKSON join. . . .

*Second.* We find nothing in what took place here which amounts to cruel and unusual punishment in the constitutional sense. The case before us does not call for an examination into any punishments except that of death. . . . The traditional humanity of modern Anglo-American law forbids the infliction of unnecessary pain in the execution of the death sentence. Prohibition against the wanton infliction of pain has come into our law from the Bill of Rights of 1688. The identical words appear in our Eighth Amendment. The Fourteenth would prohibit by its due process clause execution by a state in a cruel manner.

Petitioner's suggestion is that because he once underwent the psychological strain of preparation for electrocution, now to require him to undergo this preparation again subjects him to a lingering or cruel and unusual punishment. Even the fact that petitioner has already been subjected to a current of electricity does not make his subsequent execution any more cruel in the constitutional sense than any other execution. The cruelty against which the Constitution protects a convicted man is cruelty inherent in the method of punishment, not the necessary suffering involved in any method employed to extinguish life humanely. The fact that an unforeseeable accident prevented the prompt consummation of the sentence cannot, it seems to us, add an element of cruelty to a subsequent execution. There is no purpose to inflict unnecessary pain nor any unnecessary pain involved in the proposed execution. The situation of the unfortunate victim of this accident is just as though he had suffered the identical amount of mental anguish and physical pain in any other occurrence, such as, for example, a fire in the cell block. We cannot agree that the hardship imposed upon the petitioner rises to that level of hardship denounced as denial of due process because of cruelty.

## B. DISSENTING OPINION

MR. JUSTICE BURTON, with whom MR. JUSTICE DOUGLAS, MR. JUSTICE MURPHY and MR. JUSTICE RUTLEDGE concur, dissenting. . . .

In determining whether the proposed procedure is unconstitutional, we must measure it against a lawful electrocution. The contrast is that between instantaneous death and death by installments—caused by electric shocks administered after one or more intervening periods of complete consciousness of the victim. . . .

The all-important consideration is that the execution shall be so instantaneous and substantially painless that the punishment shall be reduced, as nearly as possible, to no more than that of death itself. . . .

If the state officials deliberately and intentionally had placed the relator in the electric chair five times and, each time, had applied electric current to his body in a manner not sufficient, until the final time, to kill him, such a form of torture would rival that of burning at the stake. Although the failure of the first attempt, in the present case, was unintended, the reapplication of the electric current will be intentional. How many deliberate and intentional reapplications of electric current does it take to produce a cruel, unusual and unconstitutional punishment?

While five applications would be more cruel and unusual than one, the uniqueness of the present case demonstrates that, today, two separated applications are sufficiently "cruel and unusual" to be prohibited. If five attempts would be "cruel and unusual," it would be difficult to draw the line between two, three, four and five. It is not difficult, however, as we here contend, to draw the line between the one continuous application prescribed by statute and any other application of the current.

*Source*: 329 U.S. 459 (1947), 460–476 (footnotes omitted).

---

## DOCUMENT 36: *Patton v. Mississippi* (1947)

---

The issue of racial discrimination in jury selection for a capital trial came before the Supreme Court in the 1947 case of *Patton v. Mississippi*.

The petitioner, Eddie (Buster) Patton, was a black man convicted and sentenced to death by an all-white jury for the murder of a white man.

Patton claimed that he had been denied equal protection of the laws as guaranteed by the Fourteenth Amendment by the exclusion of blacks from both the grand jury that indicted him and the petit jury that convicted him.

Further, he claimed that the failure to include any blacks on the jury was due not to a lack of blacks qualified for jury service in the county, but instead to a "systematic, intentional, deliberate and invariable practice on the part of [the county's] administrative officers to exclude Negroes from the jury lists, jury boxes and jury service" (68 S.Ct. 184, 185). In fact, said Patton, although the 1940 U.S. Census showed that 12,511 of Lauderdale County's 34,821 adult residents were black, no black resident had served on a grand or petit criminal court jury for thirty years or more.

Upon reviewing the evidence presented by Patton, the Court unanimously reversed the decision of the state court to uphold the conviction and sentence and ordered a new trial, setting a new precedent for the prohibition of racial discrimination in jury selection.

Mr. Justice BLACK delivered the opinion of the Court. . . .

[1] Sixty-seven years ago this Court held that state exclusion of Negroes from grand and petit juries solely because of their race denied Negro defendants in criminal cases the equal protection of the laws required by the Fourteenth Amendment. . . .

[2, 3] Whether there has been systematic racial discrimination by administrative officials in the selection of jurors is a question to be determined from the facts in each particular case. In this case the Mississippi Supreme Court concluded that petitioner had failed to prove systematic racial discrimination in the selection of jurors, but in so concluding it erroneously considered only the fact that no Negroes were on the particular venire lists from which the juries were drawn that indicted and convicted petitioner. It regarded as irrelevant the key fact that for thirty years or more no Negro had served on the grand and petit juries. This omission seriously detracts from the weight and respect that we would otherwise give to its conclusion in reviewing the facts, as we must in a constitutional question like this.

[4] It is to be noted at once that the indisputable fact that no Negro had served on a criminal court grand or petit jury for a period of thirty years created a very strong showing that during that period Negroes were systematically excluded from jury service because of race. When such a showing was made, it became the duty of the State to try to justify such an exclusion as having been brought about for some reason other than racial discrimination. The Mississippi Supreme Court did not conclude, the State did not offer any evidence, and in fact did not make any claim, that its officials had abandoned their old jury selection practices. The State Supreme Court's conclusion of justification rested upon the following reasoning. Section 1762 of the Mississippi Code enumerates the qualifications for jury service, the most important of which apparently are that one must be a male citizen and "a qualified elector." Sections 241, 242, 243 and 244 of the state constitution set forth the prerequisites for qualified electors. Among other things these provisions require that each elector shall pay an annual poll tax, produce satisfactory proof of such payment, and be able to read any section of the state constitution, or to understand the same when read to him, or to give a reasonable interpretation thereof. The evidence showed that a very small number of Negro male citizens (the court estimated about 25) as compared with white male citizens, had met the requirements for qualified electors, and thereby become eligible to be considered under additional test for jury service. . . .

We hold that the State wholly failed to meet the very strong evidence of purposeful racial discrimination made out by the petitioner upon the uncontradicted showing that for thirty years or more no Negro had served as a juror in the criminal courts of Lauderdale County. When a jury selection plan, whatever it is, operates in such way as always to result in the complete and long-continued exclusion of any representative at all from a large group of negroes, or any other racial group, indictments and verdicts returned against them by juries thus selected cannot stand. As we pointed out in Hill v. State of Texas . . . , our holding does not mean that a guilty defendant must go free. For indictments can be returned and convictions can be obtained by juries selected as the Constitution commands.

*Source*: 68 S.Ct. 184 (1947), 185–187 (footnotes omitted).

---

## DOCUMENT 37: San Quentin Warden Clinton Duffy (1950)

Sing Sing's Lewis E. Lawes (see Document 31) wasn't the only prison warden who opposed capital punishment. On the other side of the continent, California's Clinton Duffy (1898–1982), warden of San Quentin State Prison from 1940 to 1952, actively supported penal reform, including several proposals for a moratorium on executions (Mackey 1976:xliv).

Duffy, whose father had been a guard at San Quentin, was born and raised on the premises. Duffy served in the Marine Corps, then worked for a railroad and a construction company before finally returning to San Quentin in 1929 as an office assistant to Warden Jim Holohan.

After Holohan resigned in 1936, Court Smith, former warden of Folsom Prison, was appointed warden of San Quentin. Under his direction, San Quentin became what Duffy referred to as a "city of nightmares" by the end of 1938 (Duffy 1950:60).

Following a lengthy investigation by the governor's office, San Quentin's entire board of prison directors was ousted in 1940, and, much to his surprise, Duffy was appointed temporary warden of the prison (Duffy 1950:61). It was a thirty-day appointment that lasted twelve years.

Duffy wasted no time in implementing reforms—firing six guards who had beaten prisoners, banning the use of whips, straps, rubber hoses and other forms of corporal punishment, abolishing head shaving for new prisoners, and improving the prisoners' food and living conditions.

During his twelve years as warden, Duffy also tried to close the doors to the prison's gas chamber for good, but without success. Like Lawes, Duffy was convinced—based on research and personal experience with the condemned—that the death penalty was not an effective deterrent to murder.

Capital punishment is a tragic failure, and my heart fights it even as my hand gives the execution signal in the death house. I argued the subject for years with Warden Holohan and others, but was never able to convince them, even when I demonstrated that in one five-year period California police arrested some two thousand men and women for murder but that only forty-six of them were finally put to death at San Quentin. I knew most of these condemned men, and I have officially executed many others since then, but all of them said that the death penalty did not deter them, even momentarily, from committing their crimes.

I remember one in particular, a swarthy young farmer from one of our mountain counties, who not only knew about San Quentin's gas chamber but who borrowed its deadly principle for his own crime. He killed his best friend by generating cyanide fumes in an airtight cabin, and said afterward he thought it was rather a thoughtful way of ending his victim's life. Just a few hours before he was to get a dose of his own medicine, I said to him, "John, didn't you realize that you might have to sit in a gas chamber yourself when you used the cyanide on your friend?"

"Warden," he said, "I never gave it a thought."

More than one newspaperman has told me that murderers are rarely executed, or even sent to Condemned Row, if they have the right connections or enough money to finance the costly legal fight for their lives. This cynical attitude, which is more prevalent than most people realize, further contributes to the futility of the capital punishment law, so that the gas chamber holds terror only for those who are actually strapped into its iron chair.

*Source*: Clinton T. Duffy (with Dean Jennings), *The San Quentin Story* (Garden City, N.Y.: Doubleday & Company, 1950), 80–81.

---

## DOCUMENT 38: Public Opinion and the Death Penalty (1953)

In 1953, the Gallup Poll questioned Americans on the death penalty for the first time since 1938. No doubt with the pending executions of accused Soviet spies Julius and Ethel Rosenberg in mind (see Document 39), the January poll paid particular attention to the issue of treason (Document 38A). Not surprisingly, respondents were strongly in favor of the death penalty for treason.

Later that same year, the poll returned to the issue of capital punishment—this time with regard to those convicted of murder (Document 38B)—with similar results.

However, despite strong public support for the death penalty, fewer executions actually were taking place than in previous years. For example, an average of 83 executions were conducted between 1950 and 1954, compared to an average of 155 between 1930 and 1934 (Bowers 1984:25–26). This represented a 23 percent decline in the ratio of executions to homicides (U.S. Bureau of the Census 1975: tables 155 and 971).

## A. GALLUP POLL REPORT, JANUARY 30, 1953

**JANUARY 30**
**PUNISHMENT FOR TREASON**
Interviewing Date 1/11–16/53
Survey #510-K                                                     Question #4

*Do you approve or disapprove of the death sentence for persons convicted of treason against this country?*

| | |
|---|---|
| Approve | 73% |
| Disapprove | 21 |
| No opinion | 6 |

## B. GALLUP POLL REPORT, NOVEMBER 21, 1953

**NOVEMBER 21**
**CAPITAL PUNISHMENT**
Interviewing Date 11/1–5/53
Survey #522-K                                                     Question #7a

*Are you in favor of the death penalty for persons convicted of murder?*

| | |
|---|---|
| Yes | 68% |
| No | 25 |
| No opinion | 7 |

*Source*: George Gallup, *The Gallup Poll: Public Opinion 1935–71*, Volume Two, 1949–1958 (New York: Random House, 1972), 1117, 1187. Copyright 1972 by Scholarly Resources Inc. Reprinted by permission of Scholarly Resources Inc.

## DOCUMENT 39: The Execution of Julius and Ethel Rosenberg (1953)

Despite strong public support for the death penalty—particularly for treason (see Document 38A)—the executions of Julius and Ethel Rosenberg created an uproar. However, the focus of public protests against the executions was not capital punishment in general, but rather the execution of the Rosenbergs—whom many believed were innocent of the Soviet espionage for which they had been condemned (Mackey 1976:xli; also see Document 39B).

The Rosenbergs were arrested by the FBI in 1950 for conspiring to transmit classified information on the atomic bomb to the Soviet Union. Their accuser was Ethel's brother, David Greenglass, who had worked on the atomic bomb project at Los Alamos National Laboratory in New Mexico. He claimed that they had persuaded him to give them highly classified information on the bomb. Greenglass was sentenced to fifteen years in prison for his role in the conspiracy; two co-defendants, Morton Sobell and Harry Gold, were sentenced to thirty years each; and the Rosenbergs—who consistently maintained their innocence—were given the death penalty (Hook and Kahn 1989:7–8).

In the wake of numerous court appeals and public protests, the Supreme Court became involved in the controversy—first when Justice William O. Douglas stayed the executions on June 17, 1953, and again when a majority of the Court voted to vacate Douglas's stay during a special session convened by Chief Justice Fred M. Vinson to review the stay (Fineberg 1953:112–113; see also Document 39A). The Rosenbergs were electrocuted on June 19, 1953—making their case "the first trial to result in the execution of U.S. citizens for conspiracy to commit espionage" (Hook and Kahn 1989:7).

## A. PRESIDENT EISENHOWER AND THE SUPREME COURT UPHOLD THE DEATH SENTENCES

WASHINGTON, June 19—President Eisenhower and the Supreme Court refused today to save Julius and Ethel Rosenberg from death in the electric chair.

The high court vacated the stay granted to the atomic spies on Wednesday by Justice William O. Douglas. It upheld the legality of the death sentence imposed by Federal Judge Irving R. Kaufman.

Less than an hour after the court had announced its verdict, President Eisenhower refused Executive clemency for the second time. He had denied a similar petition on Feb. 11.

"I can only say that, by immeasurably increasing the chances of atomic war, the Rosenbergs may have condemned to death tens of millions of innocent people all over the world," the President said. "The execution of two human beings is a grave matter. But even graver is the thought of the millions of dead whose deaths may be directly attributable to what these spies have done."

He was convinced, the President said, that the Rosenbergs had received "the fullest measure of justice and due process of law."

"When in their most solemn judgment the tribunals of the United States have adjudged them guilty and the sentence just, I will not intervene in this matter," the President declared.

*Source*: Luther A. Huston, "Six Justices Agree: President Says Couple Increased 'Chances of Atomic War,'" *New York Times*, June 20, 1953, 1.


## B. PUBLIC REACTION TO THE EXECUTIONS

Sympathizers of Julius and Ethel Rosenberg bombarded judges with new appeals last night and staged rallies in a desperate last-minute flurry of efforts to save the condemned atom spies from the electric chair.

As time ran out for the doomed couple, lawyers and sympathizers tried every avenue of appeal and protest in a feverish evening that included:

• An order by Police Commissioner George P. Monaghan to all police commands to maintain a special city-wide vigil against any disorder or violence in connection with the execution.

• Three separate appeals to Federal Judge Irving R. Kaufman, who sentenced the Rosenbergs, to stay their execution. He rejected all.

• Two separate appeals to two Federal Circuit Court judges to grant a stay. These also were denied.

• A rally by an estimated 5,000 persons in Seventeenth Street, west of the north end of Union Square, where members of the New York Clemency Committee of the National Committee to Secure Justice in the Rosenberg Case denounced President Eisenhower as "bloodthirsty."

*Source*: "Eisenhower Is Denounced to 5,000 in Union Sq. Rally," *New York Times*, June 20, 1953, 1.


## DOCUMENT 40: Public Opinion and the Death Penalty (1957)

By the mid-1950s, Americans seemed ready to put four decades of turmoil—including three major wars and the Great Depression—behind them. Social reforms that had long taken a back seat to these other concerns once again moved to the forefront.

Among them was a slow but steady revival of anti-death penalty activities in the United States. At the same time, public support of capital punishment for murder dropped to 47 percent in 1957—a 21-point decrease in just four years (see Document 38B).

## OCTOBER 11
## CAPITAL PUNISHMENT

Interviewing Date 8/29–9/4/57
Survey #588-K                                              Question #27a

*Do you favor the death penalty for murder?*[1]

| | |
|---|---|
| Yes | 47% |
| No | 50 |
| No opinion | 3 |

*Source*: George Gallup, *The Gallup Poll: Public Opinion 1935–71*, Volume Two, 1949–1958 (New York: Random House, 1972), 1518. Copyright 1972 by Scholarly Resources Inc. Reprinted by permission of Scholarly Resources Inc.

### NOTE

1. According to Robert M. Bohm, "American Death Penalty Opinion, 1936–1986: A Critical Examination of the Gallup Polls" (Bohm 1991a:116), the following figures from this 1972 report on the Gallup Poll are not accurate. Bohm says original Gallup Poll databases stored at the Roper Center for Public Opinion Research in Storrs, Connecticut, state that in the August/September 1957 poll, 47 percent favored capital punishment for murder, 34 percent were opposed to it, and 18 percent were undecided.

---

## DOCUMENT 41: *Trop v. Dulles* (1958)

---

The 1958 case of *Trop v. Dulles*, like the 1910 case of *Weems v. U.S.* (see Document 27), was not a death penalty case. But, like *Weems*, it was highly significant in the capital punishment debate because it dealt once again with the Supreme Court's interpretation of the Eighth Amendment's prohibition against cruel and unusual punishment.

The petitioner, Albert Trop, had been stripped of his citizenship for deserting the U.S. Army during World War II. Although the incident—for which he had been court-martialed, dishonorably discharged, and sentenced to three years at hard labor—occurred in 1944, it was not until 1952, when he applied for a passport, that Trop discovered that he had been denationalized under the provisions of the Nationality Act of 1940. Trop appealed, and the Supreme Court was called upon to determine whether the government had the constitutional right to impose such a penalty.

Writing for the five-member majority, Chief Justice Warren held that the penalty violated the Eighth Amendment's prohibition against cruel and unusual punishment because "the basic concept underlying the Eighth Amendment is nothing less than the dignity of man" (78 S.Ct. 590, 597).

Citing the similar decision of the *Weems* court fifty years earlier, Warren went on to explain that "the Amendment must draw its meaning from the evolving standards of decency that mark the progress of a maturing society" (see Document 27).

Although the Court's opinion specifically stated that the death penalty was not unconstitutional because it still was widely accepted by the public, opponents of capital punishment were encouraged by the decision. It suggested that should the majority of the public come to reject capital punishment, it might finally be abolished as cruel and unusual under the Court's new test standard (Epstein and Kobylka 1992:42; Paternoster 1991:53).

## A. OPINION OF THE COURT

Mr. Chief Justice WARREN announced the judgment of the Court and delivered an opinion, in which Mr. Justice BLACK, Mr. Justice DOUGLAS, and Mr. Justice WHITTAKER join. . . .

The exact scope of the constitutional phrase "cruel and unusual" has not been detailed by this Court. But the basic policy reflected in these words is firmly established in the Anglo-American tradition of criminal justice. The phrase in our Constitution was taken directly from the English Declaration of Rights of 1688, and the principle it represents can be traced back to the Magna Carta. The basic concept underlying the Eighth Amendment is nothing less than the dignity of man. While the State has the power to punish, the Amendment stands to assure that this power be exercised within the limits of civilized standards. Fines, imprisonment and even execution may be imposed depending upon the enormity of the crime, but any technique outside the bounds of these traditional penalties is constitutionally suspect. This Court has had little occasion to give precise content to the Eighth Amendment, and, in an enlightened democracy such as ours, this is not surprising. But when the Court was confronted with a punishment of 12 years in irons at hard and painful labor imposed for the crime of falsifying public records, it did not hesitate to declare that the penalty was cruel in its excessiveness and unusual in its character. [*Weems v. United States*]. . . . The Court recognized in that case that the words of the Amendment are not precise, and that their scope is not static. The Amendment must draw its meaning from the evolving standards of decency that mark the progress of a maturing society.

We believe, as did Chief Judge Clark in the court below, that use of denationalization as a punishment is barred by the Eighth Amendment. There may be involved no physical mistreatment, no primitive torture. There is instead the total destruction of the individual's status in organized society. It is a form of punishment more primitive than torture, for it destroys for the individual the political existence that was centuries in the development. The punishment strips the citizen of his status in the national and international political community. His very existence is at the sufferance of the country in which he happens to find himself. While any one country may accord him some rights, and presumably as long as he remained in this country he would enjoy the limited rights of an alien, no country need do so because he is stateless. Furthermore, his enjoyment of even the limited rights of an alien might be subject to termination at any time by reason of deportation. In short, the expatriate has lost the right to have rights.

This punishment is offensive to cardinal principles for which the Constitution stands. It subjects the individual to a fate of ever-increasing fear and distress. He knows not what discriminations may be established against him, what proscriptions may be directed against him, and when and for what cause his existence in his native land may be terminated. He may be subject to banishment, a fate universally decried by civilized people. He is stateless, a condition deplored in the international community of democracies. It is no answer to suggest that all the disastrous consequences of this fate may not be brought to bear on a stateless person. The threat makes the punishment obnoxious.

## B. DISSENTING OPINION

Mr. Justice FRANKFURTER, whom Mr. Justice BURTON, Mr. Justice CLARK, and Mr. Justice HARLAN join, dissenting. . . .

Petitioner contends that loss of citizenship is an unconstitutionally disproportionate "punishment" for desertion and that it constitutes "cruel and unusual punishments" within the scope of the Eighth Amendment. Loss of citizenship entails undoubtedly severe—and in particular situations even tragic—consequences. Divestment of citizenship by the Government has been characterized, in the context of denaturalization, as "more serious than a taking of one's property, or the imposition of a fine or other penalty." . . . However, like denaturalization . . . expatriation under the Nationality Act of 1940 is not "punishment" in any valid constitutional sense. . . . Simply because denationalization was attached by Congress as a consequence of conduct that it had elsewhere made unlawful, it does not follows [sic] that denationalization is a "punishment," any more than it can be said that loss of civil rights as a result of conviction for a felony . . . is a "punishment" for any legally significant purposes. The process of denationalization, as devised by the expert Cabinet Committee on which Congress quite properly and responsibly relied and as established by Congress in the legislation before the Court, was related to the authority of Congress, pursuant to its constitutional powers, to regulate conduct free from restrictions that pertain to legislation in the field technically described as criminal justice. Since there are legislative ends within the scope of Congress' war power that are wholly consistent with a "non-penal" purpose to regulate the military forces, and since there is nothing on the face of this legislation or in its history to indicate that Congress had a contrary purpose, there is no warrant for this Court's labeling the disability imposed by §401(g) as a "punishment."

Even assuming, *arguendo*, that §401(g) can be said to impose "punishment," to insist that denationalization is "cruel and unusual" punishment is to stretch that concept beyond the breaking point. It seems scarcely arguable that loss of citizenship is within the Eighth Amendment's prohibition because disproportionate to an offense that is capital and has been so from the first year of Independence. . . . Is constitutional dialectic so empty of reason that it can be seriously urged that loss of citizenship is a fate worse than death? The seriousness of abandoning one's country when it is in the grip of mortal conflict precludes denial to Congress of the power to terminate citizenship here, unless that power is to be denied to Congress under any circumstance.

*Source*: 78 S.Ct. 590 (1958), 591–611 (footnotes omitted).

## DOCUMENT 42: *The Death Penalty* (Thorsten Sellin, 1959)

As the 1950s drew to a close, social scientist Thorsten Sellin (1896–1994), a professor at the University of Pennsylvania, added fuel to the growing abolitionist cause with a study in which he concluded that executions had no effect on homicide rates and, hence, that capital punishment was not an effective deterrent to murder.

Sellin, who has been called "the dean of America's scholarly opponents of capital punishment" (Mackey 1976:227), was among the first social science researchers to use empirical evidence generated by statistical analysis to examine the deterrent value of the death penalty (Paternoster 1991:221).

His 1959 study, which accompanied the American Law Institute's Model Penal Code, compared homicide rates in abolitionist states to homicide rates in contiguous death penalty states from 1920 to 1958. Attempting to control for other factors that might affect homicide rates, Sellin grouped together states with similar social, economic, and cultural characteristics (Sellin 1959).

Sellin's study (excerpted in the document below), which remains controversial to this day, spawned a number of other studies aimed at examining the deterrent effect (or lack thereof) of the death penalty (for example, see Documents 60 and 65).

It seems reasonable to assume that if the death penalty exercises a deterrent or preventive effect on prospective murderers, the following propositions would be true:

(a) Murders should be less frequent in states that have the death penalty than in those that have abolished it, other factors being equal. Comparisons of this nature must be made among states that are as alike as possible in all other respects—character of population, social and economic condition, etc.—in order not to introduce factors known to influence murder rates in a serious manner but present in only one of these states.

(b) Murders should increase when the death penalty is abolished and should decline when it is restored.

(c) The deterrent effect should be greatest and should therefore affect murder rates most powerfully in those communities where the crime occurred and its consequences are most strongly brought home to the population.

(d) Law enforcement officers would be safer from murderous attacks in states that have the death penalty than in those without it. . . .

The data examined reveal that

1. The *level* of the homicide death rates varies in different groups of states. It is lowest in the New England areas and in the northern states of the middle west and lies somewhat higher in Michigan, Indiana and Ohio.

2. Within each group of states having similar social and economic conditions and populations, it is impossible to distinguish the abolition state from the others.

3. The *trends* of the homicide death rates of comparable states with or without the death penalty are similar.

The inevitable conclusion is that executions have no discernible effect on homicide death rates which, as we have seen, are regarded as adequate indicators of capital murder rates. . . .

In preceding pages, one of the aspects of this issue has been considered, namely, the question of whether or not the death penalty appears to have any effect on homicide death rates. We have examined comparatively such rates in selected states that do and those that do not have the death penalty; we have compared the rates of capital crimes in specific states or countries that have experimented with abolition in order to observe the effect of the abolition or introduction of capital punishment on such rates; we have noted the specific effect of highly publicized executions on homicides in a metropolitan city; and we have tried to learn if the claim of the police is true, when they say that their lives are safer in states that have the death penalty.

Any one who carefully examines the above data is bound to arrive at the conclusion that the death penalty, as we use it, exercises no influence on the extent or fluctuating rates of capital crimes. It has failed as a deterrent. If it has utilitarian value, it must rest in some other attribute than its power to influence the future conduct of people.

*Source*: Thorsten Sellin, *The Death Penalty* (Philadelphia: The American Law Institute, 1959). In Hugo Adam Bedau, *The Death Penalty in America* (Chicago: Aldine, 1964), 276, 279, 284 (footnotes omitted).

# Part IV

# Capital Punishment in the Courts, 1960–1976

Although earlier eras discussed in this book were much longer and the detail of information available about them today is much coarser than with contemporary issues and information technology, it seems safe to say that the capital punishment debate became as heated and robust during the period between 1960 and 1976 as at any time in U.S. history. This renewed focus on the death penalty was fueled by a number of factors, which are discussed below.

## SOCIAL UNREST

The 1960s opened with the execution of convicted kidnapper Caryl Chessman (see Document 43), whose eleven-year string of appeals and best-selling books written from death row brought the issue of capital punishment to center stage (Schwed 1983:68–69).

At the same time, intense social unrest appears to have increased people's receptiveness to anti-capital punishment arguments—at least during the early to mid-1960s. For example, as Schwed (1983:95) pointed out, the civil rights movement and its focus on equality for black Americans "spurred recognition of the death penalty as one instrument of repression of blacks and minorities." Moreover, the protests against the Vietnam war and the draft that began in the mid-1960s may have contributed to the concurrent waning of support for capital punishment by heightening many people's "moral sensitivity to killing in general" and leading them to question the government's rationale for doing so, either in war or in the execution chamber (Schwed 1983:94).

Along with these changes, which challenged long-established ways of doing things, traumatic events such as the assassinations of President John F. Kennedy, Malcolm X, Dr. Martin Luther King, Jr., and Senator

Robert Kennedy within less than five years shook the country, along with riots in many black urban slums, campus unrest, illicit drug use, and the sexual revolution (Finckenauer 1988:88–89).

Amid this rapidly changing social and political climate, public support for capital punishment dropped to 42 percent in 1966—the lowest level since the Gallup Poll first began asking questions about capital punishment thirty years previously.

## A SHIFT IN ABOLITIONIST TACTICS

During the early 1960s, the debate over capital punishment also began to shift increasingly from religious, moral, and utilitarian grounds to legal philosophy. And the arena in which those debates took place shifted from the pulpit, the lecture hall, and the floor of the legislature to the courtroom.

Attorneys such as Gerald Gottlieb (Document 46) started the process by exploring the potential for challenging the death penalty's constitutionality. Then, in a 1963 dissenting opinion, Supreme Court Justice Goldberg further encouraged this approach when he alerted the legal community that he and at least two of his fellow justices might be willing to entertain Eighth and Fourteenth Amendment challenges to the constitutionality of the death penalty (see Document 47). Constitutional challenges began in earnest when the American Civil Liberties Union (ACLU) took a strong stance against capital punishment midway through the decade and authorized its lawyers to enter death penalty cases where there was evidence of race or class bias. At about the same time, the National Association for the Advancement of Colored People's Legal Defense and Educational Fund began a campaign against Southern racism in death penalty cases involving black men accused of raping white women. When the LDF expanded that campaign in 1967 to provide counsel to *all* death row prisoners, it hoped to bring about a *de facto* moratorium on the death penalty. It worked. Within a year, almost all scheduled executions were tied up in constitutional appeals.

As anti-death penalty advocates increased the number and quality of appeals, the Supreme Court ruled on important constitutional issues in a series of fluid interpretations that reflected the increasingly complex nature of the capital punishment debate.

In 1968, Anthony Amsterdam of the LDF argued against the constitutionality of juries that excluded people who opposed or had reservations about the death penalty, claiming that they were not representative and thus violated the Sixth and Fourteenth Amendments. The Supreme Court agreed in a ruling that affected nearly every prisoner on death row (see Document 52) because almost all states used only "death qualified" jurors at the time.

Three years later, the Supreme Court dealt abolitionists a setback when it ruled on two key procedural issues: (1) That it was constitutional to give juries complete discretion over whether to sentence a defendant to life in prison or death; and (2) That "unitary trials" in which issues of both guilt and punishment were decided were constitutional even though they often forced defendants to choose between self-incrimination and presentation of evidence about mitigating circumstances surrounding their actions (see Document 53).

Finally, in 1972, the Supreme Court agreed to consider Eighth Amendment issues directly and to hear three appeals claiming that the imposition and execution of the death penalty itself was cruel and unusual punishment. In a clear victory for abolitionists, a narrow majority of the Court ruled in the lead case of *Furman v. Georgia* that the death penalty, as currently administered, was applied arbitrarily and capriciously and thus violated the Eighth and Fourteenth Amendments (see Document 54). As a result, more than six hundred death row inmates had their sentences commuted to life imprisonment—and many abolitionists celebrated what they thought would be the beginning of the end of capital punishment in the United States.

## ABOLITIONIST SENTIMENT DECLINES AS CRIME INCREASES

Ironically, by the late 1960s, when abolitionist lawyers were beginning to claim victories against capital punishment in the courtroom, public support for the abolition of the death penalty actually was declining.

In fact, as criminologist Robert M. Bohm has pointed out, just 54 weeks after support for the death penalty reached its Gallup Poll low of 42 percent in 1966, public opinion swung the other way. The 1967 poll reported that 53 percent of the American public favored the death penalty. "Thus, instead of marking the beginning of the end to popular support for the sanction, 1966 represented a turning point. . . . although there have been other significant short-term changes in death penalty opinions in the United States, the change between 1966 and 1967 was pivotal because it marked the end of a 13-year nonlinear decline and the beginning of a 20-plus-year nonlinear increase in support of the death penalty" (Bohm 1992b:524).

In his historical analysis of these changes, Bohm argues that the strength of support and opposition for the death penalty is an indicator of the "level of dread and angst in a society" and that transitions such as occurred between 1966 and 1967 mark the threshold of "people's tolerance of media-reported crime" and social change (1992b:539).

Indeed, increasing crime presented social reformers with one of their most difficult conundrums during this era. Although income, employment, education, and health care had improved substantially since World War II, per capita crimes reported to police began to increase precipitously. In 1960, five out of every 100,000 people in the United States was murdered. By 1970, the proportion was up 60 percent to eight homicide victims per 100,000 population, peaking in 1974 at nearly double the 1960 rate. Reporting on other violent crimes such as robbery, rape, and aggravated assault almost tripled between 1960 and 1976 (see Maguire and Pastore 1995:Table 3.94).

Much of the increase in crime reflected fundamental changes in the way people lived their lives. For example, increasing population density and urbanization provided more opportunities for potential victims to cross paths with potential offenders, and growing female participation in the work force increased opportunities for women (who a decade earlier had spent much more of their time in the home) to become victims (Cohen and Felson 1979:588–608).

Shifts in the age structure of society further magnified the crime potential of these ecological changes. The demographic shock wave known as the baby boom that rolled through hospital nurseries and schools in the 1950s began to hit the streets in the 1960s and 1970s. Adolescents and young adults are, on average, much more likely to commit crime or become victims of crime than any other age group, and in 1970 there were more than fourteen million more of them than there had been in 1950. As the proportion of the population in these age groups increased, so, inevitably, did crime (see Gottfredson and Hirschi 1990:124–130).

At the same time that crime was increasing rapidly, it also is possible that the public was becoming more sensitive to crime and more fearful because of increasingly complete reporting of crime by criminal justice agencies (O'Brien 1996) and a growing focus on crime by news media and pollsters (Erskine 1974:131–145). The extensive publicity associated with the convictions of two especially reprehensible individuals for multiple murders may have helped swing public opinion back in favor of the death penalty. The "Boston Strangler," Albert Desalvo, who claimed to have murdered thirteen women, was convicted in January 1967. Three months later, Richard Speck was convicted for murdering eight student nurses in Chicago. Two months after that, interviews were conducted for the 1967 Gallup Poll (see Bohm 1992b:531).

## RETENTIONISTS RALLY

Hence, while abolitionists cheered over their apparent victory in the 1972 case of *Furman v. Georgia*, they had not won the war against capital punishment. On the defensive for the first time in American history, retentionists immediately went to work to draft capital laws that would meet the Supreme Court's requirements. Backed by massive public support, within a year more than half the states and the federal government had enacted new capital laws designed to lead to less arbitrary and capricious application of the death penalty—and more than 600 prisoners had received death sentences under those laws. But before executions could resume, the constitutionality of those new laws had to be tested.

In 1976 the Supreme Court further refined its position on capital punishment, upholding new "guided discretion" statutes in three states in the lead case of *Gregg v. Georgia* (see Documents 62A and 62B). Each of the laws that met the court's standards included important procedural reforms such as splitting trials into guilt and penalty phases, statements of aggravating and mitigating factors to help guide juries, and appellate review of all death sentences. However, the Court also ruled against mandatory death penalty statutes in two Southern states (see Documents 62C and 62D). Six months later, Gary Mark Gilmore became the first U.S. prisoner to be executed in a decade (see Document 63).

## DOCUMENT 43: The Execution of Caryl Chessman (1960)

From the late 1950s until his execution in 1960, one death row inmate's long yet ultimately unsuccessful fight for life did much to revive the capital punishment controversy in the United States.

Caryl Chessman (1921–1960) was arrested in 1948 on suspicion of being Los Angeles' notorious "Red Light Bandit"—a man who impersonated a police officer using a red spotlight in order to rob couples parked on a "lover's lane." In at least two instances, he had abducted the woman and forced her to perform fellatio on him. Chessman was convicted of these crimes and sentenced to death under California's "Little Lindbergh" kidnapping law of 1933 (Hook and Kahn 1989:8–9; Mackey 1976:225; Schwed 1983:73).

Through appeals and legal maneuvering, Chessman—who many believe did not receive a fair trial for a number of reasons (Hook and Kahn 1989:8; Schwed 1983:73–78)—received eight stays of execution over what then was an unprecedented period of eleven years and ten months on death row (Bedau 1977:30).

During that time, Chessman attracted worldwide attention to his case—and to the capital punishment controversy in general—through books that he wrote from his cell, including the bestselling *Cell 2455 Death Row* (1954), *Trial by Ordeal* (1955), and *The Face of Justice* (1957).

While Chessman's books won him many supporters, they also helped to motivate much of the public, who saw them as self-serving propaganda, against him (Schwed 1983:78–79). But regardless of which side people were on, it was not Chessman's guilt or innocence, but rather the issue of capital punishment itself that took center stage throughout the controversy (Schwed 1983:90–91).

Chessman eventually ran out of appeals, and California Governor Edmund G. (Pat) Brown, though himself a staunch abolitionist, ultimately denied clemency to Chessman. His execution on May 2, 1960, marked the beginning of a new wave of abolitionist activity in the United States (Schwed 1983:88–91).

Following is an excerpt from a newspaper account of Chessman's execution.

SAN FRANCISCO, Calif., May 2—Caryl Chessman was executed today.

After a series of last-hour legal maneuvers in state and Federal courts on opposite sides of the country, the convict-author kept his ninth scheduled appointment in the gas chamber at San Quentin Prison. He had lived nearly twelve years in the prison's death row. . . .

Chessman was escorted into the little octagonal steel room, with its dark green walls, and strapped into the right hand one of two chairs just after 10 A.M., Pacific Coast time. . . .

At 10:03:15, cyanide pellets were dropped from a container under the chair into a basin of sulphuric acid solution. At 10:12, prison doctors said Chessman was dead of the resulting acid fumes.

Warden Fred Dickson said Chessman's last request to him had been "to specifically state that he was not the red-light bandit" for whose crimes he was paying the penalty.

Chessman, 38 years old, was convicted in 1948 on numerous felony counts growing out of depredations against parked couples in lonely places around Los Angeles. The counts invoking the death penalty included kidnapping, "with bodily harm."

An hour and fifty-five minutes ahead of the scheduled execution hour the seven-justice State Supreme Court began discussion in near-by San Francisco of a petition filed on Saturday afternoon. The petition had sought a writ of habeas corpus.

At 9:10 A.M. the court ruled, 4 to 3, against the first request. Fifteen minutes later George T. Davis of Chessman counsel asked for a stay so that the decision might be appealed to the United States Supreme Court.

This was denied at 9:50 by the same vote.

Five minutes later Mr. Davis and Miss Rosalie Asher, co-counsel, were in the chamber of Federal District Judge Louis E. Goodman. They wanted a brief stay, time enough to argue on a request to petition the United States Supreme Court for a writ of review.

At almost the same time Associate Justice William O. Douglas of the Supreme Court had sent word of his denial of a plea for a stay of execution. The papers had been airmailed to him in Washington.

Judge Goodman listened to Mr. Davis and Miss Asher, then sent his clerk, Edward Evansen, to ask Miss Celeste Hickey, his secretary, to put a phone call through to the warden at San Quentin at 10:03.

The prison number was passed along to Miss Hickey orally through several persons and somehow, in the noise and tension, a digit was dropped. She had to dial again after having verified the number. Associate Warden Louis Nelson told her that the cyanide pellets had just been dropped.

Miss Asher emerged, weeping, from the judge's chambers.

### Wanted an Hour's Stay

Judge Goodman told reporters he had planned to ask the warden to stay the execution one hour.

At Sacramento, Gov. Edmund G. Brown received the news of the execution as he sat in his private study in his Capitol office. Outside the Capitol, a group of pickets was marching. It [*sic*] leader, Dr. Isadore Ziferstein, a Los Angeles psychiatrist, called the Governor "the hangman of California."

Other pickets had marched outside the prison all night.

*Source*: Lawrence E. Davies, "Caryl Chessman Executed; Denies His Guilt to the End," *New York Times*, May 3, 1960, 1, 22.

---

## DOCUMENT 44: California Gov. Edmund G. Brown (1960)

---

Caught in the middle of the Chessman controversy (see Document 43) was California Governor Edmund G. "Pat" Brown (1906–1996). Brown was staunchly opposed to the death penalty, and yet ultimately he denied clemency to Chessman. Given the fact that Chessman was a twice-convicted felon, Brown apparently felt compelled by law to uphold the death sentence. According to one newspaper account of his career, "It would remain the one major regret of his years in office" (Michaelson 1996).

As an act of public conscience and from the experience of over a decade and a half in law enforcement work, I ask the Legislature to abolish the death penalty in California. There are powerful and compelling reasons why this should be done. It is not based on maudlin sympathy for the criminal and depraved. And although I believe the death penalty constitutes an affront to human dignity and brutalizes and degrades society, I do not merely for these reasons urge this course for our State.

I have reached this momentous resolution after 16 years of careful, intimate and personal experience with the application of the death penalty in this State. This experience embraces seven years as District Attorney of San Francisco, eight years as Attorney General of this State, and now 14 months as Governor. I have had a day-to-day, first-hand familiarity with crime and punishment surpassed by very few.

Society has both the right and moral duty to protect itself against its enemies. This natural and prehistoric axiom has never successfully been refuted. If by ordered death, society is really protected and our homes and institutions guarded, then even the most extreme of all penalties can be justified.

## DEATH PENALTY A FAILURE

But the naked, simple fact is that the death penalty has been a gross failure. Beyond its horror and incivility, it has neither protected the innocent nor deterred the wicked. The recurrent spectacle of publicly sanctioned killing has cheapened human life and dignity without the redeeming grace which comes from justice meted out swiftly, evenly, humanely.

The death penalty is invoked too randomly, too irregularly, too unpredictably, and too tardily to be defended as an effective example warning away wrong-doers.

In California, for example, in 1955, there were 417 homicides. But only 52 defendants were convicted of first degree murder. And only 8, or 2%, were in fact sentenced to death. There can be no meaningful exemplary value in a punishment the incidence of which is but one to 50.

Nor is the death penalty to be explained as society's ultimate weapon of desperation against the unregenerate and perverse. The study of executions over a 15-year period produces the startling facts that of 110 condemned cases, 49% of those executed had never previously suffered a prior felony; that 75% of them came from families which had been broken by divorce, separation or otherwise when the condemned was still in his teens.

## NO DATA TO SUPPORT PENALTY

Again I say, that if this most drastic of sanctions could be said substantially to serve the ends of legal justice by adding to our safety and security, it would deserve some greater place in our respect. But no available data from any place or time that I have been able to find from research over many years gives support to the grand argument that the presence or absence of the death penalty exerts any substantial effect upon the incidence of homicide. . . .

Specifically, the death penalty has been abolished in nine states (Minnesota, Wisconsin, Michigan, Rhode Island, North Dakota, Maine, Alaska and Hawaii) and in 30 foreign countries (as Sweden, Belgium, Norway, Italy, Western Germany, Puerto Rico, Austria and 22 others).

## ABOLITION BRINGS NO INCREASE

In none of these states has the homicide rate increased, and indeed, in comparison with other states their rates seem somewhat lower. And these rates are lower not because of the death penalty but because of particular social organization, composition of population, economic and political conditions. . . .

## MOSTLY MINORITIES

As shocking as may be the statistics in our deep South where the most extensive use of the death penalty is made and against the most defenseless and downtrodden of the population, the Negroes, let it be remembered too that in California, in the 15-year period ending in 1953, covering 110 executions, 30% were of Mexicans and Negroes, more than double the combined population percentages of these two groups at the time. Indeed, only last year, 1959, out of 48 executions in the United States, 21 only were whites, while 27 were of Negroes. These figures are not mine. I tender them to you for critical examination and comparison. But I believe you will find them compelling evidence of the gross unfairness and social injustice which has characterized the application of the death penalty. . . .

## STRUGGLE FOR DIGNITY

I am a realist and know the great resistance to what I propose. But public leadership must face up to the humane as well as economic and social issues of our communities. And it is not enough for those charged with public responsibilities to be content to cope with just the immediate and readily attainable—the basic and long range values of our society must also constantly be brought into fuller reality. I believe the entire history of our civilization is a struggle to bring about a greater measure of humanity, compassion and dignity among us. I believe those qualities will be the greater when the action proposed here is achieved—and not just for the wretches whose execution is changed to life imprisonment, but for each of us.

Finally, I urge that the deliberations on this profound issue, whatever the outcome, be conducted with reason and restraint. There is already too much senseless violence and vituperation in our lives. Conscientious people may differ, but the ultimate issue here is clear. Can law and order be maintained as well or better if capital punishment is abolished?

Whatever the decision, I urge every one of us to search his conscience carefully and fully. In the final outcome of that I have full confidence.

*Source*: Edmund G. Brown, *Message to the Legislature*, March 2, 1960.

## DOCUMENT 45: J. Edgar Hoover (1960)

As the anti-death penalty movement gained momentum in the wake of the Chessman execution, many retentionists—including J. Edgar Hoover—responded with arguments in support of capital punishment.

Hoover (1895–1972), who began his career as a lawyer with the Department of Justice in 1917, was named the first director of the FBI in 1924 and remained in that position until his death at age seventy-seven.

During that time, he became famous for solving the Lindbergh baby kidnapping and for leading the FBI crusade against John Dillinger and other gangsters during the 1930s. He also was known for capturing spies during World War II and for leading the FBI campaign against Communists during the post-war period (Graham 1972).

A highly-skilled bureaucratic entrepreneur who was perceived by many to be the leading law enforcement officer in the country, Hoover believed that the death penalty was justified both as a punishment and as a potential deterrent to murder.

The question of capital punishment has sent a storm of controversy thundering across our Nation—millions of spoken and written words seek to examine the question so that decisions may be reached which befit our civilization.

The struggle for answers concerning the taking of men's lives is one to which every American should lend his voice, for the problem in a democracy such as ours is not one for a handful of men to solve alone.

As a representative of law enforcement, it is my belief that a great many of the most vociferous cries for abolition of capital punishment emanate from those areas of our society which have been insulated against the horrors man can and does perpetrate against his fellow beings. Certainly, penetrative and searching thought must be given before considering any blanket cessation of capital punishment in a time when unspeakable crimes are being committed. The savagely mutilated bodies and mentally ravaged victims of murderers, rapists and other criminal beasts beg consideration when the evidence is weighed on both sides of the scales of Justice.

At the same time, nothing is so precious in our country as the life of a human being, whether he is a criminal or not, and on the other side of the scales must be placed all of the legal safeguards which our society demands.

Experience has clearly demonstrated, however, that the time-proven deterrents to crime are sure detection, swift apprehension, and proper punishment. Each is a necessary ingredient. Law-abiding citizens have a right to expect that the efforts of law enforcement officers in detecting and apprehending criminals will be followed by realistic punishment.

It is my opinion that when no shadow of a doubt remains relative to the guilt of a defendant, the public interest demands capital punishment be invoked where the law so provides.

Who, in all good conscience, can say that Julius and Ethel Rosenberg, the spies who delivered the secret of the atomic bomb into the hands of the Soviets, should have been spared when their treachery caused the shadow of annihilation to fall upon all of the world's peoples? What place would there have been in civilization for these two who went to their deaths unrepentant, unwilling to the last to help their own country and their own fellow men? What would have been the chances of rehabilitating Jack Gilbert Graham, who placed a bomb in his own mother's luggage and blasted her and 43 other innocent victims into oblivion as they rode an airliner across a peaceful sky?

A judge once said, "The death penalty is a warning, just like a lighthouse throwing its beams out to sea. We hear about shipwrecks, but we do not hear about the ships the lighthouse guides safely on their way. We do not have proof of the number of ships it saves, but we do not tear the lighthouse down."

Despicable crimes must be dealt with realistically. To abolish the death penalty would absolve other Rosenbergs and Grahams from fear of the consequences for committing atrocious crimes. Where the death penalty is provided, a criminal's punishment may be meted out commensurate with his deeds. While a Power transcending man is the final Judge, this same Power gave man reason so that he might protect himself. Capital punishment is an instrument with which he may guard the righteous against the predators among men.

We must never allow misguided compassion to erase our concern for the hundreds of unfortunate, innocent victims of bestial criminals.

*Source*: J. Edgar Hoover, "Statement of Director J. Edgar Hoover," *F.B.I. Law Enforcement Bulletin* 29 (June 1960):1–2.

---

## DOCUMENT 46: "Testing the Death Penalty" (Gerald Gottlieb, 1961)

---

Prior to the 1960s, the capital punishment debate in America had focused on such universal issues as moral and religious philosophies, potential rehabilitation of the criminal, and the deterrent value—or lack thereof—of the death penalty.

But during the early 1960s, the debate began to shift as lawyers and academics for the first time began to question the basic constitutionality of capital punishment (Epstein and Kobylka 1992:40–41; Meltsner 1973:23; Paternoster 1991:41; Schwed 1983:105).

One pioneer in this territory was Gerald Gottlieb, a Los Angeles antitrust lawyer and a volunteer for the American Civil Liberties Union's Southern California chapter. In a May 1960 memo to his fellow chapter members, Gottlieb suggested that the Eighth Amendment's prohibition against cruel and unusual punishment could provide the basis for a legal challenge to capital punishment. He argued that the death penalty violated contemporary moral standards—what the Supreme Court had called "evolving standards of decency that mark the progress of a maturing society" in *Trop v. Dulles* (see Document 41)—and therefore could be considered unconstitutional under the Eighth Amendment.

Gottlieb's memo was published as an article in the *Southern California Law Review* in 1961. But although it received widespread attention, it seems likely that few people at the time actually believed that a constitutional challenge to capital punishment ever would hold up in court (Schwed 1983:105–106).

## I. Capital Punishment: A Measure for Cruel and Unusual Punishment

The phrase "cruel and unusual" is profoundly ambiguous. It refers to certain dynamic realities of society and of men's states of mind. Although those realities have been changing during the many centuries since the phrase was coined, judicial definition of the phrase in terms of contemporary society has only recently begun and is incomplete.

One of the punishments yet fully to be tested under the Eighth Amendment, within the context and findings of modern penology, psychology, morals and social requirements, is the death penalty. To proceed with such a test would seem important, if for no other reason than that this penalty is practiced by the federal government and forty-one of our states.

The constitutionality of the death penalty in the present social setting comprises a substantial and justiciable question and it may tenably be urged that capital punishment is unconstitutional. Capital punishment may, on a sufficient factual showing, be found violative of the Eighth Amendment, since death by means of the gas chamber, gun, rope or electric chair may now with good reason be alleged to be "cruel and unusual" punishment and within the reach of the Eighth Amendment and its state counterparts. An issue of law dependent upon judicially noticeable facts awaits its day in court. . . .

## II. Decency as a Measure

The sentence of death violates the Eighth Amendment to the United States Constitution if the sentence and its execution are repugnant to the evolving standards of decency that mark the progress of our maturing society. . . .

Is the death penalty unconstitutional today within the context of the social and cultural conditions of this nation and of the world? The *Trop* and *Weems* cases hold that the concept of cruelty is a dynamic one. Necessarily, those holdings cause the constitutional question of the validity of capital punishment to be a combined question of law and fact. The facts to be adduced refer to the injuries done to society and to the family of the executed man, the extent of pain, both physical and psychological, and generally the social context in such aspects as are relevant to the problem of crime, crime prevention, punishment and the developing culture and humanity of our country. The issue of constitutionality then requires the judges to be acute observers of the times and of the imperatives which spring from an "evolving standard of decency." If the death penalty is now repugnant to our evolved standards "that mark the progress of a maturing society," then it seems that capital punishment ought to be struck down by judicial action.

## III. The Test of Necessity

Whether capital punishment and the processes and proceedings necessarily associated therewith violate the Eighth Amendment can be said to depend upon whether the processes are cruel by definition. Cruelty is properly definable as "the infliction of pain or loss without necessity or justification." . . .

As against life imprisonment, and other penological programs, is the death penalty necessary? If it is not, then under several tests, common sense, ethical and legal, the punishment of death constitutes cruelty.

## IV. A Proper Function for Punishment

Some recent decisions of our state courts suggest another criterion. Under this view capital punishment may be said to comprise unconstitutional cruelty if that institution cannot secure a proper function of society within civilized standards. . . .

Can the death penalty be shown to have a proper function? Certainly its function cannot be that of rehabilitation, nor can it be that of confinement, a function which is thoroughly and efficiently served by imprisonment. The burden is to show that the death penalty constitutes, as compared to life imprisonment, and differentially, a deterrent upon future criminal activities. Unless the death penalty has such a proper function in our society, it would seem to be cruel by definition.

## V. THE COMPARATIVE TEST

Another test, somewhat more mechanical, should be included in the constitutional review. If a penalty is more cruel than another punishment already held to violate these constitutional provisions, then the death penalty is unconstitutional as a matter of simple logic. Thus, comparison becomes the relevant factor.

In *Trop v. Dulles*, the Supreme Court held that a punishment generally considered *less* than death, the punishment of deprivation of citizenship, was nevertheless "cruel and unusual" and violative of the Eighth Amendment. . . .

If *Trop v. Dulles* is now the standard, does the death penalty constitute cruelty as a matter of law, based on comparison to the *Trop* case? . . .

## VI. THE CONTEXT OF MAN'S DIGNITY

Repeatedly the courts advert to still another touchstone of cruelty. Under this test the question whether capital punishment violates the Eighth Amendment is to be answered affirmatively if the punishment violates conscience, morality, humanity, or the dignity of mankind. . . .

It might be shown to the courts that historically, the more harsh and the more severe is the scale of punishment, the more degraded is the society as a correlative thereof. It further might be shown that the very act of the sovereign, descending in his majesty upon an offender to vengeful or unnecessarily severe punishment, a punishment that has been prepared by the sovereign with premeditation, coldness and infinite planning, has a symbolic effect upon society far beyond the fact that a life is then taken. This act by the state tends to cheapen the very values that refer to humanity itself, to lower the opinion of humanity regarding itself and to diminish its standards of decency, of conscience and of culture. The practice of capital punishment might be proven to violate the dignity of mankind.

*Source*: Gerald H. Gottlieb, "Testing the Death Penalty," *Southern California Law Review* 34 (1961): 269–278 (footnotes omitted).

---

## DOCUMENT 47: *Rudolph v. Alabama* (1963)

Although it was never actually heard by the Supreme Court, the 1963 case of *Rudolph v. Alabama* opened the door for the constitutional challenges to capital punishment proposed by Gerald Gottlieb (see Document 46)—and hence a new era in the death penalty debate.

The case itself—involving a Southern rape for which the defendant had received death—was not particularly significant. The defendant's appeal was based on arguments surrounding the voluntariness of his confession. No constitutional challenges to the death penalty were included in the appeal.

However, prior to their meeting to decide whether to grant certiorari in the case, Justice Arthur Goldberg informed his fellow justices that he planned to raise the issue of constitutionality in the case. Specifically, said his memo to the other justices, he would ask: "Whether and under what circumstances, the imposition of the death penalty is proscribed by the Eighth and Fourteenth Amendments of the U.S. Constitution?" (quoted in Epstein and Kobylka 1992:42).

The majority of the Court apparently felt that Goldberg was trying to overstep the bounds of the Court's authority (Epstein and Kobylka 1992:43), and subsequently denied certiorari in the case. In response, Justice Goldberg—joined by Justices Douglas and Brennan—wrote a dissenting opinion to the Court's decision to deny certiorari in which he raised the same questions he had intended to raise in court had the Rudolph case been heard.

While Goldberg's dissent made no difference in the Rudolph case, the widely-circulated opinion alerted the legal community to the fact that at least three Supreme Court Justices might be willing to entertain constitutional challenges to the death penalty (Bedau 1977:12–13; Epstein and Kobylka 1992:43).

MR. JUSTICE GOLDBERG, with whom MR. JUSTICE DOUGLAS and MR. JUSTICE BRENNAN join, dissenting.

I would grant certiorari in this case and in No. 169, Misc., *Snider* v. *Cunningham, supra*, to consider whether the Eighth and Fourteenth Amendments to the United States Constitution permit the imposition of the death penalty on a convicted rapist who has neither taken nor endangered human life.

The following questions, *inter alia*, seem relevant and worthy of argument and consideration:

(1) In light of the trend both in this country and throughout the world against punishing rape by death, does the imposition of the death penalty by those States which retain it for rape violate "evolving standards of decency that mark the progress of [our] maturing society," or "standards of decency more or less universally accepted"?

(2) Is the taking of human life to protect a value other than human life consistent with the constitutional proscription against "punishments

which by their excessive . . . severity are greatly disproportioned to the offenses charged"?

(3) Can the permissible aims of punishment (*e.g.*, deterrence, isolation, rehabilitation) be achieved as effectively by punishing rape less severely than by death (*e.g.*, by life imprisonment); if so, does the imposition of the death penalty for rape constitute "unnecessary cruelty"?

*Source*: 375 U.S. 889 (1963), 889–891 (footnotes omitted).

---

## DOCUMENT 48: The ACLU Takes a Stand Against the Death Penalty (1965)

---

Prior to 1965, the American Civil Liberties Union (ACLU) had steered clear of the capital punishment controversy, maintaining that the death penalty was not a civil liberties issue (Meltsner 1973:55).

However, not all of the organization's members agreed with this position. Following "much internal debate" (Dorsen 1968:278), the ACLU board adopted a new policy against the death penalty—detailed in the document below—in June of 1965.

In announcing this change in policy, the ACLU board stated that it would seek, "as a matter of civil liberties concern, the commutation of death sentences, until such time as the death penalty is eliminated as part of law and practice of the United States" (quoted in Epstein and Kobylka 1992:46).

The board also authorized ACLU lawyers to enter cases in which it was claimed that the death penalty had been imposed on the basis of race or class, "provided that a factual study has been made that seems to justify this conclusion" (quoted in Meltsner 1973:55).

The ACLU's new policy on capital punishment was especially significant to abolitionists, given the fact that the organization's mission is to promote and enforce the civil rights afforded by the U.S. Constitution and the Bill of Rights. As philosopher Hugo Adam Bedau (see Documents 81–83) put it, "If the ACLU thinks capital punishment is unconstitutional, perhaps it is" (1977:13).

The American Civil Liberties Union believes that capital punishment is so inconsistent with the underlying values of a democratic system that the imposition of the death penalty for any crime is a denial of civil liberties. We believe that past decisions to the contrary are in error, and we will seek the repeal of existing laws imposing the death penalty, and will seek reversal of convictions carrying a sentence of death.

## Denial of Equal Protection

. . . The disproportionately large number of executions of members of the Negro race indicates that this penalty is often imposed as the result of racial bias. Certainly no statute could require that the death penalty be imposed upon a Negro, but not upon a white person, because such provision would be a denial of equal protection of the law. A law which permits such a result is also an unconstitutional denial of equal protection of the law.

There is also evidence of a compelling nature that the death penalty is more likely to be imposed upon one who is poor, regardless of his race, than upon one who has significant financial resources. For example, a rich man accused of a crime may avoid the death penalty by employing legal counsel and compensating him fully for the excessive time necessary to pursue the multiple remedies available to those under penalty of death. A poor man, while given the right to counsel, has only that counsel which is volunteered, or which is either compelled or compensated by the state. While such publicly provided counsel is almost always dedicated, it is an avoidance of reality to believe that such counsel can give the kind, range, and detail of service which can come from those compensated at the usual rate paid the most competent lawyers of our time. To make punishment of the irrevocable and final nature of death depend upon the availability of funds is clearly a denial of equal protection to the man whose funds are inadequate or nonexistent. . . .

## Cruel and Unusual Punishment

. . . The fact that capital punishment has been acceptable in the past is no reason for its continuation. The rack and the screw; drawing and quartering; flogging—all have been used and subsequently rejected as maturing and sensitizing notions of the essential commands of human decency demonstrated the barbarity of the practices. . . .

To ask today the question whether the imposition of the death penalty is cruel is to answer it. Anglo-American law, and indeed, much of human experience, has been devoted to postponement of death. So committed is the society to the maintenance of life that it does not permit the life of a hopeless invalid to be taken in order to end the greatest of pain. If society's respect for life denies men the right to take life in order to prevent or end pain, or because one is tired of life, surely the state should not be permitted to take a life so as to punish for past behavior. . . .

Contemporary discomfort with the death penalty is further revealed by the reversal of verdicts of guilty for technical errors which to laymen and lawyers both would be insubstantial were it not for the fact that to permit the judgment to stand would result in the ending of a life. . . .

Because the poor man and the member of the minority group are the most likely to be the victims of a death penalty, the punishment is, as to the rest of society, not only cruel, but also unusual. It is, for most members of the society, a punishment that the society for reasons of conscience refuses to inflict.

We believe, therefore, that contemporary notions of the significance of human life make imposition of the death penalty cruel and unusual punishment prohibited by the Constitution of the United States.

**Denial of Due Process**

The irreversibility of the death penalty means that error discovered after the penalty has been imposed cannot be corrected. Thus one who suffers the death penalty, and subsequently is found to have been improperly convicted, has been denied due process of law.

It can be argued that the death penalty is in and of itself a denial of due process. Life is the *sine qua non* of the right to due process. A dead man cannot be given due process. A dead man has no rights. The right to have rights—the right to due process—depends upon the existence of life. The state should not be permitted to deprive the citizen of all rights—including the right to have rights—by taking his life for any reason.

*Source*: "ACLU's New Stand on the Death Penalty," *Civil Liberties* 227 (June 1965): 2.

---

## DOCUMENT 49: Public Opinion and the Death Penalty (1966)

---

In 1966, the Gallup Poll reported the lowest level of public support for the death penalty since the question first had been asked in 1936 (and reported in 1937).

While the renewed attack on the death penalty may have been partly responsible for this decline in public support for capital punishment, other factors, such as the rapid social and political changes that occurred during the 1960s, also were likely to have contributed to the change (Schwed 1983:72).

**JULY 1**
**CAPITAL PUNISHMENT**
Interviewing Date 5/19–24/66
Survey #729-K                                   Question #7          Index #13
*Are you in favor of the death penalty for persons convicted of murder?*
Yes                              42%

No                          47
No opinion                  11

*Source*: George Gallup, *The Gallup Poll: Public Opinion 1935–71*, Volume Three, 1959–1971 (New York: Random House, 1972), 2016. Copyright 1972 by Scholarly Resources Inc. Reprinted by permission of Scholarly Resources Inc.

---

## DOCUMENT 50: President's Commission Report on Law Enforcement and Administration of Justice (1967)

In 1965, President Lyndon B. Johnson established the Commission on Law Enforcement and Administration of Justice to study the increasing problem of crime in the United States and to provide recommendations for how it might best be resolved. Two years later the commission—composed of judges, attorneys, academics, police chiefs and others—submitted its report, *The Challenge of Crime in a Free Society*.

The lengthy report included more than two hundred recommendations pertaining to crime and the criminal justice system. Included among these recommendations was what seemed to some a surprisingly brief assessment of the continuing problem of capital punishment—especially considering the widespread public attention the issue had once again received in recent years (Bedau 1977:1).

But despite its brevity on the subject, the Commission report brought up several particularly salient issues pertaining to capital punishment, including the increasing rareness of its imposition, the ambiguity of its deterrent value, its impact on the criminal justice system, the lengthy appeals process, and evidence of possible discrimination in the imposition of death sentences—issues that would become even more prominent during the coming years.

According to James Vorenberg, a professor at Harvard Law School who served as the first director of the Department of Justice's Office of Criminal Justice and executive director of the President's Commission staff, "[I]t was clear from an early date that the Commission would not be able to agree on anything that would be helpful if it tried to take sides on the basic issue. The focus on discrimination and delay seemed to us to be helpful and avoided what would have been divisive without being constructive."[1]

### NOTE
1. From a letter to the authors dated March 1, 1996.

As the abolition or the retention of the death penalty is being widely debated in the States, it is appropriate to point out several aspects of its administration that bear on the issue.

The most salient characteristic of capital punishment is that it is infrequently applied. During 1966 only 1 person was executed in the United States; the trend over the last 36 years shows a continual decline in the number of executions, from a high of 200 in 1935 to last year's low of one. Furthermore, all available data indicate that judges, juries, and governors are becoming increasingly reluctant to impose, or authorize the carrying out of a death sentence. Only 67 persons were sentenced to death by the courts in 1965, a decline of 31 from the previous year, and 62 prisoners were reprieved from their death sentences. In a few States in which the penalty exists on the statute books, there has not been an execution in decades.

The decline in the application of the death penalty parallels a substantial decline in public support for capital punishment. The most recent Gallup Poll, conducted in 1966, revealed that less than half of those interviewed favored retaining the death penalty. In the last 3 years, 5 States either totally abolished capital punishment or severely limited its use, thus bringing to 13 the number of States which have effectively repealed capital punishment. . . .

It is impossible to say with certainty whether capital punishment significantly reduces the incidence of heinous crimes. The most complete study on the subject, based on a comparison of homicide rates in capital and noncapital jurisdictions, concluded that there is no discernible correlation between the availability of the death penalty and the homicide rate. . . .

Whatever views one may have on the efficacy of the death penalty as a deterrent, it clearly has an undesirable impact on the administration of criminal justice. Capital cases take longer to litigate at the trial level; the selection of a jury often requires several days, and each objection or point of law requires inordinate deliberation because of the irreversible consequences of error. In addition, the inherent sensationalism of a trial for life distorts the factfinding process and increases the danger that public sentiment will be aroused for the defendant, regardless of his guilt of the crime charged. . . .

Furthermore, the imposition of a death sentence is but the first stage of a protracted process of appeals, collateral attacks, and petitions for executive clemency. At the end of 1965 there were 331 prisoners awaiting execution in the United States, and since then this number undoubtedly has increased. These prisoners then were under sentence for an average of 30.8 months, and the average time between imposition and execution was almost 4 years. The spectacle of men living on death row for years while their lawyers pursue appellate and collateral remedies tarnishes

our image of humane and expeditious justice. But no one seriously proposes to limit the right of a condemned man to have errors at his trial
corrected or to obtain the mercy of the executive.

Finally there is evidence that the imposition of the death sentence and
the exercise of dispensing power by the courts and the executive follow
discriminatory patterns. The death sentence is disproportionately imposed and carried out on the poor, the Negro, and the members of unpopular groups.

Some members of the Commission favor the abolition of capital punishment, while other members favor its retention. Some would support
its abolition if more adequate safeguards against the release of dangerous
offenders were devised. All members of the Commission agree that the
present situation in the administration of the death penalty in many
States is intolerable for the reasons stated above.

*The Commission recommends*:

**The question whether capital punishment is an appropriate sanction
is a policy decision to be made by each State. Where it is retained, the
types of offenses for which it is available should be strictly limited,
and the law should be enforced in an evenhanded and nondiscrimi-
natory manner, with procedures for review of death sentences that are
fair and expeditious. When a State finds that it cannot administer the
penalty in such a manner, or that the death penalty is being imposed
but not carried into effect, the penalty should be abandoned.**

*Source*: *The Challenge of Crime in a Free Society, A Report by the President's Commission on Law Enforcement and Administration of Justice* (Washington, D.C.: U.S.
Government Printing Office, 1967), 143.

---

## DOCUMENT 51: The "Last Aid Kit" (circa 1967)

During the mid-1960s, the National Association for the Advancement of Colored People's Legal Defense and Educational Fund Inc.,
also known as the Legal Defense Fund (LDF), launched a full-scale
litigation campaign against capital punishment.

The LDF's initial efforts against capital punishment focused on Southern racism in death penalty cases involving black men accused of raping white women (Epstein and Kobylka 1992:48; also see Document
57).

However, in 1967, the LDF changed course dramatically with a new
campaign to provide counsel to all prisoners on death row. Through a

nationwide litigation strategy that would keep death penalty cases tied up in the courts for years, they hoped to achieve a national moratorium on the death penalty (Epstein and Kobylka 1992:53; Meltsner 1973: 107; Schwed 1983:107).

Key to implementing this plan were Anthony Amsterdam, a University of Pennsylvania law professor who had been a consultant to the LDF since 1963 (also see Documents 52, 57, 71 and 77), and Jack Himmelstein, a 26-year-old Harvard graduate hired by the LDF to serve as managing attorney for the campaign.

Their first joint project was to put together a collection of "Documents for Proceeding in Federal Habeas Corpus in a Capital Case in which Execution is Imminent," which contained virtually everything a lawyer needed to get a court to postpone an execution—including petitions for habeas corpus, applications for stay of execution, and legal briefs outlining every significant constitutional argument against the death penalty. They distributed the collection of documents—dubbed the "Last Aid Kit"—to hundreds of LDF-cooperating attorneys nationwide (Epstein and Kobylka 1992:54; Meltsner 1973:112).

The strategy worked. By the spring of 1967, more than fifty death row inmates had LDF-supported counsel (Epstein and Kobylka 1992: 54). And by May of 1968, it had been nearly a year since an execution had occurred in the United States (Meltsner 1973:113).

## Documents for Proceeding in Federal Habeas Corpus in a Capital Case in which Execution is Imminent

### INDEX

Form No.

1. Petition for Habeas Corpus, United States District Court

2. Attorney's Verification

3. *Forma pauperis* affidavit

4. Writ of Habeas Corpus

5. Order to Show Cause

6. Order Staying Execution

7. Order allowing Petitioner to proceed *in forma pauperis*

8. Order denying all relief on the face of the petition

9. Application for a certificate of probable cause and for leave to appeal *in forma pauperis*; together with certificate and order allowing appeal as a pauper

10. Application for a stay of execution pending appeal

11. Order staying execution pending appeal

12. Notice of Appeal

13. Application in the Court of Appeals for a Certificate of Probable Cause and for leave to appeal *in forma pauperis*

14. Application in Court of Appeals for a Stay of Execution

15. Application for an original writ of Habeas Corpus directed to a Circuit Judge, with applications for a stay of execution and for leave to proceed *in forma pauperis*

16. Memorandum in Court of Appeals

17. Order of the Court of Appeals staying execution, and granting a certificate of probable cause and leave to proceed on appeal *in forma pauperis*

*Source*: "Documents for Proceeding in Federal Habeas Corpus in a Capital Case in which Execution is Imminent" (New York: NAACP Legal Defense and Educational Fund, Inc., 1971). The above index is from the 1971 version of this document. The original "Last Aid Kit," which several sources indicate was compiled in 1967, was not available.

## DOCUMENT 52: *Witherspoon v. Illinois* (1968)

The abolitionist movement achieved one of its most significant court victories in the 1968 case of *Witherspoon v. Illinois*.

William Witherspoon had been convicted and sentenced to death in 1960 for shooting and killing a police officer. After eight years on death row and fifteen postponements of his execution, Witherspoon's appeal was heard by the U.S. Supreme Court.

Witherspoon's lawyer, Albert Jenner, Jr., claimed that an Illinois law (similar to laws in other states at the time) that allowed prosecutors to eliminate potential jurors who opposed or had reservations about the death penalty resulted in a "prosecution-prone" jury—that is, a jury more likely to be biased in favor of the prosecution and against the defendant, in both its verdict and sentencing. He based this claim on two unpublished opinion surveys (Epstein and Kobylka 1992:56; Meltsner 1973:120).

Fearing that Jenner's argument was too broad and his supporting evidence too preliminary to convince the Court—and therefore might be likely to lead to an adverse ruling that could harm the LDF's overall litigation strategy—LDF lawyers intervened in the case as *amicus curiae*, or "friend of the court" (Epstein and Kobylka 1992:57; Meltsner 1973:120).

In his lengthy brief, Anthony Amsterdam urged the Court to postpone any decision on Jenner's claim of prosecution bias until more detailed research evidence was available on the subject. He argued that Witherspoon's death sentence should be vacated on the grounds that "death qualified" juries do not represent cross-sections of the population because they exclude those opposed to the death penalty and therefore are in violation of the Sixth Amendment right to an impartial jury (Epstein and Kobylka 1992:57; Meltsner 1973:120–121).

The Supreme Court agreed with Amsterdam, dismissing Jenner's prosecution-proneness argument on the grounds that the evidence presented thus far was too tentative (Schwed 1983:122). In a 6–3 decision, the Court ruled that the practice of excluding prospective jurors who have reservations about the death penalty from capital trials resulted in juries whose sentencing decisions could be considered biased and therefore unconstitutional.

At the time, many lawyers believed that the *Witherspoon* ruling—which applied retroactively and therefore affected nearly every prisoner on death row—could lead to the virtual abolition of capital punishment, both through resentencing and the addition of those who opposed capital punishment to the pool of eligible jurors (Epstein and Kobylka 1992:58; Meltsner 1973:123–124; Schwed 1983:122).

However, important as the ruling was, it did not have nearly the overall impact that had been expected. The "Witherspoon rule" still allowed judges to exclude jurors who claimed they would vote against the death penalty under any and all circumstances, regardless of the evidence presented at trial. In addition, many lower courts and legislatures found various ways to circumvent the new rule. As a result, although many death sentences were overturned by the Court's decision, a substantial number simply were reinstated by new penalty hearings (Epstein and Kobylka 1992: 58; Meltsner 1973:125; Schwed 1983: 122).

## A. OPINION OF THE COURT

MR. JUSTICE STEWART delivered the opinion of the Court. . . .

I.

The issue before us is a narrow one. It does not involve the right of the prosecution to challenge for cause those prospective jurors who state that their reservations about capital punishment would prevent them from making an impartial decision as to the defendant's guilt. Nor does it involve the State's assertion of a right to exclude from the jury in a capital case those who say that they could never vote to impose the death penalty or that they would refuse even to consider its imposition in the

case before them. For the State of Illinois did not stop there, but authorized the prosecution to exclude as well all who said that they were opposed to capital punishment and all who indicated that they had
conscientious scruples against inflicting it.

In the present case the tone was set when the trial judge said early in
the *voir dire*, "Let's get these conscientious objectors out of the way, without wasting any time on them." . . .

## II.

The petitioner contends that a State cannot confer upon a jury selected
in this manner the power to determine guilt. He maintains that such a
jury, unlike one chosen at random from a cross-section of the community, must necessarily be biased in favor of conviction, for the kind of
juror who would be unperturbed by the prospect of sending a man to
his death, he contends, is the kind of juror who would too readily ignore
the presumption of the defendant's innocence, accept the prosecution's
version of the facts, and return a verdict of guilt. To support this view,
the petitioner refers to what he describes as "competent scientific evidence that death-qualified jurors are partial to the prosecution on the
issue of guilt or innocence."

The data adduced by the petitioner, however, are too tentative and
fragmentary to establish that jurors not opposed to the death penalty
tend to favor the prosecution in the determination of guilt. We simply
cannot conclude, either on the basis of the record now before us or as a
matter of judicial notice, that the exclusion of jurors opposed to capital
punishment results in an unrepresentative jury on the issue of guilt or
substantially increases the risk of conviction. In light of the presently
available information, we are not prepared to announce a *per se* constitutional rule requiring the reversal of every conviction returned by a jury
selected as this one was.

## III.

It does not follow, however, that the petitioner is entitled to no relief.
For in this case the jury was entrusted with two distinct responsibilities:
first, to determine whether the petitioner was innocent or guilty; and
second, if guilty, to determine whether his sentence should be imprisonment or death. It has not been shown that this jury was biased with
respect to the petitioner's guilt. But it is self-evident that, in its role as
arbiter of the punishment to be imposed, this jury fell woefully short of
that impartiality to which the petitioner was entitled under the Sixth and
Fourteenth Amendments. . . .

A man who opposes the death penalty, no less than one who favors
it, can make the discretionary judgment entrusted to him by the State
and can thus obey the oath he takes as a juror. But a jury from which
all such men have been excluded cannot perform the task demanded of

it. Guided by neither rule nor standard, "free to select or reject as it [sees] fit," a jury that must choose between life imprisonment and capital punishment can do little more—and must do nothing less—than express the conscience of the community on the ultimate question of life or death. Yet, in a nation less than half of whose people believe in the death penalty, a jury composed exclusively of such people cannot speak for the community. Culled of all who harbor doubts about the wisdom of capital punishment—of all who would be reluctant to pronounce the extreme penalty—such a jury can speak only for a distinct and dwindling minority.

If the State had excluded only those prospective jurors who stated in advance of the trial that they would not even consider returning a verdict of death, it could argue that the resulting jury was simply "neutral" with respect to penalty. But when it swept from the jury all who expressed conscientious or religious scruples against capital punishment and all who opposed it in principle, the State crossed the line of neutrality. In its quest for a jury capable of imposing the death penalty, the State produced a jury uncommonly willing to condemn a man to die. . . .

Whatever else might be said of capital punishment, it is at least clear that its imposition by a hanging jury cannot be squared with the Constitution. The State of Illinois has stacked the deck against the petitioner. To execute this death sentence would deprive him of his life without due process of law.

## B. DISSENTING OPINION

MR. JUSTICE BLACK, with whom MR. JUSTICE HARLAN and MR. JUSTICE WHITE join, dissenting. . . .

I believe that the Court's decision today goes a long way to destroying the concept of an impartial jury as we have known it. This concept has been described most eloquently by Justice Story:

To insist on a juror's sitting in a cause when he acknowledges himself to be under influences, no matter whether they arise from interest, from prejudices, or from religious opinions, which will prevent him from giving a true verdict according to law and evidence, would be to subvert the objects of a trial by jury, and to bring into disgrace and contempt, the proceedings of courts of justice. We do not sit here to produce the verdicts of partial and prejudiced men; but of men, honest and indifferent in causes. This is the administration of justice [which is required]. . . .

It is just as necessary today that juries be impartial as it was in 1820 when Justice Story made this statement. I shall not contribute in any way to the destruction of our ancient judicial and constitutional concept of trial by an impartial jury by forcing the States through "constitutional doctrine" laid down by this Court to accept jurors who are bound to be biased.

*Source*: 391 U.S. 510 (1968), 512–540 (footnotes omitted).

## DOCUMENT 53: *McGautha v. California* and *Crampton v. Ohio* (1971)

The next major constitutional challenge to existing death penalty procedures came in November 1970, when the Supreme Court heard oral arguments in a pair of cases in which the petitioners claimed that their Fourteenth Amendment rights had been violated.

Both petitioners had been convicted of first-degree murder, and in both cases the decision whether the defendant should be condemned to death or given a life sentence had been left to the absolute discretion of the jury. The petitioners argued that giving juries such complete discretion in sentencing—without any standards or guidelines upon which to base their decisions—was unacceptable under the due process clause of the Fourteenth Amendment because it allowed too much room for whim, caprice, or prejudice to enter into their decisions (Bedau 1977:77; Paternoster 1991:48).

In addition, Crampton challenged the constitutionality of the kind of trial used in his capital proceeding. At the time, Ohio law provided for a unitary trial in which the jury determined guilt and punishment after a single trial and in a single verdict. Crampton argued that such a unitary trial forces the defendant to decide between taking the stand to speak on his own behalf and therefore possibly incriminating himself, or remaining silent and therefore forfeiting his chance to present mitigating circumstances that might convince the jury to give him a lesser sentence (Bedau 1977:77; Paternoster 1991:47–48). This procedure, he claimed, was a violation of his Fourteenth Amendment right to due process. (In McGautha's case the jury, in accordance with California law, had determined punishment in a separate proceeding following the trial.)

In a 6–3 opinion, delivered May 3, 1971, the Court ruled against both petitioners, upholding both standardless juries and unitary trials as constitutional.

Abolitionists, though not particularly surprised by the decision, were none too pleased. As one LDF attorney explained, "After six years of

litigation the Supreme Court had finally and decisively rejected the two
mainstays of the moratorium strategy" (Meltsner 1973:244–245).

## A. OPINION OF THE COURT

MR. JUSTICE HARLAN delivered the opinion of the Court. . . .

### III

We consider first McGautha's and Crampton's common claim: that the
absence of standards to guide the jury's discretion on the punishment
issue is constitutionally intolerable. . . .

### B

. . .

In light of history, experience, and the present limitations of human
knowledge, we find it quite impossible to say that committing to the
untrammeled discretion of the jury the power to pronounce life or death
in capital cases is offensive to anything in the Constitution. The States
are entitled to assume that jurors confronted with the truly awesome
responsibility of decreeing death for a fellow human will act with due
regard for the consequences of their decision and will consider a variety
of factors, many of which will have been suggested by the evidence or
by the arguments of defense counsel. For a court to attempt to catalog
the appropriate factors in this elusive area could inhibit rather than expand the scope of consideration, for no list of circumstances would ever
be really complete. The infinite variety of cases and facets to each case
would make general standards either meaningless "boilerplate" or a
statement of the obvious that no jury would need.

### IV

As we noted at the outset of this opinion, McGautha's trial was in two
stages, with the jury considering the issue of guilt before the presentation
of evidence and argument on the issue of punishment. Such a procedure
is required by the laws of California and of five other States. Petitioner
Crampton, whose guilt and punishment were determined at a single
trial, contends that a procedure like California's is compelled by the Constitution as well. . . .

### B

We turn first to the privilege against compelled self incrimination. The
contention is that where guilt and punishment are to be determined by
a jury at a single trial the desire to address the jury on punishment
unduly encourages waiver of the defendant's privilege to remain silent
on the issue of guilt, or, to put the matter another way, that the single-

verdict procedure unlawfully compels the defendant to become a witness against himself on the issue of guilt by the threat of sentencing him to death without having heard from him. It is not contended, nor could it be successfully, that the mere force of evidence is compulsion of the sort forbidden by the privilege. . . . It does no violence to the privilege that a person's choice to testify in his own behalf may open the door to otherwise inadmissible evidence which is damaging to his case. . . . The narrow question left open is whether it is consistent with the privilege for the State to provide no means whereby a defendant wishing to present evidence or testimony on the issue of punishment may limit the force of his evidence (and the State's rebuttal) to that issue. We see nothing in the history, policies, or precedents relating to the privilege which requires such means to be available. . . .

We conclude that the policies of the privilege against compelled self-incrimination are not offended when a defendant in a capital case yields to the pressure to testify on the issue of punishment at the risk of damaging his case on guilt. . . .

V

Before we conclude this opinion, it is appropriate for us to make a broader observation than the issues raised by these cases strictly call for. It may well be, as the American Law Institute and the National Commission on Reform of Federal Criminal Laws have concluded, that bifurcated trials and criteria for jury sentencing discretion are superior means of dealing with capital cases if the death penalty is to be retained at all. But the Federal Constitution, which marks the limits of our authority in these cases, does not guarantee trial procedures that are the best of all worlds, or that accord with the most enlightened ideas of students of the infant science of criminology, or even those that measure up to the individual predilections of members of this Court. . . . The Constitution requires no more than that trials be fairly conducted and that guaranteed rights of defendants be scrupulously respected. From a constitutional standpoint we cannot conclude that it is impermissible for a State to consider that the compassionate purposes of jury sentencing in capital cases are better served by having the issues of guilt and punishment determined in a single trial than by focusing the jury's attention solely on punishment after the issue of guilt has been determined.

## B. DISSENTING OPINION

Mr. Justice Douglas, with whom Mr. Justice Brennan and Mr. Justice Marshall concur, dissenting in No. 204 [*Crampton*]. . . .

In my view the unitary trial which Ohio provides in first-degree murder cases does not satisfy the requirements of procedural Due Process under the Fourteenth Amendment. . . .

If a defendant wishes to testify in support of the defense of insanity or in mitigation of what he is charged with doing, he can do so only if he surrenders his right to be free from self-incrimination. Once he takes the stand he can be cross-examined not only as respects the crime charged but also on other misdeeds. In Ohio impeachment covers a wide range of subjects: prior convictions for felonies and statutory misdemeanors, pending indictments, prior convictions in military service, and dishonorable discharges. Once he testifies he can be recalled for cross-examination in the State's case in rebuttal.

While the defendant in Ohio has the right of allocution, that right even in first-degree murder cases occurs only after the jury's verdict has been rendered. Unless there is prejudicial error vitiating the conviction or insufficient evidence to convict, the jury's verdict stands and the judge must enter the verdict. Allocution, though mandatory, is thus a ritual only.

If the right to be heard were to be meaningful, it would have to accrue before sentencing; yet, except for allocution, any attempt on the part of the accused during the trial to say why the judgment of death should not be pronounced against him entails a surrender of his right against self-incrimination. It therefore seems plain that the single-verdict procedure is a burden on the exercise of the right to be free of compulsion as respects self-incrimination. For he can testify on the issue of insanity or on other matters in extenuation of the crime charged only at the price of surrendering the protection of the Self-Incrimination Clause of the Fifth Amendment made applicable to the States by the Fourteenth.

## C. DISSENTING OPINION

MR. JUSTICE BRENNAN, with whom MR. JUSTICE DOUGLAS and MR. JUSTICE MARSHALL join, dissenting [in both cases].

These cases test the viability of principles whose roots draw strength from the very core of the Due Process Clause. The question that petitioners present for our decision is whether the rule of law, basic to our society and binding upon the States by virtue of the Due Process Clause of the Fourteenth Amendment, is fundamentally inconsistent with capital sentencing procedures that are purposely constructed to allow the maximum possible variation from one case to the next, and provide no mechanism to prevent that consciously maximized variation from reflecting merely random or arbitrary choice. The Court does not, however, come to grips with that fundamental question. Instead, the Court misapprehends petitioners' argument and deals with the cases as if petitioners contend that due process requires capital sentencing to be carried out under predetermined standards so precise as to be capable of purely mechanical application, entirely eliminating any vestiges of flexibility or discretion in their use. This misapprehended question is then treated in the context of the Court's assumption that the legislatures of Ohio and California are incompetent to express with clarity the bases upon which they have determined that some persons guilty of some crimes should be killed, while others should live—an assumption that, significantly, finds no support in the arguments made by those States in these cases. With the issue so polarized, the Court is led to conclude that the rule of law and the power of the States to kill are in irreconcilable conflict. This conflict the Court resolves in favor of the States' power to kill.

In my view the Court errs at all points from its premises to its conclusions.

*Source*: 402 U.S. 183 (1971), 185–249 (footnotes omitted).

## DOCUMENT 54: *Furman v. Georgia* (1972)

As a result of the Supreme Court's decision in *McGautha* and *Crampton* (see Document 53), the abolitionists' litigation strategy appeared to be on shaky ground. Now that the major procedural claims against the death penalty had been rejected, all that remained to be tried was an Eighth Amendment challenge of the death penalty itself—suggested by Gerald Gottlieb more than a decade earlier (see Document 46).

The opportunity to test that challenge came less than two months after the *McGautha* decision, when the Supreme Court announced its intention to review four death penalty cases with regard to one question: "Does the imposition and carrying out of the death penalty in this case constitute cruel and unusual punishment in violation of the Eighth and Fourteenth Amendments?" (quoted in Epstein and Kobylka 1992: 70; Meltsner 1973:246; Schwed 1983:130).

The cases were *Furman v. Georgia, Jackson v. Georgia, Branch v. Texas*, and *Aikens v. California*. *Aikins v. California* was dismissed after the California Supreme Court declared capital punishment unconstitutional under the state constitution early in February of 1972,[1] thus changing Aikens's sentence to life imprisonment (Epstein and Kobylka 1992:77; Schwed 1983:132; Tushnet 1994:47). *Jackson v. Georgia* and

*Branch v. Texas* were consolidated under *Furman v. Georgia* for the Supreme Court's review.

As in *McGautha* and *Crampton*, the issue of standardless juries was central to the legal argument in all three cases. However, instead of attacking the constitutionality of the procedure, the petitioners in *Furman* focused on the *results* of the procedure—which they claimed were arbitrary and capricious death sentences that amounted to the kind of cruel and unusual punishment prohibited by the Eighth Amendment (Paternoster 1991:53).

In a landmark decision handed down on June 29, 1972, the Supreme Court agreed—ruling that the death penalty, as it was then being administered, was "cruel and unusual punishment in violation of the Eighth and Fourteenth Amendments."

As a result of the decision, more than six hundred death row inmates in thirty-two states had their sentences commuted to life imprisonment—a clear victory for the abolitionists (Bedau 1977:82; Paternoster 1991:58; Schwed 1983:135).

However, the issue of capital punishment still was far from resolved. The Court's majority had been a narrow one (5–4) and lacked a plurality opinion (all nine justices wrote separate opinions in the case). Further, the majority opinion had not declared the death penalty unconstitutional under all circumstances—only as it then was being administered by the states. Hence, the justices had left the door open for states to devise death penalty procedures that could be considered constitutional (Epstein and Kobylka 1992:82; Paternoster 1991:58).

## NOTE

1. California reinstated the death penalty in September of 1973 (Epstein and Kobylka 1992:85), although executions did not actually resume in that state until 1992 (see Document 98).

## A. OPINION OF THE COURT

Per Curiam

Petitioner in No. 69–5003 was convicted of murder in Georgia and was sentenced to death pursuant to Ga. Code Ann. §26–1005. . . . Petitioner in No. 69–5030 was convicted of rape in Georgia and was sentenced to death pursuant to Ga. Code Ann. §26–1302. . . . Petitioner in No. 69–5031 was convicted of rape in Texas and was sentenced to death pursuant to Tex. Penal Code, Art. 1189. . . . Certiorari was granted limited to the following question: "Does the imposition and carrying out of the death penalty in [these cases] constitute cruel and unusual punishment in violation of the Eighth and Fourteenth Amendments?" . . . The Court holds that the imposition and carrying out of the death penalty in these cases constitute cruel and unusual punishment in violation of the Eighth and Fourteenth Amendments. The judgment in each case is therefore reversed insofar as it leaves undisturbed the death sentence imposed, and the cases are remanded for further proceedings.

## B. CONCURRING OPINION OF JUSTICE DOUGLAS

MR. JUSTICE DOUGLAS, concurring. . . .

In a Nation committed to equal protection of the laws there is no permissible "caste" aspect of law enforcement. Yet we know that the discretion of judges and juries in imposing the death penalty enables the penalty to be selectively applied, feeding prejudices against the accused if he is poor and despised, and lacking political clout, or if he is a member of a suspect or unpopular minority, and saving those who by social position may be in a more protected position. . . .

The high service rendered by the "cruel and unusual" punishment clause of the Eighth Amendment is to require legislatures to write penal laws that are evenhanded, nonselective, and nonarbitrary, and to require judges to see to it that general laws are not applied sparsely, selectively, and spottily to unpopular groups.

A law that stated that anyone making more than $50,000 would be exempt from the death penalty would plainly fall, as would a law that in terms said that blacks, those who never went beyond the fifth grade in school, those who made less than $3,000 a year, or those who were unpopular or unstable should be the only people executed. A law which in the overall view reaches that result in practice has no more sanctity than a law which in terms provides the same.

Thus, these discretionary statutes are unconstitutional in their operation. They are pregnant with discrimination and discrimination is an ingredient not compatible with the idea of equal protection of the laws that is implicit in the ban on "cruel and unusual" punishments.

## C. CONCURRING OPINION OF JUSTICE BRENNAN

MR. JUSTICE BRENNAN, concurring. . . .

The outstanding characteristic of our present practice of punishing criminals by death is the infrequency with which we resort to it. The evidence is conclusive that death is not the ordinary punishment for any crime.

There has been a steady decline in the infliction of this punishment in every decade since the 1930's, the earliest period for which accurate statistics are available. In the 1930's, executions averaged 167 per year; in the 1940's, the average was 128; in the 1950's, it was 72; and in the years 1960–1962, it was 48. There have been a total of 46 executions since then, 36 of them in 1963–1964. Yet our population and the number of capital crimes committed have increased greatly over the past four decades. . . .

When a country of over 200 million people inflicts an unusually severe punishment no more than 50 times a year, the inference is strong that the punishment is not being regularly and fairly applied. . . .

Although there are no exact figures available, we know that thousands of murders and rapes are committed annually in States where death is an authorized punishment for those crimes. However the rate of infliction is characterized—as "freakishly" or "spectacularly" rare, or simply as rare—it would take the purest sophistry to deny that death is inflicted in only a minute fraction of these cases. How much rarer, after all, could the infliction of death be?

When the punishment of death is inflicted in a trivial number of the cases in which it is legally available, the conclusion is virtually inescapable that it is being inflicted arbitrarily. Indeed, it smacks of little more than a lottery system.

## D. CONCURRING OPINION OF JUSTICE STEWART

MR. JUSTICE STEWART, concurring. . . .

These death sentences are cruel and unusual in the same way that being struck by lightning is cruel and unusual. For, of all the people convicted of rapes and murders in 1967 and 1968, many just as reprehensible as these, the petitioners are among a capriciously selected random handful upon whom the sentence of death has in fact been imposed. My concurring Brothers have demonstrated that, if any basis can be discerned for the selection of these few to be sentenced to die, it is the constitutionally impermissible basis of race. . . . But racial discrimination has not been proved, and I put it to one side. I simply conclude that the Eighth and Fourteenth Amendments cannot tolerate the infliction of a sentence of death under legal systems that permit this unique penalty to be so wantonly and so freakishly imposed.

## E. CONCURRING OPINION OF JUSTICE WHITE

MR. JUSTICE WHITE, concurring. . . .

The imposition and execution of the death penalty are obviously cruel in the dictionary sense. But the penalty has not been considered cruel and unusual punishment in the constitutional sense because it was thought justified by the social ends it was deemed to serve. At the moment that it ceases realistically to further these purposes, however, the emerging question is whether its imposition in such circumstances would violate the Eighth Amendment. It is my view that it would, for its imposition would then be the pointless and needless extinction of life with only marginal contributions to any discernible social or public purposes. A penalty with such negligible returns to the State would be patently excessive and cruel and unusual punishment violative of the Eighth Amendment.

It is also my judgment that this point has been reached with respect to capital punishment as it is presently administered under the statutes involved in these cases. Concededly, it is difficult to prove as a general proposition that capital punishment, however administered, more effectively serves the ends of the criminal law than does imprisonment. But however that may be, I cannot avoid the conclusion that as the statutes before us are now administered, the penalty is so infrequently imposed that the threat of execution is too attenuated to be of substantial service to criminal justice.

## F. CONCURRING OPINION OF JUSTICE MARSHALL

MR. JUSTICE MARSHALL, concurring. . . .

It has often been noted that American citizens know almost nothing about capital punishment. Some of the conclusions arrived at in the preceding section and the supporting evidence would be critical to an informed judgment on the morality of the death penalty: *e.g.*, that the death penalty is no more effective a deterrent than life imprisonment, that convicted murderers are rarely executed, but are usually sentenced to a term in prison; that convicted murderers usually are model prisoners, and that they almost always become law-abiding citizens upon their release from prison; that the costs of executing a capital offender exceed the costs of imprisoning him for life; that while in prison, a convict under sentence of death performs none of the useful functions that life prisoners perform; that no attempt is made in the sentencing process to ferret out likely recidivists for execution; and that the death penalty may actually stimulate criminal activity.

This information would almost surely convince the average citizen that the death penalty was unwise, but a problem arises as to whether it would convince him that the penalty was morally reprehensible. This problem arises from the fact that the public's desire for retribution, even though this is a goal that the legislature cannot constitutionally pursue as its sole justification for capital punishment, might influence the citizenry's view of the morality of capital punishment. The solution to the problem lies in the fact that no one has ever seriously advanced retribution as a legitimate goal of our society. Defenses of capital punishment are always mounted on deterrent or other similar theories. This should not be surprising. It is the people of this country who have urged in the past that prisons rehabilitate as well as isolate offenders, and it is the people who have injected a sense of purpose into our penology. I cannot believe that at this stage in our history, the American people would ever knowingly support purposeless vengeance. Thus, I believe that the great mass of citizens would conclude on the basis of the material already considered that the death penalty is immoral and therefore unconstitutional.

## G. DISSENTING OPINION OF CHIEF JUSTICE BURGER

MR. CHIEF JUSTICE BURGER, with whom MR. JUSTICE BLACKMUN, MR. JUSTICE POWELL, and MR. JUSTICE REHNQUIST join, dissenting. . . .

Today the Court has not ruled that capital punishment is *per se* violative of the Eighth Amendment; nor has it ruled that the punishment is barred for any particular class or classes of crimes. The substantially similar concurring opinions of MR. JUSTICE STEWART and MR. JUSTICE WHITE, which are necessary to support the judgment setting aside petitioners' sentences, stop short of reaching the ultimate question. The actual scope of the Court's ruling, which I take to be embodied in these concurring opinions, is not entirely clear. This much, however, seems apparent: if the legislatures are to continue to authorize capital punishment for some crimes, juries and judges can no longer be permitted to make the sentencing determination in the same manner they have in the past. This approach—not urged in oral arguments or briefs—misconceives the nature of the constitutional command against "cruel and unusual punishments," disregards controlling case law, and demands a rigidity in capital cases which, if possible of achievement, cannot be regarded as a welcome change. Indeed, the contrary seems to be the case. . . .

While I would not undertake to make a definitive statement as to the parameters of the Court's ruling, it is clear that if state legislatures and the Congress wish to maintain the availability of capital punishment, significant statutory changes will have to be made. Since the two pivotal concurring opinions turn on the assumption that the punishment of death is now meted out in a random and unpredictable manner, legislative bodies may seek to bring their laws into compliance with the Court's ruling by providing standards for juries and judges to follow in determining the sentence in capital cases or by more narrowly defining the crimes for which the penalty is to be imposed.

## H. DISSENTING OPINION OF JUSTICE BLACKMUN

MR. JUSTICE BLACKMUN, dissenting. . . .

[W]ere I a legislator, I would do all I could to sponsor and to vote for legislation abolishing the death penalty. And were I the chief executive of a sovereign State, I would be sorely tempted to exercise executive clemency as Governor Rockefeller of Arkansas did recently just before he departed from office. There—on the Legislative Branch of the State or Federal Government, and secondarily, on the Executive Branch—is where the authority and responsibility for this kind of action lies. The authority should not be taken over by the judiciary in the modern guise of an Eighth Amendment issue.

I do not sit on these cases, however, as a legislator, responsive, at least in part, to the will of constituents. Our task here, as must so frequently be emphasized and re-emphasized, is to pass upon the constitutionality of legislation that has been enacted and that is challenged. This is the sole task for judges. We should not allow our personal preferences as to the wisdom of legislation and congressional action, or our distaste for such action, to guide our judicial decision in cases such as these. The temptations to cross that policy line are very great. In fact, as today's decision reveals, they are almost irresistible. . . .

Although personally I may rejoice at the Court's result, I find it difficult to accept or to justify as a matter of history, of law, or of constitutional pronouncement. I fear the Court has overstepped. It has sought and has achieved an end.

## I. DISSENTING OPINION OF JUSTICE POWELL

MR. JUSTICE POWELL, with whom THE CHIEF JUSTICE, MR. JUSTICE BLACKMUN, and MR. JUSTICE REHNQUIST join, dissenting. . . .

It is important to keep in focus the enormity of the step undertaken by the Court today. Not only does it invalidate hundreds of state and federal laws, it deprives those jurisdictions of the power to legislate with respect to capital punishment in the future, except in a manner consistent with the cloudily outlined views of those Justices who do not purport to undertake total abolition. Nothing short of an amendment to the United

States Constitution can reverse the Court's judgments. Meanwhile, all flexibility is foreclosed. The normal democratic process, as well as the opportunities for the several States to respond to the will of their people expressed through ballot referenda (as in Massachusetts, Illinois, and Colorado), is now shut off. . . .

With deference and respect for the views of the Justices who differ, it seems to me . . . that, as a matter of policy and precedent, this is a classic case for the exercise of our oft-announced allegiance to judicial restraint. I know of no case in which greater gravity and delicacy have attached to the duty that this Court is called on to perform whenever legislation—state or federal—is challenged on constitutional grounds. It seems to me that the sweeping judicial action undertaken today reflects a basic lack of faith and confidence in the democratic process. Many may regret, as I do, the failure of some legislative bodies to address the capital punishment issue with greater frankness or effectiveness. Many might decry their failure either to abolish the penalty entirely or selectively, or to establish standards for its enforcement. But impatience with the slowness, and even the unresponsiveness, of legislatures is no justification for judicial intrusion upon their historic powers.

## J. DISSENTING OPINION OF JUSTICE REHNQUIST

MR. JUSTICE REHNQUIST, with whom THE CHIEF JUSTICE, MR. JUSTICE BLACKMUN, and MR. JUSTICE POWELL join, dissenting. . . .

[T]oday's holding necessarily brings into sharp relief the fundamental question of the role of judicial review in a democratic society. . . .

The most expansive reading of the leading constitutional cases does not remotely suggest that this Court has been granted a roving commission, either by the Founding Fathers or by the framers of the Fourteenth Amendment, to strike down laws that are based upon notions of policy or morality suddenly found unacceptable by a majority of this Court. . . .

If there can be said to be one dominant theme in the Constitution, perhaps more fully articulated in the Federalist Papers than in the instrument itself, it is the notion of checks and balances. The Framers were well aware of the natural desire of office holders as well as others to seek to expand the scope and authority of their particular office at the expense of others. They sought to provide against success in such efforts by erecting adequate checks and balances in the form of grants of authority to each branch of the government in order to counteract and prevent usurpation on the part of others.

The philosophy of the Framers is best described by one of the ablest and greatest of their number, James Madison, in Federalist No. 51:

In framing a government which is to be administered by men over men, the great difficulty lies in this: You must first enable the government to controul the governed; and in the next place, oblige it to controul itself.

Madison's observation applies to the Judicial Branch with at least as much force as to the Legislative and Executive Branches. While overreaching by the Legislative and Executive Branches may result in the sacrifice of individual protections that the Constitution was designed to secure against action of the State, judicial overreaching may result in sacrifice of the equally important right of the people to govern themselves.

*Source*: 408 U.S. 238 (1972), 239–470 (footnotes omitted).

---

## DOCUMENT 55: States' Response to the *Furman* Decision (1973)

As abolitionists rejoiced over the Supreme Court's decision in *Furman* (see Document 54), retentionists went to work to restore capital punishment.

The focus of the pro-death penalty campaign was on drafting new state death penalty laws that would be deemed constitutional by the Supreme Court. Keeping in mind the requirements that seemed to have been established by the Court's decision in *Furman*, the new state laws included mandatory and guided-discretion statutes. Such statutes were designed to lead to less arbitrary, more consistent sentencing by giving juries less discretion in choosing a defendant's sentence, or none at all (Paternoster 1991:63; Schwed 1983:143–144).

During the year following *Furman*, bills to restore capital punishment were introduced in more than half of the state legislatures nationwide. By the mid-1970s, thirty-four states had signed new capital statutes, and more than six hundred prisoners had been sentenced to death under the new laws (Schwed 1983:145). However, none of the executions had been carried out. In fact, they could not be carried out because it still was not known if these new state death penalty laws were constitutionally acceptable under the standards set by the Supreme Court in *Furman*. Before executions could resume, the Supreme Court would have to issue a ruling on the new statutes (Epstein and Kobylka 1992:89; Paternoster 1991:63; Schwed 1983:145).

Legislatures in more than half the states are considering a reinstitution of the death penalty.

On Monday, Governor Rockefeller was given thunderous applause when he told a labor conference that he was giving "very serious consideration" to proposing the penalty for figures in organized crime who are convicted of drug selling.

In Nevada, when Gov. Mike O'Callaghan made his hour-long State of the State message to the Legislature he was interrupted by applause just once: When he called for the death penalty for the killing of police officers or the killing of prison staff members by inmates.

In California, where voters approved a restoration of the death penalty, Gov. Ronald Reagan told the Legislature when he asked for the law, "The people of California gave us a mandate to restore capital punishment."

The passage of such legislation may be difficult, but the bills introduced, often backed by a governor, indicate that a sizable proportion of elected officials still consider the death penalty a strong crime deterrent.

### Death Penalty Voided

Last June, the Supreme Court ruled in a 5-to-4 decision that capital punishment as administered in this country was "cruel and unusual" punishment and, therefore, unconstitutional. The decision spared the lives of 631 sentenced to death in 32 states, but, in fact, there have been no executions in the United States since June of 1967.

Chief Justice Warren E. Burger, who voted against the majority, suggested that legislatures might overcome some of the majority's objections.

People "are sick and tired of heinous crimes being committed," said Keith Ashworth, a Las Vegas Democrat who is Speaker of Nevada's Assembly, and "the criminal walking out of prison to commit the same crimes again." In Nevada, he said, two issues bother the people: drug abuse and capital punishment.

"It is time that a cold-blooded and premeditated murderer pay for his crime by suffering the death penalty," the Hawaii Catholic Herald, the official Roman Catholic newspaper on the islands, said in an editorial.

The legislation that has been offered in several states generally tried to reinstate the death penalty for the killing of a policeman who is acting in the line of duty, but the measures sometimes cover airplane hijacking, rape or murder tied to other criminal acts.

Several legislatures have already approved a new version of the death penalty, although no one has been executed under these new laws.

### Several Laws Passed

In Ohio, for example, the legislature revised the criminal code last fall, effective Jan. 1, 1974, imposing the death penalty essentially for premeditated and felony murders where there were no mitigating circumstances, such as mental illness.

In Georgia, the legislature passed last month a bill reinstating the penalty for the killing of a policeman who is acting in the line of duty and for rape and kidnapping for ransom when there are aggravating circumstances, such as lasting mental and physical damage to a rape victim. Each death sentence must be reviewed by the state Supreme Court for even application.

Georgia's Gov. Jimmy Carter has said he will sign the bill, although there is some question of its constitutionality.

And the problem of constitutionality still exists.

"We are trying to figure out what the Supreme Court says, so it will be constitutional," says Senator Leo Corbet, a Republican of Phoenix, Ariz., who is chairman of the state Senate's Judiciary Committee. "We are guessing—throwing darts at the board."

*Source*: Jerry M. Flint, "States on Move: Half of Legislatures Considering Bills on Capital Offenses," *New York Times*, March 11, 1973, 1, 55.

## DOCUMENT 56: President Nixon's Response to the *Furman* Decision (1973)

As many states drafted new death penalty laws that they hoped would meet the Supreme Court's newly-defined standard for constitutionality under the Eighth Amendment (see Document 55), the Nixon administration sponsored a federal capital punishment bill of its own that would restore the death penalty for a number of federal crimes, including assassination, treason, kidnapping, air hijacking, and murder of law enforcement officials and prison guards (Epstein and Kobylka 1992:84; Meltsner 1973:309).

The bill was passed in the Senate by a vote of 54–33 on March 13, 1974. The House passed a segment of it later that year. However, as with the state laws, the constitutionality of the new federal legislation had yet to be determined by the Supreme Court.

WASHINGTON, March 10—President Nixon called on Congress today to restore the death penalty for certain Federal crimes and to enact a new program of stringent minimum jail sentences for heroin pushers.

In a radio speech scornful of what he termed "soft-headed judges" and the "permissive philosophy" that says social injustice breeds crime, the President announced that he had asked Attorney General Richard G.

Kleindienst to draft a capital punishment law that would survive review by the Supreme Court.

Mr. Nixon said that the proposal would revive the death penalty for assassination, treason, kidnapping, air hijacking and the murder of law enforcement officials and prison guards. He did not say whether the punishment would be mandatory, or merely available to a sentencing judge or jury. . . .

Throughout his speech, the sixth in a series on his domestic programs, Mr. Nixon took a stiffly uncompromising attitude on the need for heavier penalties and stronger public weapons against crime and on the deterrent effect of threatening criminals with harsher laws.

"Americans in the last decade," he said, "were often told that the criminal was not responsible for his crimes against society, but that society was responsible. I totally disagree with this permissive philosophy.

"Society is guilty of crime only when we fail to bring the criminal to justice. When we fail to make the criminal pay for his crime, we encourage him to think that crime will pay. Such an attitude will never be reflected in the laws supported by this Administration, nor in the manner in which we enforce those laws."

*Source*: Warren Weaver, Jr., "President Asks Law to Restore Death Penalty: Gives Drug Plan," *New York Times*, March 11, 1973, 1, 55.

## DOCUMENT 57: "Race, Judicial Discretion, and the Death Penalty" (Marvin E. Wolfgang and Marc Riedel, 1973)

The Supreme Court's decision in *Furman* (see Document 54) helped to revive the issue of racial discrimination in capital sentencing—an issue that had been raised during the 1960s by the NAACP Legal Defense and Educational Fund and University of Pennsylvania sociologist Marvin Wolfgang but had been rejected by several courts.

Responding in a 1973 article to the Supreme Court's assertion that the death penalty as it then was being administered by the states constituted cruel and unusual punishment—in part because it was infrequently and arbitrarily applied—Wolfgang and Marc Riedel, then a lecturer in the University of Pennsylvania's School of Social Work, pointed out that "although the death penalty may be infrequently imposed, it is not imposed arbitrarily. . . . [R]acial variables are systematically and consistently related to the imposition of the death penalty" (Wolfgang and Riedel 1973:120).

In support of this assertion, the article included findings from several studies of race and capital punishment, including a previously unpublished 1965 review of racial discrimination in the imposition of the death penalty for rape in the south[1] conducted under the direction of Wolfgang and the LDF's Anthony Amsterdam (see Documents 51, 52, 71 and 77).

The study analyzed data on more than three thousand rape convictions in eleven southern states from 1945 to 1965. A large number of factors were taken into account, including offender characteristics, victim characteristics, offense characteristics, the nature of the relationship between the offender and victim, and details of the trial. After controlling for all of these factors, the researchers found strong evidence of racial discrimination in capital sentencing for rape, particularly for African Americans convicted of raping white women.

### NOTE

1. It wasn't until 1977 that the Supreme Court ruled that the death penalty was excessive and disproportionate punishment for the rape of an adult woman whose life was not taken (see Document 64).

Among 1,265 cases in which the race of the defendant and the sentence are known, nearly seven times as many blacks were sentenced to death as were whites. Among the 823 blacks convicted of rape, 110, or 13 percent, were sentenced to death; among the 442 whites convicted of rape, only 9, or 2 percent, were sentenced to death. The statistical probability that such a disproportionate number of blacks could be sentenced to death by chance alone is less than one out of a thousand. More particularly, a statistically significantly higher proportion of black defendants whose victims were white were sentenced to death. From a total of 1,238 convicted rape defendants, 317 were black defendants with white victims, and 921 were all other racial combinations of defendant and victim—including black/black, white/white, and white/black. Of the 317 black defendants whose victims were white, 113, or approximately 36 percent, were sentenced to death. Of the 921 defendants involved in all other racial combinations of defendant and victim, only 19, or 2 percent, were sentenced to death. In short, black defendants whose victims were white were sentenced to death approximately eighteen times more frequently than defendants in any other racial combination of defendant and victim. Again, the probability of such a distribution, or such a relationship between the sentence of death and black defendants with white victims is, by chance alone, less than one out of a thousand.

*Source*: Marvin E. Wolfgang and Marc Riedel, "Race, Judicial Discretion, and the Death Penalty." *Annals of the American Academy of Political and Social Science* 407 (May 1973):129–130.

## DOCUMENT 58: Charles Black (1974)

In 1974, Yale Law School professor Charles L. Black, Jr., published a brief but well-received book, *Capital Punishment: The Inevitability of Caprice and Mistake.*

Black contended that the criminal justice system was not capable of administering capital punishment without a degree of arbitrariness and susceptibility to mistake—either of which he considered intolerable when a person's life or death was at stake (Black 1974:9–10).

Black backed up this claim with a detailed look at the criminal justice system as it then operated with regard to capital cases, showing that "standardless discretion, as well as mistake-proneness . . . permeates the whole series of choices that have to be made on the way from street to gallows" (Black 1974:56).

Further, looking specifically at the new capital punishment statutes enacted by the states since *Furman*, Black concluded that they "*do not effectively restrict* the discretion of juries by any real standards. They never will. No society is going to kill everybody who meets certain preset verbal requirements, put on the statute books without awareness or coverage of the infinity of special factors the real world can produce" (Black 1974:67).

Black's arguments were hailed as "brilliant" by one noted abolitionist, who said, "No other work states so well the contemporary, post-*Furman* case against the death penalty" (Bedau 1977:99–100).

[D]ecisions on charging, on acceptance of guilty plea, on determination of the offense for which conviction is warranted, on sentencing, and on clemency add up . . . to a process containing too much chance for mistake and too much standardless "discretion" for it to be decent for us to use it any longer as a means of choosing for death. We have to keep using it as a means of choosing for other punishment, even as we slowly try to make it better, but for the death of a person it will not do, and it cannot be reformed enough to do.

Suppose all the mistake-proneness and standardlessness I have laid out, step by step, were concentrated in the decision of one man. We would regard that as so evidently intolerable as to be undiscussable. But it might be better than what we have, for responsibility would at least be fixed. All our system does is to diffuse this same responsibility nearly to the point of its elimination, so that each participant in this long process, though perhaps knowing his own conclusions to be uncertain and inadequately based on lawful standards, can comfort himself with the thought, altogether false and vain, that the lack has been made up, or will be made up, somewhere else.

How have we allowed ourselves to get here? I suggest it is because of our seeing the whole process through the medium of a radically false mythology. We tend, I believe, to think of persons' being "clearly guilty" of crimes for which they ought to die. Then some of them, by acts of pure grace, are spared—by prosecutors' discretion, by jury leniency, by clemency. After all, who can complain at not receiving a pure favor? (There is here perhaps a touch of Calvinism—but to a true Calvinist a blasphemous touch, for the "grace" comes from humans all too human.)

The trouble is that the system may just as well be viewed, and with enormously higher accuracy, if numbers count, must be viewed, as one in which a few people are selected, without adequately shown or structured reason for their being selected, to die. The inevitable corollary of sparing some people through mere grace or favor is standardless condemnation of others. The thing that ought to impress us is the standardless condemnation; we have been looking too long at its mirror image; we should take courage and turn around.

*Source*: Charles L. Black, Jr., *Capital Punishment: The Inevitability of Caprice and Mistake* (New York: W. W. Norton, 1974), 92–93.

## DOCUMENT 59: Ernest van den Haag (1975)

One of the most prominent proponents of capital punishment during the modern era is Ernest van den Haag, who today is the John M. Olin Professor of Jurisprudence and Public Policy at Fordham University in New York and a Distinguished Scholar of the Heritage Foundation.

A conservative and controversialist, van den Haag's intellectual interests are diverse. Born in the Hague and educated in Germany, Italy, and France, van den Haag came to the United States in 1940. He received his master's degree from the University of Iowa in 1942, taught as an adjunct professor of social philosophy at New York University and as a lecturer in sociology at the New School for Social Research, and received his doctorate in economics from New York University in 1952.

Van den Haag, whose research interests have covered such topics as civil disorders, race, and Jewish history, became increasingly interested in the issue of crime and punishment during the late 1960s.

An advocate of harsh punishments—including the death penalty—as a deterrent to crime, van den Haag's widely-reviewed 1975 book on the subject, *Punishing Criminals*, was considered "thought-provoking" even by those who were critical of his views (Contemporary Biography Yearbook 1983:423).

In the book, van den Haag rejected the modern liberal characterization of the criminal as a victim of society, and instead he argued that criminal behavior is essentially conscious and voluntary, and therefore that harsher punishments would likely deter crime by increasing its cost to the criminal.

In addition to punishment in general, van den Haag devoted two chapters of the book to a discussion of the death penalty. In these chapters, he responded to a number of modern arguments for and against the death penalty. His responses to a few of these arguments are excerpted in the document below.

### The Only Threat Available

It is always difficult to know how many crimes are not committed because of a threat. But it can be shown logically that the death penalty is the only threat that could (could, not necessarily will) deter members of three groups.

1. Convicts already serving a life term are incapacitated insofar as the world beyond prison walls is concerned, but are left quite capable of committing crimes within. Such crimes are frequent. Without the death penalty, these convicts are immune to threats of further punishment. It seems unwise to grant convicted criminals this heady immunity not available to non-convicts, who are less dangerous. . . .

2. Without the death penalty, those already threatened with a life term for kidnapping, skyjacking, or murder, but not yet apprehended, have no reason to refrain from additional crimes. They may murder third persons or the kidnap victim. Above all, they will be able to kill the arresting officer with impunity. This won't make the policeman's job easier. The effective impunity granted for additional crimes to suspects already threatened with a life term invites them to murder the officers trying to apprehend them. . . .

3. Prospective spies in wartime, or violent revolutionaries in acute situations when there is a present danger of the government being overthrown, can be restrained, if at all, only by the death penalty. They believe that they will be released from prison when their side wins. They may even expect a reward. In an acute situation only the threat of an irrevocable penalty could effectively deter them. Unlike imprisonment, death cannot be revoked; it may cause the expected victory to come too late. . . .

### The Symbolic Meaning of Abolition

. . .

No matter what can be said for abolition of the death penalty, it will be perceived symbolically as a loss of nerve: social authority no longer is willing to pass an irrevocable judgment on anyone. Murder is no longer thought grave enough to take the murderer's life, no longer horrendous enough to deserve so fearfully irrevocable a punishment. When murder no longer forfeits the murderer's life (though it will interfere with his freedom), respect for life itself is diminished, as the price for taking it is. Life becomes cheaper as we become kinder to those who wantonly take it. . . .

## Injustice

. . .

Injustice justifies abolition only if the losses to justice outweigh the gains—if more innocents are lost than saved by imposing the penalty compared to whatever net result alternatives (such as no punishment or life imprisonment) would produce. If innocent victims of future murderers are saved by virtue of the death penalty imposed on convicted murderers, it must be retained, just as surgery is, even though some innocents will be lost through miscarriages of justice—as long as more innocent lives are saved than lost. More justice is done with than without the death penalty. It is always a logical error to reject a rule because of individual cases. Rules and the results they produce must be compared with alternative rules and with the results they produce, not with individual cases.

## Discriminatory Application

. . .

Penalties themselves are not inherently discriminatory; distribution, the process which selects the persons who suffer the penalty, can be. Unjust distribution—either through unjust convictions or through unjust (unequal and biased) penalization of equally guilty convicts—can occur with respect to any penalty. The vice must be corrected by correcting the distributive process that produces it. There is no reason to limit such a correction to any specific penalty. Nor can much be accomplished by abolishing any penalty, since all penalties can be meted out discriminatorily. The defect to be corrected is in the courts.

*Source*: Ernest van den Haag, *Punishing Criminals* (New York: Basic Books, 1975). [Lanham, Md.: University Press of America, 1991, 208–210, 212–213, 219–220, 221 (footnotes omitted).]

## DOCUMENT 60: "The Deterrent Effect of Capital Punishment: A Question of Life and Death" (Isaac Ehrlich, 1975)

In 1975, the capital punishment debate returned to the issue of deterrence when University of Chicago economist Isaac Ehrlich[1] published a study which seemed to indicate that the death penalty was, indeed, a significant deterrent to murder.

Using a statistical technique called multiple regression analysis, Ehrlich compared national execution rates with national murder rates for a 36-year period (1933–1969). Controlling for a number of other variables, he concluded that "an additional execution per year over the period in question may have resulted, on average, in 7 or 8 fewer murders" (Ehrlich 1975a:414).

Ehrlich's study—and his results—were unique: his was the first econometric analysis of the death penalty's deterrent effect and the first statistical study to find evidence of such an effect (Zimring and Hawkins 1986:175). As a result, the study was widely publicized and highly controversial. Many researchers were critical of Ehrlich's results, attacking both his data and his analysis (Baldus and Cole 1975; Bowers and Pierce 1975; Passell and Taylor 1977), while others conducted econometric studies of their own that reported findings similar to Ehrlich's (Layson 1983, 1985; Phillips and Ray 1982; Wolpin 1978).

Ehrlich responded to his critics and defended his work in numerous subsequent articles on the issue of deterrence and capital punishment (e.g., Ehrlich 1975b, 1977a; Ehrlich and Mark 1977). In one of these rebuttals, published in the *Yale Law Journal*, Ehrlich pointed out, "The bulk of my critics' analyses challenges neither the theoretical formulation of the deterrence hypothesis nor the statistical techniques used in the theory's empirical implementation" (Ehrlich 1975b:226). And in 1977, he published a sequel to his 1975 time-series study in which he used cross-state data from 1940 and 1950, reporting similar findings (Ehrlich 1977b).

As a result of the controversy surrounding Ehrlich's 1975 findings, the National Academy of Sciences Panel on Deterrence and Incapacitation commissioned a team of researchers to conduct a detailed reanalysis of Ehrlich's data. The team's findings, the NAS panel's report, and Ehrlich's rebuttal are excerpted in Document 65.

### NOTE
1. Ehrlich currently is a Leading Professor and Executive Officer of Economics, and the Melvin H. Baker Professor of American Enterprise at the State University of New York at Buffalo.

Contrary to previous observations, this investigation, although by no means definitive, does indicate the existence of a pure deterrent effect of capital punishment. In fact, the empirical analysis suggests that on the average the tradeoff between the execution of an offender and the lives of potential victims it might have saved was of the order of magnitude of 1 for 8 for the period 1933–67 in the United States. . . .

Previous investigations, notably those by Sellin, have developed evidence used to unequivocally deny the existence of any deterrent or preventive effects of capital punishment. This evidence stems by and large from what amounts to informal tests of the sign of the simple correlation between the legal status of the death penalty and the murder rate across states and over time in a few states. Studies performing these tests have not considered systematically the actual enforcement of the death penalty, which may be a far more important factor affecting offenders' behavior than the legal status of the penalty. Moreover, these studies have generally ignored other parameters characterizing law enforcement activity against murder, such as the probability of apprehension and the conditional probability of conviction, which appear to be systematically related to the probability of punishment by execution. In addition, the direction of the causal relationship between the rate of murder and the probabilities of apprehension, conviction, and execution is not obvious, since a high murder rate may generate an upward adjustment in the levels of these probabilities in accordance with optimal law enforcement. Thus the sign of the simple correlation between the murder rate and the legal status, or even the effective use of capital punishment, cannot provide conclusive evidence for or against the existence of a deterrent effect.

The basic strategy I have attempted to follow in formulating an adequate analytic procedure has been to develop a simple economic model of murder and defense against murder, to derive on the basis of this model a set of specific behavioral implications that could be tested against available data, and, accordingly, to test those implications statistically. The theoretical analysis provided sharp predictions concerning the signs and the relative magnitudes of the elasticities of the murder rate with respect to the probability of apprehension and the conditional probabilities of conviction and execution for murder. It suggested also the existence of a systematic relation between employment and earning opportunities and the frequency of murder and other related crimes. Although in principle the negative effect of capital punishment on the incentive to commit murder may be partly offset, for example, by an added incentive to eliminate witnesses, the results of the empirical investigation are not inconsistent with the hypothesis that, on balance, capital punishment reduces the murder rate. But even more significant is the finding that the ranking of the elasticities of the murder rate with respect to . . . [the probability of apprehension; conviction, given apprehension; and execution, given conviction] conforms to the specific theoretical predictions. The murder rate is also found negatively related to the labor force participation rate and positively to the rate of unemployment. None of these results is compatible with a hypothesis that offenders do not respond to incentives. In particular, the results concerning the effects of the estimates of the probabilities of apprehension, conviction, and execution are not consistent with the hypothesis that execution or imprisonment decrease the rate of murder only by incapacitating or preventing apprehended offenders from committing further crimes.

These observations do not imply that the empirical investigation has proved the existence of the deterrent or preventive effect of capital punishment. The results may be biased by the absence of data on the severity of alternative punishments for murder, by the use of national rather than state statistics, and by other imperfections. At the same time it is not obvious whether the net effect of all these shortcomings necessarily exaggerates the regression results in favor of the theorized results. In view of the new evidence presented here, one cannot reject the hypothesis that law enforcement activities in general and executions in particular do exert a deterrent effect on acts of murder. Strong inferences to the contrary drawn from earlier investigations appear to have been premature.

Even if one accepts the results concerning the partial effect of the conditional probability of execution on the murder rate as valid, these results do not imply that capital punishment is necessarily a desirable form of punishment. Specifically, whether the current level of application of capital punishment is optimal cannot be determined independently of the question of whether the levels of alternative punishments for murder are optimal. For example, one could argue . . . that if the severity of punishments by means other than execution had been greater in recent years, the apparent elasticity of the murder rate with respect to the conditional probability of punishment by execution would have been lower, thereby making capital punishment ostensibly less efficient in deterring or preventing murders. Again, this observation need not imply that the effective period of incarceration imposed on convicted capital offenders should be raised. . . . [I]ncarceration or execution are not exhaustive alternatives for effectively defending against murders. Indeed, these conventional punishments may be considered imperfect means of deterrence relative to monetary fines and other related compensations because the high "price" they exact from convicted offenders is not transferrable to the rest of society. Moreover, the results of the empirical investigation indicate that the rate of murder and other related crimes may also be reduced through increased employment and earning opportunities. The range of effective methods for defense against murder thus extends beyond conventional means of law enforcement and crime prevention. There is no unambiguous method for determining whether capital punishment should be utilized as a legal means of punishment without considering at the same time the optimal values of all other choice variables that can affect the level of capital crimes.

*Source*: Isaac Ehrlich, "The Deterrent Effect of Capital Punishment: A Question of Life and Death," *American Economic Review* LXV (June 1975): 398, 415–417.

---

## DOCUMENT 61: Public Opinion and the Death Penalty (1976)

By 1976—just four years after the Supreme Court's decision in *Furman*—national support for the death penalty reached its highest level since 1953, when 68 percent of the American public favored the death penalty (see Document 38B).

At 65 percent, public support for the death penalty had increased 23 points since a 1966 low of 42 percent (Document 49) and 15 points since a March 1972 poll taken before the *Furman* decision put a halt to executions in the United States (*Gallup Opinion Index*, April 1972: 14).

According to the 1976 Gallup report:

Since 1972 there have been shifts toward a "harder line" on capital punishment among virtually all major population groups, to the point where today large majorities in every socioeconomic group—with the single exceptions of non-whites—favor death for convicted murderers.

One of the most dramatic shifts in opinion has taken place among women. Normally somewhat liberal on social issues, women now are 2-to-1 in favor of the death penalty. In 1972 they were about evenly divided in their views (*Gallup Opinion Index* July 1976:23).

What led to this marked increase in support for the death penalty over such a short period of time? The Gallup report pointed out that the increase coincided with Americans' rapidly rising fear of crime—noting that in a recent study of crime and victimization, nearly half of those polled nationwide said they were fearful of going out after dark in their own neighborhoods (*Gallup Opinion Index*, July 1976:23).

### CAPITAL PUNISHMENT

Question: "Are you in favor of the death penalty for persons convicted of murder?"

April 9–12, 1976

| | Yes | No | No Opinion | Change since 1972 in percent saying "Yes" |
|---|---|---|---|---|
| NATIONAL | 65% | 28% | 7% | +8 |

*Source*: *Gallup Opinion Index* (July 1976), 24. Copyright 1976 by Scholarly Resources Inc. Reprinted by permission of Scholarly Resources Inc.

## DOCUMENT 62: *Gregg v. Georgia* and *Woodson v. North Carolina* (1976)

In 1976, the Supreme Court reviewed five death penalty cases from five states that had enacted new capital punishment laws.[1] Three of the states (Georgia, Florida and Texas) had adopted guided discretion statutes, and two (North Carolina and Louisiana) had adopted mandatory capital punishment statutes. The Court's decisions in these five cases were expected to resolve many unsettled issues regarding the constitutionality of these new laws and of the death penalty itself.

In three 7–2 decisions handed down on July 2, 1976, the Court upheld the new guided discretion statutes of Georgia, Florida and Texas.

Writing for the majority in the lead case of *Gregg v. Georgia* (see Document 62A), Justice Stewart first clarified the Court's position on the basic constitutionality of the death penalty. He went on to point out that thirty-five states and the federal government had established new death penalty laws since the Court's decision in *Furman*. This, he said, argued strongly against the petitioners' claims that due to "evolving standards of decency," the American public would no longer tolerate capital punishment.

With regard to the new Georgia death penalty statute, Stewart pointed out several important procedural reforms: a bifurcated trial with a guilt phase and a penalty phase; statutory factors to help guide jurors' decision making during the penalty phase with regard to both aggravating and mitigating factors; and state appellate court review of all death sentences. These factors were common to all three of the new statutes upheld by the Court and thus seemed to establish guidelines for what the Court would consider constitutional death penalty legislation (Bedau 1977:113; Schwed 1983:151–152).

But while abolitionists had lost a major battle with the Court's decision in *Gregg et al.*, they had not completely lost the war.

In a 5–4 opinion delivered the same day, the Court ruled against both mandatory sentencing statutes. Writing for the majority in the lead case of *Woodson v. North Carolina* (see Document 62C), Justice Stewart explained that historically, mandatory statutes had led juries to acquit guilty defendants deemed not deserving of a death sentence (thus allowing the possibility of arbitrary death sentences), and that mandatory statutes did not allow the sentencing jury to take mitigating circumstances into account. As a result of the Court's decision, about 170 death row prisoners in North Carolina and Louisiana had their sentences commuted to life imprisonment (Schwed 1983:152).

Though still considered somewhat ambiguous (Weisberg 1984:322), the Court's ruling in these five cases gave both the states and Congress a much clearer vision of what types of capital punishment statutes would be considered constitutional (Bedau 1977:115).

## NOTE

1. The cases were *Gregg v. Georgia, Proffitt v. Florida, Jurek v. Texas, Woodson v. North Carolina*, and *Roberts v. Louisiana.*

## A. OPINION OF THE COURT IN *GREGG V. GEORGIA*

Judgment of the Court and opinion of MR. JUSTICE STEWART, MR. JUSTICE POWELL, and MR. JUSTICE STEVENS, announced by MR. JUSTICE STEWART. . . .

### III

. . .

We now hold that the punishment of death does not invariably violate the Constitution. . . .

### C

. . .

The imposition of the death penalty for the crime of murder has a long history of acceptance both in the United States and in England. . . .

It is apparent from the text of the Constitution itself that the existence of capital punishment was accepted by the Framers. At the time the Eighth Amendment was ratified, capital punishment was a common sanction in every State. Indeed, the First Congress of the United States enacted legislation providing death as the penalty for specified crimes. . . .

Four years ago, the petitioners in *Furman* and its companion cases predicated their argument primarily upon the asserted proposition that standards of decency had evolved to the point where capital punishment no longer could be tolerated. The petitioners in those cases said, in effect, that the evolutionary process had come to an end, and that standards of decency required that the Eighth Amendment be construed finally as prohibiting capital punishment for any crime regardless of its depravity and impact on society. This view was accepted by two Justices. Three other Justices were unwilling to go so far; focusing on the procedures by which convicted defendants were selected for the death penalty rather than on the actual punishment inflicted, they joined in the conclusion that the statutes before the Court were constitutionally invalid.

The petitioners in the capital cases before the Court today renew the "standards of decency" argument, but developments during the four years since *Furman* have undercut substantially the assumptions upon which their argument rested. Despite the continuing debate, dating back to the 19th century, over the morality and utility of capital punishment, it is now evident that a large proportion of American society continues to regard it as an appropriate and necessary criminal sanction.

The most marked indication of society's endorsement of the death penalty for murder is the legislative response to *Furman*. The legislatures of at least 35 States have enacted new statutes that provide for the death penalty for at least some crimes that result in the death of another person. And the Congress of the United States, in 1974, enacted a statute providing the death penalty for aircraft piracy that results in death. . . .

As we have seen, however, the Eighth Amendment demands more than that a challenged punishment be acceptable to contemporary society. The Court also must ask whether it comports with the basic concept of human dignity at the core of the Amendment [*Trop v. Dulles*]. . . . Although we cannot "invalidate a category of penalties because we deem less severe penalties adequate to serve the ends of penology" [*Furman v. Georgia*], . . . the sanction imposed cannot be so totally without penological justification that it results in the gratuitous infliction of suffering. . . .

The death penalty is said to serve two principal social purposes: retribution and deterrence of capital crimes by prospective offenders.

In part, capital punishment is an expression of society's moral outrage at particularly offensive conduct. This function may be unappealing to many, but it is essential in an ordered society that asks its citizens to rely on legal processes rather than self-help to vindicate their wrongs. . . .

Statistical attempts to evaluate the worth of the death penalty as a deterrent to crimes by potential offenders have occasioned a great deal of debate. The results simply have been inconclusive. . . .

Finally, we must consider whether the punishment of death is disproportionate in relation to the crime for which it is imposed. . . . But we are concerned here only with the imposition of capital punishment for the crime of murder, and when a life has been taken deliberately by the offender, we cannot say that the punishment is invariably disproportionate to the crime. It is an extreme sanction, suitable to the most extreme of crimes. . . .

## V

The basic concern of *Furman* centered on those defendants who were being condemned to death capriciously and arbitrarily. Under the procedures before the Court in that case, sentencing authorities were not directed to give attention to the nature or circumstances of the crime committed or to the character or record of the defendant. Left unguided, juries imposed the death sentence in a way that could only be called freakish. The new Georgia sentencing procedures, by contrast, focus the jury's attention on the particularized nature of the crime and the particularized characteristics of the individual defendant. While the jury is permitted to consider any aggravating or mitigating circumstances, it must find and identify at least one statutory aggravating factor before it may impose a penalty of death. In this way the jury's discretion is channeled. No longer can a jury wantonly and freakishly impose the death sentence: it is always circumscribed by the legislative guidelines. In addition, the review function of the Supreme Court of Georgia affords additional assurance that the concerns that prompted our decision in *Furman* are not present to any significant degree in the Georgia procedure applied here.

For the reasons expressed in this opinion, we hold that the statutory system under which Gregg was sentenced to death does not violate the Constitution.

## B. DISSENTING OPINION IN *GREGG V. GEORGIA*

MR. JUSTICE BRENNAN, dissenting. . . .

This Court inescapably has the duty, as the ultimate arbiter of the meaning of our Constitution, to say whether, when individuals condemned to death stand before our Bar, "moral concepts" require us to hold that the law has progressed to the point where we should declare that the punishment of death, like punishments on the rack, the screw, and the wheel, is no longer morally tolerable in our civilized society. My opinion in *Furman v. Georgia* concluded that our civilization and the law had progressed to this point and that therefore the punishment of death, for whatever crime and under all circumstances, is "cruel and unusual" in violation of the Eighth and Fourteenth Amendments of the Constitution. I shall not again canvass the reasons that led to that conclusion. I emphasize only that foremost among the "moral concepts" recognized in our cases and inherent in the [Cruel and Unusual Punishments] Clause is the primary moral principle that the State, even as it punishes, must treat its citizens in a manner consistent with their intrinsic worth as human beings—a punishment must not be so severe as to be degrading to human dignity. A judicial determination whether the punishment of death comports with human dignity is therefore not only permitted but compelled by the Clause. . . .

The fatal constitutional infirmity in the punishment of death is that it treats "members of the human race as nonhumans, as objects to be toyed with and discarded. [It is] thus inconsistent with the fundamental premise of the Clause that even the vilest criminal remains a human being possessed of common human dignity." . . . As such it is a penalty that "subjects the individual to a fate forbidden by the principle of civilized treatment guaranteed by the [Clause]." I therefore would hold, on that ground alone, that death is today a cruel and unusual punishment prohibited by the Clause.

*Source*: 428 U.S. 153 (1976), 158–231 (footnotes omitted).

## C. OPINION OF THE COURT IN *WOODSON V. NORTH CAROLINA*

Judgment of the Court, and opinion of MR. JUSTICE STEWART, MR. JUSTICE POWELL, and MR. JUSTICE STEVENS, announced by MR. JUSTICE STEWART . . .

### III

. . .

### A

. . .

[O]ne of the most significant developments in our society's treatment of capital punishment has been the rejection of the common-law practice of inexorably imposing a death sentence upon every person convicted of a specified offense. North Carolina's mandatory death penalty statute for first-degree murder departs markedly from contemporary standards respecting the imposition of the punishment of death and thus cannot be applied consistently with the Eighth and Fourteenth Amendments' requirement that the State's power to punish "be exercised within the limits of civilized standards." . . .

### B

A separate deficiency of North Carolina's mandatory death sentence statute is its failure to provide a constitutionally tolerable response to *Furman's* rejection of unbridled jury discretion in the imposition of capital sentences. . . .

## C

A third constitutional shortcoming of the North Carolina statute is its failure to allow the particularized consideration of relevant aspects of the character and record of each convicted defendant before the imposition upon him of a sentence of death.... A process that accords no significance to relevant facets of the character and record of the individual offender or the circumstances of the particular offense excludes from consideration in fixing the ultimate punishment of death the possibility of compassionate or mitigating factors stemming from the diverse frailties of humankind. It treats all persons convicted of a designated offense not as uniquely individual human beings, but as members of a faceless, undifferentiated mass to be subjected to the blind infliction of the penalty of death....

[T]he penalty of death is qualitatively different from a sentence of imprisonment, however long. Death, in its finality, differs more from life imprisonment than a 100-year prison term differs from one of only a year or two. Because of that qualitative difference, there is a corresponding difference in the need for reliability in the determination that death is the appropriate punishment in a specific case.

For the reasons stated, we conclude that the death sentences imposed upon the petitioners under North Carolina's mandatory death sentence statute violated the Eighth and Fourteenth Amendments and therefore must be set aside.

## D. DISSENTING OPINION IN *WOODSON V. NORTH CAROLINA*

MR. JUSTICE REHNQUIST, dissenting....

I

. . .

The plurality relies first upon its conclusion that society has turned away from the mandatory imposition of death sentences, and second upon its conclusion that the North Carolina system has "simply papered over" the problem of unbridled jury discretion which two of the separate opinions in *Furman* v. *Georgia* . . . identified as the basis for the judgment rendering the death sentences there reviewed unconstitutional. The third "constitutional shortcoming" of the North Carolina statute is said to be "its failure to allow the particularized consideration of relevant aspects of the character and record of each convicted defendant before the imposition upon him of a sentence of death." . . .

I do not believe that any of these reasons singly, or all of them together, can withstand careful analysis. Contrary to the plurality's assertions, they would import into the Cruel and Unusual Punishments Clause procedural requirements which find no support in our cases. Their application will result in the invalidation of a death sentence imposed upon a defendant convicted of first-degree murder under the North Carolina system, and the upholding of the same sentence imposed on an identical defendant convicted on identical evidence of first-degree murder under the Florida, Georgia, or Texas systems—a result surely as "freakish" as that condemned in the separate opinions in *Furman*. . . .

IV

. . .

The plurality also relies upon the indisputable proposition that "death is different." . . . But the respects in which death is "different" from other punishment which may be imposed upon convicted criminals do not seem to me to establish the proposition that the Constitution requires individualized sentencing.

One of the principal reasons why death is different is because it is irreversible; an executed defendant cannot be brought back to life. This aspect of the difference between death and other penalties would undoubtedly support statutory provisions for especially careful review of the fairness of the trial, the accuracy of the factfinding process, and the fairness of the sentencing procedure where the death penalty is imposed. But none of those aspects of the death sentence is at issue here. Petitioners were found guilty of the crime of first-degree murder in a trial the constitutional validity of which is unquestioned here. And since the punishment of death is conceded by the plurality not to be a cruel and unusual punishment for such a crime, the irreversible aspect of the death penalty has no connection whatever with any requirement for individualized consideration of the sentence.

*Source*: 428 U.S. 280 (1976), 282–323 (footnotes omitted).

# Part V

---

# The Debate Begins
# Anew,
# 1977–1989

## EXECUTIONS AND APPEALS RESUME

The post-*Furman* resumption of executions in 1977 marked the beginning of a new era of debate over capital punishment. In the midst of mounting public support for the death penalty, the Supreme Court was inundated with habeas challenges to the new capital laws. These challenges led to a series of decisions that refined legal issues such as what kinds of offenders could be eligible for death sentences and for execution, what types of crimes could be punishable by death, and what kinds of evidence properly could be presented during the penalty phase of trials. As we discuss later, the interminable delays in carrying out capital sentences associated with these challenges also were important.

Some of the cases were "categorical" challenges of the use of the death penalty for crimes such as rape (see Document 64) or against juveniles (Document 86) or for people who were insane or retarded (Documents 76, 88) or were accomplices to felony murder whose roles had been relatively minor (Documents 66, 69). Other appeals attempted to broaden the range of mitigating factors that could—and should—be considered by juries and judges in the sentencing portion of capital trials (Document 70). In deciding in favor of considering more mitigating factors, the Supreme Court increased the possibility for more fully informed sentencing decisions, but it also increased the likelihood of arbitrary death sentences (Paternoster 1991:76–77; Schwed 1983: 164). Substantially less than one out of ten people sentenced to death row were eventually executed, and many abolitionists argued that the difference between them and people who were not killed by the state often had little to do with legitimate aggravating or mitigating factors (Document 68).

In counterpoint to the move to expand the range of relevant mitigating factors, the Court also ruled on the constitutionality of broadening the types of aggravating factors that might be considered during sentencing. Here, however, it held the line more rigidly. On one hand, the Court ruled that prosecutors could introduce psychiatric testimony regarding a defendant's potential future dangerousness—even though such testimony often is unreliable (Document 72). On the other, the Court denied prosecution attempts to introduce victim impact statements, ruling that they were not relevant for determining whether the death penalty should be invoked (Document 78).

## THE BACKLOG OF CAPITAL CASES MOUNTS

Each year from 1977 to 1989, on average, 242 more offenders were sentenced to death while fewer than 10 were executed. As a consequence, the number of prisoners in the United States under sentence of death climbed steadily from 423 in 1977 to 2,250 in 1989 (Maguire and Pastore 1995: table 6.76). By 1994, the last year for which data were available, about 17 percent of the prisoners sentenced to die during this period had had their sentences or convictions overturned on appeal, and 7 percent had been executed.

Increased use of habeas challenges, many of them frivolous or timed so as to trigger last-minute stays of execution, steadily lengthened average death row stays. So did other abolitionist tactics such as petitions for grants of clemency, public demonstrations, and legislative lobbying (Schwed 1983:154). Prisoners executed between 1977 and 1983 spent an average of 51 months on death row after sentencing. By 1989, the average elapsed time from sentence to execution was 95 months (Stephan and Snell 1996: table 11 and Appendix table 1).

These delays frustrated both the public and the courts. By the early 1980s, the Supreme Court's decisions and treatment of applications for stays of execution began to reflect this frustration. Retired Justice Powell, who earlier had played a major role in reshaping capital laws, questioned whether it was in the public interest to retain a punishment that was not being enforced, noting that excessive delays for appellate review—which rarely had to do with questions of innocence—undermined confidence and respect for the criminal justice system (Bodine 1988). He characterized the common practice of manipulating the "malfunctioning" judicial system in order to stall executions as an "abuse of process" that "is unfair to the hundreds of persons confined anxiously on death row" and a disservice to the public interest (White

1987:12). He called on Congress and the courts to either find a speedier way to handle death penalty appeals or abolish capital punishment (Document 71).

Soon after Justice Powell's call for reform of the habeas appeal process, the federal judiciary began expediting its review procedures—a move that could hasten the execution of death row inmates (Documents 72, 77, 112). Abolitionists argued that these expedited procedures failed to provide appellants with sufficient time to research and present their appeals in legal matters that the justices themselves had characterized as "byzantine," "exceedingly complex," and "contradictory" (Acker 1993:65). Routine civil matters might take years to move through the appeals process, but irreversible executions were being expedited. As Welsh S. White noted, this led to a bizarre twist in death penalty law that caused capital defendants "to lose rights rather than gain additional protections" (1987:13), as a series of rulings held that minor imperfections in the deliberative process were no longer sufficient grounds to set aside lower court judgments.

## PUBLIC OPINION SOLIDIFIES

Public support for the death penalty continued to grow in the 1970s and 1980s while public opposition declined (Documents 75 and 84). Nearly twice as many people responding to the Gallup Poll in 1987 favored the death penalty for murder as had in 1967 (Bohm 1991a: 116; Longmire forthcoming). However, the level of support varied substantially within the population; men, whites, Republicans, and those with moderate (as opposed to either high or low) levels of education or who resided in rural areas were significantly more likely to support capital punishment (Bohm 1991a; Longmire forthcoming). According to criminal justice professor Robert Bohm, who has studied public opinion regarding the death penalty extensively, the opinions of both proponents and opponents of the death penalty—although fairly constant—are "not the product of rational deliberation, but, instead, are the result of irrationality, emotion, ritualism, and conformity to reference group pressures" (1991a:137).

Perhaps part of the increase in public opinion in support of the death penalty was a backlash from the social activism of the previous fifteen years. The 1980s seemed in many ways to harken back to post–World War I levels of materialism and self-centeredness. Following President Carter's rather bland progressivism, Americans returned to the politics of influence and money with the election of Ronald Reagan. Baby boomers were beginning to mature. Productivity was up, unemployment was declining, constant dollar prices were down while personal incomes and expenditures were up. In spite of general prosperity, crime rates generally were increasing, although much more slowly than during the previous fifteen years. Thus, another source of public support for capital punishment may have been frustration with the intractability of crime.

After all, most people expect crime to decline during times of prosperity. Yet many people reported during this period that they were afraid to walk alone in areas near their homes at night. And a majority of those polled believed that government spent too little on crime control and that courts were too lenient on criminals. Few reported a great deal of confidence in Congress (see Maguire and Pastore 1995: Chapter 2). In this environment, honing capital statutes became a popular legislative activity.

However, the 1985 Gallup Poll (and subsequent polls) also found that support for capital punishment dropped significantly when life without parole was mentioned as an alternative punishment (Document 75), suggesting to sociologist William Bowers that "[p]erhaps the expressed support they reflect is not a deep-seated or strongly held commitment to capital punishment but actually a reflection of the public's desire for a genuinely harsh but meaningful punishment for convicted murderers" (1993:162).

## LEGISLATION REFINED

Legislative bodies were actively involved in developing new capital statutes and revising existing statutes in response to evolving legal standards and public concerns throughout this period. Revisions to state laws often added factors such as drug-related murders, drug trafficking, and multiple murders to the list of aggravating factors to be considered in the sentencing phase of first-degree murder trials.

The U.S. Congress also was active, adding to federal capital punishment statutes remaining in effect from the pre-*Furman* era. The new federal laws allowed the death penalty for murder associated with continuing criminal enterprises and murder of a law enforcement officer while evading apprehension or imprisonment for a felony (21 USC §848(e)); several categories of espionage relating to vital national defense interests (10 USC §906(a)); and aircraft hijacking resulting in a death (49 USC §§1472 and 1473) (see Greenfield 1990:11).

## RESEARCH CONTINUES

Expanding on the earlier work of Thorsten Sellin (Document 42), Marvin Wolfgang (Document 57), and Isaac Ehrlich (Document 60), researchers continued to shed new light on the deterrent effect of the death penalty, the role of racism in capital cases, and the potential for executing innocent people. As was the case in earlier centuries, the qualitative work of historians, philosophers, and legal scholars continued to contribute to our understanding of capital punishment. Many influential studies were based on newly-developed quantitative techniques that enabled researchers to study issues in a much more complex—and thus realistic—manner.

In 1978, a National Academy of Sciences–commissioned study replicated Ehrlich's results but disputed his interpretation of them, concluding that they were not sufficiently strong to warrant making a judgment about the general deterrent effect of the death penalty (Document 65). Ten years later, sociologist William J. Bowers attempted to assess brutalization effects, an issue that had been the subject of speculation since the Enlightenment. His results suggested that any deterrence associated with executions was more than offset by brutalizing effects (Document 85).

A series of exhaustive studies by David C. Baldus and his associates that began in 1983 carefully examined the role of race in capital cases, finding that significant prosecutorial and jury bias against murderers of whites and against black defendants persisted despite statutory post-*Furman* reforms (Document 74). While acknowledging the quality of these studies, however, the Supreme Court ignored them (see Hanson 1988), ruling that the general tendency toward racial bias in capital cases was not sufficient grounds for black defendants to claim that death penalty convictions violated the Fourteenth Amendment. Instead, each defendant had to demonstrate that race had been a factor in his or her particular case. This was consistent with the Court's general tendency to downplay research results—even when they had direct bearing on the factual issues being considered (Document 79). (See Acker 1993 for a thoughtful review of this issue.) Attempts to enact federal legislation allowing defendants to offer statistical evidence as proof of discrimination in the late 1980s were unsuccessful (Hanson 1988:317).

Bedau and Radelet's examination of capital cases over an 85-year period (Document 82) provided support for the abolitionist contention that the execution of innocent people was more than a hypothetical issue. They identified 350 people out of 7,000 cases who had been wrongfully convicted in capital or potentially capital cases—23 of whom actually were executed. Other researchers, even though questioning some of Bedau and Radelet's cases, interpreted their results as indicating that the contemporary justice system is sufficiently accurate so as to be employed in good conscience (Document 83).

Another study during this period took advantage of the opportunity for a natural experiment presented by the release of over 600 death row inmates subsequent to the *Furman* decision. James W. Marquart and Jonathan R. Sorensen (Document 89) examined the fundamental necessity of the death penalty by examining the behavior of former death row inmates who had been released into general prison populations, some of whom eventually had been paroled. Their findings suggested that it was unacceptable to use capital punishment to incapacitate convicted offenders because most of those released from death row did not represent a significant threat to society—and it was not possible to distinguish the few who did from the rest.

## DOCUMENT 63: The Execution of Gary Gilmore (1977)

The ten-year moratorium on executions in the United States ended on January 17, 1977, with the "voluntary" execution of convicted murderer Gary Mark Gilmore in Utah.

Gilmore was convicted and sentenced to death for killing a motel night clerk during a robbery just months after being paroled from prison in April of 1976. He refused to appeal his sentence at a post-trial hearing held November 1, 1976. "I believe I was given a fair trial, and I think the sentence was proper, and I'm willing to accept it like a man and wish it to be carried out without delay," Gilmore contended, according to a November 11, 1976 *New York Times* article (quoted in Schwed 1983:155).

Although Gilmore dismissed his lawyers shortly after the post-trial hearing, they filed an appeal on his behalf with the Utah Supreme Court. Despite his written protests to the court, Gilmore then received two consecutive stays of execution—one from the Utah court and one from the Governor (Tushnet 1994:96).

After meeting to discuss the case, the state Board of Pardons refused to extend the Governor's stay, and Gilmore's execution was rescheduled for December 6. At that point, Gilmore's mother, Bessie, assisted by the American Civil Liberties Union, sought a stay of execution for her son from the U.S. Supreme Court (Tushnet 1994:96–97).

The Court granted a temporary stay on December 3 in order to receive and review transcripts of the case from the Utah courts and the Board of Pardons. After reviewing those documents—and Bessie Gilmore's questionable right to challenge her son's death penalty against his wishes—the Court ruled in a 5–4 decision to lift its temporary stay.

Gilmore, who had attempted suicide twice during the months in which the court battles ensued, was executed by firing squad on the morning of January 17, 1977. His last words were "Let's do it" (*Associated Press*, Jan. 17, 1977).

Although Gilmore's execution provoked an immediate reaction from capital punishment opponents, it was not expected to have much legal impact on the 358 other convicts who remained on death rows nationwide at the time. For those who chose not to waive their appeal rights, the court battles most likely would continue for years to come.

## A. CONCURRING OPINION OF CHIEF JUSTICE BURGER

MR. CHIEF JUSTICE BURGER, with whom MR. JUSTICE POWELL joins, concurring. . . .

After examining with care the pertinent portions of the transcripts and reports of state proceedings, and the response of Gary Mark Gilmore filed on December 8, I am in complete agreement with the conclusion expressed in the Court's order that Gary Mark Gilmore knowingly and intelligently, with full knowledge of his right to seek an appeal in the Utah Supreme Court, has waived that right. I further agree that the State's determinations of his competence to waive his rights knowingly and intelligently were firmly grounded.

When the record establishing a knowing and intelligent waiver of Gary Mark Gilmore's right to seek appellate review is combined with the December 8 written response submitted to this Court, it is plain that the Court is without jurisdiction to entertain the "next friend" application filed by Bessie Gilmore. This Court has jurisdiction pursuant to Art. III of the Constitution only over "cases and controversies," and we can issue stays only in aid of our jurisdiction. . . . There is no dispute, presently before us, between Gary Mark Gilmore and the State of Utah, and the application of Bessie Gilmore manifestly fails to meet the statutory requirements to invoke this Court's power to review the action of the Supreme Court of Utah. No authority to the contrary has been brought to our attention, and nothing suggested in dissent bears on the threshold question of jurisdiction.

In his dissenting opinion, MR. JUSTICE WHITE suggests that Gary Mark Gilmore is "unable" as a matter of law to waive the right to state appellate review. Whatever may be said as to the merits of this suggestion, the question simply is not before us. Gilmore, duly found to be competent by the Utah courts, has had available meaningful access to this Court and has declined expressly to assert any claim here other than his explicit repudiation of Bessie Gilmore's effort to speak for him as next friend. It follows, therefore, that the Court is without jurisdiction to consider the question posed by the dissent.

## B. DISSENTING OPINION

MR. JUSTICE MARSHALL, dissenting.

I fully agree with my Brother WHITE that a criminal defendant has no power to agree to be executed under an unconstitutional statute. I believe that the Eighth Amendment not only protects the right of individuals not to be victims of cruel and unusual punishment, but that it also expresses a fundamental interest of society in ensuring that state authority is not used to administer barbaric punishments. Irrespective of this, however, I cannot agree with the view expressed by THE CHIEF JUSTICE that Gilmore has competently, knowingly, and intelligently decided to let himself be killed. Less than five months have passed since the commission of the crime; just over two months have elapsed since sentence was imposed. That is hardly sufficient time for mature consideration of the question, nor does Gilmore's erratic behavior—from his suicide attempt to his state habeas petition—evidence such deliberation. No adversary hearing has been held to examine the experts, all employed by the State of Utah, who have pronounced Gilmore sane. The decision of the Utah Supreme Court finding a valid waiver can be given little weight. In the transcripts that the court prepared for us, it omitted a portion of its proceedings as having "no pertinency" to the issue of Gilmore's "having voluntarily and intelligently waived his right to appeal." That "irrelevant" portion involved a discussion by Gilmore's trial counsel of his opinion of Gilmore's competence and the constitutionality of the Utah statute. It is appalling that any court could consider these questions irrelevant to that determination. It is equally shocking that the Utah court, in a matter of such importance, failed even to have a court reporter present to transcribe the proceeding, instead relying on recordings made by dictating machines which have produced a partly unintelligible record. These inexplicable actions by a court charged with life or death responsibility underscore the failure of the State to determine adequately the validity of Gilmore's purported waiver and the propriety of imposing capital punishment.

*Source*: 429 U.S. 1012 (1976), 1013–1020 (footnotes omitted).

---

## DOCUMENT 64: *Coker v. Georgia* (1977)

Unlike Gary Gilmore (see Document 63), most convicts on death row did not object to appealing their sentences. With the assistance of lawyers from the ACLU, the LDF, and others, hundreds of capital cases went to court in the years following the Supreme Court's decision in *Gregg* (Epstein and Kobylka 1992:117).

Among these were several "categorical" challenges to the new state death penalty statutes in which defendants argued that "under no circumstances could people like them be executed" (Tushnet 1994:73).

The 1977 case of *Coker v. Georgia* was the first such challenge to be heard by the Supreme Court. The petitioner in the case—who had been convicted of rape and sentenced to death under the new Georgia statute approved in *Gregg*—claimed that execution was an excessive punishment for rape and therefore was unconstitutional under the Eighth Amendment.

In a 6–2–1 decision,[1] the Court agreed with the petitioner, ruling that the death penalty was excessive and disproportionate punishment for the rape of an adult woman whose life was not taken.

Since Georgia was the only state that had reinstated the death penalty for the rape of an adult, only a few prisoners were resentenced as a result of the Court's ruling in *Coker*. However, because it further narrowed the scope of the death penalty, *Coker* was considered an important victory for abolitionists (Schwed 1983:160). It seemed likely that from that point on, the death penalty would be considered unconstitutional for any crime that did not involve the deliberate taking of human life (Paternoster 1991:101).

**NOTE**

1.  Chief Justice Burger and Justice Rehnquist dissented, while Justice Powell concurred in part and dissented in part.

## A. OPINION OF THE COURT

MR. JUSTICE WHITE announced the judgment of the Court and filed an opinion in which MR. JUSTICE STEWART, MR. JUSTICE BLACKMUN, and MR. JUSTICE STEVENS, joined. . . .

IV.

. . .

We do not discount the seriousness of rape as a crime. It is highly reprehensible, both in a moral sense and in its almost total contempt for the personal integrity and autonomy of the female victim and for the latter's privilege of choosing those with whom intimate relationships are to be established. Short of homicide, it is the "ultimate violation of self." . . . It is also a violent crime because it normally involves force, or the threat of force or intimidation, to overcome the will and the capacity of the victim to resist. Rape is very often accompanied by physical injury to the female and can also inflict mental and psychological damage. . . . Because it undermines the community's sense of security, there is public injury as well.

Rape is without doubt deserving of serious punishment; but in terms of moral depravity and of the injury to the person and to the public, it does not compare with murder, which does involve the unjustified taking of human life. Although it may be accompanied by another crime, rape by definition does not include the death of or even the serious injury to another person. The murderer kills; the rapist, if no more than that, does not. Life is over for the victim of the murderer; for the rape victim, life may not be nearly so happy as it was, but it is not over and normally is not beyond repair. We have the abiding conviction that the death penalty, which "is unique in its severity and irrevocability," [*Gregg* v. *Georgia*] . . . is an excessive penalty for the rapist who, as such, does not take human life.

## B. DISSENTING OPINION

MR. CHIEF JUSTICE BURGER, with whom MR. JUSTICE REHNQUIST joins, dissenting. . . .

(3)

. . .

(b)

. . .

The clear implication of today's holding appears to be that the death penalty may be properly imposed only as to crimes resulting in death of the victim. This casts serious doubt upon the constitutional validity of statutes imposing the death penalty for a variety of conduct which, though dangerous, may not necessarily result in any immediate death, *e.g.*, treason, airplane hijacking, and kidnaping. In that respect, today's holding does even more harm than is initially apparent. We cannot avoid taking judicial notice that crimes such as airplane hijacking, kidnaping, and mass terrorist activity constitute a serious and increasing danger to the safety of the public. It would be unfortunate indeed if the effect of today's holding were to inhibit States and the Federal Government from experimenting with various remedies—including possibly imposition of the penalty of death—to prevent and deter such crimes.

*Source*: 433 U.S. 584 (1977), 586–621 (footnotes omitted).

---

## DOCUMENT 65: The Deterrence Controversy (1977–1978)

The efficacy of capital punishment as a deterrent to murder—an issue that had received widespread attention as a result of economist

Isaac Ehrlich's 1975 study (see Document 60)—was one of the topics addressed by the National Academy of Sciences' Panel on Deterrence and Incapacitation.[1] The goal of the panel was to provide "an objective technical assessment of the available studies of the deterrent and incapacitative effects of sanctions on crime rates" (Zimring and Hawkins 1986:179).

As part of its investigation of the deterrent and incapacitative effects of criminal sanctions, the panel commissioned several papers, including "The Deterrent Effect of Capital Punishment: An Assessment of the Estimates" by Nobel Prize–winning economist Lawrence Klein, the Benjamin Franklin Professor of Economics and Finance at the University of Pennsylvania; Brian Forst, director of research at the Institute for Law and Social Research in Washington, D.C.; and University of Pennsylvania graduate student Victor Filatov (Document 65A).

Klein and his colleagues focused primarily on Ehrlich's 1975 finding of a deterrent effect for capital punishment—a finding other researchers had tried and failed to replicate fully using their own data sets. Using Ehrlich's data set, which he provided to one of the researchers, Klein et al. were able to replicate Ehrlich's findings. However, although they applauded Ehrlich and others for "opening up a fascinating area of research," they noted several problems with his research methods and conclusions that led them to conclude that "Ehrlich's results cannot be used at this time to pass judgment on the use of the death penalty" (Klein et al. 1978:358–359).

In its 1978 report "Deterrence and Incapacitation: Estimating the Effects of Criminal Sanctions on Crime Rates" (Document 65B), the NAS panel went a step further. It not only concluded that "the results of the analyses on capital punishment provide no useful evidence on the deterrent effect of capital punishment," but added that "we are skeptical that the death penalty, so long as it is used relatively rarely, can ever be subjected to the kind of statistical analysis that would validly establish the presence or absence of a deterrent effect" (Blumstein et al. 1978:62).

In a June 1977 article (Document 65C), Ehrlich responded to a draft of the NAS panel's report, strongly disagreeing with the conclusions of both Klein et al. and the panel. In the article, Ehrlich noted that Klein et al. had been able to replicate his results and that they had found no substantive errors in his research. He also discussed in detail several technical errors in their reanalysis of his data. With regard to the NAS panel itself, Ehrlich contended that "the authors were not so much interested in rational and objective evaluation of the empirical evidence on deterrence as they were intent on showing that evidence to be defective" (Ehrlich and Mark 1977:311).

Numerous studies on the issue of the potential deterrent value of the death penalty since have been conducted. Several studies using data from the United States, England, and Canada have confirmed Ehrlich's findings (Ehrlich 1977b; Layson 1983, 1985; Phillips and Ray 1982; Wolpin 1978; also see Ehrlich 1996), while others have found that homicide rates are more likely to fall than rise following abolition of capital punishment (Archer and Gartner 1984; Fattah 1972), that the "brutalization" effect of executions is greater than the deterrent effect (Bowers 1988, see Document 85), and that televised execution publicity appears to have neither a deterrent nor a brutalization effect on homicides (Bailey 1990, see Document 92). Research on this controversial subject continues.

## NOTE

1. Chairman of the panel was Alfred Blumstein, School of Urban and Public Affairs, Carnegie-Mellon University. Other members of the panel were Franklin M. Fisher, Department of Economics, Massachusetts Institute of Technology; Gary G. Koch, Department of Biostatistics, School of Public Health, University of North Carolina, Chapel Hill; Paul E. Meehl, Department of Psychology, University of Minnesota; Albert J. Reiss, Jr., Department of Sociology, Yale University; James Q. Wilson, John Fitzgerald Kennedy School and Department of Government, Harvard University; Marvin E. Wolfgang, Center for Studies in Criminology and Criminal Law, University of Pennsylvania; Franklin E. Zimring, Department of Law and The Center for Studies in Criminal Justice, University of Chicago; and Samuel Krislov, Department of Political Science, University of Minnesota.

## A. EXCERPTS FROM THE NAS-COMMISSIONED PAPER BY KLEIN ET AL.

The building and use of statistical models of structural relationships in the field of criminal behavior, human capital, and the broader interface between sociological and economic relationships is in its infancy. Many results look very promising, suggestive, and provocative. We might well classify this research effort as being at the stage that econometric modeling reached in the 1940's and 1950's. A great deal of further painstaking developmental work was necessary to build up econometrics to the point at which the numerical findings ceased to be just interesting from an academic viewpoint and became applicable in public policy analysis. We believe that current results must undergo the same kind of testing and scholarly scrutiny over a period of years before they are ready to be used in an application as serious as the one that is associated with the use of the death penalty.

In the first instance, application might be made to general questions of public policy in the field of criminology—such questions as budgetary allocations for police work, deployment of police personnel, or use of training programs. But it seems unthinkable to us to base decisions on the use of the death penalty on Ehrlich's findings, as the Solicitor General of the United States has urged. . . . They simply are not sufficiently powerful, robust, or tested at this stage to warrant use in such an important case. They are as fragile as the most tentative of econometric estimates of parameters, and we know full well how uncertain such results are under extrapolation. It is not that Ehrlich's estimates are demonstrably wrong; it is merely that they are too uncertain and must, at best, be interpreted as tentative at this stage.

There is nothing wrong with Ehrlich's particular numerical findings. His arithmetic is correct; his formulation is imaginative; but application to the most serious of issues is premature. In short, we see too many plausible explanations for his finding a deterrent effect other than the theory that capital punishment deters murder. . . .

Sellin, Ehrlich, Passell, and others are to be congratulated on opening up a fascinating area of research with much scholarly potential. It remains to pursue this line of research to the point at which it can be used in the future for making important contributions to legal policy. The deterrent effect of capital punishment is definitely not a settled matter, and this is the strongest social scientific conclusion that can be reached at the present time.

*Source*: Lawrence R. Klein, Brian Forst, and Victor Filatov, "The Deterrent Effect of Capital Punishment: An Assessment of the Estimates." In Alfred Blumstein, Jacqueline Cohen, and Daniel Nagin, eds., *Deterrence and Incapacitation: Estimating the Effects of Criminal Sanctions on Crime Rates* (Washington, D.C.: National Academy of Sciences, 1978), 357–359.

## B. EXCERPTS FROM THE NAS PANEL'S REPORT

Ehrlich . . . , using time-series data for 1933–1969 in which homicides and executions were aggregated for the entire United States, reports a deterrent effect for executions. There have been a number of reanalyses of data equivalent to that used by Ehrlich. All of these reanalyses have shown that Ehrlich's findings are sensitive to minor technical variations in the analysis. These variations include changes in the mathematical form of the relationship of homicide rates to their determinants (*e.g.*, a multiplicative form compared to a linear one) and the variables included as determinants of homicide (*e.g.*, including the aggregate crime index as a determinant). These reanalyses either reversed the direction of the presumed effect or greatly reduced its magnitude.

The most striking sensitivity of Ehrlich's findings is to the time period over which the analysis is conducted. No negative association is found for 1933–1961, so that the results are determined by the effect in 1962–1969. But during those eight years, *all* crime rates rose dramatically, and the frequency of executions declined (and had ceased by 1968). Thus, to conclude that a deterrent effect exists, one must assume that the steady rise in homicides over this eight-year period was caused at least in part by the decline in executions and that the trends in executions and in homicides were not generated either independently or by some common third cause, which might also account for the rise in other crimes. If one makes these assumptions, statistical analyses contribute no further information to the test of the deterrence hypothesis. Moreover, the failure to discern any deterrent effect in the earlier 1933–1961 period, when there was more fluctuation in both homicide and execution rates, still remains unexplained.

In summary, the flaws in the null-effect results and the sensitivity of the Ehrlich results to minor variations in model specification and their serious temporal instability lead the Panel to conclude that the results of the analyses on capital punishment provide no useful evidence on the deterrent effect of capital punishment.

Our conclusion should not be interpreted as meaning that capital punishment does not have a deterrent effect, but rather that there is currently no evidence for determining whether it does have a deterrent effect. Furthermore, we are skeptical that the death penalty, so long as it is used relatively rarely, can ever be subjected to the kind of statistical analysis that would validly establish the presence or absence of a deterrent effect.

Our conclusion on the current evidence does not imply that capital punishment should or should not be imposed. The deterrent effect of capital punishment and its magnitude reflect only one aspect of the many considerations involved in the choice of the use of the death penalty. Those considerations include issues related to the value of human life, the moral justification of killing by government, and the appropriate form of public outrage at heinous crimes—all of which are likely to dominate policy decisions in comparison to inevitably crude estimates of the deterrent effects.

*Source*: Alfred Blumstein, Jacqueline Cohen, and Daniel Nagin, eds., *Deterrence and Incapacitation: Estimating the Effects of Criminal Sanctions on Crime Rates* (Washington, D.C.: National Academy of Sciences, 1978), 61–62 (footnotes omitted).

## C. EXCERPTS FROM EHRLICH'S REBUTTAL TO THE NAS PANEL'S REPORT

Given the prominence of my research in the Report of the Panel, it appears appropriate that I reply to the substance of the criticism. . . .

Before examining the analytical issues in detail, a remark on the composition of the Panel seems appropriate. While the methodological advances in recent research on deterrence have, to a considerable extent, come from work by economists, and while studies following the economic approach are a major focus of the Panel's work, not a single practitioner of the economic approach to crime is to be found among the Panel's interdisciplinary roster of members. In contrast, the Panel does include scholars who have pursued approaches in criminology that are seriously challenged by the economic approach and whose past work exhibits considerable skepticism, if not philosophical hostility, toward the deterrence hypothesis. These comments are not intended, of course, to impugn the intellectual integrity of these respected scholars, nor to question the desirability of having their views represented. However, the imbalanced composition of the Panel may be partly responsible for the shortcomings of its work and conclusions, which are elaborated in the following sections. . . .

Despite its own recognition that the evidence from the empirical studies of the deterrence hypothesis clearly leans toward a proposition supporting deterrence, the panel admits to a reluctance to "assert that the evidence warrants an affirmative conclusion regarding deterrence." That results based on observational statistics, as opposed to truly "controlled" experiments, cannot constitute a proof for any proposition is, of course, well recognized in statistical literature as well as in careful studies of the deterrence hypothesis. Hardly any empirical study in the behavioral sciences is immune to this basic limitation. However, the Panel's reticence in properly recognizing the preponderance of the accumulated evidence apparently derives primarily from those reviewers' arguments addressed in the preceding section: possible measurement errors, "missing" variables, and an identification bias. Yet, as particularly points 2, 3, 4, 5, and 7 of Section II.A and points 1–6 in Section II.B have demonstrated, the arguments are variously sciolistic, selectively advanced, and, almost invariably, speculative.

In maintaining steadfast pessimism regarding the accumulated evidence, and even the prospects for future research, the Panel ignores the most basic, albeit unhighlighted, conclusions arising from its commissioned reanalysis and surveys. Most fundamentally, the surveys challenge neither the propriety of the theoretical structure underlying the economic approach to crime nor the general statistical methodology used to implement the theory against available data. Moreover, the reanalyses replicate to a high degree previously published results and attest to numerical accuracy of the computations and of the data. In other words, the Panel's extensive investigations of studies pursuing the economic approach reveal no substantive errors in research that has applied, in the Panel's words, "complex" scientific methods and that has, by implication, exhibited at the very least conventional care in derivations of the results.

Thus, the Panel's reservations toward the reported findings of apparent deterrent effects stem not from any mistakes uncovered or from any fundamental methodological disagreements but instead are founded upon various conjectures—a level of criticism quite different in kind. Indeed, the impression derived from the entire document of the Panel is that the authors were not so much interested in rational and objective evaluation of the empirical evidence on deterrence as they were intent on showing that evidence to be defective. While the specific interpretations of statistical findings may quite rightly become the object of scholarly dispute, none of the work of the Panel and its commissioned papers attempts to provide a systematic and comprehensive alternative explanation for the amalgam of cross-sectional and time series evidence consistent with the deterrence hypothesis. It seems inappropriate that evidence consistent with a set of detailed behavioral propositions emanating from a theory that also has proven useful in explaining a variety of other expressions of human behavior is hardly given equal weight to a set of speculations and some ad hoc behavioral propositions which do not derive from logical principles of general applicability.

Inescapably, a review of the sort undertaken by the Panel begs the question of who is to review the reviewers. On the one level, the Panel must shoulder responsibility for the scholarship of the papers commissioned and, of course, those by its staff and members. The control brought to bear by the Panel as a scientific review board is open to serious questions when these papers present largely irrelevant exercises as substantive, accept uncritically those findings denying deterrence while viewing those supporting deterrence as inherently suspicious, cite patently erroneous exercises as informative, and present published work incompletely and inaccurately, while referring repeatedly to previous work by Panel members, staff, and contributors as particularly instructive.

*Source*: Isaac Ehrlich (in cooperation with Randall Mark), "Fear of Deterrence: A Critical Evaluation of the 'Report of the Panel on Research on Deterrent and Incapacitative Effects,'" *Journal of Legal Studies* VI (June 1977), 294–295, 310–312.

## DOCUMENT 66: *Lockett v. Ohio* (1978)

In the years that followed *Gregg* (see Document 62), the Supreme Court not only narrowed the scope of capital crimes (see Document

64), it also broadened the range of mitigating factors that could be introduced in a capital trial.

In the 1978 case of *Lockett v. Ohio*, 21-year-old Sandra Lockett had driven the getaway car during an armed robbery in which a pawnshop owner was shot and killed by one of her accomplices. While the gunman had plea-bargained for a prison sentence, Lockett had refused to do so. She stood trial and was convicted and sentenced to death under Ohio's aiding-and-abetting statute.

Ohio's new capital punishment law required the death penalty for defendants convicted of capital murder unless the sentencing judge found evidence of at least one of three mitigating circumstances: that the victim had somehow induced the murder; that the defendant was under duress, coercion, or strong provocation; or that the defendant's offense was the product of psychosis or mental deficiency (Schwed 1983:162). None of these three factors applied in Lockett's case, and the fact that she had not actually committed the murder or even been at the scene when the shot was fired had not been considered an allowable mitigating circumstance under the Ohio law.[1]

Upon hearing the case, the Supreme Court reversed Lockett's death sentence and struck down Ohio's capital statute as unconstitutional, explaining that in a capital case, the jury must be allowed to consider the full spectrum of mitigating circumstances.

As a result of the Court's ruling, approximately one hundred Ohio death row inmates were resentenced. In addition, it appeared that only nine of the thirty-three states that had reinstituted the death penalty since *Furman* had statutes that would meet the Court's new requirements for mitigating circumstances (Schwed 1983:163–164).

The ruling was considered another major victory for abolitionists because it would allow a defendant to present all pertinent mitigating factors to the jury for consideration, and also was likely to give the jury greater discretion to vote against the death penalty. However, in giving juries stronger discretionary power in sentencing, it also increased the likelihood of arbitrary death sentences—the very problem the Court had tried to solve in *Furman* (Paternoster 1991:76–77; Schwed 1983: 164).

## NOTE

1. Four years later, the Supreme Court would rule that the death penalty was excessive punishment for those whose participation in a felony murder was minor and who did not kill or have intent to kill (see Document 69, *Enmund v. Florida*, 1982).

## A. OPINION OF THE COURT

MR. CHIEF JUSTICE BURGER delivered the opinion of the Court. . . .

[T]he Eighth and Fourteenth Amendments require that the sentencer, in all but the rarest kind of capital case, not be precluded from considering, *as a mitigating factor*, any aspect of a defendant's character or record and any of the circumstances of the offense that the defendant proffers as a basis for a sentence less than death. We recognize that, in noncapital cases, the established practice of individualized sentences rests not on constitutional commands, but on public policy enacted into statutes. The considerations that account for the wide acceptance of individualization of sentences in noncapital cases surely cannot be thought less important in capital cases. Given that the imposition of death by public authority is so profoundly different from all other penalties, we cannot avoid the conclusion that an individualized decision is essential in capital cases. The need for treating each defendant in a capital case with that degree of respect due the uniqueness of the individual is far more important than in noncapital cases. A variety of flexible techniques—probation, parole, work furloughs, to name a few—and various postconviction remedies may be available to modify an initial sentence of confinement in noncapital cases. The nonavailability of corrective or modifying mechanisms with respect to an executed capital sentence underscores the need for individualized consideration as a constitutional requirement in imposing the death sentence.

There is no perfect procedure for deciding in which cases governmental authority should be used to impose death. But a statute that prevents the sentencer in all capital cases from giving independent mitigating weight to aspects of the defendant's character and record and to circumstances of the offense proffered in mitigation creates the risk that the death penalty will be imposed in spite of factors which may call for a less severe penalty. When the choice is between life and death, that risk is unacceptable and incompatible with the commands of the Eighth and Fourteenth Amendments.

## B. DISSENTING OPINION

MR. JUSTICE REHNQUIST . . . dissenting in part. . . .

If a defendant as a matter of constitutional law is to be permitted to offer as evidence in the sentencing hearing any fact, however bizarre, which he wishes, even though the most sympathetically disposed trial judge could conceive of no basis upon which the jury might take it into account in imposing a sentence, the new constitutional doctrine will not eliminate arbitrariness or freakishness in the imposition of sentences, but will codify and institutionalize it. By encouraging defendants in capital cases, and presumably sentencing judges and juries, to take into consideration anything under the sun as a "mitigating circumstance," it will not guide sentencing discretion but will totally unleash it.

*Source*: 438 U.S. 602 (1978), 589–631 (footnotes omitted).

---

## DOCUMENT 67: *For Capital Punishment* (Walter Berns, 1979)

One of the most vociferous proponents of the death penalty in the 1970s was political theorist Walter Berns (1919–   ), then the John M. Olin Professor at Georgetown University in Washington, D.C., and an adjunct scholar at the American Enterprise Institute.

In his 1979 book *For Capital Punishment: Crime and the Morality of the Death Penalty*, Berns criticized the modern penal system for placing too much emphasis on rehabilitation and deterrence, rather than on punishment. He went on to argue that Americans are entitled to "demand that criminals be paid back, and that the worst of them be made to pay back with their lives" (Berns 1979:189).

As one reviewer of the book explained, "The nub of Walter Berns's argument . . . is that the awesomeness of the death penalty reflects the horror of murder, and paradoxically, endorses the sanctity of life. In author Berns's words, the death penalty 'serves to remind us of the majesty of the moral order'; its purpose is not primarily to deter but to enact justice and assuage the public anger that demands it" (Gardner 1979:120).

Although Berns was commended by some for offering "a calm and reasoned case for inflicting the death penalty for certain crimes" (Canavan 1979:1042), his retributivist theory also received heavy criticism, from both abolitionists and retentionists alike.

For example, well-known retentionist Ernest van den Haag (see Document 59) said, "I, too, am for capital punishment. But I find Berns' compilation careless and too often confused. . . . Berns could not be expected to solve the basic problems of deontological retributionism which have puzzled political philosophers for centuries. But he could have met them. Rhetoric—conservative or liberal—is of no help" (van den Haag 1982:40–41).

Capital punishment, like Shakespeare's dramatic and Lincoln's political poetry (and it is surely that, and was understood by him to be that) serves to remind us of the majesty of the moral order that is embodied in our law and of the terrible consequences of its breach. The law must not be understood to be merely statute that we enact or repeal at our will and obey or disobey at our convenience, especially not the criminal law. Wherever law is regarded as merely statutory, men will soon enough disobey it, and they will learn how to do so without any inconvenience to themselves. The criminal law must possess a dignity far beyond that possessed by mere statutory enactment or utilitarian and self-interested calculations; the most powerful means we have to give it that dignity is to authorize it to impose the ultimate penalty. The criminal law must be made awful, by which I mean, awe-inspiring, or commanding "profound respect or reverential fear." It must remind us of the moral order by which alone we can live as *human* beings, and in our day the only punishment that can do this is capital punishment.

*Source*: Walter Berns, *For Capital Punishment: Crime and the Morality of the Death Penalty* (New York: Basic Books, 1979), 172–173.

## DOCUMENT 68: The Execution of John Spenkelink[1] (1979)

On May 25, 1979, John Arthur Spenkelink became the second person to be executed since the Supreme Court had deemed certain types of guided-discretion death penalty statutes constitutional in *Gregg* (see Document 62), and the first to be put to death against his will since the 1967 execution of Aaron Mitchell in Colorado (Schwed 1983:166).

Spenkelink, an escaped felon, had been sentenced to death for the murder of a fellow drifter and ex-con, Joseph Szymankiewicz. Szymankiewicz, whom Spenkelink had picked up hitchhiking in Nebraska, had raped Spenkelink, forced him to play Russian roulette, and stolen his money on the trip from Nebraska to Tallahassee, Florida. Bent on retrieving his money, the 24-year-old Spenkelink had shot and killed Szymankiewicz while he slept in their Tallahassee motel room.

Unlike Gary Gilmore, who practically had demanded to be executed in 1977, Spenkelink fought his death sentence tooth and nail—through seven years of court battles, habeas corpus petitions and clemency pleas. The U.S. Supreme Court denied certiorari in the case, the federal appeals courts upheld Spenkelink's sentence, and the governor of Florida denied clemency in the case (Schwed 1983:165; Tushnet 1994: 100).

Eventually, Supreme Court Justice Thurgood Marshall granted a stay of execution so the Court could consider Spenkelink's case. Elbert Tuttle, a Federal district judge, also granted a stay. However, on May 24, 1979, both stays were vacated, and the execution was permitted to proceed (Tushnet 1994:100–101).

Abolitionists, who denounced the execution as "official homicide," pointed out that Spenkelink's crime was no worse than that of many others who had not received the death penalty. Hence they contended that despite the new death penalty legislation enacted since *Furman*, capital punishment still was being applied arbitrarily and therefore still was unconstitutional.

**NOTE**

1. Although many state and federal courts spelled Spenkelink's surname "Spinkellink" (see *Spinkellink v. Wainwright*, 578 F.2d (1978)), the correct spelling, according to a footnote to *Spinkellink v. Wainwright* that cites the petitioner's brief, is "Spenkelink."

Opponents of capital punishment reacted with anger and bitterness to yesterday's execution of John A. Spenkelink. Several protests were staged around the country, including one outside the Supreme Court in Washington, where 13 demonstrators were arrested.

"Thou shalt not kill, thou shalt not kill," the protesters chanted. They went limp and had to be dragged into the small police station on the court's ground floor. It is against the law to demonstrate on Supreme Court property.

The execution was the first in the United States since Gary Mark Gilmore, who asked to die, faced a firing squad in Utah on Jan. 17, 1977, and only the second in the last dozen years.

According to an Associated Press check, there are 531 inmates on Death Rows around the country. In the vast majority of these cases, legal remedies are far from being exhausted.

### Execution Called 'Homicide'

"The official homicide of John Spenkelink this morning is a constitutional, legal, social and human outrage," said Henry Schwartzchild [*sic*], director of the American Civil Liberties Union's capital punishment project. Mr. Schwartzchild [*sic*] said he did not expect executions to take place quickly or in great quantity.

Jack Greenberg, director-counsel of the NAACP Legal Defense and Educational Fund Inc., suggested that starting in a year or two there might be 10 to 20 executions at the same level as in the early 1960's.

According to the legal defense fund's figures, slightly less than half of the Death Row inmates are black or have Spanish surnames. More are in Florida, the site of Mr. Spenkelink's execution, than in any other state.

More than 30 other states have death penalty statutes, but most inmates sentenced to death are concentrated in Southern states. Texas has 122 inmates on Death Row, and Georgia follows with 68. . . .

Ira Glasser, A.C.L.U. executive director, said yesterday that he viewed Mr. Spenkelink's death as a "human sacrifice," a phrase that was used yesterday by several opponents of capital punishment.

Both Mr. Glasser and Mr. Greenberg of the NAACP fund stressed that the nature of Mr. Spenkelink's crime suggested that the death penalty could never be equitably applied. Therefore, they said, it was unconstitutional.

Mr. Spenkelink admitted shooting a man, but he maintained that the slaying had been in self-defense. A second man charged in the slaying cooperated with the prosecution and was freed.

"Spenkelink's crime was no worse that [sic] tens of thousands for which lesser penalties regularly are imposed," said Mr. Greenberg. "It was committed against a man who sodomized and violently assaulted him. Spenkelink's accomplice now freely walks the streets; the deliberate murderer of San Francisco's Mayor was this week sentenced to five years."

Source: Tom Goldstein, "Death Penalty Opponents Embittered by Execution," New York Times, May 26, 1979.

## DOCUMENT 69: *Enmund v. Florida* (1982)

In 1982, the Supreme Court issued a ruling in yet another categorical challenge to the death penalty that further narrowed its scope.

On April 1, 1975, Earl Enmund drove the getaway car for two accomplices—Jeanette and Sampson Armstrong—during a robbery in which an elderly couple was shot and killed in front of their home by one or both of the Armstrongs.

Under Florida's felony-murder statute, Enmund and both Armstrongs were indicted for first-degree murder and robbery. The statute, which considered any homicide committed during the course of another felony (such as robbery) to be first-degree murder, also considered aiders and abettors such as Enmund to be equally responsible for the crimes (Paternoster 1991:102; Tushnet 1994:74).

Enmund and Sampson Armstrong were tried together, and both were sentenced to death. Enmund appealed his death sentence to the U.S. Supreme Court on the ground that it was unconstitutionally disproportionate to his crime, since he had not taken life, attempted to take life, nor intended to take life.

The Court agreed, ruling in a 5–4 decision that the death penalty was excessive punishment for Enmund and others like him whose participation in a felony murder was minor and who did not kill or have intent to kill.

As in *Coker v. Georgia* (see Document 64) and other previous categorical challenges to the death penalty, the Court based its decision in part on an examination of the laws of other death penalty states, only eight of which allowed the death penalty for those with very minor roles in a felony-murder. The Court also noted that "American juries have repudiated imposition of the death penalty for crimes such as petitioner's" (458 U.S. 782, 794).

After presenting these and other facts as evidence of societal rejection of the death penalty for crimes such as Enmund's, the Court concluded with its own judgment: "As was said of the crime of rape in *Coker*, we have the abiding conviction that the death penalty . . . is an excessive penalty for the robber who, as such, does not take human life."[1]

## NOTE

1. Six years later, in the 1988 case of *Tison v. Arizona*, the Supreme Court would further define the *Enmund* rule regarding the extent of personal involvement required for a defendant to be eligible for the death penalty for felony murder. In *Tison*, "[t]he Court concluded that people who did not actually kill could receive a death sentence if they were major participants in the felony and had 'the culpable mental state of reckless indifference to human life' " (Tushnet 1994:76).

## A. OPINION OF THE COURT

JUSTICE WHITE delivered the opinion of the Court. . . .

### III

Although the judgments of legislatures, juries, and prosecutors weigh heavily in the balance, it is for us ultimately to judge whether the Eighth Amendment permits imposition of the death penalty on one such as Enmund who aids and abets a felony in the course of which a murder is committed by others but who does not himself kill, attempt to kill, or intend that a killing take place or that lethal force will be employed. We have concluded, along with most legislatures and juries, that it does not.

We have no doubt that robbery is a serious crime deserving serious punishment. It is not, however, a crime "so grievous an affront to humanity that the only adequate response may be the penalty of death."

[*Gregg* v. *Georgia*]. . . . "[I]t does not compare with murder, which does involve the unjustified taking of human life. Although it may be accompanied by another crime, [robbery] by definition does not include the death of or even the serious injury to another person. The murderer kills; the [robber], if no more than that, does not. Life is over for the victim of the murderer; for the [robbery] victim, life . . . is not over and normally is not beyond repair." [*Coker* v. *Georgia*]. . . . As was said of the crime of rape in *Coker*, we have the abiding conviction that the death penalty, which is "unique in its severity and irrevocability," [*Gregg* v. *Georgia*] . . . is an excessive penalty for the robber who, as such, does not take human life. . . .

It would be very different if the likelihood of a killing in the course of a robbery were so substantial that one should share the blame for the killing if he somehow participated in the felony. But competent observers have concluded that there is no basis in experience for the notion that death so frequently occurs in the course of a felony for which killing is not an essential ingredient that the death penalty should be considered as a justifiable deterrent to the felony itself. . . . This conclusion was based on three comparisons of robbery statistics, each of which showed that only about one-half of one percent of robberies resulted in homicide. The most recent national crime statistics strongly support this conclusion. In addition to the evidence that killings only rarely occur during robberies is the fact, already noted, that however often death occurs in the course of a felony such as robbery, the death penalty is rarely imposed on one only vicariously guilty of the murder, a fact which further attenuates its possible utility as an effective deterrence. . . .

For purposes of imposing the death penalty, Enmund's criminal culpability must be limited to his participation in the robbery, and his punishment must be tailored to his personal responsibility and moral guilt. Putting Enmund to death to avenge two killings that he did not commit and had no intention of committing or causing does not measurably contribute to the retributive end of ensuring that the criminal gets his just deserts. This is the judgment of most of the legislatures that have recently addressed the matter, and we have no reason to disagree with that judgment for purposes of construing and applying the Eighth Amendment.

## B. DISSENTING OPINION

JUSTICE O'CONNOR, with whom THE CHIEF JUSTICE, JUSTICE POWELL, and JUSTICE REHNQUIST join, dissenting. . . .

II

. . .

C

. . .

The Court's holding today is especially disturbing because it makes intent a matter of federal constitutional law, requiring this Court both to review highly subjective definitional problems customarily left to state criminal law and to develop an Eighth Amendment meaning of intent. As JUSTICE BLACKMUN pointed out in his concurring opinion in *Lockett*, the Court's holding substantially "interfere[s] with the States' individual statutory categories for assessing legal guilt." . . . Although the Court's opinion suggests that intent can be ascertained as if it were some historical fact, in fact it is a legal concept, not easily defined. Thus, while proportionality requires a nexus between the punishment imposed and the defendant's blameworthiness, the Court fails to explain why the Eighth Amendment concept of proportionality requires rejection of standards of blameworthiness based on other levels of intent, such as, for example, the intent to commit an armed robbery coupled with the knowledge that armed robberies involve substantial risk of death or serious injury to other persons. Moreover, the intent-to-kill requirement is crudely crafted; it fails to take into account the complex picture of the defendant's knowledge of his accomplice's intent and whether he was armed, the defendant's contribution to the planning and success of the crime, and the defendant's actual participation during the commission of the crime. Under the circumstances, the determination of the degree of blameworthiness is best left to the sentencer, who can sift through the facts unique to each case. Consequently, while the type of *mens rea* of the defendant must be considered carefully in assessing the proper penalty, it is not so critical a factor in determining blameworthiness as to require a finding of intent to kill in order to impose the death penalty for felony murder.

In sum, the petitioner and the Court have failed to show that contemporary standards, as reflected in both jury determinations and legislative enactments, preclude imposition of the death penalty for accomplice felony murder. Moreover, examination of the qualitative factors underlying the concept of proportionality do not show that the death penalty is disproportionate as applied to Earl Enmund. In contrast to the crime in *Coker*, the petitioner's crime involves the very type of harm that this Court has held justifies the death penalty. Finally, because of the unique and complex mixture of facts involving a defendant's actions, knowledge, motives, and participation during the commission of a felony murder, I believe that the factfinder is best able to assess the defendant's blameworthiness. Accordingly, I conclude that the death penalty is not disproportionate to the crime of felony murder, even though the defendant did not actually kill or intend to kill his victims.

*Source*: 458 U.S. 782 (1982), 783–826 (footnotes omitted).

## DOCUMENT 70: *Eddings v. Oklahoma* (1982)

In the 1978 case of *Lockett v. Ohio* (see Document 66), the Supreme Court held that "the Eighth and Fourteenth Amendments require that the sentencer . . . not be precluded from considering, *as a mitigating factor,* any aspect of a defendant's character or record and any of the circumstances of the offense that the defendant proffers as a basis for a sentence less than death." The Supreme Court reaffirmed this decision in the 1982 case of *Eddings v. Ohio,* when it overturned the death sentence of Monty Lee Eddings.

Eddings, who had pleaded guilty and been sentenced to death for the 1977 shooting death of an Oklahoma police officer, had committed the murder at the age of sixteen. During the penalty phase of his trial, Eddings had presented substantial evidence of his troubled youth as mitigating evidence, including the fact that his parents had divorced when he was very young, that his mother had neglected him, and that his father had subjected him to severe physical punishment.

However, the sentencing judge apparently had refused even to consider this mitigating evidence when weighing the aggravating and mitigating circumstances. The only mitigating factor he had considered was the defendant's extreme youth, and although giving it "serious consideration," he had not found this one factor alone sufficient to outweigh the aggravating factors in the case. According to his own statements at trial: "[T]he Court cannot be persuaded entirely by the . . . fact that the youth was sixteen years old when this heinous crime was committed. *Nor can the Court in following the law, in my opinion, consider the fact of this young man's violent background*" (quoted, with emphasis added, in 455 U.S. 104, 109).

Because the sentencing judge had refused to consider the full range of mitigating circumstances pertaining to Eddings's disturbed youth, in violation of the rule established in *Lockett,* the Supreme Court vacated the death sentence.

## A. OPINION OF THE COURT

JUSTICE POWELL delivered the opinion of the Court. . . .

### III

. . .

We find that the limitations placed by these courts upon the mitigating evidence they would consider violated the rule in *Lockett.* Just as the State may not by statute preclude the sentencer from considering any mitigating factor, neither may the sentencer refuse to consider, *as a matter of law*, any relevant mitigating evidence. In this instance, it was as if the trial judge had instructed a jury to disregard the mitigating evidence Eddings proffered on his behalf. The sentencer, and the Court of Criminal Appeals on review, may determine the weight to be given relevant mitigating evidence. But they may not give it no weight by excluding such evidence from their consideration.

Nor do we doubt that the evidence Eddings offered was relevant mitigating evidence. Eddings was a youth of 16 years at the time of the murder. Evidence of a difficult family history and of emotional disturbance is typically introduced by defendants in mitigation.... In some cases, such evidence properly may be given little weight. But when the defendant was 16 years old at the time of the offense there can be no doubt that evidence of a turbulent family history, of beatings by a harsh father, and of severe emotional disturbance is particularly relevant.

The trial judge recognized that youth must be considered a relevant mitigating factor. But youth is more than a chronological fact. It is a time and condition of life when a person may be most susceptible to influence and to psychological damage. Our history is replete with laws and judicial recognition that minors, especially in their earlier years, generally are less mature and responsible than adults. Particularly "during the formative years of childhood and adolescence, minors often lack the experience, perspective, and judgment" expected of adults....

Even the normal 16-year-old customarily lacks the maturity of an adult. In this case, Eddings was not a normal 16-year-old; he had been deprived of the care, concern, and paternal attention that children deserve. On the contrary, it is not disputed that he was a juvenile with serious emotional problems, and had been raised in a neglectful, sometimes even violent, family background. In addition, there was testimony that Eddings' mental and emotional development were at a level several years below his chronological age. All of this does not suggest an absence of responsibility for the crime of murder, deliberately committed in this case. Rather, it is to say that just as the chronological age of a minor is itself a relevant mitigating factor of great weight, so must the background and mental and emotional development of a youthful defendant be duly considered in sentencing.

## B. DISSENTING OPINION

CHIEF JUSTICE BURGER, with whom JUSTICE WHITE, JUSTICE BLACKMUN, and JUSTICE REHNQUIST join, dissenting....

We held in *Lockett* that the "Eighth and Fourteenth Amendments require that the sentencer . . . not be precluded from considering, *as a mitigating factor*, any aspect of a defendant's character or record and any of the circumstances of the offense that the defendant proffers as a basis for a sentence less than death." . . . We therefore found the Ohio statute flawed, because it did not permit individualized consideration of mitigating circumstances—such as the defendant's comparatively minor role in the offense, lack of intent to kill the victim, or age. . . . We did not, however, undertake to dictate the *weight* that a sentencing court must ascribe to the various factors that might be categorized as "mitigating," nor did we in any way suggest that this Court may substitute its sentencing judgment for that of state courts in capital cases. . . .

In its attempt to make out a violation of *Lockett*, the Court relies entirely on a single sentence of the trial court's opinion delivered from the bench at the close of the sentencing hearing. After discussing the aggravated nature of petitioner's offense, and noting that he had "given very serious consideration to the youth of the Defendant when this particular crime was committed," the trial judge said that he could not

be persuaded entirely by the . . . fact that the youth was sixteen years old when this heinous crime was committed. Nor can the Court in following the law, in my opinion, consider the fact of this young man's violent background. . . .

From this statement, the Court concludes "it is clear that the trial judge did not evaluate the evidence in mitigation and find it wanting as a matter of fact, rather he found that *as a matter of law* he was unable even to consider the evidence." . . . This is simply not a correct characterization of the sentencing judge's action.

In its parsing of the trial court's oral statement, the Court ignores the fact that the judge was delivering his opinion extemporaneously from the bench, and could not be expected to frame each utterance with the specificity and precision that might be expected of a written opinion or statute. Extemporaneous courtroom statements are not often models of clarity. Nor does the Court give any weight to the fact that the trial court had spent considerable time listening to the testimony of a probation officer and various mental health professionals who described Eddings' personality and family history—an obviously meaningless exercise if, as the Court asserts, the judge believed he was barred "as a matter of law" from "considering" their testimony. Yet even examined in isolation, the trial court's statement is at best ambiguous; it can just as easily be read to say that, while the court had taken account of Eddings' unfortunate childhood, it did not consider that either his youth or his family background was sufficient to offset the aggravating circumstances that the evidence revealed. Certainly nothing in *Lockett* would preclude the court from making such a determination.

*Source*: 455 U.S. 104 (1982), 105–125 (footnotes omitted).

---

## DOCUMENT 71: "Justice Powell Urges End to Death Sentence Delaying" (*Washington Post*, 1983)

---

During the seven years following the Supreme Court's decision in *Gregg* (see Document 62), few executions actually had taken place. The nation's death row population grew larger with each passing year, while the court system was once again inundated with capital case appeals.

Addressing a group of judges from the Eleventh Circuit at a conference in Savannah, Georgia, Supreme Court Justice Lewis F. Powell, Jr., made clear his dissatisfaction with the increasingly time-consuming capital appeals process.

Powell pointed out that more than one thousand convicted murderers were then on death row—"an intolerable situation"—and that many of those persons had been convicted and sentenced several years previously. He blamed the system of repetitive review, as well as last-minute applications for stays of execution, for the large backlog in executions, and advocated measures to reduce habeas corpus filings and speed up the appeals process.

Powell, a conservative 1972 Nixon appointee, was himself "neither enthusiastically for nor categorically against capital punishment" (Jeffries 1994:409). However, during his tenure on the Supreme Court, he had gained a reputation as "a fervent partisan of capital punishment—or rather of the constitutionality of capital punishment" (Jeffries 1994: 409). He had voted against the majority opinion in *Furman*, and he wrote the majority opinion in *Gregg*, basing both decisions primarily on the constitutional permissibility of the death penalty.

Not surprisingly, Powell's speech was received with dismay by many opponents of capital punishment. As noted defense attorney Anthony Amsterdam (see Documents 51, 52, 57, and 77) later explained, "the conscience of the Court had turned a corner where capital punishment was concerned" (Amsterdam 1987:50).

Supreme Court Justice Lewis F. Powell Jr., citing an "intolerable" backlog of more than 1,000 death-row inmates, yesterday urged the courts and Congress to end the long delays and repetitive appeals that he said have stalled implementation of capital punishment sentences across the country.

If the death penalty can't be implemented more efficiently, he said, states should abolish it.

Powell's comments, prepared for delivery to a conference of judges of the 11th U.S. Circuit Court of Appeals, were among the strongest off-the-bench remarks by a justice on the subject of the death penalty, and came as the court is considering a major case involving appeals procedures for death-row inmates.

Seven persons have been executed since capital punishment was reinstated in 1976, while 1,156 people—some on death row for six to seven years—are awaiting execution.

"This malfunctioning of our system of justice is unfair to the hundreds of persons confined anxiously on death row," Powell said. "It also disserves the public interest in the implementation of lawful sentences" and "undermines public confidence in our system of justice and the will and ability of the courts to administer it."

Powell placed part of the blame on resourceful defense lawyers who take "every advantage of a system that irrationally permits abuse" of the process. "The primary fault lies with our permissive system," he said, "that both Congress and the courts tolerate."

Powell said Congress should consider legislation to "inhibit unlimited filings" of habeas corpus petitions, in which prisoners protest their sentences or convictions long after exhausting the regular appeals process.

He suggested that the courts put death penalty cases on "an accelerated schedule. . . . When a prisoner is on death row, his interest—as well as that of the state—demands that judges at all levels expedite their consideration" of appeals.

*Source*: Fred Barbash, "Justice Powell Urges End to Death Sentence Delaying," *Washington Post*, May 10, 1983.

---

## DOCUMENT 72: *Barefoot v. Estelle* (1983)

Shortly after Justice Powell's speech at the judge's conference in Georgia (see Document 71), it began to appear that not only he, but a majority of the Supreme Court justices, had adopted a new attitude toward capital punishment. The case of *Barefoot v. Estelle* illustrates this attitude shift and its ramifications.

Thomas Barefoot had been sentenced to death for the 1978 murder of a Texas police officer. Barefoot appealed his sentence on the grounds that psychiatric testimony regarding the strong likelihood of his future dangerousness presented by the prosecution during his penalty trial was unreliable and therefore should not have been presented to the jury as evidence.

The Court of Appeals for the Fifth Circuit denied Barefoot a stay of execution, ruling that his petition had no substantial merit. Subsequently, the U.S. Supreme Court granted certiorari in the case to decide both on the substantive issue of whether Barefoot's claim had merit and—perhaps even more importantly—on a procedural issue pertaining to the federal court's handling of Barefoot's appeal.

Addressing the procedural issue first, the Supreme Court upheld the somewhat unusual and expedited procedures used by the Fifth Circuit court, which had heard oral arguments and issued a judgment denying Barefoot's application for a stay within a two-day period. In its decision, the Supreme Court affirmed that a federal appeals court may make a single summary decision both on the merits of a petitioner's legal claim and his request for a stay of execution, thus clearing the way for widespread use of expedited federal review procedures.

Turning to the issue of the merit of the appeal itself, the Court also ruled against Barefoot. Although the Court acknowledged evidence provided by the American Psychiatric Association that showed that psychiatric testimony regarding future dangerousness often is unreliable (Paternoster 1991:79), it pointed out that during a penalty hearing, the defense is free to call expert witnesses of its own who can argue against the prosecution witnesses' assessment of the defendant's future dangerousness.

The Court's ruling in *Barefoot* was significant because it established a legal climate that was favorable to hastening the execution of death row inmates through speedier federal habeas proceedings. It also suggested that the Court henceforth might take a more "hands-off" approach to the states' death penalty trials and procedures (Paternoster 1991:79–81).

## A. OPINION OF THE COURT

JUSTICE WHITE delivered the opinion of the Court. . . .

II

. . .

Federal courts are not forums in which to relitigate state trials. Even less is federal habeas a means by which a defendant is entitled to delay an execution indefinitely. The procedures adopted to facilitate the orderly consideration and disposition of habeas petitions are not legal entitlements that a defendant has a right to pursue irrespective of the contribution these procedures make toward uncovering constitutional error. . . .

## A

Petitioner urges that the Court of Appeals improperly denied a stay of execution while failing to act finally on his appeal. He suggests the possibility of remanding the case to the Court of Appeals without reaching the merits of the District Court's judgment. The heart of petitioner's submission is that the Court of Appeals, unless it believes the case to be entirely frivolous, was obligated to decide the appeal on its merits in the usual course and must, in a death case, stay the execution pending such disposition. The State responds that the Court of Appeals reached and decided the merits of the issues presented in the course of denying the stay and that petitioner had ample opportunity to address the merits. . . .

Approving the execution of a defendant before his appeal is decided on the merits would clearly be improper. . . . However, a practice of deciding the merits of an appeal, when possible, together with the application for a stay, is not inconsistent with our cases. . . .

Although the Court of Appeals did not formally affirm the judgment of the District Court, there is no question that the Court of Appeals ruled on the merits of the appeal, as its concluding statements demonstrate:

This Court has had the benefit of the full trial court record except for a few exhibits unimportant to our considerations. We have read the arguments and materials filed by the parties. The petitioner is represented here, as he has been throughout the habeas corpus proceedings in state and federal courts, by a competent attorney experienced in this area of the law. We have heard full arguments in open court. Finding no patent substantial merit, or semblance thereof, to petitioner's constitutional objections, we must conclude and order that the motion for stay should be DENIED.

Although the Court of Appeals moved swiftly to decide the stay, this does not mean that its treatment of the merits was cursory or inadequate. On the contrary, the court's resolution of the primary issue on appeal, the admission of psychiatric testimony on dangerousness, reflects careful consideration. For these reasons, to remand to the Court of Appeals for verification that the judgment of the District Court was affirmed would be an unwarranted exaltation of form over substance. . . .

## III

. . .

A

The suggestion that no psychiatrist's testimony may be presented with respect to a defendant's future dangerousness is somewhat like asking us to disinvent the wheel. In the first place, it is contrary to our cases. If the likelihood of a defendant's committing further crimes is a constitutionally acceptable criterion for imposing the death penalty, which it is, ... and if it is not impossible for even a lay person sensibly to arrive at that conclusion, it makes little sense, if any, to submit that psychiatrists, out of the entire universe of persons who might have an opinion on the issue, would know so little about the subject that they should not be permitted to testify. . . .

Acceptance of petitioner's position that expert testimony about future dangerousness is far too unreliable to be admissible would immediately call into question those other contexts in which predictions of future behavior are constantly made. . . .

In the second place, the rules of evidence generally extant at the federal and state levels anticipate that relevant, unprivileged evidence should be admitted and its weight left to the factfinder, who would have the benefit of cross-examination and contrary evidence by the opposing party. Psychiatric testimony predicting dangerousness may be countered not only as erroneous in a particular case but also as generally so unreliable that it should be ignored. If the jury may make up its mind about future dangerousness unaided by psychiatric testimony, jurors should not be barred from hearing the views of the State's psychiatrists along with opposing views of the defendant's doctors.

Third, petitioner's view mirrors the position expressed in the *amicus* brief of the American Psychiatric Association (APA). As indicated above, however, the same view was presented and rejected in *Estelle v. Smith*. We are no more convinced now that the view of the APA should be converted into a constitutional rule barring an entire category of expert testimony. We are not persuaded that such testimony is almost entirely unreliable and that the factfinder and the adversary system will not be competent to uncover, recognize, and take due account of its shortcomings.

## B. DISSENTING OPINION OF JUSTICE MARSHALL

Justice Marshall, with whom Justice Brennan joins, dissenting. . . .

II

. . .

[I] frankly do not understand how the Court can conclude that the Court of Appeals' treatment of this case was "tolerable." . . . If, as the

Court says, the Court of Appeals was "obligated to decide the merits of the appeal," . . . it most definitely failed to discharge that obligation, for the court never ruled on petitioner's appeal. It is simply false to say that "the Court of Appeals ruled on the merits of the appeal." . . . The record plainly shows that the Court of Appeals did no such thing. It neither dismissed the appeal as frivolous nor affirmed the judgment of the District Court. The Court of Appeals made one ruling and one ruling only: it refused to stay petitioner's execution. Had this Court not granted a stay, petitioner would have been put to death without his appeal ever having been decided one way or the other. . . .

The Court offers no justification for the procedure followed by the Court of Appeals because there is none. A State has no legitimate interest in executing a prisoner before he has obtained full review of his sentence. A stay of execution pending appeal causes no harm to the State apart from the minimal burden of providing a jail cell for the prisoner for the period of time necessary to decide his appeal. By contrast, a denial of a stay on the basis of a hasty finding that the prisoner is not likely to succeed on his appeal permits the State to execute him prior to full review of a concededly substantial constitutional challenge to his sentence. If the court's hurried evaluation of the appeal proves erroneous, as is entirely possible when difficult legal issues are decided without adequate time for briefing and full consideration, the execution of the prisoner will make it impossible to undo the mistake.

Once a federal judge has decided, as the District Judge did here, that a prisoner under sentence of death has raised a substantial constitutional claim, it is a travesty of justice to permit the State to execute him before his appeal can be considered and decided. If a prisoner's statutory right to appeal means anything, a State simply cannot be allowed to kill him and thereby moot his appeal.

### III

. . .

In view of the irreversible nature of the death penalty and the extraordinary number of death sentences that have been found to suffer from some constitutional infirmity, it would be grossly improper for a court of appeals to establish special summary procedures for capital cases. The only consolation I can find in today's decision is that the primary responsibility for selecting the appropriate procedures for these appeals lies, as the Court itself points out, . . . with the court of appeals. . . . Notwithstanding the profoundly disturbing attitude reflected in today's opinion, I am hopeful that few circuit judges would ever support the adoption of procedures that would afford less consideration to an appeal in which a man's life is at stake than to an appeal challenging an ordinary money judgment.

## C. DISSENTING OPINION OF JUSTICE BLACKMUN

JUSTICE BLACKMUN, with whom JUSTICE BRENNAN and JUSTICE MAR-
SHALL join as to Parts I–IV, dissenting. . . .

The Court holds that psychiatric testimony about a defendant's future
dangerousness is admissible, despite the fact that such testimony is
wrong two times out of three. The Court reaches this result—even in a
capital case—because, it is said, the testimony is subject to cross-
examination and impeachment. In the present state of psychiatric knowledge, this is too much for me. One may accept this in a routine lawsuit
for money damages, but when a person's life is at stake—no matter how
heinous his offense—a requirement of greater reliability should prevail.
In a capital case, the specious testimony of a psychiatrist, colored in the
eyes of an impressionable jury by the inevitable untouchability of a medical specialist's words, equates with death itself.

*Source*: 463 U.S. 880 (1983), 883–916 (footnotes omitted).

## DOCUMENT 73: Death Penalty Debate (1983)

In 1983, Ernest van den Haag (see Document 59) and John P. Conrad, former director of research for the California Department of Corrections and a firm abolitionist, engaged in what is possibly the liveliest
and best-known death penalty debate since that of Clarence Darrow
and Alfred J. Talley in 1924 (see Document 29).

Their balanced and thought-provoking exchange did not take place
in front of an audience, but rather was published as a book: *The Death
Penalty: A Debate* (New York: Plenum Press, 1983).

In his foreword to the book, former Supreme Court Justice Arthur J.
Goldberg stated, "During my tenure on the Supreme Court, I read
many briefs concerning the death penalty by distinguished lawyers.
Many of these briefs cannot hold a candle to this book, written by two
non-lawyer scholars. Even in treating the constitutional issues, the opposing views in the debate are presented with keen analysis frequently
lacking in the writings and arguments of members of the Bar" (in van
den Haag and Conrad 1983:vi).

Following are excerpts from concluding statements made by Conrad
and van den Haag in the book.

## A. JOHN CONRAD

The question that I have raised so often in this debate must be confronted again: *Why should we retain capital punishment when a life sentence in prison will serve the deterrent purpose at least as well?*

Implicit in that question is my complete disbelief that there exists a population of potential murderers who would be deterred by the gallows—or the lethal needle—but would proceed with their killings if the worst they could expect was a life sentence in prison. If such extraordinary people exist, a supposition for which there is absolutely no evidence, they would be balanced by an equally extraordinary, and equally hypothetical, few who are tempted to commit murder to achieve the notoriety of public execution. There may be a few in each of these classes, but in the absence of any positive evidence of their existence in significant numbers, no debating points can be claimed for them by either side.

The adequacy of a life sentence in prison as a deterrent to murder—if deterrence is truly our aim—is obvious to those who know what that experience does to the prisoner. The term begins in ignominy. It is lived out in squalor. It ends when youth is long since gone, or, more often than most people know, in the death of the senile in a prison ward for the aged and infirm. Those who fancy that life in prison bears any resemblance to the gaiety of a resort hotel or the luxury of a country club have been beguiled by dishonest demagogues. Commitment to an American prison is a disaster for all but the most vicious human predators, men who discover a false manhood in the abuse of the weak. The unique combination of ennui and chronic dread of one's fellows, of idleness and wasted years, and of lives spent with wicked, vicious, or inane men and women should be—and for most people certainly is—a terrifyingly deterrent prospect. Those who find it tolerable are manifesting the meaninglessness of their lives before commitment. . . .

The executioner does what he has to do in behalf of the citizens of the state that employs him. His hand is on the lever that releases the cyanide, switches on the current, or springs the trap. We, as citizens, cannot escape a full share of his responsibility. We voted into office the legislators who make killers of us all. If the deliberate killing of another human being is the most abhorrent of crimes, we are all guilty, even though we shall be scot-free from legal punishment. The pity and terror that an execution inspires in even the most callous is punishment enough for the perceptive citizen. Pity and terror, mixed with the knowledge that what has been done is futile.

As my stoical opponent has repeatedly reminded us, we must all die. Many of us will die in conditions far more painful than sudden oblivion from a whiff of gas or a lethal charge of electricity. None of us has to inflict death on another. The statutes that make such deaths occasionally possible must be repealed in the interest of decency and good conscience. The sooner the better.

## B. ERNEST VAN DEN HAAG

I see no evidence for society somehow not having "the right" to execute murderers. It has always done so. Traditional laws and Scriptures have always supported the death penalty. I know of no reasoning, even in a religious (theocratic) state, that denies the right of secular courts to impose it. We in America have a secular republic, of course, and therefore, the suggestion that the right to punish belongs only to God, or that the right to impose capital punishment does, is clearly out of place. It is not a religious but a secular task to put murderers to death. Our Constitution does provide for it (Amendments V and XIV). However much we believe in divine justice, it is to occur after, not in, this life. As for justice here and now, it is done by the courts, which are authorized in certain cases to impose the death penalty. A secular state cannot leave it to God. And incidentally, no theocratic state ever has. If they make mistakes, one can hope that God will correct the courts hereafter—but this is no ground for depriving courts of their duty to impose the penalties provided by law where required, nor is it a ground for depriving the law of the ability to prescribe the punishments felt to be just, including the death penalty. . . .

Where there is life there is hope. This certainly is one major argument in favor of the death penalty. The murderer who premeditates his crime—and crimes of passion are not subject to capital punishment—if he contemplates the risk of life imprisonment is not likely to believe that, if convicted, he will remain in prison for life. He knows, however inchoately, about parole, pardons, commutations—he believes above all that he, a smart and superior fellow, will find a way to escape. Few prisoners actually do escape. But practically all "lifers" believe that they will, at least when they start their sentence. So believing, they do not greatly fear a sentence of life imprisonment and are not deterred by it. This is why the rate of stranger-murders—murders in which victim and murderer do not know one another and to which the threat of the death penalty should apply—as a proportion of all murders has steadily climbed in the last twenty years. The murderers knew that in practice they would get away with life imprisonment, from which they would be paroled after a few years. Or they hoped they would escape. After all, we executed all of five prisoners in 1981, only one of whom was executed against his wishes. (All of them were white, to the great disappointment of the civil liberties lobby.) At this rate no murderer can foresee execution or be deterred by it. . . .

The lives of the innocents that will or may be spared because of the death penalty are more valuable to me, and to any civilized society, than the lives of murderers. I do not want to risk their lives for the sake of the lives of murderers.

The reader will have to decide for himself on which side he wants to be.

*Source*: Ernest van den Haag and John P. Conrad, *The Death Penalty: A Debate* (New York: Plenum Press, 1983), 293–300.

---

## DOCUMENT 74: "Comparative Review of Death Sentences: An Empirical Study of the Georgia Experience" (David C. Baldus, Charles Pulaski, and George Woodworth, 1983)

In 1983, a study conducted by David Baldus, a professor of law at the University of Iowa, and colleagues Charles Pulaski, professor of law at Arizona State University, and George Woodworth, associate professor of statistics at the University of Iowa, shed new light on the subject of race and capital sentencing.

The main goal of the study was to examine the effectiveness of Georgia's post-*Furman* comparative sentence review procedures, used by the courts to determine "whether a death sentence is consistent with the usual pattern of sentencing decisions in similar cases or is comparatively excessive" (Baldus et al. 1983:663). Such procedures were designed to help protect against the kinds of arbitrary and capricious death sentences forbidden by the Supreme Court in *Furman* (see Document 54).

In their exhaustive study, Baldus et al. analyzed the cases of 594 defendants tried and sentenced for murder under Georgia's post-*Furman* statutes between 1973 and 1978. In 190 (32 percent) of these cases, the prosecutor had sought the death penalty, resulting in 203 penalty trials.[1] Among this group, 113 death sentences were imposed upon 100 offenders.

Baldus et al. found that the prosecutors in these 594 cases were significantly more likely to *seek* the death penalty in white-victim cases as opposed to black-victim cases. In fact, the death penalty was sought in 44 percent of the cases involving a white victim and only 15 percent of those in which the victim was black—nearly a 3–1 difference. This racial disparity persisted even when the researchers conducted a multivariate analysis that simultaneously controlled for more than 150 aggravating and mitigating factors (Paternoster 1991:132–133).

Turning to the 190 cases in which the prosecutors had sought the death penalty, Baldus et al. found that Georgia juries also were more likely to *impose* the death penalty on a murderer whose victim was white than on one whose victim was black.[2] However, jurors' racial biases appeared much less pronounced than those of prosecutors in determining the fate of the offender, leading the researchers to conclude that "[t]he leading source of race-of-victim disparities in Georgia's death sentencing system for defendants convicted of murder at trial is clearly the decision to advance the case to a penalty trial" (Baldus et al., 1983:710, note 131).

These findings, which Baldus and his co-researchers expanded on and reconfirmed in subsequent analyses of the Georgia data in 1985 and 1990, were an early and significant contribution to the growing body of post-*Furman* research that indicated the persistence of racial disparities in capital sentencing, despite reformed capital punishment statutes (Paternoster 1991:23).

**NOTES**

1. In some cases, two or more penalty trials were held.

2. Georgia juries imposed the death sentence in 97 out of 166 (58 percent) penalty trials of killers whose victims were white and in 16 out of 37 (43 percent) penalty trials of killers whose victims were black (Baldus et al., 1983: 710, Table 7).

There appear to be two principal explanations for Georgia's generally low death-sentencing rates. The first is that prosecutors do not routinely seek death sentences in death-eligible cases. In fact, in only forty percent of the cases in which the jury convicted the defendant of a murder involving a statutory aggravating circumstance did the prosecution even seek a death sentence. Although the Georgia statute states that there "shall" be a penalty trial in all cases resulting in a murder conviction, in practice a penalty trial will not occur unless the prosecution so requests. The impact of this exercise of prosecutorial discretion to forego a penalty trial is enormous. When penalty trials do occur, Georgia juries impose death sentences in fifty-five percent of the cases; among the more aggravated cases the death-sentencing rates are particularly high.

Georgia's relatively low overall post-*Furman* death-sentencing rate also reflects a very low death-sentencing rate in black victim cases. Specifically, the rate is .06 (15/246) for black victim cases versus .24 (85/348) for white victim cases. This disparity is particularly apparent when prosecutors are deciding whether to seek a death sentence, and its effect persists after one adjusts for the aggravation level of different cases. In other words, our data strongly suggest that Georgia is operating a dual system, based upon the race of the victim, for processing homicide cases. Georgia juries appear to tolerate greater levels of aggravation without imposing the death penalty in black victim cases; and, as compared to white victim cases, the level of aggravation in black victim cases must be substantially greater before the prosecutor will even seek a death sentence.

Source: David C. Baldus, Charles Pulaski, and George Woodworth, "Comparative Review of Death Sentences: An Empirical Study of the Georgia Experience," Journal of Criminal Law & Criminology 74 (1983): 706–710 (footnotes omitted).

## DOCUMENT 75: Public Opinion and the Death Penalty (1985)

In 1985, seven in ten Americans were in favor of capital punishment—the highest recorded level of public support in the nearly fifty years since the Gallup Poll had first begun asking questions about the death penalty in 1936 (Gallup 1985:3; also see Document 33).

However, the 1985 survey also found that support for capital punishment dropped significantly—from 72 percent to 56 percent—when life-without-parole was mentioned as an alternative punishment.

### Death Penalty for Murder
QUESTION:

Are you in favor of the death penalty for persons convicted of murder?

January 11–14, 1985

|  | Favor | Oppose | No Opinion | Number of interviews |
|---|---|---|---|---|
| NATIONAL | 72% | 20% | 8% | 1,523 |

### Death Penalty vs. Life Imprisonment
QUESTION:

What do you think should be the penalty for murder—the death penalty or life imprisonment, with absolutely no possibility of parole?

January 11–14, 1985

| | Death penalty | Life imprisonment | Neither (vol.) | No opinion | Number of interviews |
|---|---|---|---|---|---|
| NATIONAL | 56% | 34% | 4% | 6% | 1,523 |

*Source*: *Gallup Report* (January/February 1985): 4–5. Copyright 1985 by Scholarly Resources Inc. Reprinted by permission of Scholarly Resources Inc.

## DOCUMENT 76: *Ford v. Wainwright* (1986)

In 1986, no state allowed for the imposition of the death sentence on someone who was insane at the time of his or her crime. But what about the convict who went insane during the long years of waiting on death row to be executed? The Supreme Court addressed this issue in the case of *Ford v. Wainwright*.

Alvin Bernard Ford had shown no signs of mental illness at the time of his offense or when he was convicted of murder and sentenced to death by a Florida jury in 1974. However, in 1982, after eight years on Florida's death row, Ford began to develop an apparent mental disorder characterized by one psychiatrist as resembling paranoid schizophrenia with suicide potential (477 U.S. 399, 402–403).

Ford's lawyer sought to have his client's death penalty reversed on the grounds that he had become insane and therefore was incompetent for execution. Under a Florida statute governing the determination of a condemned prisoner's competency, the governor appointed three psychiatrists, who together interviewed Ford for about half an hour. Although their diagnoses varied, all three psychiatrists agreed that Ford was fit enough for execution, and the governor subsequently signed his death warrant.

After being denied a new competency hearing for Ford in the state court and an evidentiary hearing in the Federal District Court, Ford's lawyer appealed to the Supreme Court. The Court granted certiorari to resolve the issue of whether the Eighth Amendment prohibits the execution of the insane and, if so, whether the district court should have held a hearing on Ford's claim.

The Court held that the execution of the insane was indeed unconstitutional under the Eighth Amendment, based on the nation's "common law heritage" in which the execution of the insane was considered "savage and inhuman" (477 U.S. 399, 406). It also found

Florida's procedure for determining Ford's competence to be sorely lacking and therefore "inadequate to preclude federal redetermination of the constitutional issue" (477 U.S. 399, 416), thus reversing the decision of the lower court that had denied Ford a new competency hearing.

## A. OPINION OF THE COURT

JUSTICE MARSHALL announced the judgment of the Court and delivered the opinion of the Court with respect to Parts I and II and an opinion with respect to Parts III, IV, and V, in which JUSTICE BRENNAN, JUSTICE BLACKMUN, and JUSTICE STEVENS join. . . .

### II

. . .

### B

. . .

Today, no State in the Union permits the execution of the insane. It is clear that the ancient and humane limitation upon the State's ability to execute its sentences has as firm a hold upon the jurisprudence of today as it had centuries ago in England. The various reasons put forth in support of the common-law restriction have no less logical, moral, and practical force than they did when first voiced. For today, no less than before, we may seriously question the retributive value of executing a person who has no comprehension of why he has been singled out and stripped of his fundamental right to life. . . . Similarly, the natural abhorrence civilized societies feel at killing one who has no capacity to come to grips with his own conscience or deity is still vivid today. And the intuition that such an execution simply offends humanity is evidently shared across this Nation. Faced with such widespread evidence of a restriction upon sovereign power, this Court is compelled to conclude that the Eighth Amendment prohibits a State from carrying out a sentence of death upon a prisoner who is insane. Whether its aim be to protect the condemned from fear and pain without comfort of understanding, or to protect the dignity of society itself from the barbarity of exacting mindless vengeance, the restriction finds enforcement in the Eighth Amendment.

### III

The Eighth Amendment prohibits the State from inflicting the penalty of death upon a prisoner who is insane. Petitioner's allegation of insanity in his habeas corpus petition, if proved, therefore, would bar his execution. The question before us is whether the District Court was under an obligation to hold an evidentiary hearing on the question of Ford's sanity. . . .

## IV

### A

The first deficiency in Florida's procedure lies in its failure to include the prisoner in the truth-seeking process. . . . In all other proceedings leading to the execution of an accused, we have said that the factfinder must "have before it all possible relevant information about the individual defendant whose fate it must determine." . . . And we have forbidden States to limit the capital defendant's submission of relevant evidence in mitigation of the sentence. . . . It would be odd were we now to abandon our insistence upon unfettered presentation of relevant information, before the final fact antecedent to execution has been found.

Rather, consistent with the heightened concern for fairness and accuracy that has characterized our review of the process requisite to the taking of a human life, we believe that any procedure that precludes the prisoner or his counsel from presenting material relevant to his sanity or bars consideration of that material by the factfinder is necessarily inadequate. . . .

### B

A related flaw in the Florida procedure is the denial of any opportunity to challenge or impeach the state-appointed psychiatrists' opinions. . . . Cross-examination of the psychiatrists, or perhaps a less formal equivalent, would contribute markedly to the process of seeking truth in sanity disputes by bringing to light the bases for each expert's beliefs, the precise factors underlying those beliefs, any history of error or caprice of the examiner, any personal bias with respect to the issue of capital punishment, the expert's degree of certainty about his or her own conclusions, and the precise meaning of ambiguous words used in the report. Without some questioning of the experts concerning their technical conclusions, a factfinder simply cannot be expected to evaluate the various opinions, particularly when they are themselves inconsistent. . . .

### C

Perhaps the most striking defect in the procedures of Fla. Stat. §922.07 . . . , as noted earlier, is the State's placement of the decision wholly within the executive branch. Under this procedure, the person who appoints the experts and ultimately decides whether the State will be able to carry out the sentence that it has long sought is the Governor, whose subordinates have been responsible for initiating every stage of the prosecution of the condemned from arrest through sentencing. The commander of the State's corps of prosecutors cannot be said to have the neutrality that is necessary for reliability in the factfinding proceeding.

## B. DISSENTING OPINION

JUSTICE REHNQUIST, with whom THE CHIEF JUSTICE joins, dissenting. . . .

The Court places great weight on the "impressive historical credentials" of the common-law bar against executing a prisoner who has lost his sanity. . . . What it fails to mention, however, is the equally important and unchallenged fact that at common law it was the *executive* who passed upon the sanity of the condemned. . . . So when the Court today creates a constitutional right to a determination of sanity outside of the executive branch, it does so not in keeping with but at the expense of "our common-law heritage." . . .

Creating a constitutional right to a judicial determination of sanity before that sentence may be carried out, whether through the Eighth Amendment or the Due Process Clause, needlessly complicates and postpones still further any finality in this area of the law. The defendant has already had a full trial on the issue of guilt, and a trial on the issue of penalty; the requirement of still a third adjudication offers an invitation to those who have nothing to lose by accepting it to advance entirely spurious claims of insanity. A claim of insanity may be made at any time before sentence and, once rejected, may be raised again; a prisoner found sane two days before execution might claim to have lost his sanity the next day, thus necessitating another judicial determination of his sanity and presumably another stay of his execution. . . .

Since no State sanctions execution of the insane, the real battle being fought in this case is over what procedures must accompany the inquiry into sanity. The Court reaches the result it does by examining the common law, creating a constitutional right that no State seeks to violate, and then concluding that the common-law procedures are inadequate to protect the newly created but common-law based right. I find it unnecessary to "constitutionalize" the already uniform view that the insane should not be executed, and inappropriate to "selectively incorporate" the common-law practice.

*Source*: 477 U.S. 399 (1986), 401–435 (footnotes omitted).

---

## DOCUMENT 77: Anthony G. Amsterdam (1987)

Beginning with his involvement as a consultant to the NAACP Legal Defense and Educational Fund in 1963 (see Document 51), Anthony

G. Amsterdam (1935–   ) long has been one of the best-known and most influential legal scholars and litigating attorneys in the modern death penalty debate.

Amsterdam, who served as lead attorney for the NAACP in numerous landmark death penalty cases, including *Furman v. Georgia* (see Document 54), often is described as a brilliant, dynamic, dedicated, and tireless champion of civil rights (Epstein and Kobylka 1992:49–50; Meltsner 1973:78–84; Tushnet 1994:29).

Amsterdam received his A.B. from Haverford College in Pennsylvania in 1957 and his LL.B. from the University of Pennsylvania in 1960. In 1960 he was admitted to the bar in Washington, D.C., where he served as a law clerk to U.S. Supreme Court Justice Felix Frankfurter and as an assistant U.S. attorney.

In 1962 Amsterdam became a professor of law at the University of Pennsylvania Law School, where he remained until 1969. From 1969 to 1981, he was a professor of law at Stanford Law School. In 1981, he became a professor of law and director of clinical programs and trial advocacy at New York University Law School in New York City.

In addition to his consulting work for the NAACP, Amsterdam is a trustee of the National Coalition to Abolish the Death Penalty, general counsel to the New York ACLU, and advisory counsel to the Northern California chapter of the ACLU, among other organizations.

Following is an excerpt from a 1987 article by Amsterdam in which he criticized the Supreme Court's increasing trend toward expediting executions.

For centuries it has been an historical commonplace and a proud boast of the Anglo-American system of criminal justice that the courts were especially solicitous to protect the rights of the accused in capital cases. In his classic *History of English Criminal Law*, Sir Leon Radzinowicz has demonstrated the extent to which the judiciary mitigated the rigor of England's "bloody code" by scrupulous insistence upon procedural regularity in prosecutions where life was at stake. Thirty years ago, Mr. Justice Harlan spoke in the voice of a long tradition when he wrote that "[s]o far as capital cases are concerned, I think they stand on quite a different footing than other offenses. In such cases the law is especially sensitive to demands for . . . procedural fairness. . . . I do not concede that whatever process is 'due' an offender faced with a fine or a prison sentence necessarily satisfies the requirements of the Constitution in a capital case. The distinction is by no means novel . . . nor is it negligible, being literally that between life and death." A few years earlier, Mr. Justice Jackson put the matter in more earthy terms, saying that "[w]hen the penalty is death, we, like state court judges, are tempted to strain the evidence and even, in close cases, the law in order to give a doubt-fully condemned man another chance."

We have witnessed a startling reversal of this centuries-old attitude during the past three or four years. Today, the temptation that appears to afflict a majority of the Supreme Court of the United States is to give death-sentenced inmates less, not more, of a chance than other litigants. And there is strong evidence that the Court is succumbing to the temptation in at least one important area: the administration of the federal *habeas corpus* jurisdiction which serves as a last-ditch safeguard against violations of federal constitutional rights. In federal *habeas corpus* cases coming to the Court since 1983, an impatience to decide the cases quickly, so as to avoid delaying executions, seems increasingly to be taking precedence over any concern to decide them fairly or reliably. . . .

## V.

The irrevocability of an executed death sentence and the fallibility of human judgment have forever been important objections to capital punishment. Nothing can be done about the first, and little can be done about the second; but if a society chooses to use the death penalty, it seems not too much to ask that the courts of that society do whatever they can. This has been the view of Anglo-American judges for more than two hundred years. Patient, painstaking review of the legal claims of condemned inmates has been the rule of judicial responsibility, not because the task was convenient, efficient or gratifying, but because its omission was unthinkable. That it should come to be begrudged in our generation tells us much about ourselves.

*Source*: Anthony G. Amsterdam, "*In Favorem Mortis*: The Supreme Court and Capital Punishment," *Human Rights* 14, no. 1 (1987): 14–16, 57–58 (footnotes omitted).

---

## DOCUMENT 78: *Booth v. Maryland* (1987)

With its 1977 ruling in *Lockett* (see Document 66) and several subsequent cases, the Supreme Court ensured a capital defendant's right to present all relevant mitigating evidence during the penalty phase of his or her trial. Turning to the flip side of this issue, the Court in 1987 ruled on the prosecution's constitutional right to present a certain type of evidence, called a victim-impact statement (VIS), to the jury during the sentencing hearing.

John Booth had been convicted and sentenced to death for the 1983 murders of Irvin and Rose Bronstein, an elderly couple living in West Baltimore, Maryland. The Bronsteins were bound, gagged, and stabbed to death with a kitchen knife during an apparent robbery by Booth and his partner, Willie Reid.

During the penalty phase of Booth's trial, the jury had been presented with a presentence report by the state of Maryland which included, according to a state statute, a victim-impact statement. The VIS, which was based on interviews with the victims' family, described the severe emotional impact of the murders on the family, along with the family members' perceptions of the crimes and of Booth.

The state court had denied the defense's motion to suppress the VIS, and the Maryland Court of Appeals affirmed Booth's conviction and death sentence, concluding that "the VIS serves an important interest by informing the sentencer of the full measure of harm caused by the crime" (quoted in 107 S.Ct. 2529).

However, in a 5–4 decision, the Supreme Court reversed this decision, holding that "[t]he introduction of a VIS at the sentencing phase of a capital murder trial violates the Eighth Amendment, and therefore the Maryland statute is invalid to the extent it requires consideration of this information. Such information is irrelevant to a capital sentencing decision, and its admission creates a constitutionally unacceptable risk that the jury may impose the death penalty in an arbitrary and capricious manner."

## A. OPINION OF THE COURT

Justice POWELL delivered the opinion of the Court. . . .

II

. . .

While the full range of foreseeable consequences of a defendant's actions may be relevant in other criminal and civil contexts, we cannot agree that it is relevant in the unique circumstance of a capital sentencing hearing. In such a case, it is the function of the sentencing jury to "express the conscience of the community on the ultimate question of life or death." . . . When carrying out this task the jury is required to focus on the defendant as a "uniquely individual human bein[g]." . . . The focus of a VIS, however, is not on the defendant, but on the character and reputation of the victim and the effect on his family. These factors may be wholly unrelated to the blameworthiness of a particular defendant. As our cases have shown, the defendant often will not know the victim, and therefore will have no knowledge about the existence or characteristics of the victim's family. Moreover, defendants rarely select their victims based on whether the murder will have an effect on anyone other than the person murdered. Allowing the jury to rely on a VIS therefore could result in imposing the death sentence because of factors about which the defendant was unaware, and that were irrelevant to the decision to kill. This evidence thus could divert the jury's attention away from the defendant's background and record, and the circumstances of the crime.

It is true that in certain cases some of the information contained in a VIS will have been known to the defendant before he committed the offense. As we have recognized, a defendant's degree of knowledge of the probable consequences of his actions may increase his moral culpability in a constitutionally significant manner. . . . We nevertheless find that because of the nature of the information contained in a VIS, it creates an impermissible risk that the capital sentencing decision will be made in an arbitrary manner. . . .

We also note that it would be difficult—if not impossible—to provide a fair opportunity to rebut such evidence without shifting the focus of the sentencing hearing away from the defendant. A threshold problem is that victim impact information is not easily susceptible to rebuttal. Presumably the defendant would have the right to cross-examine the declarants, but he rarely would be able to show that the family members have exaggerated the degree of sleeplessness, depression, or emotional trauma suffered. Moreover, if the state is permitted to introduce evidence of the victim's personal qualities, it cannot be doubted that the defendant also must be given the chance to rebut this evidence. . . . Putting aside the strategic risks of attacking the victim's character before the jury, in appropriate cases the defendant presumably would be permitted to put on evidence that the victim was of dubious moral character, was unpopular, or was ostracized from his family. The prospect of a "mini-trial" on the victim's character is more than simply unappealing; it could well distract the sentencing jury from its constitutionally required task—determining whether the death penalty is appropriate in light of the background and record of the accused and the particular circumstances of the crime. We thus reject the contention that the presence or absence of emotional distress of the victim's family, or the victim's personal characteristics, are proper sentencing considerations in a capital case.

## B. DISSENTING OPINION

Justice WHITE, with whom THE CHIEF JUSTICE, Justice O'CONNOR, and Justice SCALIA join, dissenting. . . .

The Court's judgment is based on the premises that the harm that a murderer causes a victim's family does not in general reflect on his blameworthiness, and that only evidence going to blameworthiness is relevant to the capital sentencing decision. Many if not most jurors, however, will look less favorably on a capital defendant when they appreciate the full extent of the harm he caused, including the harm to the victim's family. There is nothing aberrant in a juror's inclination to hold a murderer accountable not only for his internal disposition in committing the crime but also for the full extent of the harm he caused; many if not most persons would also agree, for example, that someone who drove his car recklessly through a stoplight and unintentionally killed a pedestrian merits significantly more punishment than someone who drove his car recklessly through the same stoplight at a time when no pedestrian was there to be hit. I am confident that the Court would not overturn a sentence for reckless homicide by automobile merely because the punishment exceeded the maximum sentence for reckless driving; and I would hope that the Court would not overturn the sentence in such a case if a judge mentioned, as relevant to his sentencing decision, the fact that the victim was a mother or father. But if punishment can be enhanced in noncapital cases on the basis of the harm caused, irrespective of the offender's specific intention to cause such harm, I fail to see why the same approach is unconstitutional in death cases. If anything, I would think that victim impact statements are particularly appropriate evidence in capital sentencing hearings: the State has a legitimate interest in counteracting the mitigating evidence which the defendant is entitled to put in . . . by reminding the sentencer that just as the murderer should be considered as an individual, so too the victim is an individual whose death represents a unique loss to society and in particular to his family.

*Source*: 107 S.Ct. 2529 (1987), 2530–2540 (footnotes omitted).

---

## DOCUMENT 79: *McCleskey v. Kemp* (1987)

---

On April 22, 1987, the U.S. Supreme Court issued a ruling in what was quite possibly the most controversial capital punishment case since *Furman* (see Document 54).

The case was *McCleskey v. Kemp*. At issue was the petitioner's claim that "the Georgia capital sentencing process was administered in a racially discriminatory manner in violation of the Eighth and Fourteenth Amendments" (481 U.S. 279, 286).

In support of his claim McCleskey—who was black and had killed
a white police officer during a 1978 furniture store robbery—produced
as evidence a detailed statistical study of capital sentencing procedures
in Georgia conducted by University of Iowa law professor David Baldus and his colleagues, Charles Pulaski and George Woodworth. The
"Baldus study," as it became known, actually consisted of two sophisticated research programs—a 1983 procedural reform study (see
Document 74) and a subsequent (and larger) charging and sentencing
study—that examined more than two thousand murder cases that occurred in Georgia during the 1970s.

Controlling for 230 variables that might explain disparities in sentencing on nonracial grounds, the studies still found evidence of racial
discrimination in Georgia's capital sentencing—particularly with regard to the race of the victim. For example, one of the models used in
the studies indicated that defendants charged with killing whites were
4.3 times as likely to receive a death sentence as those charged with
killing blacks. The model also showed that black defendants were 1.1
times as likely to receive a death sentence as other defendants (481
U.S. 279, 287).

Although the Court accepted the statistical validity of the Baldus
study, it rejected McCleskey's petition on the basis that these statistics
still were "clearly insufficient to support an inference that any of the
decisionmakers in McCleskey's case acted with discriminatory purpose" (481 U.S. 279, 297).

Writing for the majority, Justice Powell explained that a successful
Fourteenth Amendment claim must prove purposeful discrimination
against the defendant, which the Baldus data did not. Furthermore,
because the Baldus study did not prove that race had been a factor in
McCleskey's particular case, the Eighth Amendment claim that his
death sentence had been influenced by an impermissible factor—
race—also was rejected by the Court.

## A. OPINION OF THE COURT

JUSTICE POWELL delivered the opinion of the Court. . . .

IV

. . .

B

. . .

Even Professor Baldus does not contend that his statistics *prove* that
race enters into any capital sentencing decisions or that race was a factor
in McCleskey's particular case. Statistics at most may show only

a likelihood that a particular factor entered into some decisions. There is, of course, some risk of racial prejudice influencing a jury's decision in a criminal case. There are similar risks that other kinds of prejudice will influence other criminal trials. . . . The question "is at what point that risk becomes constitutionally unacceptable,". . . . McCleskey asks us to accept the likelihood allegedly shown by the Baldus study as the constitutional measure of an unacceptable risk of racial prejudice influencing capital sentencing decisions. This we decline to do. . . .

## C

At most, the Baldus study indicates a discrepancy that appears to correlate with race. Apparent disparities in sentencing are an inevitable part of our criminal justice system. The discrepancy indicated by the Baldus study is "a far cry from the major systemic defects identified in *Furman*,". . . . As this Court has recognized, any mode for determining guilt or punishment "has its weaknesses and the potential for misuse." . . . Specifically, "there can be 'no perfect procedure for deciding in which cases governmental authority should be used to impose death.' " . . . Despite these imperfections, our consistent rule has been that constitutional guarantees are met when "the mode [for determining guilt or punishment] itself has been surrounded with safeguards to make it as fair as possible." . . . Where the discretion that is fundamental to our criminal process is involved, we decline to assume that what is unexplained is invidious. In light of the safeguards designed to minimize racial bias in the process, the fundamental value of jury trial in our criminal justice system, and the benefits that discretion provides to criminal defendants, we hold that the Baldus study does not demonstrate a constitutionally significant risk of racial bias affecting the Georgia capital sentencing process.

## B. DISSENTING OPINION

JUSTICE BRENNAN, with whom JUSTICE MARSHALL joins, and with whom JUSTICE BLACKMUN and JUSTICE STEVENS join in all but Part I, dissenting. . . .

## II

. . .

The Court today holds that Warren McCleskey's sentence was constitutionally imposed. It finds no fault in a system in which lawyers must tell their clients that race casts a large shadow on the capital sentencing process. The Court arrives at this conclusion by stating that the Baldus study cannot "*prove* that race enters into any capital sentencing decisions or that race was a factor in McCleskey's particular case." . . . Since, according to Professor Baldus, we cannot say "to a moral certainty" that race influenced a decision . . . , we can identify only "a likelihood that a particular factor entered into some decisions," . . . and "a discrepancy that appears to correlate with race." . . . This "likelihood" and "discrepancy," holds the Court, is insufficient to establish a constitutional violation. The Court reaches this conclusion by placing four factors on the scales opposite McCleskey's evidence: the desire to encourage sentencing discretion, the existence of "statutory safeguards" in the Georgia scheme, the fear of encouraging widespread challenges to other sentencing decisions, and the limits of the judicial role. The Court's evaluation of the significance of petitioner's evidence is fundamentally at odds with our consistent concern for rationality in capital sentencing, and the considerations that the majority invokes to discount that evidence cannot justify ignoring its force. . . .

                                    III

    . . .

                                     B

    . . .

    The statistical evidence in this case . . . relentlessly documents the risk that McCleskey's sentence was influenced by racial considerations. This evidence shows that there is a better than even chance in Georgia that race will influence the decision to impose the death penalty: a majority of defendants in white-victim crimes would not have been sentenced to die if their victims had been black. In determining whether this risk is acceptable, our judgment must be shaped by the awareness that "[t]he risk of racial prejudice infecting a capital sentencing proceeding is especially serious in light of the complete finality of the death sentence," . . . and that "[i]t is of vital importance to the defendant and to the community that any decision to impose the death sentence be, and appear to be, based on reason rather than caprice or emotion," . . . In determining the guilt of a defendant, a State must prove its case beyond a reasonable doubt. That is, we refuse to convict if the chance of error is simply less likely than not. Surely, we should not be willing to take a person's life if the chance that his death sentence was irrationally imposed is *more* likely than not. In light of the gravity of the interest at stake, petitioner's statistics on their face are a powerful demonstration of the type of risk that our Eighth Amendment jurisprudence has consistently condemned.

*Source*: 481 U.S. 279 (1987), 282–328 (footnotes omitted).

## DOCUMENT 80: *Death Penalty for Juveniles* (Victor Streib, 1987)

In 1987, Cleveland State University law professor Victor L. Streib (1941–   ) published a book devoted entirely to a discussion of the death penalty for juveniles.

In his book, Streib, a specialist in juvenile justice, procedural reform, and the social control of violence, provided the history and demographics of juvenile executions in the United States, and chronicled the evolution of death penalty laws pertaining to juveniles.

As philosophy professor and noted abolitionist Hugo Adam Bedau (see Documents 81–83), pointed out in his foreword to Streib's book: "For the first time we have at our fingertips the answers to myriad questions about juveniles and the death penalty. The book is a model of patient and resourceful investigation and is bound to advance understanding in legislatures, courts, and the general public. Anyone who reads it will find it difficult not to agree that it is high time to recognize the injustice of the death penalty for the young and to regard it as the 'cruel and unusual punishment' it really is" (in Streib 1987:viii).

This nation and its colonial antecedents have executed 281 juveniles over the past three and one-half centuries. The practice of juvenile executions, like that of criminal executions in general, peaked in the 1930s and 1940s. Executions of juvenile offenders ended temporarily in 1964 but began again in 1985.

While some persons have been executed for crimes committed as young as age ten, most of the juvenile offenders were age sixteen or seventeen when they committed their crimes; the average age was just over sixteen years. The younger offenders, particularly those under age fourteen, were executed in the greatest numbers before 1900. That is also true of the nine female juveniles executed. The last female juvenile execution was in 1912.

Whites constitute only one-quarter of the executed juveniles and only 20 percent of those executed since 1900. In striking contrast, the victims of these capital crimes were overwhelmingly whites, 89 percent overall and 93 percent since 1900. Eighty-one percent of these executions were for murder and 15 percent for rape. All forty-three rape offenders were black, all but one of their victims were white, and all the states that executed them were southern.

In line with the historical pattern for all executions in this country, the southern states predominate in juvenile executions, with 65 percent of the total. Georgia is the leader, with forty-one juvenile executions. Other leading states are North Carolina, Ohio, New York, Texas, and Virginia. Thirty-five states and the federal government have executed juveniles for their crimes.

This summary of the characteristics of these executed children and their crimes raises more questions than it answers. But perhaps it will at least serve to refute the commonly held belief that the death penalty has always been reserved for our most hardened criminals, the middle-aged three-time losers. While they are often the ones executed, offenders of more tender years, down even to prepubescence, also have been killed lawfully, hanging from our gallows, restrained in our gas chambers, sitting in our electric chairs, and lying on our hospital gurneys. . . .

The long-term solution to violent juvenile crime—or all crime, for that matter—cannot come from harsh criminal punishment, whether it is imprisonment or death. Given the individual freedom enjoyed in our society, the resultant ample opportunities for violent juvenile crime, and the low probability of being caught and punished, prevention through threatened punishment will always be insufficiently effective.

Our society must be willing to devote enormous resources to a search for the causes and cures of violent juvenile crime, just as we have done in the search for the causes and cures of such killer diseases as cancer. And we must not demand a complete cure in a short time, since no one knows how long it will take. We must at the same time beware of those persons who loudly proclaim that they have the cure now. Unfortunately, no one yet has the cure for violent juvenile crime. It seems clear, however, that the death penalty for juveniles has been given a long trial period and has been found wanting. Its societal costs are enormous, and it delays our search for a rational and acceptable means of reducing violent juvenile crime.

*Source*: Victor L. Streib, *Death Penalty for Juveniles* (Bloomington: Indiana University Press, 1987), 71, 189.

## DOCUMENT 81: Hugo Adam Bedau (1987)

Philosopher Hugo Adam Bedau is one of the most prominent scholarly opponents of the death penalty in the modern era.

Bedau first became interested in the issue of capital punishment in 1957, while teaching a course on ethics at Princeton University. In the years that followed, as the American death penalty debate grew increasingly intense, Bedau participated in death penalty reform efforts in New Jersey as both a scholar and an activist (Mackey 1976:300).

After receiving his Ph.D. from Harvard in 1961, Bedau joined the faculty of Reed College in his hometown of Portland, Oregon. There, he continued his work toward death penalty reform as research director for the Oregon Council to Abolish the Death Penalty and a leader in Oregon's referendum campaign to abolish capital punishment, which succeeded in 1964.

In 1966, Bedau accepted a position as professor and chairman of the Department of Philosophy at Tufts University in Medford, Massachusetts. There, he became the research director for the Massachusetts Council to Abolish the Death Penalty and president of the American League to Abolish Capital Punishment. He also provided research assistance to the NAACP Legal Defense and Educational Fund, and worked to help promote increased social science research on capital punishment (Mackey 1976:300).

Today, Bedau is the Austin Fletcher Professor of Philosophy at Tufts, a position he has held since 1970. He recently served as chairman of the National Coalition to Abolish the Death Penalty.

He is the author of numerous books and articles on capital punishment, including *In Spite of Innocence* (co-author, 1992), *Death is Different* (1987), *The Courts, the Constitution, and Capital Punishment* (1977), *Capital Punishment in the United States* (co-editor, 1976), and *The Death Penalty in America* (editor, 1964).

Following is an excerpt from one of Bedau's more recent books in which he discusses his reasons for opposing the death penalty.

During earlier centuries, the death penalty played a plausible, perhaps even justifiable, role in society's efforts to control crime and mete out just deserts to convicted offenders. After all, the alternative of imprisonment—the modern form of banishment—had yet to be systematically developed. Consequently, society in an earlier age could tolerate the death penalty with a clearer conscience than we can today. For us, however, the true dimension in which to assess this mode of punishment is neither its crime-fighting effectiveness nor its moral necessity, but its symbolism. Mistaken faith in deterrent efficacy, confusion over the requirements of justice, indifference to unfair administration, ignorance of non-lethal methods of social control—all these can explain only so much about the current support for the death penalty. The rest of the explanation lies elsewhere, in what executions symbolize, consciously or unconsciously, for those who favor them.

This symbolism deserves a closer look. The death penalty, today as in the past, symbolizes the ultimate power of the state, and of the government of society, over the individual citizen. Understandably, the public wants visible evidence that the authority of its political leaders is intact, their powers competent to deal with every social problem, and their courage resolute in the face of any danger. Anxiety about war, fear of crime, indignation at being victimized provoke the authorities to use the power of life and death as a public gesture of strength, self-confidence, and reassurance. Not surprisingly, many are unwilling to abandon the one symbol a society under law in peacetime has at its disposal that, above all others, expresses this power with awe-inspiring finality: the death penalty.

This is precisely why, in the end, we should oppose the death penalty in principle and without exception. As long as capital punishment is available under law for any crime, it is a temptation to excess. Tyrannical governments, from Idi Amin's Uganda to the Ayatollah's Iran, teach this lesson. At best the use of the death penalty here and elsewhere has been and continues to be capricious and arbitrary. The long history of several of our own states, notably Michigan and Wisconsin, quite apart from the experience of other nations, proves that the government of a civilized society does not *need* the death penalty. The citizenry should not clamor for it. Their political leaders should know better—as, of course, the best of them do—than to cultivate public approval for capital statutes, death sentences, and executions. Instead a civilized government should explain why such practices are ill-advised, and why they are ineffective in reducing crime, removing its causes, and responding to victimization.

*Source*: Hugo Adam Bedau, *Death Is Different: Studies in the Morality, Law, and Politics of Capital Punishment* (Boston: Northeastern University Press, 1987), 246–247 (footnotes omitted).

---

## DOCUMENT 82: "Miscarriages of Justice in Potentially Capital Cases" (Hugo Adam Bedau and Michael Radelet, 1987)

In 1987, Hugo Adam Bedau (see Document 81) and his colleague Michael Radelet, then an associate professor of sociology at the University of Florida, published a study in the *Stanford Law Review* in which they identified 350 people who had been wrongly convicted in capital (or potentially capital) cases in the United States between 1900 and 1985. Although some of these wrongful convictions took place in abolitionist states or were quickly overturned, many occurred in death penalty states and went uncorrected for years. And, according to Bedau and Radelet, twenty-three of those wrongly convicted actually were put to death (Bedau and Radelet 1987:36).

As the authors later explained, one of the goals of the study was to "show how the risk of executing the innocent was relevant to the on-

going debate over whether to retain, expand, or abolish the death penalty" (Radelet, Bedau, and Putnam 1992:ix). Following is an excerpt
from the 1987 study in which the authors discuss their findings.

Is it possible that the availability of the death penalty spurs the system
to work more reliably than it otherwise might? If the possibility of executing convicted murderers were abolished, would society lose the
greatest possible incentive to avoid tragic error? We think not. If this
were true, the proportion of erroneous convictions in potentially capital
cases should be higher in non-death penalty states than in death penalty
states—assuming equal probability for the discovery of errors in capital
and noncapital jurisdictions. Without data on the number of homicide
convictions in each state since the turn of the century, the results of our
research do not suffice to test this hypothesis.

Our results lead us to believe that the small number of cases in our
catalogue in which major doubts remain about the guilt of the executed
is an indication not of the reliability and fairness of the system, but rather
of its power and finality. For a variety of reasons, very few cases in this
century have managed to attract the sustained interest of persons in a
position to undertake the research necessary to challenge successfully a
guilty verdict meted out to a defendant later executed. Rarely are funds
available to investigate executions of the allegedly innocent; there are
not even funds available to investigate most of the convictions of those
allegedly wrongly imprisoned, whether or not they are under death sentence. The 1974 Florida case of James Adams illustrates this point: Once
the defendant is dead, the best source of evidence is gone, as is the main
motive to reinvestigate. Further, the limited resources of those who
might challenge the deceased's guilt are quickly absorbed by the legal
battles involved in trying to save the lives of others still on death row.
The result is that, as time passes, relevant evidence of a miscarriage remains undiscovered. Today or tomorrow, it may be virtually unobtain-
able. In addition, no organization exists whose purpose is to gather and
sift the evidence of a defendant's possible innocence after he or she has
been executed. The Court of Last Resort did a remarkable job in a few
capital cases, and our catalogue of errors is indebted to its labors. But
this organization never confined its attention to capital cases, and its
work spanned less than two decades (1947 to 1960). More to the point,
we know of no instance where it attempted to reopen any case of allegedly erroneous execution.

Finally, officials and citizens involved in a death penalty case, from
arrest to denial of commutation, tend to close ranks and resist admission
of error. They have been known to obstruct others from investigating
the charge of erroneous execution. Silent witnesses or true culprits are
even less likely to step forward if their failure to do so earlier has cost

the life of an innocent man. Our study of the records in hundreds of cases where error but no execution occurred confirms that all these factors play a role. Even if this were not so, exoneration of the innocent is thwarted from another direction. As others have noted, no forum save that of public opinion exists to present evidence in favor of the belief that some innocent person went to his death.

*Source*: Hugo Adam Bedau and Michael L. Radelet, "Miscarriages of Justice in Potentially Capital Cases," *Stanford Law Review* 40 (November 1987): 85–86.

## DOCUMENT 83: The "Miscarriage of Justice" Controversy (1988)

Shortly after Bedau and Radelet published their study "Miscarriages of Justice in Potentially Capital Cases" (see Document 82), two attorneys from the U.S. Department of Justice—Stephen J. Markman and Paul G. Cassell—wrote a rebuttal to the article at the request of then-Attorney General Edwin Meese, III (Radelet, Bedau, and Putnam 1992: ix).

The rebuttal (see Document 83A), in which Markman and Cassell harshly criticized the study, appeared in a subsequent edition of the *Stanford Law Review*, along with a response from Bedau and Radelet (see Document 83B), in which they staunchly defended their work.

### A. MARKMAN AND CASSELL'S REBUTTAL TO THE BEDAU-RADELET STUDY

The use of capital punishment entails some risk that an innocent person will be executed. Proponents of the death penalty have commonly taken the position that this risk is not great. The Bedau-Radelet study confirms this view. After "sustained and systematic" research, they point to only twenty-three out of more than 7000 executions as erroneous. Their judgments of error are unconvincing with respect to the twelve cases in which sufficient facts are available to test them. Their methodology makes their conclusion in the other eleven cases suspect as well. Assuming, however, for the sake of argument that as many as twenty-three innocent persons have been executed, the rate of error would be only about one-third of one percent over the past eighty-seven years. Moreover, even accepting the authors' claims, this minuscule rate of error has been reduced by more than one-third since 1943. . . .

According to Bedau and Radelet, ninety-four defendants have been the subjects of "miscarriages of justice" in capital or potentially capital cases since 1960. However, only twenty-six of these persons were sentenced to death. Only two were executed, and the authors give unconvincing reasons for concluding that these executions were erroneous. There is, in short, no persuasive evidence that any innocent person has been put to death in more than twenty-five years. . . .

The likely explanation for the absence of errors in capital cases during the past quarter century is the greater care taken by the courts to assure the correct resolution of such cases and, particularly, the painstaking reviews that occur in cases in which the death sentence is actually imposed. The point is illustrated by the very few "miscarriages of justice" claimed by Bedau and Radelet to have occurred in the decade after the Supreme Court upheld the constitutionality of the death penalty. Out of approximately 50,000 murder convictions during the period from 1977 to 1986, the authors point to only thirty-one persons who, they claim, were wrongly convicted of capital offenses or potential capital crimes. Even if one accepts their claim that all of these convictions were mistaken, the authors' accounts of these cases demonstrate that current postconviction procedures work reasonably well in discovering and correcting errors. After all, in each of these cases the mistake was discovered. Furthermore, in more than three-fourths of the cases the error was discovered within four years of conviction, resulting in the defendant's acquittal or release from prison, or in the dismissal of charges; and in eight of the cases the error was discovered within one year. . . .

Ultimately, the Bedau-Radelet study offers little to opponents of capital punishment. The eighty-four percent of Americans who support the death penalty do so not because they believe its administration is perfect, but because they believe it to be prudently administered in a manner consistent with the society's interest in justice and the protection of the innocent. Nothing presented by Bedau and Radelet undermines that conviction.

*Source*: Stephen J. Markman and Paul G. Cassell, "Protecting the Innocent: A Response to the Bedau-Radelet Study," *Stanford Law Review* 41 (November 1988): 146, 150, 151–152, 160 (footnotes omitted). Copyright © 1988 by the Board of Trustees of the Leland Stanford Junior University.

## B. BEDAU AND RADELET'S RESPONSE TO MARKMAN AND CASSELL

The Department of Justice under the Reagan Administration has made quite clear its support for the death penalty, and the critique of our research by Markman and Cassell is but one more indication of that support. We view this hostile attention as evidence of how influential the Department thinks our research may prove to be. Since Markman and Cassell begin their critique by conceding that human judgments are not infallible and that "the possibility exists" that innocent defendants will be executed, they evidently concede one of the basic assumptions of our research. The fundamental questions in dispute are thus how to measure the risk of such error, the extent to which our research enables one to make that measurement, the role this risk should play in a rational assessment of the death penalty, and the adequacy of the evidence to convince the unbiased observer that such errors have indeed occurred. In their zeal to attack our research, our critics have failed to shed light on these important issues. Their efforts appear to spring largely from unacknowledged political roots; as a result, they either obfuscate the issues or merely trumpet the limits of our research as though we had failed to state them in the first place.

The basic problem with Markman and Cassell's response is that it seems bent on defending the criminal justice system in every regard that bears on the death penalty and its administration. This inflexible stance requires our critics to deny that anyone actually innocent has ever been executed, lest the criminal justice system itself be charged with such an error. It may be that the failure of the criminal justice system to acknowledge error of this sort is itself part of the problem rather than evidence that no such errors have occurred. Criticism of Markman and Cassell's sort seems to us not seriously intended to show how the death penalty is "Protecting the Innocent." Instead, it is an effort to protect the myth of systemic infallibility: the myth that prosecutors in capital cases never indict an innocent person; that if they do the trial courts can be counted on to acquit; that if the courts convict they sentence to prison rather than to death; that if courts do convict and sentence to death the appellate courts may be relied on to rectify an erroneous conviction; and that if the appellate courts fail then the chief executive will come to the rescue. We do not believe this myth, we do not sympathize with the effort to protect it, and we trust that anyone who studies our research will agree with us in rejecting the myth. We stand firmly behind every conclusion reached in our original essay.

*Source*: Hugo Adam Bedau and Michael L. Radelet, "The Myth of Infallibility: A Reply to Markman and Cassell," *Stanford Law Review* 41 (November 1988): 169–170 (footnotes omitted). Copyright © 1988 by the Board of Trustees of the Leland Stanford Junior University.

## DOCUMENT 84: Public Opinion and the Death Penalty (1988)

By 1988, public support for the death penalty had increased by another 7 points since the 1985 high of 72 percent reported by the Gallup Poll (see Document 75). Nearly eight in ten Americans (79 percent) now were in favor of executing persons convicted of murder.

The poll also found that 63 percent of Americans were in favor of the death penalty for persons who attempted to assassinate the president, 51 percent supported the death penalty for rapists, and 49 percent felt that airplane hijackers should be executed.

**DECEMBER 4**
**DEATH PENALTY**

Interviewing Date: 9/25–10/1/87
Special Telephone Survey

*Do you favor or oppose the death penalty for persons convicted of murder?*

| | |
|---|---|
| Favor | 79% |
| Oppose | 16 |
| No opinion | 5 |

*Source*: *The Gallup Poll: Public Opinion 1988* (Wilmington, Del.: Scholarly Resources Inc., 1988), 250. Copyright 1988 by Scholarly Resources Inc. Reprinted by permission of Scholarly Resources Inc.

## DOCUMENT 85: Deterrence or Brutalization? (William J. Bowers, 1988)

In 1988, sociologist William J. Bowers reported the findings of his extensive review of empirical studies that examined the relationship between executions and violence. Rather than discovering evidence of a deterrent effect, Bowers noted, most of these studies found a clear, short-term "brutalizing" effect that occurred within the first one or two months after an execution.

In his report, Bowers paid special attention to a 1980 study conducted by David Phillips.[1] Phillips' highly controversial study of execution publicity on homicides in London from 1858 to 1921 indicated that fifteen of the twenty-two executions during that period resulted in a significantly lower number of homicides during the week of the execution. The more newspaper coverage an execution had received, the more significant the reduction in execution-week homicides. While homicide rates remained lower than average during the first week following the execution, they then increased during the next three weeks. Thus, the deterrent effect, if any, was short-lived and offset by the subsequent increase in homicides (Bowers 1988:69–70; Paternoster 1991: 231).

In his critique of Phillips' study, Bowers extended the execution and homicide data to encompass a ten-week period before and after each execution, as well as the execution week itself. He found that the number of homicides committed during the ten weeks following an execution was significantly higher than during the ten weeks prior to an execution, and that this "brutalization effect" increased according to the amount of publicity the execution had received.

## NOTE
1. David Phillips, "The Deterrent Effect of Capital Punishment: New Evidence on an Old Controversy," *American Journal of Sociology* 86 (1980): 139–147.

These data on executions and homicides in London during the period 1858–1921 are obviously *not* the "first compelling statistical evidence" that executions deter homicides, as Phillips claimed. Quite the contrary, they show that executions encourage homicides, more so the more they are publicized.

Such a brutalizing pattern also appears (upon close scrutiny) in most previous studies of homicides in the days, weeks, or months following executions. Yet, these studies usually examined too few executions with too few homicide observations to conclude that a brutalizing effect of as few as two or three homicides per execution was statistically reliable. The first exception was our study of some 600 executions over a 57-year period in New York State. With 692 monthly homicide observations, a rise of two homicides in the first month after an execution was statistically significant. The second exception is Phillips's study as replicated and reanalyzed here. Though Phillips selected only 22 executions for study with 462 weekly homicide observations (week $-10$ through $+10$), an average increase of 2.7 homicides per execution (b = .27 per week over ten weeks) is significant beyond the .05 probability level (two-tailed test).

What these London data show for the first time is that the rise in homicides following an execution is associated with the publicity accorded the case. Although homicides rose following the less as well as the more publicized of these cases, the rise was considerably more pronounced among the more publicized ones. This effect of publicity is consistent with the notion that the message executions convey is one of "lethal vengeance"—to strike back with deadly force against someone who has gravely offended—and that this message is more effectively conveyed the more broadly executions are publicized.

Potential offenders who learn about an execution do not appear to identify, as we wish they would, with the murderer who is executed, but may instead identify with the state as an "enforcer" and "executioner" seeking lethal vengeance. The example of an execution may release inhibitions against killing or reinforce justifications for killing, at least among those few who have reached a state of "readiness to kill." . . . Moreover, the evidence of brutalization is consistent with a growing body of evidence that publicized acts of lethal violence—suicide . . . , homicide . . . , and fatal accidents . . . —are followed in kind, and with the longstanding judicial wisdom that "brutal punishment brutalizes."

*Source*: William J. Bowers, "The Effect of Executions Is Brutalization, Not Deterrence." In Kenneth C. Haas and James A. Inciardi, eds., *Challenging Capital Punishment: Legal and Social Science Approaches* (Newbury Park, Calif.: Sage Publications, 1988), 78–79 (footnotes omitted).

---

## DOCUMENT 86: *Thompson v. Oklahoma* (1988)

In the 1982 case of *Eddings v. Oklahoma* (see Document 71), the U.S. Supreme Court overturned the death sentence of Monty Lee Eddings, who had been sixteen at the time of his crime, on the grounds that the sentencing judge had failed to consider the full range of mitigating circumstances in the case, including Eddings' youth and difficult upbringing. However, the Court had made no ruling as to what might be considered the constitutionally permissible minimum age for execution.

In 1988, after being repeatedly petitioned to make a decision on the issue (Paternoster 1991:97–98; Tushnet 1994:77), the Court finally issued a minimum age ruling in the case of *Thompson v. Oklahoma.*

William Wayne Thompson had been fifteen years old when he actively participated (with three older friends) in the 1983 murder of his former brother-in-law, who apparently had abused Thompson's sister. Thompson was tried as an adult, convicted, and sentenced to death by an Oklahoma jury. The Oklahoma appeals court affirmed both his conviction and sentence.

The U.S. Supreme Court granted certiorari in the case specifically to determine "whether the execution of that sentence would violate the constitutional prohibition against the infliction of 'cruel and unusual punishments' because petitioner was only 15 years old at the time of his offense" (108 S.Ct. 2687, 2690).

In a 5–3 opinion (one justice did not participate in this decision), the Court held that the Eighth Amendment did indeed prohibit the execution of an individual who was under sixteen years of age at the time of his or her offense.

Writing the opinion of the Court, Justice Stevens pointed out that (1) of the eighteen states that had set a minimum age for the death penalty, that age was never younger than sixteen; (2) other countries of Anglo-American heritage and "leading members of the Western European community" appeared to share the opinion that executing individuals under the age of sixteen "would offend civilized standards of decency"; and (3) that modern juries typically were reluctant to impose the death penalty on persons under the age of sixteen.

In addition to these three indicators that "contemporary standards of decency" had evolved to the point where it was no longer constitutionally acceptable to execute individuals under the age of sixteen, Justice Stevens emphasized the importance of youth as a mitigating factor in determining an individual's level of culpability for a crime, and he noted that the death penalty was very unlikely to have any deterrent effect on those under sixteen.

## A. OPINION OF THE COURT

Justice STEVENS announced the judgment of the Court and delivered an opinion in which Justice BRENNAN, Justice MARSHALL, and Justice BLACKMUN join. [Justice O'CONNOR filed a separate opinion concurring in the judgment]. . . .

V

. . .

[T]he Court has already endorsed the proposition that less culpability should attach to a crime committed by a juvenile than to a comparable crime committed by an adult. The basis for this conclusion is too obvious to require extended explanation. Inexperience, less education, and less intelligence make the teenager less able to evaluate the consequences of his or her conduct while at the same time he or she is much more apt to be motivated by mere emotion or peer pressure than is an adult. The reasons why juveniles are not trusted with the privileges and responsibilities of an adult also explain why their irresponsible conduct is not as morally reprehensible as that of an adult. . . .

In *Gregg* we concluded that as "an expression of society's moral outrage at particularly offensive conduct," retribution was not "inconsistent with our respect for the dignity of men." . . . Given the lesser culpability of the juvenile offender, the teenager's capacity for growth, and society's fiduciary obligations to its children, this conclusion is simply inapplicable to the execution of a 15-year-old offender.

For such a young offender, the deterrence rationale is equally unacceptable. The Department of Justice statistics indicate that about 98% of the arrests for willful homicide involved persons who were over 16 at the time of the offense. Thus, excluding younger persons from the class that is eligible for the death penalty will not diminish the deterrent value of capital punishment for the vast majority of potential offenders. And even with respect to those under 16 years of age, it is obvious that the potential deterrent value of the death sentence is insignificant for two reasons. The likelihood that the teenage offender has made the kind of cost-benefit analysis that attaches any weight to the possibility of execution is so remote as to be virtually nonexistent. And, even if one posits such a cold-blooded calculation by a 15-year-old, it is fanciful to believe that he would be deterred by the knowledge that a small number of persons his age have been executed during the 20th century. In short, we are not persuaded that the imposition of the death penalty for offenses committed by persons under 16 years of age has made, or can be expected to make, any measurable contribution to the goals that capital punishment is intended to achieve. It is, therefore, "nothing more than the purposeless and needless imposition of pain and suffering" *Coker v. Georgia,* . . . and thus an unconstitutional punishment.

## B. DISSENTING OPINION

Justice SCALIA, with whom THE CHIEF JUSTICE and Justice WHITE join, dissenting. . . .

II

A

. . .

[T]he statistics of executions demonstrate nothing except the fact that our society has always agreed that executions of 15-year-old criminals should be rare, and in more modern times has agreed that they (like all other executions) should be even rarer still. There is no rational basis for discerning in that a societal judgment that no one so much as a day under 16 can *ever* be mature and morally responsible enough to deserve that penalty; and there is no justification except our own predilection for converting a statistical rarity of occurrence into an absolute constitutional ban. One must surely fear that, now that the Court has taken the first step of requiring an individualized consideration in capital cases, today's decision begins a second stage of converting into constitutional rules the general results of that individuation. One could readily run the same statistical argument with respect to other classes of defendants. Between 1930 and 1955, for example, 30 women were executed in the United States. Only three were executed between then and 1986—and none in the 22-year period between 1962 and 1984. Proportionately, the drop is as impressive as that which the plurality points to in 15-year-old executions. (From 30 in 25 years to 3 in the next 31 years, versus from 18 in 50 years to potentially one—the present defendant—in the next 40 years.) Surely the conclusion is not that it is unconstitutional to impose capital punishment upon a woman.

If one believes that the data the plurality relies upon are effective to establish, with the requisite degree of certainty, a constitutional consensus in this society that no person can ever be executed for a crime committed under the age of 16, it is difficult to see why the same judgment should not extend to crimes committed under the age of 17, or of 18. The frequency of such executions shows an almost equivalent drop in recent years, . . . and of the 18 States that have enacted age limits upon capital punishment, only 3 have selected the age of 16, only 4 the age of 17, and all the rest the age of 18. . . . It seems plain to me, in other words, that there is no clear line here, which suggests that the plurality is inappropriately acting in a legislative rather than a judicial capacity. Doubtless at some age a line does exist—as it has always existed in the common law . . . —below which a juvenile can *never* be considered fully responsible for murder. The evidence that the views of our society, so steadfast and so uniform that they have become part of the agreed-upon laws that we live by, regard that absolute age to be 16 is nonexistent.

*Source*: 108 S.Ct. 2687 (1988), 2690–2718 (footnotes omitted).

## DOCUMENT 87: *Stanford v. Kentucky* (1989)

One year after the Supreme Court ruled that the Eighth Amendment prohibited the execution of an individual who was under sixteen years of age at the time of his or her offense (see Document 86), it further clarified its position on the execution of juveniles in the case of *Stanford v. Kentucky* and its companion case, *Wilkins v. Missouri.*

Kevin Stanford had been approximately seventeen years and four months old in 1981 when he and an accomplice repeatedly raped and sodomized a gas station attendant, Barbel Poore, after robbing the gas station, then drove her to a secluded area and shot her in the face and again in the back of the head. Heath Wilkins had been approximately sixteen years and six months old in 1985 when he stabbed to death Nancy Allen, a 26-year-old mother of two who was working behind the counter of a convenience store she owned with her husband. Both had been tried as adults, convicted, and sentenced to death for their crimes. Both appealed their death sentences to the Supreme Court on the grounds that, under "evolving standards of decency" (see Document 41), the Eighth Amendment prohibits the punishment for individuals who were only sixteen or seventeen years old at the time they committed their crimes.

The Court rejected their Eighth Amendment argument on the grounds that neither a historical nor a modern societal consensus forbade the imposition of capital punishment on individuals who commit murder at the age of sixteen or seventeen.

## A. OPINION OF THE COURT

JUSTICE SCALIA announced the judgment of the Court and delivered the opinion of the Court with respect to Parts I, II, III, and IV-A, and an opinion with respect to Parts IV-B and V, in which THE CHIEF JUSTICE, JUSTICE WHITE, and JUSTICE KENNEDY join. . . .

II

The thrust of both Wilkins' and Stanford's arguments is that imposition of the death penalty on those who were juveniles when they committed their crimes falls within the Eighth Amendment's prohibition against "cruel and unusual punishments." . . . Wilkins would have us define juveniles as individuals 16 years of age and under; Stanford would draw the line at 17.

Neither petitioner asserts that his sentence constitutes one of "those modes or acts of punishment that had been considered cruel and unusual at the time that the Bill of Rights was adopted." . . . Nor could they support such a contention. At that time, the common law set the rebuttable presumption of incapacity to commit any felony at the age of 14, and theoretically permitted capital punishment to be imposed on anyone over the age of 7. . . . In accordance with the standards of this common-law tradition, at least 281 offenders under the age of 18 have been executed in this country, and at least 126 under the age of 17. . . .

Thus petitioners are left to argue that their punishment is contrary to the "evolving standards of decency that mark the progress of a maturing society," . . . They are correct in asserting that this Court has "not confined the prohibition embodied in the Eighth Amendment to 'barbarous' methods that were generally outlawed in the 18th century," but instead has interpreted the Amendment "in a flexible and dynamic manner." . . . In determining what standards have "evolved," however, we have looked not to our own conceptions of decency, but to those of modern American society as a whole. . . .

### III

"[F]irst" among the " 'objective indicia that reflect the public attitude toward a given sanction' " are statutes passed by society's elected representatives. . . . Of the 37 States whose laws permit capital punishment, 15 decline to impose it upon 16-year-old offenders and 12 decline to impose it on 17-year-old offenders. This does not establish the degree of national consensus this Court has previously thought sufficient to label a particular punishment cruel and unusual. . . .

Petitioners make much of the recently enacted federal statute providing capital punishment for certain drug-related offenses, but limiting that punishment to offenders 18 and over. . . . That reliance is entirely misplaced. To begin with, the statute in question does not embody a judgment by the Federal Legislature that no murder is heinous enough to warrant the execution of such a youthful offender, but merely that the narrow class of offense it defines is not. The congressional judgment on the broader question, if apparent at all, is to be found in the law that permits 16- and 17-year-olds (after appropriate findings) to be tried and punished as adults for all federal offenses, including those bearing a capital penalty that is not limited to 18-year-olds. . . . Moreover, even if it were true that no federal statute permitted the execution of persons under 18, that would not remotely establish—in the face of a substantial number of state statutes to the contrary—a national consensus that such punishment is inhumane, any more than the absence of a federal lottery establishes a national consensus that lotteries are socially harmful. To be sure, the absence of a federal death penalty for 16- or 17-year-olds (if it existed) might be evidence that there is no national consensus in favor of such punishment. It is not the burden of Kentucky and Missouri, however, to establish a national consensus approving what their citizens have voted to do; rather, it is the "heavy burden" of petitioners, . . . to establish a national consensus against it. As far as the primary and most reliable indication of consensus is concerned—the pattern of enacted laws—petitioners have failed to carry that burden.

## IV

## A

Wilkins and Stanford argue, however, that even if the laws themselves do not establish a settled consensus, the application of the laws does. That contemporary society views capital punishment of 16- and 17-year-old offenders as inappropriate is demonstrated, they say, by the reluctance of juries to impose, and prosecutors to seek, such sentences. Petitioners are quite correct that a far smaller number of offenders under 18 than over 18 have been sentenced to death in this country. From 1982 through 1988, for example, out of 2,106 total death sentences, only 15 were imposed on individuals who were 16 or under when they committed their crimes, and only 30 on individuals who were 17 at the time of the crime. . . . And it appears that actual executions for crimes committed under age 18 accounted for only about two percent of the total number of executions that occurred between 1642 and 1986. . . . As Wilkins points out, the last execution of a person who committed a crime under 17 years of age occurred in 1959. These statistics, however, carry little significance. Given the undisputed fact that a far smaller percentage of capital crimes are committed by persons under 18 than over 18, the discrepancy in treatment is much less than might seem. Granted, however, that a substantial discrepancy exists, that does not establish the requisite proposition that the death sentence for offenders under 18 is categorically unacceptable to prosecutors and juries. To the contrary, it is not only possible, but overwhelmingly probable, that the very considerations which induce petitioners and their supporters to believe that death should never be imposed on offenders under 18 cause prosecutors and juries to believe that it should rarely be imposed. . . .

## V

Having failed to establish a consensus against capital punishment for 16- and 17-year-old offenders through state and federal statutes and the behavior of prosecutors and juries, petitioners seek to demonstrate it through other indicia, including public opinion polls, the views of interest groups, and the positions adopted by various professional associations. We decline the invitation to rest constitutional law upon such uncertain foundations. A revised national consensus so broad, so clear, and so enduring as to justify a permanent prohibition upon all units of democratic government must appear in the operative acts (laws and the application of laws) that the people have approved. . . .

* * *

We discern neither a historical nor a modern societal consensus forbidding the imposition of capital punishment on any person who murders at 16 or 17 years of age. Accordingly, we conclude that such punishment does not offend the Eighth Amendment's prohibition against cruel and unusual punishment.

## B. DISSENTING OPINION

JUSTICE BRENNAN, with whom JUSTICE MARSHALL, JUSTICE BLACKMUN, and JUSTICE STEVENS join, dissenting.

I believe that to take the life of a person as punishment for a crime committed when below the age of 18 is cruel and unusual and hence is prohibited by the Eighth Amendment. . . .

### I

. . .

### A

The Court's discussion of state laws concerning capital sentencing, . . . gives a distorted view of the evidence of contemporary standards that these legislative determinations provide. Currently, 12 of the States whose statutes permit capital punishment specifically mandate that offenders under age 18 not be sentenced to death. . . . When one adds to these 12 States the 15 (including the District of Columbia) in which capital punishment is not authorized at all, it appears that the governments in fully 27 of the States have concluded that no one under 18 should face the death penalty. A further three States explicitly refuse to authorize sentences of death for those who committed their offense when under 17, . . . making a total of 30 States that would not tolerate the execution of petitioner Wilkins. Congress' most recent enactment of a death penalty statute also excludes those under 18. . . .

### D

. . .

It is unnecessary, however, to rest a view that the Eighth Amendment prohibits the execution of minors solely upon a judgment as to the meaning to be attached to the evidence of contemporary values outlined above, for the execution of juveniles fails to satisfy two well-established and independent Eighth Amendment requirements—that a punishment not be disproportionate, and that it make a contribution to acceptable goals of punishment. . . .

### III

. . .

### C

Juveniles very generally lack that degree of blameworthiness that is, in my view, a constitutional prerequisite for the imposition of capital punishment under our precedents concerning the Eighth Amendment proportionality principle. The individualized consideration of an offender's youth and culpability at the transfer stage and at sentencing has not operated to ensure that the only offenders under 18 singled out for the ultimate penalty are exceptional individuals whose level of responsibility is more developed than that of their peers. In that circumstance, I believe that the same categorical assumption that juveniles as a class are insufficiently mature to be regarded as fully responsible that we make in so many other areas is appropriately made in determining whether minors may be subjected to the death penalty. As we noted in *Thompson*, . . . it would be ironic if the assumptions we so readily make about minors as a class were suddenly unavailable in conducting proportionality analysis. I would hold that the Eighth Amendment prohibits the execution of any person for a crime committed below the age of 18.

## IV

Under a second strand of Eighth Amendment inquiry into whether a particular sentence is excessive and hence unconstitutional, we ask whether the sentence makes a measurable contribution to acceptable goals of punishment. . . . The two "principal social purposes" of capital punishment are said to be "retribution and the deterrence of capital crimes by prospective offenders." . . . Unless the death penalty applied to persons for offenses committed under 18 measurably contributes to one of these goals, the Eighth Amendment prohibits it. . . .

The deterrent value of capital punishment rests "on the assumption that we are rational beings who always think before we act, and then base our actions on a careful calculation of the gains and losses involved." . . . As the plurality noted in *Thompson*, . . . "the likelihood that the teenage offender has made the kind of cost-benefit analysis that attaches any weight to the possibility of execution is so remote as to be virtually nonexistent." First, juveniles "have less capacity . . . to think in long-range terms than adults," . . . and their careful weighing of a distant, uncertain, and indeed highly unlikely consequence prior to action is most improbable. In addition, juveniles have little fear of death, because they have "a profound conviction of their own omnipotence and immortality." . . . Because imposition of the death penalty on persons for offenses committed under the age of 18 makes no measurable contribution to the goals of either retribution or deterrence, it is "nothing more than the purposeless and needless imposition of pain and suffering," . . . and is thus excessive and unconstitutional.

*Source*: 492 U.S. 361 (1989), 364–405 (footnotes omitted).

## DOCUMENT 88: *Penry v. Lynaugh* (1989)

In 1986, the Supreme Court ruled that execution of the insane was unconstitutional under the Eighth Amendment, based on the nation's "common law heritage" in which the execution of the insane was considered "savage and inhuman" (see Document 77).

Three years later, the Court issued a ruling on a related issue—the execution of the mentally retarded—in the 1989 case of *Penry v. Lynaugh*.

Johnny Paul Penry had been convicted and sentenced to death for the 1979 rape and murder of a woman, Pamela Carpenter, in her home. Carpenter described her attacker prior to her death, and Penry, who fit the description and had a previous conviction for rape, was arrested and confessed to the crime.

Though 22 at the time of his crime, pretrial testing had indicated that Penry had the mental age of a 6½-year-old child, the social maturity of a 9- or 10-year-old, and an IQ of 54. This information, and other mitigating evidence pertaining to Penry's mental retardation, learning disabilities, and childhood abuse, had been presented during Penry's trial but had not influenced the jury's decision to impose the death penalty.

Although the Supreme Court overturned Penry's death sentence on the grounds that it had not been explained clearly enough to the jury that they could consider Penry's mental retardation as a mitigating factor, it rejected his claim that the Eighth Amendment categorically prohibits the execution of the mentally retarded.

Writing for the majority in a case consisting of numerous concurring and dissenting opinions, Justice O'Connor explained that the Eighth Amendment would likely prohibit the execution of profoundly or severely retarded persons who are unable to understand or appreciate the wrongfulness of their actions. However, the jury had found Penry competent to stand trial and had rejected his insanity defense, and therefore he did not appear to fall into this category of offender.

Furthermore, the Court rejected Penry's claim that there was a national consensus against the execution of retarded persons on the basis that only one state in the nation specifically prohibited the execution of such persons. Although Penry also had provided evidence from opinion polls that showed that a majority of Americans disapproved of the death penalty for the mentally retarded, the Court contended that such polls "do not establish a societal consensus, absent some legislative reflection of the sentiment expressed therein" (492 U.S. 302, 335).


## A. OPINION OF THE COURT

JUSTICE O'CONNOR delivered the opinion of the Court. . . .

IV

. . .

B

. . .

It was well settled at common law that "idiots," together with "lunatics," were not subject to punishment for criminal acts committed under those incapacities. . . .

The common law prohibition against punishing "idiots" for their crimes suggests that it may indeed be "cruel and unusual" punishment to execute persons who are profoundly or severely retarded and wholly lacking the capacity to appreciate the wrongfulness of their actions. Because of the protections afforded by the insanity defense today, such a person is not likely to be convicted or face the prospect of punishment. . . . Moreover, under *Ford* v. *Wainwright*, . . . someone who is "unaware of the punishment they are about to suffer and why they are to suffer it" cannot be executed. . . .

Such a case is not before us today. Penry was found competent to stand trial. In other words, he was found to have the ability to consult with his lawyer with a reasonable degree of rational understanding, and was found to have a rational as well as factual understanding of the proceedings against him. . . . In addition, the jury rejected his insanity defense, which reflected their conclusion that Penry knew that his conduct was wrong and was capable of conforming his conduct to the requirements of the law. . . .

Penry argues, however, that there is objective evidence today of an emerging national consensus against execution of the mentally retarded, reflecting the "evolving standards of decency that mark the progress of a maturing society." *Trop* v. *Dulles*. . . . Only one State, however [Georgia], currently bans execution of retarded persons who have been found guilty of a capital offense. . . . Maryland has enacted a similar statute which will take effect on July 1, 1989. . . .

In our view, the two state statutes prohibiting execution of the mentally retarded, even when added to the 14 States that have rejected capital punishment completely, do not provide sufficient evidence at present of a national consensus.

Penry does not offer any evidence of the general behavior of juries with respect to sentencing mentally retarded defendants, nor of decisions of prosecutors. He points instead to several public opinion surveys that indicate strong public opposition to execution of the retarded. For example, a poll taken in Texas found that 86% of those polled supported the death penalty, but 73% opposed its application to the mentally retarded. . . . A Florida poll found 71% of those surveyed were opposed to the execution of mentally retarded capital defendants, while only 12% were in favor. . . . A Georgia poll found 66% of those polled opposed to the death penalty for the retarded, 17% in favor, with 16% responding that it depends how retarded the person is. . . . In addition, the AAMR, the country's oldest and largest organization of professionals working with the mentally retarded, opposes the execution of persons who are mentally retarded. . . . The public sentiment expressed in these and other polls and resolutions may ultimately find expression in legislation, which is an objective indicator of contemporary values upon which we can rely. But at present, there is insufficient evidence of a national consensus against executing mentally retarded people convicted of capital offenses for us to conclude that it is categorically prohibited by the Eighth Amendment. . . .

C

. . .

In sum, mental retardation is a factor that may well lessen a defendant's culpability for a capital offense. But we cannot conclude today that the Eighth Amendment precludes the execution of any mentally retarded person of Penry's ability convicted of a capital offense simply by virtue of his or her mental retardation alone. So long as sentencers can consider and give effect to mitigating evidence of mental retardation in imposing sentence, an individualized determination whether "death is the appropriate punishment" can be made in each particular case. While a national consensus against execution of the mentally retarded may someday emerge reflecting the "evolving standards of decency that mark the progress of a maturing society," there is insufficient evidence of such a consensus today.

## B. DISSENTING OPINION

JUSTICE BRENNAN, with whom JUSTICE MARSHALL joins, . . . dissenting in part. . . .

II

. . .

A

. . .

Even if mental retardation alone were not invariably associated with a lack of the degree of culpability upon which death as a proportionate punishment is predicated, I would still hold the execution of the mentally retarded to be unconstitutional. If there are among the mentally retarded exceptional individuals as responsible for their actions as persons who suffer no such disability, the individualized consideration afforded at sentencing fails to ensure that they are the only mentally retarded offenders who will be picked out to receive a death sentence. The consideration of mental retardation as a mitigating factor is inadequate to guarantee, as the Constitution requires, that an individual who is not fully blameworthy for his or her crime because of a mental disability does not receive the death penalty. . . .

B

Because I believe that the Eighth Amendment to the United States Constitution stands in the way of a State killing a mentally retarded person for a crime for which, as a result of his or her disability, he or she is not fully culpable, I would reverse the judgment of the Court of Appeals in its entirety.

*Source*: 492 U.S. 302 (1989), 307–349 (footnotes omitted).

---

## DOCUMENT 89: "A National Study of the *Furman*-Commuted Inmates: Assessing the Threat to Society from Capital Offenders" (1989)

Potential recidivism—that is, the possibility that an individual convicted of a crime will offend again in the future—often is mentioned by retentionists to justify the death penalty and because of its ability to permanently incapacitate violent offenders.

The Supreme Court's 1972 decision in *Furman* (see Document 54), which resulted in the commutation of more than 600 death sentences nationwide, presented the ideal situation in which to study actual recidivism among former death row inmates.

In 1989, James W. Marquart, an associate professor in the College of Criminal Justice at Sam Houston State University, and doctoral student Jonathan R. Sorensen published a study in which they tracked the prison and parole (if applicable) behavior of 558 of the *Furman*-commuted prisoners for nearly fifteen years.

Marquart and Sorensen found that seven of these former death row inmates were responsible for seven additional murders—six within prisons and one in free society (Marquart and Sorensen 1989:27). However, the majority served their prison sentences with few instances of serious misconduct and were not arrested for additional crimes if paroled.

What factors contributed to this low level of recidivism? The researchers hypothesized that the relatively good prison behavior of the *Furman*-commuted inmates may have been partly due to the fact that many of them already had lived enough years on death row to become used to institutional life before joining the general prison population. Furthermore, the average age of the *Furman* commutees was thirty-one years, making them older than most "new" inmates. Similarly, those who eventually were paroled typically were in their forties when released from prison. Therefore, Marquart and Sorensen suggested that it was the aging process and its effect on criminal activity, also known as "aging out of crime," that may have had the most impact on the *Furman* inmates' low levels of recidivism in free society. "In other words," they explained, "the dual effects of long prison terms (incapacitation) and aging on these offenders—presumably the high risk offenders—effectively reduced their potential for future criminal activity" (Marquart and Sorensen 1989:26).

[Legal philosopher] H.L.A. Hart asked: "What is the weight and character of the evidence that the death penalty is required for the protection of society?" This question, in our opinion, is the most salient one in any discussion of the utility of capital punishment. Seven (1.3%) *Furman*-commuted prisoners were responsible for seven additional murders. Certainly execution of all 558 prisoners would have prevented these killings. However, such a "preemptive strike" would not have greatly protected society. In addition, four innocent prisoners would have been put to death. The question then becomes whether saving the lives of the seven victims was worth the execution of four innocent inmates.

The data in this paper suggest that these prisoners did not represent a significant threat to society. Most have performed well in the prison; those few who have committed additional violent acts are indistinguishable from those who have not. Therefore, over-prediction of secondary violence is indicated. More than two-thirds of the *Furman* inmates, using a very liberal definition of violence, were false positives—predicted to be violent but were not. We cannot conclude from these data that their execution would have protected or benefitted society.

There are numerous policy implications to be drawn from the data presented in this paper. We do not suggest that every commuted capital offender can be released into free society. Some, albeit a minority, certainly need long-term confinement in maximum security facilities. Life-without-parole statutes are not the answer either because the indiscriminate warehousing of these prisoners would not have prevented numerous killings in free society. What we are suggesting is that the great majority of the *Furman* inmates were not violent predators in the prison or free society. The data presented in this paper suggest that current capital sentencing schemes predicated on their incapacitation effect, as is the practice of many states today that include a prediction of future dangerousness to justify executions, cannot accomplish their goals accurately or with a sense of fair play.

*Source*: James W. Marquart and Jonathan R. Sorensen, "A National Study of the *Furman*-Commuted Inmates: Assessing the Threat to Society from Capital Offenders," *Loyola of Los Angeles Law Review* 23 (November 1989): 27–28 (footnotes omitted).

# Part VI

# The Death Penalty in the 1990s: Contemporary Issues

## CAPITAL POLITICS

The procedural abuses Justice Powell and many others had criticized (Document 71) were under serious attack during the 1990s. Public and political support for procedural reform was spurred on by dramatic examples of execution delays involving undisputedly guilty convicted murderers. Appeals and collateral review after sentencing delayed the execution of John Wayne Gacy, who murdered twenty-seven young boys, for fourteen years; they delayed Robert Alton Harris's execution for thirteen years; and they delayed the execution of Los Angeles-area "freeway killer" William Bonin for fourteen years.

In spite of abolitionists' efforts, the political power of public sentiment was demonstrated vividly in 1995 when New York once again instituted the death penalty (Document 109). As *Los Angeles Times* columnist Dana Parsons wryly noted:

It's almost required that major political figures support the death penalty, regardless of how seldom the officeholder actually confronts the issue. . . . It's . . . a no-lose proposition for a politician. No political harm can come from supporting executions, unless you make the mistake of being consistent or nonarbitrary in your support. For example, where was the chorus of support for O. J. Simpson facing a possible death sentence for the double murders he is accused of committing? (1996)

The political assault on habeas corpus associated with the *Antiterrorism and Effective Death Penalty Act of 1996* was a striking example of the profound potential for fallout from the capital punishment debate to affect fundamental constitutional guarantees. In a rush to develop and pass antiterrorism legislation by the first anniversary of the 1995 bombing of the Oklahoma City Federal Building, Congress abandoned habeas reforms designed by Justice Powell after his retirement (and endorsed by Chief Justice Rehnquist). In spite of strong opposition by an eclectic mix that included legal scholars, the ACLU, the National Rifle Association, leftist groups, and Arab and Muslim Americans, the act was hurriedly—and almost unanimously—passed with language that "imposed severe limits on prisoners challenging state court convictions in federal courts. Deadlines were set. Grounds for granting . . . [habeas] writ[s] were limited. And presumptions in favor of state court actions were established" (*Washington Post* 1996). As Boston University law professor Larry Yackle predicted, the immediate effect of the act was likely to be contrary to supporters' claims: "There are 20 pages of technical legal language in the bill that will take five to six years to deal with. . . . There is scarcely a line that won't require a good bit of litigation" (quoted in Marquand 1996). A month after the act was passed, the Supreme Court rushed to hear the first of what may be many cases generated by the act (Document 112).

## CAPITAL CONSERVATISM ON THE BENCH

Seven new Supreme Court justices had been appointed since the *Furman* decision—only one by a Democratic president. Abolitionists lost ground in the 1990s as this more conservative high court reduced the types of claims that could be brought before it (Document 95) and reversed its earlier exclusion of victim impact statements from consideration in the penalty phase of capital trials (Document 96).

After a dramatic last-minute judicial tug of war between Ninth Circuit appeals court judges attempting to once again stay the execution of convicted murderer Robert Alton Harris, who had filed numerous unsuccessful habeas corpus petitions during his thirteen years on death row, the Supreme Court took the unprecedented step of forbidding any further stays of Harris's death sentence by lower courts (Document 98).

In yet another move that shocked many observers, the Court refused to consider questionable "new evidence" of a convicted murderer's innocence as grounds for granting a habeas petition (Documents 101, 102), arguing that its role was to insure that prisoners were not held in violation of the Constitution—not to correct errors of fact in lower court trials.

After repeated losses in the High Court, a symbolic ray of hope for abolitionists came from Justice Blackmun, who for a quarter-century generally had voted to enforce the death penalty. Dissenting in a capital case opinion (Document 104), he asserted that—since it appeared impossible to eliminate arbitrariness, discrimination, caprice, and mistake from capital sentencing—it was impossible to constitutionally administer the death penalty.

Soon afterward, the Court gave another sign that it might be moving in a less conservative direction when it supported a defendant's claim that the trial court judge had violated his right to due process by refusing to advise his jury that he had no possibility of parole if given a life sentence rather than being sentenced to death (Document 105). Speaking before the *Antiterrorism and Effective Death Penalty Act of 1996* was passed, death penalty researcher and University of Memphis professor Richard Janikowski speculated that these and other 1995 cases indicated that the Supreme Court's "speeding train carrying death row inmates to the execution chamber may be slowing a bit" (1996). Now that the act is law, it seems possible to say only that the High Court's decisions regarding the act's constitutionality will have an important effect on whether the train accelerates to full throttle.

## NEW ABOLITIONIST TACTICS

As old arguments against the death penalty began to have less sway, and old tactics to forestall executions became less effective, abolitionists began to explore new issues in and out of court. For example, under what, if any, circumstances should health care professionals such as psychiatrists treat condemned prisoners when their recovery would make them eligible for execution (Document 99)? Is it ethical for physicians to participate in executions when state laws require their involvement in order for the execution to take place (Document 106)? One commentator even urged attorneys to avoid taking on death penalty appeals on the grounds that, without competent counsel, condemned prisoners couldn't receive due process—and thus could never be executed (Hinerfeld 1996). Other abolitionists attempted to demonstrate that, contrary to what many people assumed, it actually was much more expensive to execute a convicted murderer than to impose lifelong incarceration (Document 100).

Additional support for abolitionists came from the work of academics whose research challenged a number of assumptions about the effects and effectiveness of capital punishment and who attempted to influence public thinking by summarizing in a thoughtful and accessible fashion what was known about the topic.

During the 1990s, a number of scholars who had carefully studied the death penalty question concluded that—at least in contemporary society—capital punishment failed to meet the goals of retentionists. And, like Justice Blackmun, they concluded that it was impossible to administer the death penalty in a manner that was consistent with the ideals of the Constitution; no matter how carefully legislation was crafted, juries were instructed, or decisions were reviewed, capital punishment would be plagued by arbitrariness, discrimination, caprice, and mistake. In detailed reviews of the myriad of issues associated with capital punishment, researchers like Mark Tushnet, Raymond Paternoster, Hugo Adam Bedau, and a number of others whom we have cited extensively attempted to communicate this to the public. In the best scholarly tradition, others like Ernest van den Haag carefully articulated why capital punishment should be retained and how it could be made to work in a just and accurate manner.

## CAPITAL CELEBRITY

In addition to scholarly analyses, the public also was bombarded by evidence of the rational, legal, and moral inconsistencies associated with the death penalty during the period as one horrifying case after another—the trials of the Menendez brothers, Susan Smith, and O. J. Simpson, for example—received media attention. The Simpson spectacle, in particular, showed people first-hand how strongly who a person is and/or what legal representation a person can afford may affect whether prosecutors seek the death penalty (see Schmalleger 1996).

In the same period that the first man in fifty years was hanged in Delaware and California carried out its first execution by lethal injection, capital punishment began to be investigated and analyzed "through the lens of popular culture," suggesting that the public might be "thinking more deeply about this troubling matter than many news reports and stump speeches would suggest" (Sterritt 1996). People flocked to movies about the death penalty such as *Dead Man Walking, Last Dance, Just Cause*, and *A Time to Kill*. And they purchased millions of copies of novels dealing with the subject.

While the public was enthralled with celebrity cases, sociologist William C. Bailey examined a related issue—the question of what impact televised execution publicity had on people (Document 92). In the most sophisticated and relevant research to date, he found neither a deterrent nor a brutalization effect. Bailey's research notwithstanding, when television stations petitioned to broadcast executions live—repeating arguments raised more than one hundred fifty years earlier (Document 17)—their request was denied (Document 97).

## PUBLIC SENTIMENT AND EXECUTIONS

Another important popular assumption that was reexamined by several researchers had to do with the appearance of strong popular support for the death penalty. In spite of the sustained efforts of abolitionists in the United States and abroad (Document 93), the United States—which tends to see itself as a leader in the field of human rights—remained one of the only democracies in the world to allow the execution of prisoners (Document 110). Throughout the 1990s a strong majority of Americans polled reported that they were in favor of capital punishment.

When questioned only about their support or opposition to capital punishment for murder, an all-time high of 80 percent of Americans said that they were in favor of the death penalty in a 1994 Gallup Poll (Document 107). Sixty percent even supported the death penalty for convicted teenaged murderers. Thus, most researchers, political leaders, and commentators accepted as fact that there was a strong public consensus in favor of the death penalty. Other researchers, however, looked at public support more closely.

The 1985 Gallup Poll (Document 75) had found that public support for imposing the death penalty on convicted murderers dropped from 72 percent to 56 percent if people were given "life imprisonment with absolutely no possibility of parole" as an alternative (Document 90). Thirty-four percent favored this alternative as the penalty for murder. Six years later, this trend was even more pronounced (Document 94). When presented with the option, 35 percent now reported favoring life-without-parole while 53 percent favored the death penalty.

Other studies indicated that even more people might favor life-without-parole over executions if convicted murderers also were made to work while in prison to pay restitution to the families of their victims (Document 103). Taken together, these studies suggested that standard polling questions that were limited to general favorability or opposition well might be measuring something other than just support for capital punishment. For example, the strong support for the death penalty reported by some polls might actually be indicative of public support for harsh and meaningful punishments, rather than capital punishment itself.

One study found, for example, that "only 9% of the apparent proponents of capital punishment consistently remain in favor when presented with alternatives and the issue of the death penalty for juveniles and the mentally retarded" (Sandys and McGarrell 1995:208). According to the authors, this means that there is far less consensus on capital punishment than many believe. This may be very important because simplistic reports that "perpetuate the myth that almost three quarters of the population supports capital punishment can easily result in unnecessary, overly harsh laws that, in reality, are not preferred by a majority of the population" (Sandys and McGarrell 1995:211).

## A GROWING BACKLOG OF CASES

The steady resolution of constitutional challenges to the new capital punishment statutes enacted after *Furman* made it seem likely that the logjam of cases—which by the beginning of 1990 had 2,250 inmates on death rows across the country—soon would break, unleashing a flood of executions (Document 91).

With increasing support for capital punishment came more and more executions. As this book goes to press, the deluge of executions feared by opponents of capital punishment in recent years has failed to materialize, but the number of prisoners executed has crept upward slowly from eleven in 1990 to fifty-six in 1995. Although some have looked on the 1995 high as an indicator of a coming bloodbath (Document 111), it is important to note that the growth in executions still has not kept pace with the growth in prisoners delivered to death row by the courts each year. Thus, the population of condemned prisoners continues to grow. As one European commentator on America noted, "Despite broad and deep support among voters, a growing number of states with death-penalty laws on their books and an ever-widening circle of federal crimes for which execution can be imposed, the central truth about capital punishment in America is this: almost nobody dies" (*The Economist* 1995:19).

To the extent that support for capital punishment is a symbolic response by the American public to the violent crime rate (Vito 1995), there appears to be little likelihood that the death penalty debate will be resolved soon. This is especially true because violent crime rates have remained high in the United States relative both to levels earlier in this century and to those of other industrialized countries. Indeed, during the 1990s, although the overall crime rate was growing much more slowly than in previous decades, it still was at an all-time high. Homicide rates were 46 percent higher than they had been in 1960. Aggravated assaults reported to police were up 83 percent, and as a whole, serious violent crimes such as rape, robbery, aggravated assault, and homicide were up 57 percent. Less comforting still, just like twenty-five years ago, another baby boom is approaching its high-crime years. As noted political scientist and criminologist James Q. Wilson summed up in a recent widely-circulated analysis of crime and public policy in the United States:

I seriously doubt that this country has the will to address . . . its . . . crime problems [property crime and violent crime associated with young, urban underclass gang life], save by acts of individual self-protection. . . . We could alter the way in which at-risk children experience the first few years of life, but the opponents of this . . . are numerous and the bureaucratic problems enormous.

Instead we debate the death penalty, wring our hands about television, lobby to keep prisons from being built in our neighborhoods, and fall briefly in love with trendy nostrums that seem to cost little and promise much. Meanwhile, just beyond the horizon, there lurks a cloud that the winds will soon bring over us. The population will start getting younger again. . . . thirty thousand more young muggers, killers, and thieves than we have now. (1994:34)

If, as Wilson and many other experts predict, violent crime rates increase because of demographic shifts, it appears unlikely that public support for the death penalty will weaken substantially in the next two decades.

## DOCUMENT 90: "Life-Without-Parole: An Alternative to Death or Not Much of a Life at All?" (1990)

In addition to punishment and incapacitation, the rehabilitation of prisoners for release back into society long has been a goal of the U.S. prison system.

However, during the post-*Furman* era, many states began to adopt life-without-parole (LWOP) statutes. By March 1990, thirty states had enacted some type of life-without-parole sanction for murder, often as an alternative to the death penalty (in states with capital punishment laws). In some states, repeatedly convicted offenders eventually could receive LWOP sentences for crimes that, by themselves, would not warrant such a punishment. And a few states and the federal government had enacted laws allowing LWOP sentences for drug "kingpins" (Wright 1990:532).

In a 1990 research note in the *Vanderbilt Law Review*, Julian H. Wright, Jr., reported on the various types of these relatively new statutes, and provided examples of their application in different states. He also discussed the benefits and problems associated with LWOP sentences, and offered recommendations for states considering LWOP as an alternative to capital punishment.

For states grappling with both the problems of violent crime and a public perception that the criminal justice system fails to deal adequately with such crime, life-without-parole appears to offer a viable alternative. Life-without-parole is a punishment that does exactly what it says and adds certainty to punishment that the death penalty and regular life sentences sorely lack. The Supreme Court and lower courts have repeatedly affirmed life-without-parole's constitutionality, and a majority of states have employed life-without-parole in a variety of sentencing schemes. The availability of life-without-parole as punishment for the most heinous and violent murderers displays both an implacable hardness against the wanton taking of human life and a sensitivity to the inherent value of all human life.

Life-without-parole is employed effectively as a prosecutorial weapon against murder, and potentially saves money and lives—the lives of convicted murderers who would otherwise languish on death row as well as the innocent victims of paroled murderers who may kill again. These savings entail a cost, however, and incarcerating violent murderers for the rest of their lives poses some serious problems. If society, however, intends to use prisons to incarcerate, isolate, and punish criminals, then adequate planning and foresight can address potential overcrowding problems, needs of elderly inmates, and security risks caused by increased use of LWOP. When compared to the current, more prevalent practice of sentencing without imposing capital punishment, and the paroling of murderers supposedly serving life sentences, life-without-parole's philosophical and practical advantages outweigh its potential problems. . . .

Life-without-parole as a punishment for murder should be considered on its own merits, not in conjunction with LWOP as a punishment for habitual offenders or drug kingpins. Much of the public's perception of the sanction's potential problems stems from its possible, increased use on criminals other than violent murderers. While these uses are valid and often may be justified, life-without-parole as a punishment for murder accrues certain distinct philosophical advantages that are not shared by the sanction's other uses. Many opponents of capital punishment will champion life-without-parole as a crucial step toward abolishing the death penalty. While this argument seems sound in light of public opinion polls concerning the death penalty, the sanction also can be used effectively in tandem with capital punishment to benefit criminal justice systems and to protect citizens from violent criminals. Life-without-parole should not be seen solely as a stepping stone to eliminating capital punishment. . . .

All states that employ or are considering adopting some form of life-without-parole also should continue to study the sanction's effects on the criminal justice and corrections systems and on LWOP prisoners themselves. Extensive additional information is still necessary to measure adequately the long-term effects of the sanction. Existing information, however, indicates that life-without-parole works as an effective sanction against violent murderers. It protects society better than a normal life sentence that allows parole and is a swifter and surer penalty in most cases than the death penalty. Life-without-parole is a hard sanction, consigning individuals to live their natural lives behind bars, but it accurately reflects society's disdain for the taking of human life. Life-without-parole offers a legitimate alternative to capital punishment that provides a small measure of hope to inmates. Life-without-parole deserves greater use as a sanction against society's worst killers.

*Source*: Julian H. Wright, Jr., "Life-Without-Parole: An Alternative to Death or Not Much of a Life at All?" *Vanderbilt Law Review* 43 (March 1990): 565–568 (footnotes omitted).

## DOCUMENT 91: "Death in the States" (*U.S. News & World Report*, 1990)

By 1990, there were approximately 2,400 persons awaiting execution on death rows across the United States, with about 300 new death row inmates added each year. However, only 140 executions had taken place between 1977—when Gary Gilmore became the first person to be executed since the ten-year moratorium on executions began in 1967 (see Document 63)—and September of 1990. Overall, executions were taking place at a relatively low average rate of about ten per year (Paternoster 1991:274–275).

Moreover, although recent public opinion polls indicated that a large majority of Americans were in favor of the death penalty, there also was growing evidence that public support for capital punishment likely would decrease if life-without-parole (LWOP) was an available alternative (see Document 75). At the same time, thirty states had by 1990 adopted LWOP statutes of various types as available sanctions for murder (see Document 90).

However, despite these factors—which seemed to mitigate against increased executions during the 1990s—by September of 1990 it appeared likely that more executions would indeed occur, at least in some states, in the near future.

The long-expected expansion of capital punishment in the industrial states and California is set to happen. Most Americans favor capital punishment for murderers, but since the Supreme Court allowed states to resume executions in 1976, putting convicts to death has been almost entirely a phenomenon of the South and West. But executions by lethal injection in both Illinois and Oklahoma last week raised to 16 the number of states to carry out modern-day executions. And soon the odds may tilt against many of the more than 2,400 now on 35 death rows: Congress is expected to pass a crime law placing strict limits on habeas corpus challenges to death penalties. The largest state where a bloodbath may follow is California, with 289 death-row inmates. Both competing gubernatorial candidates are campaigning for capital punishment.

*Source*: "Death in the States," *U.S. News & World Report* 109, no. 12 (September 24, 1990): 14.

## DOCUMENT 92: "Murder, Capital Punishment, and Television: Execution Publicity and Homicide Rates" (William C. Bailey, 1990)

The role, if any, of execution publicity in deterring or promoting homicides was the subject of several studies conducted between the late 1970s and 1990 (see Document 85). Most of these studies focused on newspaper rather than television news coverage of executions, despite the fact that television has become America's primary source of news (Bailey 1990:628).

Understanding the possible effects of televised execution publicity is especially important given the fact that the same populations that are disproportionately involved in homicides—young adults, African Americans, those with low incomes, and poorly educated individuals— also are more likely to rely on television as a news source (Bailey 1990: 628).

In 1990, William C. Bailey, professor of sociology and associate dean of the graduate college at Cleveland State University, conducted a study that looked specifically at the effects of televised execution publicity on homicide rates for the period 1976–1987. His study included a series of regression analyses of monthly homicide rates, the frequency of executions, and the amount and type of television coverage devoted to executions during this time period (Bailey 1990:629).

Following is an excerpt from Bailey's 1990 study in which he discussed his findings.

In this investigation I find no evidence that the amount and/or type of television publicity devoted to executions had a significant deterrent or brutalization effect on homicides during the 1976–1987 period. Television has become the most relied upon source of news in this society. Therefore, if the death penalty is an effective deterrent to murder, one would expect to see evidence of this since our national return to capital punishment over the last dozen or so years.

That the findings do not support the deterrence argument for capital punishment does not come as a total surprise. The results are consistent with a long line of capital punishment investigations. However, proponents of capital punishment may not be persuaded by these findings. Some have argued that over the last few decades executions have been so few in number as to rob capital punishment of its effectiveness as a deterrent to murder. . . . It is possible that a certain level of execution certainty (a threshold point) must be achieved before executions and execution publicity become effective deterrents to murder, and this level may not have been reached in recent years. Over the 1976–1987 period there were a total of 93 executions; 33 received television news attention. In contrast, during the same period, FBI statistics indicate that there were a total of 53,905 felony-murders (killings that take place during the commission of another felony). These are capital homicides in virtually all death penalty jurisdictions. Treated as a measure of the certainty of capital punishment, the ratio of the number of executions to felony-homicides is very small. Thus, what television news coverage may be *communicating* to the public is that the certainty of capital punishment for murder is quite low. At this point, one can only speculate about the level of executions and the type and amount of media attention required before capital punishment might become effective in decreasing (deterrence) or increasing (brutalization) killings. What does seem clear, however, is that the current level of executions and media practices regarding executions in this country neither discourage nor promote murder.

*Source*: William C. Bailey, "Murder, Capital Punishment, and Television: Execution Publicity and Homicide Rates," *American Sociological Review* 55 (October 1990): 631–633.

---

## DOCUMENT 93: Amnesty International's Stand on the Death Penalty (1990)

In 1990, Amnesty International, a worldwide human rights organization founded in 1961, consisted of more than 750,000 members working together toward four main goals: the release of prisoners of conscience; obtaining fair trials for political prisoners; eliminating torture and cruel, inhuman, and degrading treatment; and an end to executions (Staunton and Fenn 1990:5).

According to the 1990 Amnesty International Handbook, the organization opposed the death penalty because (1) it is cruel, arbitrary, and irrevocable; (2) it is imposed disproportionately; (3) it is a violation of human rights; and (4) it does not deter crime (Staunton and Fenn 1990:11).

The organization's 1990 handbook devoted an entire chapter to addressing in detail each of these objections to the death penalty. The following excerpt focuses on the death penalty as a human rights violation.

THE REALITY OF THE DEATH PENALTY

Today in 99 countries across the world prisoners can legally be put to death for criminal offences or for political crimes. From 1985 to mid-1988 over 3,399 people were executed worldwide for crimes ranging from the violent and brutal, such as murder, rape and armed robbery, to the non-violent, such as black marketeering and bribe-taking. Those who face the death penalty are overwhelmingly the poor, the disadvantaged, ethnic minorities, the unwanted or those whom the authorities deem their political enemies. Most of those killed do not receive a fair trial; all of them are made to face the unique horror of a violent death at the hands of the state.

Amnesty International believes the death penalty to be a violation of fundamental human rights. The organization opposes the death penalty in all cases.

**Human rights and the death penalty**

The Universal Declaration of Human Rights secures the right to life, and categorically states in Article 5 that "no one shall be subjected to torture or to cruel, inhuman or degrading treatment."

While most peoples and governments (at least officially) condemn torture, acknowledging that there can be no justification for its use, many argue that the death penalty is a separate issue and indeed not a matter of human rights.

If hanging a woman by her arms until she experiences excruciating pain is rightly condemned as torture, how does one describe hanging her by the neck until she is dead? If administering 100 volts of electricity to the most sensitive parts of a man's body evokes disgust, what is the appropriate reaction to the administration of 2,000 volts to his body in order to kill him?

*Source*: Marie Staunton and Sally Fenn, eds., *Amnesty International Handbook* (London: Macdonald Optima, 1990), 53–54.

---

## DOCUMENT 94: Public Opinion and the Death Penalty (1991)

In 1991, public support for capital punishment held steady at 76 percent, only three points lower than the half-century high of 79 percent reported by the Gallup Poll in 1988 (see Document 84).

However, consistent with findings from the 1985 Gallup Poll (Document 75), support for the death penalty again was found to drop significantly when life imprisonment without possibility of parole was suggested as an alternative to capital punishment.

## JUNE 26
## DEATH PENALTY

Interviewing Date: 6/13–16/91
Survey #GO 222002

*Are you in favor of the death penalty for persons convicted of murder?*

| | |
|---|---|
| Yes | 76% |
| No | 18 |
| No opinion | 6 |

*What do you think should be the penalty for murder—the death penalty or life imprisonment, with absolutely no possibility of parole?*

| | |
|---|---|
| Death penalty | 53% |
| Life imprisonment | 35 |
| Neither (volunteered) | 3 |
| No opinion | 9 |

*Source: The Gallup Poll: Public Opinion 1991* (Wilmington, Del.: Scholarly Resources Inc., 1991), 128, 129–130. Copyright 1991 by Scholarly Resources Inc. Reprinted by permission of Scholarly Resources Inc.

---

## DOCUMENT 95: *Coleman v. Thompson* (1991)

By the early 1990s, nearly 10,000 habeas corpus petitions were being filed each year by U.S. prisoners, many of whom were on death row. In an attempt to reduce this growing number of constitutional appeals, the U.S. Supreme Court began to impose stricter limits on their admissibility (Regoli and Hewitt 1996:503).

One of the Court's first attempts to do so came in the 1991 case of *Coleman v. Thompson*. Roger Keith Coleman had been convicted and sentenced to death in Virginia for the rape and murder of his sister-in-law, Wanda McCoy. After his first appeal failed, Coleman filed a habeas corpus action in which he raised seven new constitutional claims. The County Circuit Court rejected these new claims, and Coleman, through his lawyers, filed a petition for appeal in the Virginia Supreme Court. However, his lawyers filed the appeal thirty-three days after the trial court's decision, which was three days too late under Virginia's procedural rules. As a result, Coleman's appeal was rejected by the Virginia Supreme Court and subsequently by the federal courts, which stood by the Virginia Supreme Court's procedural rule (111 S.Ct. 2546: 2552–2553).

The U.S. Supreme Court eventually granted certiorari in the case and it, too, upheld Virginia's procedural rule. The Court held that Coleman's claims were not subject to review in federal habeas, adding that his appeal would have been acceptable only if he could have shown that the state had somehow prevented his lawyers from filing it on time.

After subsequent attempts to prove his innocence—including a lie detector and DNA test (both of which pointed to his guilt rather than to his innocence)—and to obtain a stay of execution failed, Coleman was electrocuted on May 20, 1992 (Tushnet 1994:106).

Regardless of the apparent likelihood of his guilt, Coleman's execution is significant because he never was allowed to present his constitutional claims in court (Tushnet 1994:106). Thus, some claimed that he literally was "hung on a technicality" (Kaplan and Cohn 1992:56).

## A. OPINION OF THE COURT

Justice O'CONNOR delivered the opinion of the Court.

This is a case about federalism. It concerns the respect that federal courts owe the States and the States' procedural rules when reviewing the claims of state prisoners in federal habeas corpus. . . .

II

A

. . .

[8] . . . This Court has long held that a state prisoner's federal habeas petition should be dismissed if the prisoner has not exhausted available state remedies as to any of his federal claims. . . . This exhaustion requirement is also grounded in principles of comity; in a federal system, the States should have the first opportunity to address and correct alleged violations of state prisoner's federal rights. . . .

[9] These same concerns apply to federal claims that have been procedurally defaulted in state court. Just as in those cases in which a state prisoner fails to exhaust state remedies, a habeas petitioner who has failed to meet the State's procedural requirements for presenting his federal claims has deprived the state courts of an opportunity to address those claims in the first instance. A habeas petitioner who has defaulted his federal claims in state court meets the technical requirements for exhaustion; there are no state remedies any longer "available" to him.

... In the absence of the independent and adequate state ground doctrine in federal habeas, habeas petitioners would be able to avoid the exhaustion requirement by defaulting their federal claims in state court. The independent and adequate state ground doctrine ensures that the States' interest in correcting their own mistakes is respected in all federal habeas cases. . . .

IV

. . .

[20] . . . In all cases in which a state prisoner has defaulted his federal claims in state court pursuant to an independent and adequate state procedural rule, federal habeas review of the claims is barred unless the prisoner can demonstrate cause for the default and actual prejudice as a result of the alleged violation of federal law, or demonstrate that failure to consider the claims will result in a fundamental miscarriage of justice. . . . We now recognize the important interest in finality served by state procedural rules, and the significant harm to the States that results from the failure of federal courts to respect them.

## B. DISSENTING OPINION

Justice BLACKMUN, with whom Justice MARSHALL and Justice STEVENS join, dissenting. . . .

I

The Court cavalierly claims that "[t]his is a case about federalism," . . . and proceeds without explanation to assume that the purposes of federalism are advanced whenever a federal court refrains from reviewing an ambiguous state-court judgment. Federalism, however, has no inherent normative value: It does not, as the majority appears to assume, blindly protect the interests of States from any incursion by the federal courts. Rather, federalism secures to citizens the liberties that derive from the diffusion of sovereign power. . . . In this context, it cannot lightly be assumed that the interests of federalism are fostered by a rule that impedes federal review of federal constitutional claims.

Moreover, the form of federalism embraced by today's majority bears little resemblance to that adopted by the Framers of the Constitution and ratified by the original States. The majority proceeds as if the sovereign interests of the States and the Federal Government were coequal. Ours, however, is a federal republic, conceived on the principle of a supreme federal power and constituted first and foremost of citizens, not of sovereign States. . . .

Federal habeas review of state-court judgments, respectfully employed to safeguard federal rights, is no invasion of state sovereignty. . . . Since 1867, Congress has acted within its constitutional authority to " 'interpose the federal courts between the States and the people, as guardians of the people's federal rights—to protect the people from unconstitutional action.' " . . . Justice Frankfurter, in his separate opinion in *Brown v. Allen,* . . . recognized this:

Insofar as [federal habeas] jurisdiction enables federal district courts to entertain claims that State Supreme Courts have denied rights guaranteed by the United States Constitution, it is not a case of a lower court sitting in judgment on a higher court. It is merely one aspect of respecting the Supremacy Clause of the Constitution whereby federal law is higher than State law.

Thus, the considered exercise by federal courts—in vindication of fundamental constitutional rights—of the habeas jurisdiction conferred on them by Congress exemplifies the full expression of this Nation's federalism.

*Source*: 111 S.Ct. 2546 (1991), 2552–2570 (footnotes omitted).

---

## DOCUMENT 96: *Payne v. Tennessee* (1991)

---

Shortly after its decision in *Coleman* (see Document 95), the U.S. Supreme Court issued another ruling that reflected its changing attitude toward capital punishment.

The case was *Payne v. Tennessee,* in which Pervis Tyrone Payne had been convicted and sentenced to death for the murders of Charisse Christopher and her two-year-old daughter, Lacie Jo. At issue, as in the 1987 case of *Booth v. Maryland* (see Document 78), was the admissibility of victim impact evidence—specifically the testimony of Charisse's mother, Mary Zvolanek, who had described how Charisse's three-year-old son, Nicholas, who had survived Payne's assault, missed his mother and baby sister.

However, while the Court had deemed such evidence unconstitutional in *Booth* on the ground that it might result in arbitrary discrimination against the defendant, it now reversed this decision, holding that the Eighth Amendment did not, after all, prohibit the presentation of victim impact evidence during a capital trial.

Writing the opinion of the Court, Chief Justice Rehnquist explained that because a capital defendant was allowed to present all relevant mitigating evidence during the penalty phase of his trial, preventing the prosecution from presenting all relevant evidence of "the specific harm caused by the defendant" gave the defense an unfair advantage over the prosecution (111 S.Ct. 2597, 2607, 2608).

## A. OPINION OF THE COURT

Chief Justice REHNQUIST delivered the opinion of the Court....

[14] We are now of the view that a State may properly conclude that for the jury to assess meaningfully the defendant's moral culpability and blameworthiness, it should have before it at the sentencing phase evidence of the specific harm caused by the defendant. "[T]he State has a legitimate interest in counteracting the mitigating evidence which the defendant is entitled to put in, by reminding the sentencer that just as the murderer should be considered as an individual, so too the victim is an individual whose death represents a unique loss to society and in particular to his family." ... By turning the victim into a "faceless stranger at the penalty phase of a capital trial," ... *Booth* deprives the State of the full moral force of its evidence and may prevent the jury from having before it all the information necessary to determine the proper punishment for a first-degree murder.

[15] The present case is an example of the potential for such unfairness. The capital sentencing jury heard testimony from Payne's girlfriend that they met at church; that he was affectionate, caring, and kind to her children; that he was not an abuser of drugs or alcohol; and that it was inconsistent with his character to have committed the murders. Payne's parents testified that he was a good son, and a clinical psychologist testified that Payne was an extremely polite prisoner and suffered from a low IQ. None of this testimony was related to the circumstances of Payne's brutal crimes. In contrast, the only evidence of the impact of Payne's offenses during the sentencing phase was Nicholas' grandmother's description—in response to a single question—that the child misses his mother and baby sister. Payne argues that the Eighth Amendment commands that the jury's death sentence must be set aside because the jury heard this testimony. But the testimony illustrated quite poignantly some of the harm that Payne's killing had caused; there is nothing unfair about allowing the jury to bear in mind that harm at the same time as it considers the mitigating evidence introduced by the defendant. The Supreme Court of Tennessee in this case obviously felt the unfairness of the rule pronounced by *Booth* when it said: "It is an affront to the civilized members of the human race to say that at sentencing in a capital case, a parade of witnesses may praise the background, character and good deeds of Defendant (as was done in this case), without limitation as to relevancy, but nothing may be said that bears upon the character of, or the harm imposed, upon the victims." ...

[16] We thus hold that if the State chooses to permit the admission of victim impact evidence and prosecutorial argument on that subject, the Eighth Amendment erects no *per se* bar. A State may legitimately conclude that evidence about the victim and about the impact of the murder on the victim's family is relevant to the jury's decision as to whether or not the death penalty should be imposed. There is no reason to treat such evidence differently than other relevant evidence is treated.

## B. DISSENTING OPINION OF JUSTICE MARSHALL

Justice MARSHALL, with whom Justice BLACKMUN joins, dissenting.

Power, not reason, is the new currency of this Court's decisionmaking. Four Terms ago, a five-Justice majority of this Court held that "victim impact" evidence of the type at issue in this case could not constitutionally be introduced during the penalty phase of a capital trial. *Booth v. Maryland* [Document 78]. . . . By another 5–4 vote, a majority of this Court rebuffed an attack upon this ruling just two Terms ago. *South Carolina v. Gathers*. . . . Nevertheless, having expressly invited respondent to renew the attack, . . . today's majority overrules *Booth* and *Gathers* and credits the dissenting views expressed in those cases. Neither the law nor the facts supporting *Booth* and *Gathers* underwent any change in the last four years. Only the personnel of this Court did.

In dispatching *Booth* and *Gathers* to their graves, today's majority ominously suggests that an even more extensive upheaval of this Court's precedents may be in store. Renouncing this Court's historical commitment to a conception of "the judiciary as a source of impersonal and reasoned judgments," . . . the majority declares itself free to discard any principle of constitutional liberty which was recognized or reaffirmed over the dissenting votes of four Justices and with which five or more Justices *now* disagree. The implications of this radical new exception to the doctrine of *stare decisis* are staggering. The majority today sends a clear signal that scores of established constitutional liberties are now ripe for reconsideration, thereby inviting the very type of open defiance of our precedents that the majority rewards in this case. Because I believe that this Court owes more to its constitutional precedents in general and to *Booth* and *Gathers* in particular, I dissent.

## C. DISSENTING OPINION OF JUSTICE STEVENS

Justice STEVENS, with whom Justice BLACKMUN joins, dissenting. . . .

III

Victim impact evidence, as used in this case, has two flaws, both related to the Eighth Amendment's command that the punishment of
death may not be meted out arbitrarily or capriciously. First, aspects of
the character of the victim unforeseeable to the defendant at the time of
his crime are irrelevant to the defendant's "personal responsibility and
moral guilt" and therefore cannot justify a death sentence. . . .

Second, the quantity and quality of victim impact evidence sufficient
to turn a verdict of life in prison into a verdict of death is not defined
until after the crime has been committed and therefore cannot possibly
be applied consistently in different cases. The sentencer's unguided consideration of victim impact evidence thus conflicts with the principle
central to our capital punishment jurisprudence that, "where discretion
is afforded a sentencing body on a matter so grave as the determination
of whether a human life should be taken or spared, that discretion must
be suitably directed and limited so as to minimize the risk of wholly
arbitrary and capricious action." . . . Open-ended reliance by a capital
sentencer on victim impact evidence simply does not provide a "prin-
cipled way to distinguish [cases], in which the death penalty [i]s imposed, from the many cases in which it [i]s not."

*Source*: 111 S.Ct. 2597 (1991), 2601–2628 (footnotes omitted).

---

## DOCUMENT 97: "Execution in Your Living Room" (*The Progressive*, 1991)

---

Early in the 1990s, the debate over whether executions should be
made public—an issue that first rose to prominence during the mid-
1830s when executions in America shifted from public to private—
received renewed attention when a San Francisco television station
requested permission to film an execution at San Quentin and was
denied both by the prison and later by a federal district court (Hentoff
1991:16).

Although more than one hundred fifty years had passed and the
question now was whether television cameras should be allowed inside the execution chamber rather than whether executions themselves
should be held in public, many of the arguments that emerged in the
federal court case and the media coverage surrounding it were strik-
ingly similar to those of the original debate.

For example, just as Thomas Upham (see Document 17) had argued that private executions had no place in a republican society, the television station argued that the American public was entitled under the First Amendment to see what was being done in its name, with its tax dollars (Hentoff 1991:16).

Conversely, many of those who opposed the televising of executions believed, as did nineteenth-century opponents of public executions, that "such spectacles demoralized the population" (Masur 1989:117). For example, *New York Times* columnist Anthony Lewis asserted that "The First Amendment in my judgment does not require access to scenes whose broadcast would further coarsen our society and increase its already dangerous level of insensitivity" (in Hentoff 1991:16).

Following is an excerpt from an article by Nat Hentoff, author of *The First Freedom* (1980), in which he examined both sides of this issue.

The constitutional question remains: Does the Government have the right to shut the press and the public out of these stories? To invoke prior restraint on any of the allegedly ethical or sociological or psychological grounds mentioned by the opponents of access would be to open a door to all kinds of censorship for "the common good."

Moreover, shutting the press—and thereby the public—out of the death chamber is akin to the Bush Administration's command that the press could not photograph the coffins of American military personnel killed in the Gulf war as they were brought home. The great beast, the public, could not be trusted to see the fresh corpses lest some people turn on the Government and ask why these once and former Americans had been killed.

The most useful function of the press is to get the public, or at least parts of it, to ask why. In this case, what is accomplished by allowing the state to murder? And what is the state ashamed of when it continues to insist on conducting its killings in secret?

*Source*: Nat Hentoff, "Execution in Your Living Room," *The Progressive* 55, no. 11 (November 1991): 17.

## DOCUMENT 98: Robert Alton Harris (1992)

The Supreme Court's growing intolerance of repeated, frivolous, and/or last minute habeas corpus petitions by death row inmates during the 1990s is vividly evidenced by its rulings with regard to the final habeas corpus petition of condemned murderer Robert Alton Harris.

Harris already had unsuccessfully appealed his case and filed numerous unsuccessful habeas corpus petitions during his thirteen years on California's death row (Calabresi and Lawson 1992:279). As his latest execution date of April 21, 1992, approached, a class action was filed in the district court on behalf of Harris and his fellow death row inmates. The class action claimed that lethal gas was a cruel and unusual method of carrying out the death penalty and therefore prohibited by the Eighth and Fourteenth Amendments (Reinhardt 1992:207; Tushnet 1994:109).

In response, Marilyn Hall Patel, the district court judge, issued a tenday restraining order on use of California's gas chamber that would allow her to consider the merits of the action's claim. Because the action had been filed on April 17, 1992, just four days before Harris's scheduled execution, this temporary restraining order would mean yet another stay of execution for Harris (Reinhardt 1992:207; Tushnet 1994:109).

Two days later, through what has been termed an "extraordinary" (Reinhardt 1992:207) and questionably valid (Tushnet 1994:109) writ of mandamus, the three Ninth Circuit appeals court judges who originally had heard Harris's case voted (in a 2–1 decision) to vacate Judge Patel's stay. A formal order was sent to the district court late the following day, April 20 (Reinhardt 1992:208).

However, early the next morning, just half an hour before Harris was scheduled to be executed, a majority of the 28-judge appeals court voted to stay his execution until the entire court could review the case (Tushnet 1994:110). The U.S. Supreme Court quickly vacated this stay (see Document 98A) over the objections of Justices Stevens and Blackmun (Document 98B). After the stay was vacated, a Ninth Circuit judge entered another stay of Harris's execution on different grounds. However, the Supreme Court vacated this stay as well and at the same time issued an "unprecedented" (Caminker and Chemerinsky 1992:246; Reinhardt 1992:213)—and what some have called possibly unconstitutional (Calabresi and Lawson 1992:271)—order that "no further stays of Robert Alton Harris' execution shall be entered by the federal courts except upon order of this Court" (see Document 98C).

Harris was executed in the gas chamber as scheduled, at 6:21 A.M. Tuesday, April 21. He was the first person executed in California since 1967 (Caminker and Chemerinsky 1992:225).

According to the authors of one of three articles on Harris's execution that appeared in the *Yale Law Journal*:

The judicial opinions entered over these few days are shocking. The majority of the Ninth Circuit panel that overturned the district court's temporary restraining order, and the seven Supreme Court Justices who vacated the subsequent stays of execution, ignored or misapplied legal principles without justifying their departures from established law. Their understandable frustration resulting from recent experiences with delayed executions led to a last-minute rush to execution in this case. To ensure that the State executed Harris as scheduled, judges sworn to uphold the Constitution failed to exercise their responsibility to exercise detached, considered judgment. (Caminker and Chemerinsky 1992:225–226)

## A. PER CURIAM DECISION OF THE COURT

PER CURIAM.

[1] Harris claims that his execution by lethal gas is cruel and unusual in violation of the Eighth Amendment. This case is an obvious attempt to avoid the application of *McCleskey v. Zant*, . . . to bar this successive claim for relief. Harris has now filed four prior federal habeas petitions. He has made no convincing showing of cause for his failure to raise this claim in his prior petitions.

[2, 3] Even if we were to assume, however, that Harris could avoid the application of *McCleskey* to bar his claim, we would not consider it on the merits. Whether his claim is framed as a habeas petition or §1983 action, Harris seeks an equitable remedy. Equity must take into consideration the State's strong interest in proceeding with its judgment and Harris' obvious attempt at manipulation. . . . This claim could have been brought more than a decade ago. There is no good reason for this abusive delay, which has been compounded by last-minute attempts to manipulate the judicial process. A court may consider the last-minute nature of an application to stay execution in deciding whether to grant equitable relief.

The application to vacate the stay of execution of death is granted, and it is ordered that the orders staying the execution of Robert Alton Harris entered by the United States Court of Appeals for the Ninth Circuit in No. 92–70237 on April 20, 1992 are vacated.

*Source*: 112 S.Ct. 1652 (1992), 1653.

## B. DISSENTING OPINION

Justice STEVENS, with whom Justice BLACKMUN joins, dissenting.

In a time when the Court's jurisprudence concerning the imposition of the death penalty grows ever more complicated, Robert Alton Harris brings a simple claim. He argues that California's method of execution—exposure to cyanide gas—constitutes cruel and unusual punishment and therefore violates the Eighth and Fourteenth Amendments. In light of all that we know today about the extreme and unnecessary pain inflicted by execution by cyanide gas, and in light of the availability of more humane and less violent methods of execution, Harris' claim has merit. I would deny the State's application to vacate the stay imposed by the Court of Appeals and allow the courts below to hear and rule on Harris' claim.

Execution by cyanide gas is "in essence asphyxiation by suffocation or strangulation." As dozens of uncontroverted expert statements filed in this case illustrate, execution by cyanide gas is extremely and unnecessarily painful. . . .

The State contends that Harris should have brought his claim earlier. This is not reason enough to upset the stay issued by the Court of Appeals and dispatch the considered judgment of the 14 appellate judges who voted to rehear the case en banc. Indeed, although reluctant to recognize as much, the State itself could have avoided this last-minute litigation. In 1983, seven States authorized executions by exposure to cyanide gas. In that year, three Members of this Court indicated that that method of execution raised sufficiently serious questions under the Eighth Amendment to merit review by writ of certiorari. . . . Thereafter, four States (Colorado, Mississippi, Oregon, and Wyoming) abandoned cyanide gas as a method of execution. In light of these events and the decisions of other legislatures, California as well should have revisited its 55-year-old statute.

More fundamentally, if execution by cyanide gas is in fact unconstitutional, then the State lacks the *power* to impose such punishment. Harris' delay, even if unjustified, cannot endow the State with the authority to violate the Constitution. . . . For these reasons, the State's interest in an immediate execution must yield to a deliberate and careful study of the merits of Harris' claims.

*Source*: 112 S.Ct. 1652 (1992), 1653–1656 (footnotes omitted).


## C. MEMORANDUM DECISION NO. A-768

April 21, 1992. The application to vacate the stay of execution of sentence of death presented to Justice O'CONNOR and by her referred to the Court is granted, and it is ordered that the order staying the execution entered by the United States Court of Appeals for the Ninth Circuit on April 21, 1992 is vacated. No further stays of Robert Alton Harris' execution shall be entered by the federal courts except upon order of this Court.

Justice BLACKMUN and Justice STEVENS would deny the application.

*Source*: 112 S.Ct. (1992), 1713–1714.

---

## DOCUMENT 99: "The Debate on Treating Individuals Incompetent for Execution" (Kirk Heilbrun, Michael L. Radelet, and Joel Dvoskin, 1992)

---

In the 1986 case of *Ford v. Wainwright* (see Document 76), the U.S. Supreme Court held that executing the insane—including those who apparently went insane after being sentenced to death, such as Alvin Bernard Ford—was unconstitutional under the Eighth Amendment.

This ruling, along with the rapid growth of the nation's death row population during the years that followed, led to increased interest in the debate over whether mental health professionals should treat death row inmates who have been deemed incompetent for execution. The main moral and ethical dilemma facing the health care professionals who provide treatment in such cases is the possibility that the patient will be put to death if the treatment is successful (Heilbrun et al. 1992: 596–597).

In their 1992 article in the *American Journal of Psychiatry*, Kirk Heilbrun, Michael L. Radelet, and Joel Dvoskin addressed this issue and other objections to treating mentally incompetent death row inmates. They also discussed arguments in favor of providing professional help for mentally incompetent persons under sentence of death, including the need to respect the wishes of the prisoner.

Following is an excerpt from the article in which the authors presented their conclusions and recommendations.

One of the recommendations made elsewhere is that mental health professionals should consider very carefully the decision about whether to participate in the assessment of competency for execution. This recommendation seems equally apt for the decision about providing treatment. Clinicians should carefully weigh any decision to participate under these circumstances. However, it also seems appropriate to conclude that such a decision should be made on an individual basis rather than as a profession. We have argued that any decision about treating persons incompetent for execution should involve a variety of considerations. A blanket recommendation against participation does not seem indicated on ethical grounds.

There are, however, some unresolved questions about how to participate that might be usefully addressed by the professional psychiatric and psychological associations. To what extent is treatment of incompetent prisoners a clinical situation, emphasizing the principles of beneficence and nonmaleficence, and to what extent is it a forensic situation, in which the needs of society may be weighed more heavily than those of the individual? Clearer answers may await our professions' responses to [the] call for the development of a comprehensive set of forensic ethical standards.

Competency for execution presents a very complex set of ethical and moral problems for mental health professionals involved with these cases. The discussion in this article leads us to conclude that there is no single, ethically proper position on the treatment of persons found incompetent for execution. It appears unethical to administer against the prisoner's wishes treatment that is highly relevant to competency, such as antipsychotic medication for psychotic disorders. It may not be unethical if the prisoner consents to receiving such medication, although there are problems in determining what constitutes "consent." If the treatment is unlikely to affect competency-relevant symptoms, however, then it is not unethical to provide it. Finally, the circumstances of each case will influence some of the treatment decisions for which there are no clear ethical mandates. We hope that these conclusions, and the discussion on which they are based, will introduce more shades of gray into a debate that has often been treated in black and white.

*Source*: Kirk Heilbrun, Michael L. Radelet, and Joel Dvoskin, "The Debate on Treating Individuals Incompetent for Execution," *American Journal of Psychiatry* 149 (May 1992): 603–604 (footnotes omitted).

## DOCUMENT 100: The Cost of the Death Penalty (Richard Dieter, 1992)

While the moral and ethical debate over the death penalty has been waged for centuries, in more recent years the controversy has expanded to cover purely practical issues as well—including financial costs.

At first glance, it might seem that executing serious offenders would be less expensive than paying for their lifelong incarceration. However, on closer examination, this does not appear to be the case.

By 1992, several studies had shown that, after taking into account automatic review of death sentences and the often numerous appeals filed by death row prisoners, it typically costs much more to execute a person than to keep him or her in prison for life.

In his 1992 report *Millions Misspent: What Politicians Don't Say About the High Costs of the Death Penalty*, Richard Dieter, executive director of the Death Penalty Information Center in Washington, D.C., summarized the findings of many of these studies. Following is an excerpt from his report.

### The Financial Costs of the Death Penalty

Death penalty cases are much more expensive than other criminal cases and cost more than imprisonment for life with no possibility of parole. In California, capital trials are six times more costly than other murder trials. A study in Kansas indicated that a capital trial costs $116,700 more than an ordinary murder trial. Complex pre-trial motions, lengthy jury selections, and expenses for expert witnesses are all likely to add to the costs in death penalty cases. The irreversibility of the death sentence requires courts to follow heightened due process in the preparation and course of the trial. The separate sentencing phase of the trial can take even longer than the guilt or innocence phase of the trial. And defendants are much more likely to insist on a trial when they are facing a possible death sentence. After conviction, there are constitutionally mandated appeals which involve both prosecution and defense costs.

Most of these costs occur in every case for which capital punishment is sought, regardless of the outcome. Thus, the true cost of the death penalty includes all the added expenses of the "unsuccessful" trials in which the death penalty is sought but not achieved. Moreover, if a defendant is convicted but not given the death sentence, the state will still incur the costs of life imprisonment, in addition to the increased trial expenses.

For the states which employ the death penalty, this luxury comes at a high price. In Texas, a death penalty case costs taxpayers an average of $2.3 million, about three times the cost of imprisoning someone in a single cell at the highest security level for 40 years. In Florida, each execution is costing the state $3.2 million. In financially strapped California, one report estimated that the state could save $90 million each year by abolishing capital punishment. The New York Department of Correctional Services estimated that implementing the death penalty would cost the state about $118 million *annually.*

*Source*: Richard C. Dieter, *Millions Misspent: What Politicians Don't Say About the High Costs of the Death Penalty* (Washington, D.C.: Death Penalty Information Center Report, October 1992), 3 (footnotes omitted).

## DOCUMENT 101: *Herrera v. Collins* (1993)

In the 1993 case of *Herrera v. Collins*, the U.S. Supreme Court issued a 6–3 ruling in which it held that a claim of innocence based on newly discovered evidence is not ground for federal habeas relief. Many people were outraged by this ruling (see Document 102), which they perceived as the Court's sanctioning of the execution of a possibly innocent person. Indeed, in a strong dissenting opinion, Justice Blackmun asserted that "[t]he execution of a person who can show that he is innocent comes perilously close to simple murder" (see Document 101B).

In the Court's defense, it is important to note the facts in the case. Leonel Torres Herrera had been convicted of the murders of two Texas police officers and sentenced to death in 1982. The evidence against him had been overwhelming in both cases—his Social Security card was found at the scene of the first murder; blood from the first victim was on his jeans, his wallet, and the car he had been driving; a handwritten note implying his guilt in the first murder had been found on him when he was arrested; and he had been identified by the second victim (and another witness) before that victim's death. Herrera also had pleaded guilty to the first murder after being convicted and sentenced to death for the second murder (113 S.Ct. 853:857).

Herrera had unsuccessfully challenged his conviction and sentence on appeal. Then, ten years later, he had filed a second habeas petition in which he claimed that he was innocent of the crimes, and that his now dead brother, Raúl, had instead committed them. To back up this claim, Herrera submitted the affidavits of Hector Villarreal, Raúl's lawyer, and Juan Franco Palacious, one of Raúl's former cellmates, both of whom claimed that Raúl, who died in 1984, had told them that it was he who had killed the police officers. He also presented affidavits from Raúl's son, who claimed that he had witnessed his father shoot the two officers, and one of Raúl's friends, Jose Ybarra, who claimed that Raúl had told him about the murders in 1983 (113 S.Ct. 853:858).

However, the question of Herrera's guilt or innocence was not the main issue that concerned the Court. Writing the opinion of the Court, Chief Justice Rehnquist stated that "federal habeas courts sit to insure that individuals are not imprisoned in violation of the Constitution— not to correct errors of fact" (113 S.Ct. 853:860).

Rehnquist went on to note that Herrera was not left "without a forum in which to raise his actual innocence claim" (113 S.Ct. 853:866), explaining that traditionally "[e]xecutive clemency has provided the 'fail safe' in our criminal justice system" (113 S.Ct. 853:868).

In addition to these reasons for rejecting Herrera's claim, the Court also made it clear that it did not find Herrera's new claim of innocence credible.

Herrera was executed on May 12, 1993.

## A. OPINION OF THE COURT

Chief Justice REHNQUIST delivered the opinion of the Court. . . .

[8] . . . [I]n state criminal proceedings the trial is the paramount event for determining the guilt or innocence of the defendant. Federal habeas review of state convictions has traditionally been limited to claims of constitutional violations occurring in the course of the underlying state criminal proceedings. Our federal habeas cases have treated claims of "actual innocence" not as an independent constitutional claim, but as a basis upon which a habeas petitioner may have an independent constitutional claim considered on the merits, even though his habeas petition would otherwise be regarded as successive or abusive. History shows that the traditional remedy for claims of innocence based on new evidence, discovered too late in the day to file a new trial motion, has been executive clemency.

[9] We may assume, for the sake of argument in deciding this case, that in a capital case a truly persuasive demonstration of "actual innocence" made after trial would render the execution of a defendant unconstitutional, and warrant federal habeas relief if there were no state avenue open to process such a claim. But because of the very disruptive effect that entertaining claims of actual innocence would have on the need for finality in capital cases, and the enormous burden that having to retry cases based on often stale evidence would place on the States, the threshold showing for such an assumed right would necessarily be extraordinarily high. The showing made by petitioner in this case falls far short of any such threshold.

Petitioner's newly discovered evidence consists of affidavits. In the new trial context, motions based solely upon affidavits are disfavored because the affiants' statements are obtained without the benefit of cross-examination and an opportunity to make credibility determinations. . . . Petitioner's affidavits are particularly suspect in this regard because, with the exception of Raul Herrera, Jr.'s affidavit, they consist of hearsay. Likewise, in reviewing petitioner's new evidence, we are mindful that defendants often abuse new trial motions "as a method of delaying enforcement of just sentences." . . . Although we are not presented with a new trial motion *per se*, we believe the likelihood of abuse is as great—or greater—here.

The affidavits filed in this habeas proceeding were given over eight years after petitioner's trial. No satisfactory explanation has been given as to why the affiants waited until the 11th hour—and, indeed, until after the alleged perpetrator of the murders himself was dead—to make their statements. . . . Equally troubling, no explanation has been offered as to why petitioner, by hypothesis an innocent man, pleaded guilty to the murder of Rucker.

Moreover, the affidavits themselves contain inconsistencies, and therefore fail to provide a convincing account of what took place on the night Officers Rucker and Carrisalez were killed. For instance, the affidavit of Raul Jr., who was nine years old at the time, indicates that there were three people in the speeding car from which the murderer emerged, whereas Hector Villarreal attested that Raul Sr. told him that there were two people in the car that night. Of course, Hernandez testified at petitioner's trial that the murderer was the only occupant of the car. The affidavits also conflict as to the direction in which the vehicle was heading when the murders took place, and petitioner's whereabouts on the night of the killings.

Finally, the affidavits must be considered in light of the proof of petitioner's guilt at trial—proof which included two eyewitness identifications, numerous pieces of circumstantial evidence, and a handwritten letter in which petitioner apologized for killing the officers and offered to turn himself in under certain conditions. . . . That proof, even when considered alongside petitioner's belated affidavits, points strongly to petitioner's guilt.

This is not to say that petitioner's affidavits are without probative value. Had this sort of testimony been offered at trial, it could have been weighed by the jury, along with the evidence offered by the State and petitioner, in deliberating upon its verdict. Since the statements in the affidavits contradict the evidence received at trial, the jury would have had to decide important issues of credibility. But coming 10 years after petitioner's trial, this showing of innocence falls far short of that which would have to be made in order to trigger the sort of constitutional claim which we have assumed, *arguendo*, to exist.

## B. DISSENTING OPINION

Justice BLACKMUN, with whom Justice STEVENS and Justice SOUTER join with respect to Parts I–IV, dissenting. . . .

V

I have voiced disappointment over this Court's obvious eagerness to do away with any restriction on the States' power to execute whomever and however they please. . . . I have also expressed doubts about whether, in the absence of such restrictions, capital punishment remains constitutional at all. . . . Of one thing, however, I am certain. Just as an execution without adequate safeguards is unacceptable, so too is an execution when the condemned prisoner can prove that he is innocent. The execution of a person who can show that he is innocent comes perilously close to simple murder.

*Source:* 113 S.Ct. 853 (1993), 856–884.

---

## DOCUMENT 102: "Lethal Expediency" (*The Progressive,* 1993)

Following is an editorial that appeared in *The Progressive,* a monthly political magazine based in Madison, Wisconsin, shortly after the Supreme Court's January 25, 1993 decision in *Herrera v. Collins* (see Document 101).

The U.S. Supreme Court has plunged to a depth of barbarity surprising even to its harshest critics. It has ruled that solid evidence of innocence can be considered *irrelevant* to the case of a prisoner condemned to death. It ruled that the courts don't have to listen to the evidence. It ruled that the state may kill the probably innocent prisoner anyway, because he missed a filing deadline.

Leaving aside the question of the fundamental inhumanity of capital punishment, we note that no argument we've ever heard or read by even the most rabid advocates of state-sanctioned death supports the notion that it's okay to execute *innocent* people.

This ruling in the Texas case of *Herrera v. Collins,* decided by a vote of six-to-three (Justices Harry Blackmun, John Paul Stevens, and David Souter dissented), is the latest in a series designed to "unclog" the Federal courts and make it harder for death-row prisoners to delay their executions with strings of appeals. The earlier rulings were bad enough, sending many with perfectly legitimate grounds for appeal to premature deaths. But this one is absurd; it is housekeeping gone berserk.

Leonel Herrera was convicted in 1982 of the murder of two police officers. Ten years later, new evidence surfaced: several affidavits stating that Herrera's brother Raúl had confessed to the killings before his death in 1984 and a statement by Raúl's son that he had witnessed the killings as a nine-year-old boy. The Texas courts refused to reopen the case, though, saying Herrera was just too late.

The majority opinion did offer other condemned men and women a sliver of hope: If they have "truly persuasive" evidence of innocence, the courts must hear it. We wonder, though, what meaning that sliver has if Leonel Herrera's evidence is not persuasive enough.

And so it goes in this Supreme Court defined by twelve years of Reagan and Bush appointees. Their injury to the rule of right and reason was clear: They gave the state of Texas the green light to lead Herrera to the death chamber and inject a lethal dose of poison into his body.

But the Reagan-Bush Court also took the occasion to insult the memory of Thurgood Marshall, in recent years the Court's most vehement opponent of state murder, a Justice who time and again wrote that the death penalty under *any* circumstances is cruel and unusual punishment forbidden by the Eighth Amendment.

On the Monday morning in January when the Justices condemned Herrera, the flag above the Supreme Court building flew at half-mast for Marshall, who was not yet resting in his grave. We expect it'll be awhile before he rests easy.

*Source*: "Lethal Expediency," *The Progressive* 57, no. 3 (March 1993): 10.

## DOCUMENT 103: Misperceptions About Public Support for Capital Punishment (William Bowers, 1993)

In his 1993 article "Capital Punishment and Contemporary Values: People's Misgivings and the Court's Misperceptions," sociologist William Bowers (also see Document 85) hypothesized that the Supreme Court's new attitude toward capital punishment since its 1976 decision in *Gregg v. Georgia* (see Document 62) was likely due in part to "the Court's misplaced apprehension about public opinion."

Bowers explained that public opinion polls showed a strong increase in support for capital punishment during the past two decades (see Documents 61, 75, 84, and 94). Therefore, the Court's change of attitude "may reflect the Court's belief that the public wants capital punishment and to do away with it would be disastrous for the Court's credibility with the public" (Bowers 1993:159).

However, Bowers hypothesized that perhaps "we all, including the Court, have misinterpreted the polls. Perhaps the expressed support they reflect is not a deep-seated or strongly held commitment to capital punishment but actually a reflection of the public's desire for a genuinely harsh but meaningful punishment for convicted murderers" (Bowers 1993:162). The findings from his study, excerpted below, appear to support this hypothesis.

In a series of surveys beginning with one conducted by Amnesty International USA in Florida in 1985 and followed up by surveys in other states, the following question, or one very much like it, was asked: "Suppose convicted first-degree murderers in this state could be sentenced to life in prison without parole and also be required to work in prison for money that would go to the families of their victims. Would you prefer this as an alternative to the death penalty?"

This question was asked in surveys in Florida, Georgia, New York, and California 1985–89 and replicated in our 1991 New York and Nebraska surveys. . . .

In all instances where this alternative of life without parole combined with a restitution requirement (LWOP + R) was posed, expressed death penalty support plummeted. Among the earlier surveys, it dropped 62 percentage points in Florida; 32 points in Georgia; 40 points in New York; and 54 points in California. Among our own samples, it dropped 52, 49, and 56 points, respectively, in New York State, in New York City, and in Nebraska.

What is more, this obviously harsh but meaningful punishment, which puts the offender to work to pay restitution for the loss and suffering his crime has caused, is preferred to the death penalty by a majority in every state where it was posed as an alternative. Even among respondents who said they "strongly" favored the death penalty on the standard favor/oppose question, majorities of 56%, 66%, and 57% abandoned it in favor of the LWOP + R alternative, respectively, in our New York State, New York City, and Nebraska samples. Public preference for this alternative is unmistakable. . . .

The evidence sketched out here, if replicated and confirmed in other studies, could have the critical effect of changing the perspectives of legislators, judges, the media, and the public on how people think about capital punishment. The obvious political implication of a clear public preference for an alternative to the death penalty is that it will prompt lawmakers to convert the public's punishment preference into laws or they will be replaced by those who will. The apparently exorbitant costs of maintaining a system of capital punishment . . . as well as the public's interest in restitution requirements as a component of punishment and in seeing prisoners work during their incarceration, . . . will add to the political attractiveness of an alternative that puts prisoners to work for money that would go to their victims' families.

The recognition that we have been wrong about how the public thinks about the death penalty will take time to sink in, but if and when it becomes the new wisdom on this matter, it will surely affect the Supreme Court, perhaps not directly or immediately in a shift of the Court's interpretation of contemporary values, but perhaps indirectly by fostering a renewed receptivity to death penalty challenges.

*Source*: William Bowers, "Capital Punishment and Contemporary Values: People's Misgivings and the Court's Misperceptions," *Law & Society Review* 27, no. 1 (1993): 163–164, 172–173 (footnotes omitted).

## DOCUMENT 104: *Callins v. Collins* (1994)

On February 22, 1994, Supreme Court Justice Harry A. Blackmun, then 85, renounced capital punishment in a dramatic dissent from the majority opinion in the case of *Callins v. Collins.*

The case itself was not particularly dramatic or unusual. Bruce Callins had been sentenced to death for a murder committed during a bar robbery, and had petitioned the Supreme Court for certiorari. Eight of the justices had denied his request, thereby voting to allow the execution to proceed, while Blackmun alone had dissented (Kaplan 1994).

The dissent was particularly newsworthy in view of the fact that it marked a reversal of judicial opinion for Blackmun. During his nearly twenty-five years on the Court Blackmun typically had voted to enforce the death penalty, even though he had stated publicly that he "doubted its moral, social, and constitutional legitimacy" (114 S.Ct., 1130).

In his dissent, Blackmun said that legal and procedural attempts since the Court's decision in *Furman* (see Document 54) to eliminate arbitrariness, discrimination, caprice, and mistake from capital sentencing had failed. He added that achieving these constitutional goals did not appear to be possible "without compromising an equally essential component of fundamental fairness—individualized sentencing" (114 S.Ct., 1129).

Blackmun went on to conclude that "the proper course when faced with irreconcilable constitutional commands is not to ignore one or the other, nor to pretend that the dilemma does not exist, but to admit the futility of the effort to harmonize them. This means accepting the fact that the death penalty cannot be administered in accord with our Constitution" (114 S.Ct., 1137).

As David A. Kaplan pointed out (1994), Blackmun's "about-face" would likely have no legal impact on capital punishment since the eight other members of the Court—and the majority of Americans— appeared to accept the death penalty. However, said Kaplan, the "symbolic force" of Blackmun's new official position on capital punishment might help to revive the debate over the death penalty within the Court, which had all but ended with the retirements of Justices William Brennan, Jr., and Thurgood Marshall, both of whom had been firmly opposed to capital punishment.

Justice BLACKMUN, dissenting. . . .

From this day forward, I no longer shall tinker with the machinery of death. For more than 20 years I have endeavored—indeed, I have struggled—along with a majority of this Court, to develop procedural and substantive rules that would lend more than the mere appearance of fairness to the death penalty endeavor. Rather than continue to coddle the Court's delusion that the desired level of fairness has been achieved and the need for regulation eviscerated, I feel morally and intellectually obligated simply to concede that the death penalty experiment has failed. It is virtually self-evident to me now that no combination of procedural rules or substantive regulations ever can save the death penalty from its inherent constitutional deficiencies. The basic question—does the system accurately and consistently determine which defendants "deserve" to die?—cannot be answered in the affirmative. It is not simply that this Court has allowed vague aggravating circumstances to be employed, . . . relevant mitigating evidence to be disregarded, . . . and vital judicial review to be blocked. . . . The problem is that the inevitability of factual, legal, and moral error gives us a system that we know must wrongly kill some defendants, a system that fails to deliver the fair, consistent, and reliable sentences of death required by the Constitution.

*Source*: 114 S.Ct. (1994), 1128–1130 (footnotes omitted).

## DOCUMENT 105: *Simmons v. South Carolina* (1994)

Soon after Supreme Court Justice Harry Blackmun's widely-publicized renouncement of capital punishment (see Document 104), the Court issued a ruling that some saw as a sign that the majority of the Court was turning away from the views of its most conservative justices in favor of more moderate conservatism (Greenhouse 1994).

The case was *Simmons v. South Carolina*. The petitioner, Jonathon Simmons, had been sentenced to death by a South Carolina jury for brutally beating an elderly woman to death in 1990. With two previous violent offenses on his record, Simmons was ineligible for parole under South Carolina state law should he be convicted for the murder and not sentenced to death.

During the penalty phase of the trial, the prosecution had argued that Simmons was too dangerous ever to be set free. However, jurors were not told of Simmons' ineligibility for parole. In fact, the trial judge had refused the defendant's request to present this information. And when specifically asked by the deliberating jury whether life imprisonment included the possibility of parole, the judge had replied that parole was "not a proper issue for your consideration" and that "[t]he terms life imprisonment and death sentence are to be understood in their plan [sic] and ordinary meaning." Twenty-five minutes later, the jury returned to the courtroom and sentenced Simmons to death.

In a 7–2 ruling, the Court overturned Simmons' death sentence. Writing the plurality opinion for himself and three other justices, Justice Blackmun held that the state, which had raised the issue of the defendant's future dangerousness, had violated Simmons' Fourteenth Amendment right to due process by refusing to inform the jury that, as an alternative to the death penalty, the sentence of life imprisonment carried with it no possibility of parole.

## A. PLURALITY OPINION

BLACKMUN, J., announced the judgment of the Court and delivered an opinion in which STEVENS, SOUTER, and GINSBURG, JJ., joined. . . .

II

[1, 2] The Due Process Clause does not allow the execution of a person "on the basis of information which he had no opportunity to deny or explain." . . . In this case, the jury reasonably may have believed that petitioner could be released on parole if he were not executed. To the extent this misunderstanding pervaded the jury's deliberations, it had the effect of creating a false choice between sentencing petitioner to death and sentencing him to a limited period of incarceration. This grievous misperception was encouraged by the trial court's refusal to provide the jury with accurate information regarding petitioner's parole ineligibility, and by the State's repeated suggestion that petitioner would pose a future danger to society if he were not executed. Three times petitioner asked to inform the jury that in fact he was ineligible for parole under state law; three times his request was denied. The State thus succeeded in securing a death sentence on the ground, at least in part, of petitioner's future dangerousness, while at the same time concealing from the sen-

tencing jury the true meaning of its noncapital sentencing alternative, namely, that life imprisonment meant life without parole. We think it is clear that the State denied petitioner due process.

## B. DISSENTING OPINION

Justice SCALIA, with whom Justice THOMAS joins, dissenting. . . .

As I said at the outset, the regime imposed by today's judgment is undoubtedly reasonable as a matter of policy, but I see nothing to indicate that the Constitution requires it to be followed coast-to-coast. I fear we have read today the first page of a whole new chapter in the "death-is-different" jurisprudence which this Court is in the apparently continuous process of composing. It adds to our insistence that State courts admit "all relevant mitigating evidence," . . . a requirement that they adhere to distinctive rules, more demanding than what the Due Process Clause normally requires, for admitting evidence of other sorts— Federal Rules of Death Penalty Evidence, so to speak, which this Court will presumably craft (at great expense to the swiftness and predictability of justice) year-by-year. The heavily outnumbered opponents of capital punishment have successfully opened yet another front in their guerilla war to make this unquestionably constitutional sentence a practical impossibility.

*Source*: 114 S.Ct. 2187 (1994), 2190–2205 (footnotes omitted).

## DOCUMENT 106: Physician Participation in Executions (1994)

Physician participation in executions is not new. In fact, two medical doctors, Carlos MacDonald and E. C. Spitzka, were responsible for supervising the first execution by electric chair in 1890 (American College of Physicians et al. 1994:9–10; also see Document 25).

However, the growing "popularity" of lethal injection as a mode of execution since its first use in Texas in 1982 brought increased attention to the ethical and moral issues surrounding medical participation in executions during the 1990s (American College of Physicians et al. 1994:10–11).

Considered more "humane" than other modes of execution, lethal injection was designated as either the mandatory or optional method of execution in twenty-five of the thirty-six states that authorized capital punishment as of 1994. In many of these states, physician involvement in execution by lethal injection was mandated by state law and/or specified in departmental regulations concerning execution procedures (American College of Physicians et al. 1994:17).

A 1994 report published by the American College of Physicians, Human Rights Watch, the National Coalition to Abolish the Death Penalty, and Physicians for Human Rights provided detailed information on these laws and regulations and on the actual nature of physician participation in the execution process. The report also addressed at length the policies of various state and national medical societies with regard to medical ethics and physician participation in executions.

Following is an excerpt from the report.

The contemporary ethical prohibition against medical participation in capital punishment is deeply rooted in the professional tradition of non-maleficence. In recent years, physician participation has been condemned by the World Medical Association, the World Psychiatric Association, and national medical societies throughout the industrialized world, including the United States. Some opponents of physician involvement base their objections on their belief that capital punishment is immoral or contrary to international law. Many others, including the American Medical Association, take the position that the morality of the death penalty is a matter of personal conscience but that physician complicity in its administration is nevertheless unethical.

Physician participation in executions represents a significant challenge to morality of the medical profession. For patients and the public, the credibility of physicians is inextricably linked to the medical profession's separation from activities that directly conflict with its central mission. As AMA executive vice president James Todd, M.D., recently said, "When the healing hand becomes the hand inflicting the wound, the world is turned inside out." Society trusts that physicians will work for the benefit of their patients; that trust is threatened by physician participation in executions.

Many commentators have based their opposition to physician participation in executions on the Hippocratic dictum, "first, do no harm." As one physician has written, "Doctors are not executioners. Inflicted death is antithetical to their ancient creed." The Council on Ethical and Judicial Affairs of the AMA notes, "Physician participation in executions contradicts the dictates of the medical profession by causing harm rather than alleviating pain and suffering."

Some people might suggest, however, that physician participation could be construed as compassionate and caring, rather than harmful. Lethal injection, for example, was introduced as a method that would appear to be less excruciating than electrocution, the gallows, or gas. A physician might conclude that given the inevitability of an execution, participation might be ethically acceptable. Although physician participation in some instances may arguably reduce pain, there are many countervailing arguments. First, the purpose of medical involvement may not be to reduce harm or suffering, but to give the surface appearance of humanity. Second, the physician presence also serves to give an aura of medical legitimacy to the procedure. Third, in the larger picture, the physician is taking over some of the responsibility for carrying out the punishment and in this context, becomes the handmaiden of the state as executioner. In return for possible reduction of pain, the physician, in effect, acts under the control of the state, doing harm.

Physicians are clearly out of place in the execution chamber, and their participation subverts the core of their professional ethics, which require them to "maintain the utmost respect for human life from its beginning even under threat" and to provide "competent medical service in full technical and moral independence, with compassion and respect for human dignity." These insights produce a more subtle and comprehensive prohibition on physician participation than simple reliance upon the Hippocratic dictum of *primum non nocere*. Nevertheless, the maxim, "first, do no harm" represents a powerful, evocative ideal.

*Source*: *Breach of Trust: Physician Participation in Executions in the United States* (American College of Physicians, Human Rights Watch, National Coalition to Abolish the Death Penalty, Physicians for Human Rights, 1994), 37–39 (footnotes omitted).

## DOCUMENT 107: Public Opinion and the Death Penalty (1994)

Support for the death penalty broke a new Gallup Poll record in 1994, with 80 percent of Americans in favor of capital punishment— a four-point increase since 1991 (see Document 94) and one point more than the previous high of 79 percent reported by Gallup in 1988 (see Document 84).

Sixty percent of Americans surveyed in 1994 were in favor of the death penalty for teenagers who commit murder, compared to 11 percent in 1959. The Gallup report notes that "In a year in which crime has emerged in the public's mind as the nation's most important problem, Americans today express decidedly tough attitudes about juvenile crime" (Gallup 1994:150).

**SEPTEMBER 29**
**DEATH PENALTY/JUVENILE CRIME**
Interviewing Dates: 9/6–7/94
CNN/*USA Today*/Gallup Poll
Survey #GO 22–00807–020

*Are you in favor of the death penalty for a person convicted of murder?*

| | |
|---|---|
| Favor | 80% |
| Oppose | 16 |
| No opinion | 4 |

*When a teenager commits a murder and is found guilty by a jury, do you think he should get the death penalty, or should he be spared because of his youth?*

| | |
|---|---|
| Death penalty | 60% |
| Spared | 30 |
| No opinion | 10 |

*Source*: *The Gallup Poll: Public Opinion 1994* (Wilmington, Del.: Scholarly Resources Inc., 1994), 148, 149. Copyright 1994 by Scholarly Resources Inc. Reprinted by permission of Scholarly Resources Inc.

---

## DOCUMENT 108: "Capital Punishment" (Tom Disch, 1995)

Poetry can be an especially powerful and potentially influential form of expression about capital punishment because it has the ability to communicate the strong feelings that many people may have about capital punishment—feelings that often aren't captured by legal or scholarly writings.

For example, in "Capital Punishment" noted author and poet Tom Disch (1940–   ) offered a strong view on capital punishment that demanded even more than the death of the condemned prisoner.

Murderers, said Disch, should be "instructed in remorse" and made to identify with their victims—made to learn about the lives they have taken. Ultimately, he said, the goal of capital punishment is not justice, but poetry—"a way of balancing one terrible headline with another of equal weight."

According to Disch, "Elsa Rush, to whom the poem is dedicated, is a forceful and articulate opponent of capital punishment, and more than once has persuaded me, against my own primitive urges, that capital punishment is a bad idea, if only because it is not cost-effective, the appeals process being more expensive than the cost of lifelong incarceration. Yet, away from Elsa's eloquence, I would always fall back into my old way of thinking. This poem was an attempt to account for that recidivism."[1]

Disch, who has been called "one of the most remarkably talented writers around" by a *Washington Post Book World* reviewer (August 6, 1989), is the author of dozens of novels, story collections, poetry volumes, children's books, and other publications.

## NOTE

1. In a letter to the authors dated June 18, 1996.

### CAPITAL PUNISHMENT

*For Elsa*

They should always have to ask for it—
But only after they have been instructed
In remorse. For the cannier psychotics
Understand that death is a door opening
To the Florida of their dreams and head for it
The minute it's dawned on them they've no one
To rape but themselves, no one to kill
But those who deserve it. This diminishes
The thrill to that degree Florida
Starts to look good.

                  Would this be cruel
And unusual and, so, prohibited? Not
If we can plausibly deny it. Let us say
That when, in the first stage of their greased
Slide to Lethe, they are put on round-the-clock
Electronic display, this is not done
In a spirit of cruelty or retribution
But rather as instruction. And if some of us
Who have paid for the privilege of dialing
Their 900-numbers would seem to be harassing them
Cruelly, the prisoners have every opportunity
To call their callers to account. Just so long
As they answer their questions first:
Why did you murder them? How could you be
So cruel? Would you do it again?
Have you ever been raped in prison? Are you afraid
That you'll be raped again? The same questions
Every day and all through the night, like water
    dripping
On their foreheads. Eventually, in most cases,
A dent is made.

Yet there are a few who never ask
To be advanced to the next stage of their punishment,
Who seem actually to enjoy the phone calls
From angry strangers and whose sullen defiance
Is inexhaustible as the steam of geysers.
But even the stoniest of these will break
Beneath the strain of silence and neglect.
When the headlines have forgotten them
And all the survivors have spent their rage,
When the phone stops ringing and the prisoners
Can only sit there listening to the recycling
Of earlier diatribes, at last from sheer boredom
They'll ask to be advanced to the next ledge of their
    purgatory.

Here all is upbeat, bright, and normative
As 60's sitcoms. Here the condemned are encouraged
To study the lineaments of the lives
They have smashed, reversing the tapes,
As it were, from the moment of impact, back
To some everyday of unsuspecting happiness.
As when the victim, a sophomore at Julliard,
Essayed *Les Barricades Mysteriuses*
By François Couperin. His murderer,
Aged 15, an admirer of Dr. Dre,
Will be immersed in Couperin until he learns
To love it. Only at that point
Will he be allowed to request the *coup de grace*.

But what of the more common case
When killer and victim share the same dismal
Horizon, when it's a toss-up which death
Would have represented the larger social benefit?
Should the state's iron boot be used to trample
The perp's soul till it yields some five or six
Thimbles of sympathy? Even then could we be sure
That a coerced remorse has its source
In anything more than the universal need
To appease one's torturers? We cannot, of course,
And it is incumbent that we explain
To the condemned that there is nothing he can do
To make us believe his post-Watergate
Born-again glory isn't a ploy. The brighter ex-cons
Understand this and wear their crimes
Like fur coats. Manson writes hit songs,
And North his bestsellers. In another century
They would have been the sort to deliver
A good bon mot from the gallows.

There will always be those unwilling
To share the guilt of the executioner.
Even now that Dr. Kevorkian has refashioned
The machinery so death is just a sigh away,
The old objection is still sometimes made
That killing people is wrong. As perhaps it is.
The object of capital punishment
Is not justice but poetry, a way of balancing one
Terrible headline with another of equal weight.

Source: Tom Disch, "Capital Punishment," Poetry CLXV, no. 4 (January 1995): 189–191.

---

## DOCUMENT 109: *The New York Death Penalty Statute* (1995)

On March 7, 1995, New York Governor George E. Pataki signed a state death penalty bill into law, making New York the thirty-eighth state in the union to authorize capital punishment. The law—which was strongly challenged by opponents of capital punishment—took effect September 1, 1995 (Cohen and Rosenthal 1995:3).

The bill, which Pataki called "the most effective of its kind in the nation" (*New York Times*, March 8, 1995), made death by lethal injection an available punishment for several well-defined types of first-degree murder. In an effort to eliminate racial bias and other factors leading to arbitrary or discriminatory death sentences, the new bill required an elaborate series of steps to be followed in all death penalty cases. The act also prohibited the execution of pregnant women, the mentally incompetent and the mentally retarded,[1] and provided for the assignment of defense attorneys specifically trained in capital punishment law to indigent defendants accused of capital crimes.

These and other features of the new law were described in detail in a pamphlet titled *The New York Death Penalty Statute.* Following is an excerpt from the pamphlet.

### NOTE
1. However, the mentally retarded could be eligible for execution should they commit murder while incarcerated.

On March 2, 1995, the New York State legislature passed an act, signed into law by Governor George E. Pataki on March 7, 1995, that authorizes the imposition of the death penalty for the commission of certain crimes, defined as murder in the first degree. The new legislation, which takes effect on September 1, 1995, paves the way for the resumption of executions in New York, the most recent of which took place over thirty years ago, in 1963. During this thirty-year period, existing New York death penalty statutes were held to be unconstitutional by the New York Court of Appeals on three occasions. Since 1977, death penalty bills have annually been passed by the state legislature proposing amendments to the statutory scheme—in order to conform it to constitutional requirements and allow for the imposition of the penalty—only to be vetoed by the sitting governor of the states. With the enactment of the new law, New York becomes the thirty-eighth state, in addition to the federal government, to sanction the death penalty as punishment for designated criminal conduct.

The legislation (hereinafter "the Act") inspired impassioned and heated debate concerning its morality, its effectiveness as a deterrent, its financial cost, and the possibility of its incorrect imposition. Ironically, the most recent statistical compilations have shown a dramatic decrease in the number of homicides in New York City, which account for roughly 70% of the homicides within the state. No doubt proponents of the legislation will cite its expected and realized enactment as a major contribution to the statistic, especially if the trend continues, while opponents will cite the decrease as proof that the penalty is unnecessary. One thing is clear: the legislation will spawn tremendous amounts of litigation.

The Act amends the Penal, Criminal Procedure, Judiciary, County, Correction, and Executive Laws and establishes a newly defined and limited class of murder cases, defined as murder in the first degree, for which the death penalty will be available. It also creates an elaborate procedure by which the death penalty may be imposed, including a special sentencing proceeding before the trial jury, in instances where a defendant has been found guilty of murder in the first degree. Among other things, the Act vests the District Attorney of each county with discretion in deciding whether to seek the death penalty in cases that meet the statutory criteria; it entitles either party to demand that prospective trial and sentencing jurors be examined individually outside the presence of the other prospective jurors; it allows for special consideration by the court, independent of the trial and sentencing jury's consideration, of any colorable claim that the defendant is mentally retarded, and it provides for direct review of all death penalty judgments in the New York Court of Appeals and specifically requires a "proportionality" review in which the Court of Appeals must examine other factually similar cases to determine whether the death penalty was imposed improperly by virtue of the defendant's or the victim's race. The Act also provides for the assignment of counsel to indigent defendants accused of capital crimes from a specifically designated pool of attorneys.

*Source*: Jay M. Cohen and Robert Rosenthal, *The New York Death Penalty Statute* (New York: Matthew Bender, 1995), 3–4 (footnotes omitted). Copyright © 1995 by Matthew Bender & Co., Inc. Reprinted with permission from *New York's Death Penalty Legislation*. All rights reserved.

## DOCUMENT 110: "Apartheid Lives on America's Death Row" (Jack Greenberg, 1995)

In 1995, South Africa abolished capital punishment under its post-apartheid constitution. In doing so, the South African Constitutional Court specifically referred to several American studies in which the death penalty has not been proven a greater deterrent to murder than life imprisonment.

In a *Los Angeles Times* commentary, abolitionist Jack Greenberg noted that "South Africa's decision leaves the United States even further isolated" from the world's other democracies, the majority of which have abolished the death penalty.

Greenberg, a law professor at Columbia University, served as director-counsel of the NAACP Legal Defense and Educational Fund Inc. (see Document 51) from 1961 to 1984, during which time he directed its campaign against the death penalty.

Greenberg joined the LDF as a staff attorney in 1949, after graduating from Columbia Law School (Greenberg 1994:xvii). He served as an assistant to LDF Director Thurgood Marshall, who in 1961 was appointed by President John F. Kennedy to the United States Court of Appeals and later became a U.S. Supreme Court Justice (Meltsner 1973:6, 10).

South Africa's highest court has unanimously invalidated capital punishment under its post-apartheid constitution. In a departure from the course taken by the United States Supreme Court, the South African Constitutional Court invoked its Bill of Rights provisions that prohibit "cruel, inhuman and degrading punishment." . . .

In this decision, South Africa has joined most of the world's democracies. Canada, most of Latin America, all of Western Europe, Australia, New Zealand and Namibia prohibit the death penalty as have the Czech and Slovak republics, Hungary and Romania. Russia retains it virtually only in name: Clemency has revoked the few recent death sentences. A few years ago, the Soviet Union had thousands of executions annually. India, with its population of perhaps 1 billion, executed three men in recent years.

The International Covenant on Civil and Political Rights and its pro-
tocols condemn capital punishment, as do the American and European
Human Rights Conventions. The United States, which only recently ratified the covenant, opted out of its provisions dealing with capital punishment.

South Africa's decision leaves the United States even further isolated.
In the 1980s, there were more than 1,100 executions in South Africa. In
1989, there were 60, plus unknown numbers in the "homelands" before
a moratorium went into effect. When the Constitutional Court decision
came down, 443 people were on death row; they will now be resentenced.

In recent times, the United States has executed between 30 and 40
death row inmates a year; in 1995, that number may exceed 40 and hundreds more are sentenced each year. As other countries have been abolishing capital punishment, the United States has been revving it up. Bill
Clinton advocated and Congress created about 60 new federal death penalty offenses in the last crime bill; Gov. George Pataki boasts about reinstating New York's new death-penalty law immediately following his
swearing-in. The Supreme Court has relentlessly been making capital
sentences more difficult to contest. Moreover, while more than 70 death-
penalty countries have abolished it for offenders under 18, the United
States, according to Human Rights Watch, "is a world leader in executing juvenile offenders." (Nine since the death penalty was reinstated in
1976, four in the last six months of 1993.)

Why are we so different? The best clue is that executions have taken
place overwhelmingly in the former slave-holding states. Nationwide,
anyone, particularly a black, who kills a white person, is far more likely
to be sentenced to death than someone, particularly a white, who kills a
black.

The Supreme Court has held that the intent to discriminate would
have to be proved—an impossible task—for this disparity to be unconstitutional.

Once, I was optimistic that the death penalty in America was on the
way to extinction. South Africa's humane decision has caused me to
contrast it with what has been happening here. I am afraid that until we
rid ourselves of the legacy of our own apartheid, we will have to contend
with the arbitrary, irrational, racist regime of capital justice we have today.

*Source*: Jack Greenberg, "Apartheid Lives on America's Death Row," *Los Angeles
Times*, June 26, 1995, B9.

## DOCUMENT 111: "56 Executions This Year Are Most Since 1957" (*Associated Press*, 1995)

As Americans' support for the death penalty increased during the 1990s (see Documents 94 and 107), so did executions. During 1995, a total of fifty-six executions took place in the United States—which is twenty-five more than in 1994 and forty-two more than in 1991.

The rising execution rate in America may be partly responsible for what appears to be rising public interest in the capital punishment debate, as evidenced by the popularity of books and movies that focus on the death penalty, including *Dead Man Walking* (1993), a book by Sister Helen Prejean that was made into a hit movie in 1995, and John Grisham's best-selling novel *The Chamber* (1994), which was being made into a movie at the time of this writing.

WASHINGTON, Dec. 29 (AP)—Fifty-six murderers were executed in the United States this year, the highest national figure since 1957.

And with more than 3,000 men and women now on death rows, 1996 may bring an even higher total, experts said.

"The trend is fewer legal protections, and there's a sentiment towards speeding up the process," said Richard Dieter of the Death Penalty Information Center, a Washington research group whose focus is inequality in dealing out capital punishment.

Of the 38 states with death penalty laws, 16 carried out executions in 1995. They were led by Texas, which executed 19 people; Missouri was second with 6.

"It reflects the attitude of the Texas electorate," said Larry Fitzgerald of the Texas Department of Criminal Justice. "We've got a tough-on-crime state and aggressive prosecutors."

Since the Supreme Court ended a four-year moratorium on capital punishment in 1976, there have been 313 executions in the United States, 104 of them in Texas.

Today, 411 men and 6 women are on death row in Texas. Fifteen are scheduled to die by May, and Mr. Fitzgerald said that at least five of those were "excellent candidates" whose various appeals had traveled through state and Federal courts for years.

Capital punishment remains largely, but not entirely, a Southern phenomenon. Besides Texas and Missouri, executions occurred this year in Alabama, Arizona, Arkansas, Delaware, Florida, Georgia, Illinois, Louisiana, Montana, North Carolina, Oklahoma, Pennsylvania, South Carolina and Virginia.

The 1995 total of 56 executions is a distinct increase from recent years. There were 31 executions in 1994, 38 in 1993, 31 in 1992, 14 in 1991 and 23 in 1990.

The 193 executions so far in the 1990's already surpass the 117 carried out in the 1980's. There were three in the 1970's and 191 in the 1960's.

Throughout the 1950's, the average annual execution total was 71.7. Sixty-five executions were carried out in 1957.

With some regularity since 1984, advocates and opponents of the death penalty alike have predicted that the "flood gates are opening." But that has not happened.

Still, Mr. Dieter and Mr. Fitzgerald agree that the indicators now point to a significant increase in the pace of executions.

Congress, they noted, has moved to change laws governing state prisoners' access to Federal courts, and federally financed law offices to help with death row appeals have lost financing. Also, they said, some states are speeding the appellate process in capital cases.

"There seems to be an impatience, a call for finality," Mr. Dieter said.

He said increasing the pace of executions increased the risk of killing an innocent man.

"Each year, there are people released from death row, their convictions wiped out—and not just because of some technical error in their prosecutions," Mr. Dieter said. "That speaks of the danger of mistakes being made."

*Source*: "56 Executions This Year Are Most Since 1957," *Associated Press*, December 29, 1995. In *New York Times*, December 30, 1995, 28.

---

## DOCUMENT 112: *Felkner v. Turpin* (1996)

A basic democratic freedom that dates back to the Magna Carta (1215) was modified in 1996 in order to streamline the death penalty appeals process. The *Antiterrorism and Effective Death Penalty Act of 1996* fundamentally restricts federal habeas corpus, the legal procedure by which state prisoners can go to federal courts to argue that they were unconstitutionally convicted or sentenced. In an unusual— four Justices said "unseemly"—show of speed, the Supreme Court agreed to hear a challenge to the act almost as soon as it became law. The case, *Felkner v. Turpin* (95–8836), challenged the constitutionality of a section of the act that limited the Court's authority to review habeas cases on appeal.

Habeas corpus has been a powerful weapon against unlawful detention. As many documents in the last three sections show, it has protected minorities from biased state courts, provided relief for people who were detained illegally, and been a last resort to prisoners on death row. The fact that so many prisoners sentenced to die have won new trials or been freed after habeas appeals brought appellate review emphasizes its importance as a capital punishment issue. The fact that 99 percent of the habeas petitions are not associated with death penalty appeals indicates that the "effective death penalty" provisions of this act could have a far greater impact on fundamental rights than many people would suspect.

The *Antiterrorism and Effective Death Penalty Act* that was challenged in *Felkner* makes four major changes to limit federal habeas appeals:

1. It restricts the time in which inmates may file federal appeals—which often involve an exceedingly complex set of legal issues and procedures—to one year after they lose in state-level reviews.

2. It requires that federal judges at both steps of the federal appeals process give first priority to death penalty appeals and file decisions on them within six months (i.e., six months for the federal district court decision and then another six months for the U.S. Court of Appeals).

3. It establishes a unitary appeals process under which inmates whose appeals have been rejected by state judges get only one chance to appeal in federal courts. Second and subsequent appeals are allowed only in the extreme case where a federal review panel finds "clear and convincing" proof that they are not guilty.

4. It restricts federal judges from reversing a state conviction or death sentence except in the extreme circumstance when it results from "an unreasonable application of clearly established federal law."

Senator Orrin Hatch and other legal conservatives claimed that repeated and often frivolous habeas petitions by prisoners and abolitionists block a legitimate punishment and make a mockery of the justice system and families of victims. It is argued that because of major improvements in the sensitivity of state courts to prisoners' rights, it now is appropriate to speed up the habeas process by restricting constant federal second-guessing of state courts (Marquand 1996:18).

Opponents argue that the act's habeas provisions are an unconstitutional infringement by Congress on the judicial branch; that they violate the Constitution's guarantee that the "privilege of the Writ of Habeas Corpus shall not be suspended, unless when in the cases of rebellion or invasion the public safety may require it"; that they include

unrealistic deadlines for filing court petitions; and that they place un-
due restraints on the ability of often poor, ill-educated, and marginally
represented prisoners who are fighting for their lives.

Ellis Wayne Felkner was convicted of the 1981 murder and rape of
Evelyn Joy Ludlam, a nineteen-year-old college student, in Georgia.
After being sentenced to death, he was denied relief in two rounds of
state collateral proceedings, on a direct appeal to the Supreme Court
in 1984, and in a first round of federal habeas corpus proceedings. Five
days after President Clinton signed the new 1996 death penalty law,
Felkner's lawyers tried to delay his execution yet again by filing another
federal appeal in Atlanta. The appeal was dismissed by the Atlanta
court because Felkner's claim did not meet the new law's requirements
for filing second and subsequent habeas petitions. His lawyers then
filed an emergency appeal with the Supreme Court claiming that the
act restricts the Court's jurisdiction in violation of the constitutional
stricture against suspension of habeas corpus.

In a unanimous decision, the Court denied Felkner's appeal and, as
the following document indicates, held that the act did not affect the
Supreme Court's power to hear habeas petitions. This was because,
under a law that had not been used for over seventy years—and that
apparently had been overlooked by the drafters of the legislation—the
Court still had authority to hear habeas petitions directly. Thus the *Anti-
Terrorism and Effective Death Penalty Act of 1996* withstood its first
constitutional challenge.

CHIEF JUSTICE REHNQUIST delivered the opinion of the Court. . . .

Title I of the Antiterrorism and Effective Death Penalty Act of 1996
(Act) works substantial changes to chapter 153 of Title 28 of the United
States Code, which authorizes federal courts to grant the writ of habeas
corpus. . . . We hold that the Act does not preclude this Court from
entertaining an application for habeas corpus relief, although it does
affect the standards governing the granting of such relief. We also conclude that the availability of such relief in this Court obviates any claim
by petitioner under the Exceptions Clause of Article III, §2, of the Constitution, and that the operative provisions of the Act do not violate the
Suspension Clause of the Constitution, Art. I, §9. . . .

II

We first consider to what extent the provisions of Title I of the Act
apply to petitions for habeas corpus filed as original matters in this Court
pursuant to 28 U. S. C. §§2241 and 2254. We conclude that although the
Act does impose new conditions on our authority to grant relief, it does
not deprive this Court of jurisdiction to entertain original habeas petitions.

A

. . .

[T]itle I of the Act has not repealed our authority to entertain original habeas petitions. . . . No provision of Title I mentions our authority to entertain original habeas petitions; in contrast, §103 amends the Federal Rules of Appellate Procedure to bar consideration of original habeas petitions in the courts of appeals. Although §106(b) (3)(E) precludes us from reviewing, by appeal or petition for certiorari, a judgment on an application for leave to file a second habeas petition in district court, it makes no mention of our authority to hear habeas petitions filed as original matters in this Court. As we declined to find a repeal of §14 of the Judiciary Act of 1789 as applied to this Court by implication then, we decline to find a similar repeal of §2241 of Title 28—its descendant, n. 1, *supra*—by implication now.

This conclusion obviates one of the constitutional challenges raised. The critical language of Article III, §2, of the Constitution provides that, apart from several classes of cases specifically enumerated in this Court's original jurisdiction, "[i]n all the other Cases . . . the supreme Court shall have appellate Jurisdiction, both as to Law and Fact, with such Exceptions, and under such Regulations as the Congress shall make." Previous decisions construing this clause have said that while our appellate powers "are given by the constitution," "they are limited and regulated by the [Judiciary Act of 1789], and by such other acts as have been passed on the subject." . . . The Act does remove our authority to entertain an appeal or a petition for a writ of certiorari to review a decision of a court of appeals exercising its "gatekeeping" function over a second petition. But since it does not repeal our authority to entertain a petition for habeas corpus, there can be no plausible argument that the Act has deprived this Court of appellate jurisdiction in violation of Article III, §2.

B

We consider next how Title I affects the requirements a state prisoner must satisfy to show he is entitled to a writ of habeas corpus from this Court. Title I of the Act has changed the standards governing our consideration of habeas petitions by imposing new requirements for the granting of relief to state prisoners. Our authority to grant habeas relief to state prisoners is limited by §2254, which specifies the conditions under which such relief may be granted to "a person in custody pursuant to the judgment of a State court." . . . Several sections of the Act impose new requirements for the granting of relief under this section, and they therefore inform our authority to grant such relief as well.

Section 106(b) of the Act addresses second or successive habeas petitions. Section 106(b)(3)'s "gatekeeping" system for second petitions does not apply to our consideration of habeas petitions because it applies to applications "filed in the district court." . . . There is no such limitation, however, on the restrictions on repetitive and new claims imposed by subsections 106(b)(1) and (2). These restrictions apply without qualification to any "second or successive habeas corpus application under section 2254." . . . Whether or not we are bound by these restrictions, they certainly inform our consideration of original habeas petitions.

### III

Next, we consider whether the Act suspends the writ of habeas corpus in violation of Article I, §9, clause 2, of the Constitution. This clause provides that "[t]he Privilege of the Writ of Habeas Corpus shall not be suspended, unless when in Cases of Rebellion or Invasion the public Safety may require it." . . .

The Act requires a habeas petitioner to obtain leave from the court of appeals before filing a second habeas petition in the district court. But this requirement simply transfers from the district court to the court of appeals a screening function which would previously have been performed by the district court as required by 28 U. S. C. §2254 Rule 9(b). The Act also codifies some of the pre-existing limits on successive petitions, and further restricts the availability of relief to habeas petitioners. But we have long recognized that "the power to award the writ by any of the courts of the United States, must be given by written law," . . . and we have likewise recognized that judgments about the proper scope of the writ are "normally for Congress to make." . . .

The new restrictions on successive petitions constitute a modified res judicata rule, a restraint on what is called in habeas corpus practice "abuse of the writ." In *McCleskey* v. *Zant*, . . . we said that "the doctrine of abuse of the writ refers to a complex and evolving body of equitable principles informed and controlled by historical usage, statutory developments, and judicial decisions." . . . The added restrictions which the Act places on second habeas petitions are well within the compass of this evolutionary process, and we hold that they do not amount to a "suspension" of the writ contrary to Article I, §9.

### IV

We have answered the questions presented by the petition for certiorari in this case, and we now dispose of the petition for an original writ of habeas corpus. Our Rule 20.4(a) delineates the standards under which we grant such writs:

A petition seeking the issuance of a writ of habeas corpus shall comply with the requirements of 28 U. S. C. §§2241 and 2242, and in particular with the provision in the last paragraph of §2242 requiring a statement of the "reasons for not making application to the district court of the district in which the applicant is held." If the relief sought is from the judgment of a state court, the petition shall set forth specifically how and wherein the petitioner has exhausted available remedies in the state courts or otherwise comes within the provisions of 28 U. S. C. §2254(b). To justify the granting of a writ of habeas corpus, the petitioner must show exceptional circumstances warranting the exercise of the Court's discretionary powers and must show that adequate relief cannot be obtained in any other form or from any other court. These writs are rarely granted.

Reviewing petitioner's claims here, they do not materially differ from numerous other claims made by successive habeas petitioners which we have had occasion to review on stay applications to this Court. Neither of them satisfies the requirements of the relevant provisions of the Act, let alone the requirement that there be "exceptional circumstances" justifying the issuance of the writ.

The petition for writ of certiorari is dismissed for want of jurisdiction. The petition for an original writ of habeas corpus is denied.

*Source*: Supreme Court of the United States No. 95–8836 (subject to formal revision before publication in the preliminary print of the *United States Reports*), 1–12 (footnotes omitted), 1996.

# Glossary

---

*Aliunde.* From another source.

*Allocution.* Court's formal inquiry into whether there is legal cause for not pronouncing judgment against a defendant. Often used to provide a defendant with an opportunity to make a statement on his or her own behalf and present evidence that might mitigate his sentence.

*Amicus curiae.* Friend of the court. A party with strong interest in, or views on, a matter at trial who is not actually a party to the action may petition the court for permission to file a brief.

*Arguendo.* In the course of argument. A hypothetical illustration or statement made by a judge or attorney arguing a point is said to be made *arguendo*.

*Certiorari.* A writ issued by a superior court requiring an inferior court to provide a certified record of a case it has tried. The higher court issues the writ in order to inspect the lower court's proceedings for irregularities. Certiorari usually refers to the U.S. Supreme Court's use of the writ to choose which cases it wishes to hear.

*Comity.* In general, courts in one state or jurisdiction respect the laws and judicial decisions of other states and jurisdictions as a matter of courtesy, deference, and mutual respect even though they may not be legally required to do so. This is known as the principle of comity.

*Common law.* The case law and statutory law developed in England and the American colonies before the American revolution.

*Deontological ethics.* Ethics that emphasize principles of right and wrong independent of any good or bad consequences that may result from applying those principles.

*Econometrics.* The application of statistical methods to the study of economic data and problems.

*En banc.* In the full bench. Refers to an appellate court session where all members of the court participate rather than merely a quorum.

*Habeas corpus.* Literally means "you have the body." The purpose of a writ of habeas corpus is not to determine a prisoner's guilt or innocence, but to determine whether he or she has been imprisoned unlawfully. Therefore, the only issue it is concerned with is whether a prisoner is being held without due process of law.

*Inter alia.* Among other things.

*Mens rea.* Guilty mind. An element of a criminal act requiring that it be committed intentionally, usually knowingly and willfully.

*Misprision.* An offense that does not have a specific name, such as contempt against the government or the courts, neglect or improper performance of a legal duty, or failure to attempt to prevent a crime or reveal it to authorities.

*Mulct.* Usually a monetary fine imposed as a penalty for a relatively minor offense or a civil judgment.

*Per curiam.* By the court. A brief, usually unanimous decision of a court that is rendered without elaborate discussion.

*Sanguinary.* Bloodthirsty. Describes laws that inflict death freely.

*Voire dire.* To speak the truth. A preliminary examination of a person to determine his or her competency or qualification to serve as a witness or juror.

*Writ of mandamus.* A writ issued by a superior court commanding an inferior court, board, corporation, or person to perform a specific act or duty.

*Source: Black's Law Dictionary, 1991; Cambridge Encyclopedia, 1990; Concise Oxford Dictionary, 1990; Webster's Ninth New Collegiate Dictionary, First Digital Edition, 1992.*

# APPENDIX A

# Federal and State Capital Offenses in the United States

**U.S. Federal**: Murder related to smuggling of aliens; espionage by a member of the armed forces relating to major weapons, defense strategy, nuclear weaponry, military spacecraft or satellites, war plans, communications, or cryptographic information; murder while a member of the armed forces; destruction of aircraft, motor vehicles, or related facilities resulting in death; murder committed during a drug related drive-by shooting; murder committed at an airport serving international civil aviation; retaliatory murder of a member of the immediate family of law enforcement officials; civil rights offenses resulting in death; assassination or kidnapping resulting in the death of the President or Vice President; murder of a member of Congress, an important executive official, a Supreme Court Justice, federal judge or federal law enforcement official; espionage; death resulting from offenses involving transportation of explosives, destruction of government property, or the destruction of property related to foreign or interstate commerce; murder committed by the use of a firearm during a crime of violence or a drug trafficking crime; murder committed in a federal government facility; genocide; first-degree murder; murder of a foreign official; murder by a federal prisoner; murder of a U.S. national in a foreign country; murder by an escaped federal prisoner already sentenced to life imprisonment; murder of a state or local law enforcement official or other person aiding in a federal investigation; murder of a state correctional officer; murder during a hostage-taking; murder of a court officer or juror; murder with the intent of preventing testimony by a witness, victim, or informant; retaliatory murder of a witness, victim, or informant; mailing of injurious articles with intent to kill or resulting in death; murder for hire; murder involved in a racketeering offense; willful wrecking of a train resulting in death;

bank-robbery-related murder or kidnaping; murder related to a car-jacking; murder related to rape or child molestation; murder related to sexual exploitation of children; murder committed during an offense against maritime navigation or a maritime fixed platform; terrorist murder of a U.S. national in another country; murder by the use of a weapon of mass destruction; murder involving torture; treason; intentionally ordering or causing the killing of another while engaged in a continuing criminal enterprise; intentionally ordering or causing the killing of a federal, state, or local law enforcement officer while attempting to avoid apprehension, prosecution, or service of a prison sentence for a felony associated with engaging in a continuing criminal enterprise.

**Alabama**: Murder during kidnaping, robbery, rape, sodomy, burglary, sexual assault, or arson; murder of a peace officer, correctional officer, or public official; murder while under a life sentence; murder of a defendant with a previous murder conviction; murder of a witness to a crime; murder when a victim is subpoenaed in a criminal proceeding, when the murder is related to the role of the victim as a witness; murder when a victim is less than fourteen years old; murder in which a victim is killed during a drive-by shooting.

**Alaska**: No capital offenses.

**Arizona**: First-degree murder accompanied by at least one of ten aggravating factors.

**Arkansas**: Felony murder; arson causing death; intentional murder of a law enforcement officer, teacher, or school employee; murder of prison, jail, court, or correctional personnel or of military personnel acting in line of duty; multiple murders; intentional murder of a public officeholder or candidate; intentional murder while under life sentence; contract murder.

**California**: Treason; homicide by a prisoner serving a life term; first-degree murder with special circumstances; train wrecking; perjury causing execution.

**Colorado**: First-degree murder; felony murder; intentionally killing a peace officer, firefighter, judge, referee, elected State, county, or municipal official, Federal law enforcement officer or agent; person kidnaped or being held hostage by the defendant or an associate of the defendant; being party to an agreement to kill another person; murder committed while lying in wait, from ambush, or by use of an explosive or incendiary device; murder for pecuniary gain; murder in an especially heinous, cruel, or depraved manner; murder for the purpose of avoiding or preventing a lawful arrest or prosecution or effecting an escape from custody, including the intentional killing of a witness to a criminal offense; killing two or more persons during the same incident, and murder of a child less than twelve years old; treason.

**Connecticut**: Murder of a public safety or correctional officer; murder for pecuniary gain; murder in the course of a felony; murder by a defendant with a previous conviction for intentional murder; murder while under a life sentence; murder during a kidnaping; illegal sale of cocaine, methadone, or heroin to a person who dies from using these drugs; murder during first-degree sexual assault; multiple murders; murder committed using an assault weapon.

**Delaware**: First-degree murder with aggravating circumstances, including murder of a child victim fourteen years of age or younger by an individual who was at least four years older than the victim; killing of a nongovernmental informant who provides an investigative, law enforcement, or police agency with information concerning criminal activity; premeditated murder resulting from substantial planning.

**District of Columbia**: No capital offenses.

**Florida**: Felony murder; first-degree murder; sexual battery on a child under age twelve; unlawful use of destructive devices resulting in death; capital drug trafficking.

**Georgia**: Murder; kidnaping with bodily injury when the victim dies; aircraft hijacking; treason; kidnaping for ransom when the victim dies.

**Hawaii**: No capital offenses.

**Idaho**: First-degree murder; aggravated kidnaping.

**Illinois**: First-degree murder accompanied by at least one of fourteen aggravating factors.

**Indiana**: Murder with fourteen aggravating circumstances.

**Iowa**: No capital offenses.

**Kansas**: Intentional and premeditated murder during the commission of a kidnaping; contract murder; intentional and premeditated killing by a jail or prison inmate; intentional and premeditated killing in the commission of rape or sodomy; intentional and premeditated killing of a law enforcement officer; intentional and premeditated killing of a child under the age of fourteen in the commission of kidnaping; killing two or more persons during the same incident.

**Kentucky**: Murder with aggravating factor; kidnaping with aggravating factor.

**Louisiana**: First-degree murder; treason.

**Maine**: No capital offenses.

**Maryland**: First-degree murder, either premeditated or during the commission of a felony, provided that certain death eligibility requirements are satisfied.

**Massachusetts**: No capital offenses.

**Michigan**: No capital offenses.

**Minnesota**: No capital offenses.

**Mississippi**: Murder of a peace officer or correctional officer; murder while under a life sentence; murder by bomb or explosive; contract murder; murder committed during specific felonies (rape, burglary, kidnaping, arson, robbery, sexual battery, unnatural intercourse with a child, nonconsensual unnatural intercourse); murder of an elected official; rape of a child under fourteen years old by a person eighteen years or older; aircraft piracy.

**Missouri**: First-degree murder.

**Montana**: Deliberate homicide; aggravated kidnaping when victim or rescuer dies; attempted deliberate kidnaping by a state prison inmate who has a prior conviction for deliberate homicide or who has previously been declared a persistent felony offender.

**Nebraska**: First-degree murder.

**Nevada**: First-degree murder with nine aggravating circumstances.

**New Hampshire**: Contract murder; murder of a law enforcement officer; murder of a kidnaping victim; killing another after being sentenced to life imprisonment without parole.

**New Jersey**: Purposeful or knowing murder; contract murder.

**New Mexico**: First-degree murder; felony murder with aggravating circumstances.

**New York**: First-degree murder with twelve aggravating circumstances.

**North Carolina**: First-degree murder.

**North Dakota**: No capital offenses.

**Ohio**: Aggravated murder, including assassination; contract murder; murder during escape; murder after conviction for a prior purposeful killing or prior attempted murder; murder of a peace officer; murder arising from specified felonies (rape, kidnaping, arson, robbery, burglary); murder of a witness to prevent testimony in a criminal proceeding or in retaliation.

**Oklahoma**: First-degree murder, including murder with malice aforethought; murder arising from specified felonies (forcible rape, robbery with a dangerous weapon, kidnaping, escape from lawful custody, first-degree burglary, arson); murder when the victim is a child who has been injured, tortured, or maimed.

**Oregon**: Aggravated murder.

**Pennsylvania**: First-degree murder.

**Rhode Island**: No capital offenses.

**South Carolina**: Murder with a statutory aggravating circumstance.

**South Dakota**: First-degree murder; kidnaping with gross permanent physical injury inflicted on the victim; felony murder.

**Tennessee**: First-degree murder.

**Texas**: Murder of a public safety officer, fireman, or correctional employee; murder during the commission of specified felonies (kidnaping, burglary, robbery, aggravated rape, arson); murder for remuneration; multiple murders; murder during prison escape; murder of a correctional officer; murder by a state prison inmate who is serving a life sentence for any of five offenses; murder of an individual under six years of age.

**Utah**: Aggravated murder; aggravated assault by a prisoner serving a life sentence if serious bodily injury is intentionally caused.

**Vermont**: No capital offenses.

**Virginia**: Murder during the commission or attempts to commit specified felonies (abduction, armed robbery, rape, forcible sodomy); contract murder; murder by a prisoner while in custody; murder of a law enforcement officer; multiple murders; murder of a child under twelve years during an abduction; murder arising from drug violations.

**Washington**: Aggravated first-degree premeditated murder.

**West Virginia**: No capital offenses.

**Wisconsin**: No capital offenses.

**Wyoming**: Premeditated murder; felony murder in the perpetration of (or attempts at) sexual assault, arson, robbery, burglary, escape, resisting arrest, kidnaping, or abuse of a child under sixteen years of age.

*Source*: Adapted from James J. Stephen and Tracy L. Snell, *Capital Punishment 1994*, NCJ-158023, Washington, D.C.: U.S. Government Printing Office, February 1996.

# APPENDIX B

# U.S. Executions: Colonial Times to 1995

| Year | Executions | Year | Executions | Year | Executions |
|------|-----------|------|-----------|------|-----------|
| 1600–1699 | 162 | 1946 | 131 | 1971 | 0 |
| 1700–1799 | 1,391 | 1947 | 153 | 1972 | 0 |
| 1800–1865 | 2,453 | 1948 | 119 | 1973 | 0 |
| 1866–1879 | 825 | 1949 | 119 | 1974 | 0 |
| 1880–1889 | 1,005 | 1950 | 82 | 1975 | 0 |
| 1890–1899 | 1,098 | 1951 | 105 | 1976 | 0 |
| 1900–1909 | 1,280 | 1952 | 83 | 1977 | 1 |
| 1910–1919 | 1,091 | 1953 | 62 | 1978 | 0 |
| 1920–1929 | 1,289 | 1954 | 81 | 1979 | 2 |
| 1930 | 155 | 1955 | 76 | 1980 | 0 |
| 1931 | 153 | 1956 | 65 | 1981 | 1 |
| 1932 | 140 | 1957 | 65 | 1982 | 2 |
| 1933 | 160 | 1958 | 49 | 1983 | 5 |
| 1934 | 168 | 1959 | 49 | 1984 | 21 |
| 1935 | 199 | 1960 | 56 | 1985 | 18 |
| 1936 | 195 | 1961 | 42 | 1986 | 18 |
| 1937 | 147 | 1962 | 47 | 1987 | 25 |
| 1938 | 190 | 1963 | 21 | 1988 | 11 |
| 1939 | 160 | 1964 | 15 | 1989 | 16 |
| 1940 | 124 | 1965 | 7 | 1990 | 23 |
| 1941 | 123 | 1966 | 1 | 1991 | 14 |
| 1942 | 147 | 1967 | 2 | 1992 | 31 |
| 1943 | 131 | 1968 | 0 | 1993 | 38 |
| 1944 | 120 | 1969 | 0 | 1994 | 31 |
| 1945 | 117 | 1970 | 0 | 1995 | 56 |
| | | | | **Total** | **14,766** |

*Source*: 1600–1930, Schneider and Smykla 1991:6 (but note that data prior to 1930 may not be complete); 1930–1993, Maguire and Pastore 1995:Table 6.82; 1994, Stephan and Snell 1996; 1995, *Associated Press*, December 29, 1995.

# APPENDIX C

# Selected U.S. Supreme Court Cases

# APPENDIX D

# Capital Punishment Interest Groups and Related Organizations

Following is a partial list of national organizations associated either directly or indirectly with capital punishment issues. For further information, the *Abolitionist's Directory*—an extensive listing of both national and state organizations—is available for a modest fee from the National Coalition to Abolish the Death Penalty (see listing below).

American Civil Liberties Union
Capital Punishment Project
122 Maryland Ave. NE
Washington, D.C. 20002
(202) 675–2321/2319

Amnesty International USA
Program to Abolish the Death Penalty
322 Eighth Ave.
New York, N.Y. 10001
(212) 807–8400

Center for Constitutional Rights
666 Broadway, 7th Floor
New York, N.Y. 10012
(212) 614–6464

Death Penalty Information Center
1606 20th St. NW, 2d Floor
Washington, D.C. 20009
(202) 347–2531

Death Row Support Project
P.O. Box 600
Liberty Mills, Ind. 46496
(219) 982–7480

Friends Committee on National Legislation
245 Second St. NE
Washington, D.C. 20002–5795
(202) 547–6000

Human Rights Watch
485 Fifth Avenue
New York, N.Y. 10017–6104
(212) 972–4013

Martin Luther King Center for
    Nonviolent Social Change
449 Auburn Ave. NE
Atlanta, Ga. 30312
(404) 524–1956

NAACP Legal Defense Fund
99 Hudson St., 16th Floor
New York, N.Y. 10013
(212) 219–1900

National Association of Criminal
  Defense Lawyers
Death Penalty Committee
343 Third St.
Roumain Building, Suite 400
Baton Rouge, La. 70801
(504) 387–5786

National Coalition to Abolish the Death
  Penalty
918 F St. NW, Suite 601
Washington, D.C. 20004
(202) 347–2411

National Committee Against Repressive
  Legislation
3321 12th St. NE, 3d Floor
Washington, D.C. 20017
(202) 529–4225

National Execution Alert Network
  (NCADP)
918 F St. NW, Suite 601
Washington, D.C. 20004
(202) 347–2411

# Select Bibliography

## GENERAL WORKS

Acker, James R. "A Different Agenda: The Supreme Court, Empirical Research Evidence, and Capital Punishment Decisions, 1986–1989." *Law and Society Review* 27, no. 1 (1993): 65–88.

American College of Physicians, Human Rights Watch, The National Coalition to Abolish the Death Penalty, Physicians for Human Rights. *Breach of Trust: Physician Participation in Executions in the United States,* 1994.

Amsterdam, Anthony. "*In Favorem Mortis*: The Supreme Court and Capital Punishment." *Human Rights* 14, no. 1 (1987).

Archer, Dane, and Rosemary Gartner. *Violence and Crime in Cross-National Perspective.* New Haven: Yale University Press, 1984.

*Associated Press,* February 8, 1924. "Gas Kills Convict Almost Instantly." In *New York Times,* February 9, 1924, 15.

———, January 17, 1977. "A Partial Transcript of Remarks by Witness to Gilmore Execution." In *New York Times,* January 18, 1977, 4.

———, December 29, 1995. "56 Executions This Year Are Most Since 1957." In *New York Times,* December 30, 1995, 28.

Bailey, William C. "Murder, Capital Punishment, and Television: Execution Publicity and Homicide Rates." *American Sociological Review* 55 (October 1990).

Baldus, David C., and James W. L. Cole. "The Illusion of Deterrence in Isaac Ehrlich's Research on Capital Punishment." *Yale Law Journal* 85 (1975).

Baldus, David C., Charles Pulaski, and George Woodworth. "Comparative Review of Death Sentences: An Empirical Study of the Georgia Experience." *Journal of Criminal Law & Criminology* 74 (1983).

Baldus, David, George Woodworth, and Charles A. Pulaski, Jr. *Equal Justice and the Death Penalty: A Legal and Empirical Analysis.* Boston: Northeastern University Press, 1990.

Barbash, Fred. "Justice Powell Urges End to Death Sentence Delaying." *Washington Post,* May 10, 1983.

Beccaria, Cesare. *On Crimes and Punishments*, 1764. [Translated by Henry Paolucci; Englewood Cliffs, N.J.: Prentice-Hall, 1963.]

Bedau, Hugo Adam, ed. *The Death Penalty in America*. Chicago: Aldine, 1964; New York: Oxford University Press, 1982, and 1997 (forthcoming).

———. *The Courts, the Constitution, and Capital Punishment*. Lexington, Mass.: Lexington Books, 1977.

———. *Death Is Different: Studies in the Morality, Law, and Politics of Capital Punishment*. Boston: Northeastern University Press, 1987.

Bedau, Hugo Adam, and Chester M. Pierce, eds. *Capital Punishment in the United States*. New York: AMS Press, 1975, 1976.

Bedau, Hugo Adam, and Michael L. Radelet. "Miscarriages of Justice in Potentially Capital Cases." *Stanford Law Review* 40 (November 1987).

———. "The Myth of Infallibility: A Reply to Markman and Cassell." *Stanford Law Review* 41 (November 1988).

Bercovitch, Sacvan, ed. *Execution Sermons*. New York: AMS Press, 1994.

Berkson, Larry Charles. *The Concept of Cruel and Unusual Punishment*. Lexington, Mass.: D. C. Heath, 1975.

Berns, Walter. *For Capital Punishment: Crime and the Morality of the Death Penalty*. New York: Basic Books, 1979.

Black, Charles L., Jr. *Capital Punishment: The Inevitability of Caprice and Mistake*. New York: W. W. Norton, 1974, 1981.

Blumstein, Alfred, Jacqueline Cohen, and Daniel Nagin, eds. *Deterrence and Incapacitation: Estimating the Effects of Criminal Sanctions on Crime Rates*. Washington, D.C.: National Academy of Sciences, 1978.

Bodine, Laurence. "Reform Call: Powell on Capital Punishment." *ABA Journal* 1 (October 1988): 19.

*The Body of Liberties*. 1641. In William H. Whitmore, *A Bibliographical Sketch of the Laws of the Massachusetts Colony from 1630 to 1686*. Boston: Rockwell and Churchill, 1890.

Bohm, Robert M. "American Death Penalty Opinion, 1936–1986: A Critical Examination of the Gallup Polls." In Robert M. Bohm, ed., *The Death Penalty in America: Current Research*. Cincinnati: Anderson Publishing, 1991a.

———. "Retribution and Capital Punishment: Toward a Better Understanding of Death Penalty Opinion." *Journal of Criminal Justice* 20, no. 3 (1992a): 227–236.

———. "Toward an Understanding of Death Penalty Change in the United States: The Pivotal Years, 1966 and 1967." *Humanity and Society* 16, no. 4 (1992b): 524–542.

Bohm, Robert M., ed. *The Death Penalty in America: Current Research*. Cincinnati: Anderson Publishing, 1991b.

Bowers, William. "Capital Punishment and Contemporary Values: People's Misgivings and the Court's Misperceptions." *Law & Society Review* 27, no. 1 (1993).

Bowers, William J. "The Effect of Executions Is Brutalization, Not Deterrence." In Kenneth C. Haas and James A. Inciardi, eds., *Challenging Capital Punishment: Legal and Social Science Approaches*. Newbury Park, Calif.: Sage Publications, 1988.

Bowers, William J. (with Glenn L. Pierce and John F. McDevitt). *Legal Homicide: Death as Punishment in America, 1864–1982*. Boston: Northeastern University Press, 1984.

Bowers, William J., and Glenn L. Pierce. "The Illusion of Deterrence in Isaac Ehrlich's Research on Capital Punishment." *Yale Law Journal* 85, no. 2 (1975).

Bradford, William. *An Enquiry How Far the Punishment of Death Is Necessary in Pennsylvania*. Philadelphia: Dobson, 1793. [Early American Imprints; New York: Readex Microprint, 1985.]

Brown, Edmund G. *Message to the Legislature*. Sacramento, Calif.: California State Government, March 2, 1960.

Calabresi, Steven G., and Gary Lawson. "Equity and Hierarchy: Reflections on the Harris Execution." *Yale Law Journal* 102, no. 1 (October 1992).

Caminker, Evan, and Erwin Chemerinsky. "The Lawless Execution of Robert Alton Harris." *Yale Law Journal* 102, no. 1 (October 1992).

Camus, Albert. *Reflections on the Guillotine*. Translated by Richard Howard. Michigan City, Ind.: Fridtjof-Karla, 1959.

Canavan, Francis. Book review. *National Review* 31 (August 17, 1979).

Carrington, Frank G. *Neither Cruel Nor Unusual*. New Rochelle, N.Y.: Arlington House, 1978.

Channing, Henry. *God Admonishing His People of Their Duty as Parents and Masters*, second edition. New York: T. Green, 1786. [Early American Imprints; New York: Readex Microprint, 1985.]

Cheever, George B. *Capital Punishment, The Argument of Rev. George B. Cheever in Reply to J. L. O'Sullivan, Esq*. New York: Saxton and Miles, 1843.

Child, Lydia Maria (Francis). *Letters from New York*, third edition. New York: C. S. Francis, 1845. [Freeport, N.Y.: Books for Libraries Press, American Fiction Reprint Series, 1970.]

*Civil Liberties* 227 (June 1965). "ACLU's New Stand on the Death Penalty."

Cohen, Daniel A. "In Defense of the Gallows: Justifications of Capital Punishment in New England Execution Sermons, 1674–1825." *American Quarterly* 40, no. 2 (1988): 147–164.

Cohen, Jay M., and Robert Rosenthal. *The New York Death Penalty Statute*. New York: Matthew Bender, 1995.

Cohen, Lawrence E., and Marcus Felson. "Social Change and Crime Rate Trends: A Routine Activity Approach." *American Sociological Review* 44 (1979): 588–608.

Combe, George. *Essays on Phrenology*. Edinburgh: Bell & Bradfute, 1819.

Cunliffe, Marcus. "Testing a Union." In Arthur M. Schlesinger, Jr., ed., *The Almanac of American History*. New York: Barnes and Noble, 1993.

Darrow, Clarence S. *Resist Not Evil*. Chicago: Charles H. Kerr, 1902.

Darrow, Clarence, and Alfred J. Talley. *Is Capital Punishment a Wise Public Policy?* New York: League for Public Discussion, 1924. [Chicago: Chicago Historical Bookworks, 1991.]

Davies, Lawrence E. "Caryl Chessman Executed; Denies His Guilt to the End." *New York Times*, May 3, 1960.

Dicks, Shirley. *Death Row: Interviews with Inmates, Their Families and Opponents of Capital Punishment*. Jefferson, N.C.: McFarland, Inc., 1990.

Dieter, Richard. *Millions Misspent: What Politicians Don't Say About the High Costs of the Death Penalty.* Washington, D.C.: Death Penalty Information Center Report, October 1992.

———. "Secondary Smoke Surrounds the Capital Punishment Debate." *Criminal Justice Ethics* 13, no. 1 (Winter/Spring 1994).

Disch, Tom. "Capital Punishment." *Poetry* CLXV, no. 4 (January 1995).

Dorsen, Norman. *Frontiers of Civil Liberties.* New York: Pantheon Books, 1968.

Draper, Thomas, ed. *Capital Punishment.* New York: The H. W. Wilson Company, 1985.

Duffy, Clinton T. (with Dean Jennings). *The San Quentin Story.* Garden City, N.Y.: Doubleday, 1950.

*The Economist.* April 1, 1995: 19–20. "American Survey: The Waiting Game."

Eddy, Thomas. *An Account of the State Prison or Penitentiary House, in the City of New-York.* New York: Isaac Collins and Son, 1801.

Ehrlich, Isaac. "The Deterrent Effect of Capital Punishment: A Question of Life and Death." *American Economic Review* LXV (June 1975a): 397–417.

———. "Deterrence: Evidence and Inference." *Yale Law Journal* 85 (December 1975b): 209–227.

———. "The Deterrent Effect of Capital Punishment: A Reply." *American Economic Review* (June 1977a).

———. "Capital Punishment and Deterrence: Some Further Thoughts and Additional Evidence." *Journal of Political Economy* (August 1977b).

———. "Crime, Punishment, and the Market for Offenses." *Journal of Economic Perspectives* 10 (Winter 1996): 43–67.

Ehrlich, Isaac, and Joel C. Gibbons. "On the Measurement of the Deterrent Effect of Capital Punishment and the Theory of Deterrence." *Journal of Legal Studies* VI (January 1977): 35–50.

Ehrlich, Isaac, and Randall Mark. "Fear of Deterrence: A Critical Evaluation of the 'Report of the Panel on Research on Deterrent and Incapacitative Effects.'" *Journal of Legal Studies* VI (June 1977): 293–316.

Epstein, Lee, and Joseph F. Kobylka. *The Supreme Court and Legal Change: Abortion and the Death Penalty.* Chapel Hill: The University of North Carolina Press, 1992.

Erskine, Hazel. "The Polls: Fear of Violence and Crime." *Public Opinion Quarterly* 38 (1974): 131–145.

Espy, M. Watt, and John Ortiz Smykla. *Executions in the United States, 1608–1987: The Espy File.* Ann Arbor, Mich.: Inter-university Consortium for Political and Social Research, 1987.

Fattah, Ezzat A. *A Study of the Deterrent Effect of Capital Punishment, with Special Reference to the Canadian Situation.* Ottawa: Information Canada, 1972.

Filler, Louis. "Movements to Abolish the Death Penalty in the United States." *Annals of the American Academy of Political and Social Science* 284 (1952): 124–136. In Thorsten Sellin, ed., *Capital Punishment.* New York: Harper & Row, 1967.

Finckenauer, James O. "Public Support for the Death Penalty: Retribution as Just Deserts or Retribution as Revenge?" *Justice Quarterly* 5 (1988): 81–100.

Fineberg, S. Andhil. *The Rosenberg Case: Fact and Fiction.* New York: Oceana, 1953.

Flint, Jerry M. "States on Move: Half of Legislatures Considering Bills on Capital Offenses." *New York Times*, March 11, 1973.

Galliher, John F., Gregory Ray, and Brent Cook. "Abolition and Reinstatement of Capital Punishment During the Progressive Era and Early 20th Century." *Journal of Criminal Law & Criminology* 83, no. 3 (1992).

Gallup, George. *The Gallup Poll: Public Opinion 1935–71*, Volume One, 1935–1948, Volume Two, 1949–1958, Volume Three, 1959–1971. New York: Random House, 1972.

*Gallup Opinion Index*. April 1972. Princeton, N.J.: American Institute of Public Opinion.

———. July 1976. Princeton, N.J.: American Institute of Public Opinion.

*The Gallup Report*. January/February 1985. Princeton, N.J.: The Gallup Poll.

*The Gallup Poll: Public Opinion 1988*. Wilmington, Del.: Scholarly Resources Inc., 1988.

*The Gallup Poll: Public Opinion 1991*. Wilmington, Del.: Scholarly Resources Inc., 1991.

*The Gallup Poll: Public Opinion 1994*. Wilmington, Del.: Scholarly Resources Inc., 1994.

Gardner, Peter. Book review. *Psychology Today* 13 (June 1979).

Goldstein, Tom. "Death Penalty Opponents Embittered by Execution." *New York Times*, May 26, 1979.

Gottfredson, Michael R., and Travis Hirschi. *A General Theory of Crime*. Palo Alto, Calif.: Stanford University Press, 1990.

Gottlieb, Gerald. "Testing the Death Penalty." *Southern California Law Review* 34 (1961).

Graham, Fred P. "J. Edgar Hoover Dies; Will Lie in State in Capitol." *New York Times*, May 3, 1972.

Greeley, Horace. "Death by Human Law." 1850. In Philip English Mackey, ed., *Voices Against Death: American Opposition to Capital Punishment, 1786–1975*. New York: Burt Franklin, 1976.

Greenberg, Jack. *Crusaders in the Courts*. New York: Basic Books, 1994.

———. "Apartheid Lives on America's Death Row." *Los Angeles Times*, June 26, 1995.

Greenfield, Lawrence A. *Capital Punishment 1989*. (NCJ-124545). Washington, D.C.: U.S. Government Printing Office, 1990.

Greenhouse, Linda. "High Court Overturns a Death Sentence, Signaling a Turn Away from Conservatives." *New York Times*, June 18, 1994, 13.

Grisham, John. *The Chamber*. New York: Doubleday, 1994.

Gross, Samuel R., and Robert Mauro. *Death and Discrimination: Racial Disparities in Capital Sentencing*. Boston: Northeastern University Press, 1989.

Haas, Kenneth C., and James A. Inciardi, eds. *Challenging Capital Punishment: Legal and Social Science Approaches*. Newbury Park, Calif.: Sage Publications, 1988.

Haines, Charles G. *Report on the Penitentiary System in the United States*. New York: Mahlon Day, 1822.

Hamilton, Luther, ed. *Memoirs, Speeches and Writings of Robert Rantoul, Jr*. Boston: John P. Jewett, 1854.

Hanson, Kwéku. "Racial Disparities and the Law of Death: The Case for a New Hard Look at Race-Based Challenges to Capital Punishment." *National Black Law Journal* X, no. 3 (1988): 298–317.

Heilbrun, Kirk, Michael L. Radelet, and Joel Dvoskin. "The Debate on Treating Individuals Incompetent for Execution." *American Journal of Psychiatry* 149 (May 1992): 603–604.

Hentoff, Nat. *The First Freedom*. New York: Delacorte, 1980.

———. "Execution in Your Living Room." *The Progressive* 55, no. 11 (November 1991).

Hinerfeld, Daniel S. "No Appeal Means No Execution." *Los Angeles Times*, July 5, 1996.

Hirsch, Adam Jay. *The Rise of the Penitentiary: Prisons and Punishment in Early America*. New Haven: Yale University Press, 1992.

*The Holy Bible, King James Version*. New York: World Publishing Company.

Hook, Donald D., and Lothar Kahn. *Death in the Balance: The Debate Over Capital Punishment*. Lexington, Mass.: Lexington Books, 1989.

Hoover, J. Edgar. "Statement of Director J. Edgar Hoover." *F.B.I. Law Enforcement Bulletin* 29 (June 1960).

Howard, Derek Lionel. *John Howard: Prison Reformer*. New York: Archer House, 1958.

Huie, William Bradford. *The Execution of Private Slovik*. New York: Duell, Sloan and Pearce, 1954.

Huston, Luther A. "Six Justices Agree: President Says Couple Increased 'Chances of Atomic War.' " *New York Times*, June 20, 1953.

Janikowski, Richard. Statement at "The Future of Capital Punishment" round-table discussion at the Academy of Criminal Justice Sciences annual meeting in Las Vegas, Nevada, March 15, 1996.

Jefferson, Thomas. *A Bill for Proportioning Crimes and Punishments in Cases Heretofore Capital*, 1779. In Julian P. Boyd, ed., *The Papers of Thomas Jefferson*, Vol. 2. Princeton: Princeton University Press, 1950.

Jeffries, John C., Jr. *Justice Lewis F. Powell, Jr.* New York: Scribner's, 1994.

Kaplan, David A. "Death Be Not Proud at the Court: Justice Blackmun Renounces Executions." *Newsweek*, March 7, 1994.

Kaplan, David, and Bob Cohn. "Hung on a Technicality." *Newsweek*, April 6, 1992.

Klein, Lawrence R., Brian Forst, and Victor Filatov. "The Deterrent Effect of Capital Punishment: An Assessment of the Estimates." In Alfred Blumstein, Jacqueline Cohen, and Daniel Nagin, eds., *Deterrence and Incapacitation: Estimating the Effects of Criminal Sanctions on Crime Rates*. Washington, D.C.: National Academy of Sciences, 1978.

Klofas, John, and Stan Stojkovic, eds. *Crime and Justice in the Year 2010*. Belmont, Calif.: Wadsworth, 1995.

Koestler, Arthur. *Reflections on Hanging*. New York: Macmillan, 1957.

Lane, Roger. *Violent Death in the City: Suicide, Accident, and Murder in Nineteenth-Century Philadelphia*. Cambridge, Mass.: Harvard University Press, 1979.

Lane, Roger, and John J. Turner, Jr., eds. *Riot, Rout, and Tumult: Readings in American Social and Political Violence*. Westport, Conn.: Greenwood Press, 1978.

Lawes, Lewis E. *Life and Death in Sing Sing*. Garden City, N.Y.: Doubleday, Doran, 1928.

Layson, Stephen. "Homicide and Deterrence: Another View of the Canadian Time-Series Evidence." *Canadian Journal of Economics* 16 (February 1983): 52–73.

———. "Homicide and Deterrence: A Reexamination of the United States Time-Series Evidence." *Southern Economic Journal* 52 (July 1985): 68–89.

Lester, David. *The Death Penalty: Issues and Answers*. Springfield, Ill.: Charles C. Thomas, 1987.

Lewis, David W. *From Newgate to Dannemora: The Rise of the Penitentiary in New York, 1796–1848*. Ithaca, N.Y.: Cornell University Press, 1965.

Lindert, Peter H. "English Population, Wages, and Prices: 1541–1913." *Journal of Interdisciplinary History* 15 (1985): 609–634.

Livingston, Edward. "Introductory Report to the Code of Crimes and Punishments." 1825. In *The Complete Works of Edward Livingston on Criminal Jurisprudence*, Vol 1. The National Prison Association, 1873. [Montclair, N.J.: Patterson Smith, 1968.]

Longmire, Dennis R. "Americans; Attitudes about the Ultimate Weapon: Capital Punishment." In Timothy J. Flanagan and Dennis R. Longmire, eds., *Americans View Crime and Justice: A National Public Opinion Survey*. Thousand Oaks, Calif.: Sage Publications (forthcoming).

Lownes, Caleb. *An Account of the Alteration and Present State of the Penal Laws of Pennsylvania*. Lexington, Mass.: J. Bradford, 1794. [Early American Imprints; New York: Readex Microprint, 1985.]

Lyons, Eugene. *The Life and Death of Sacco and Vanzetti*. New York: International Publishers Co., 1927. [New York: Da Capo Press, 1970.]

Mackey, Philip English, ed. *Voices Against Death*. New York: Burt Franklin, 1976.

Maguire, Kathleen, and Ann L. Pastore. *Sourcebook of Criminal Justice Statistics— 1994*. Washington, D.C.: USGPO, 1995.

Markman, Stephen J., and Paul G. Cassell. "Protecting the Innocent: A Response to the Bedau-Radelet Study." *Stanford Law Review* 41 (November 1988).

Marquand, Robert. "Congress Sets Stage for Swift Executions." *Christian Science Monitor*, April 8, 1996: 1, 18.

Marquart, James W., and Jonathan R. Sorensen. "A National Study of the *Furman*-Commuted Inmates: Assessing the Threat to Society from Capital Offenders." *Loyola of Los Angeles Law Review* 23 (November 1989).

Masur, Louis P. *Rites of Execution: Capital Punishment and the Transformation of American Culture, 1776–1865*. New York: Oxford University Press, 1989.

Mather, Increase. *A Sermon Occasioned by the Execution of a Man Found Guilty of Murder*. Boston: R. P. [Richard Pierce], 1687. In Sacvan Bercovitch, ed., *Execution Sermons*. New York: AMS Press, 1994.

Meltsner, Michael. *Cruel and Unusual: The Supreme Court and Capital Punishment*. New York: Random House, 1973.

Michaelson, Judith. "Ex-Governor Brown Led Building Boom." *Los Angeles Times*, February 19, 1996.

Morison, Samuel Eliot, Henry Steele Commager, and William E. Leuchtenburg. *A Concise History of the American Republic*. New York: Oxford University Press, 1983.

NAACP Legal Defense and Educational Fund, Inc. "Documents for Proceeding in Federal Habeas Corpus in a Capital Case in which Execution Is Imminent." New York: 1971.

Nakell, Barry, and Kenneth A. Hardy. *The Arbitrariness of the Death Penalty*. Philadelphia: Temple University Press, 1987.

*New York Times*, June 20, 1953. "Eisenhower Is Denounced to 5,000 in Union Sq. Rally."

O'Brien, Robert M. "Police Productivity and Crime Rates: 1973–1992." *Criminology* 34, no. 2 (1996): 183–207.

O'Sullivan, John L. *Report in Favor of the Abolition of the Punishment of Death by Law*. New York: J. & H. G. Langley, 1841. [New York: Arno Press, 1974.]

Otterbein, Keith F. *The Ultimate Coercive Sanction: A Cross-Cultural Study of Capital Punishment*. New Haven, Conn.: HRAF Press, 1986.

Parsons, Dana. "A Front–Row Seat at Death Row's Theater of the Absurd." *Los Angeles Times*, August 16, 1996.

Passell, Peter, and John B. Taylor. "The Deterrent Effect of Capital Punishment: Another View." *American Economic Review* 67, no. 3 (June 1977): 445–451.

Paternoster, Raymond. *Capital Punishment in America*. New York: Lexington Books, 1991.

Penn, William. *The Frame of the Government of the Province of Pensilvania in America*. 1682. Philadelphia: B. Franklin, 1740. [Early American Imprints; New York: Readex Microprint, 1985.]

Phillips, David. "The Deterrent Effect of Capital Punishment: New Evidence on an Old Contorversy." *American Journal of Sociology* 86 (1980): 139–147.

Phillips, Llad, and Subhash Ray. "Evidence on the Identification and Causality Dispute about the Death Penalty." In *Applied Time Series Analysis*. Amsterdam: North-Holland, 1982, 313–340.

Powers, Edwin. *Crime and Punishment in Early Massachusetts, 1620–1692: A Documentary History*. Boston: Beacon Press, 1966.

Prejean, Helen. *Dead Man Walking*. New York: Random House, 1993.

President's Commission. *The Challenge of Crime in a Free Society: A Report by the President's Commission on Law Enforcement and Administration of Justice*. Washington, D.C.: U.S. Government Printing Office, February 1967.

*The Progressive* 57, no. 3 (March 1993). "Lethal Expediency."

Purrington, Tobias. *Report on Capital Punishment Made to the Maine Legislature in 1836*. Washington, D.C.: Gideon, 1852.

Radelet, Michael L. "Executions of Whites for Crimes Against Blacks: Exceptions to the Rule?" *Sociological Quarterly* 30, no. 4 (1989a).

———, ed. *Facing the Death Penalty: Essays on a Cruel and Unusual Punishment*. Philadelphia: Temple University Press, 1989b.

Radelet, Michael L., Hugo Adam Bedau, and Constance E. Putnam. *In Spite of Innocence: Erroneous Convictions in Capital Cases*. Boston: Northeastern University Press, 1992.

Rantoul, Robert, Jr. *Report on the Abolition of Capital Punishment*. 1836. In Luther Hamilton, ed., *Memoirs, Speeches and Writings of Robert Rantoul, Jr*. Boston: John P. Jewett, 1854.

Regoli, Robert M., and John D. Hewitt. *Criminal Justice*. Englewood Cliffs, N.J.: Prentice-Hall, 1996.

Reid, Sue Titus. *Criminal Justice*. New York: Macmillan, 1987.

Reinhardt, Stephen. "The Supreme Court, the Death Penalty, and the *Harris Case.*" *Yale Law Journal* 102, no. 1 (October 1992).

Rotunda, Ronald D. *Modern Constitutional Law,* fourth edition. St. Paul, Minn.: West Publishing, 1993, 355–359.

Rush, Benjamin. *An Enquiry into the Effects of Public Punishments Upon Criminals and Upon Society.* Philadelphia: Joseph James, 1787. [Early American Imprints; New York: Readex Microprint, 1985.]

Sandys, Marla, and Edmund F. McGarrell. "Attitudes Toward Capital Punishment: Preference for the Penalty or Mere Acceptance?" *Journal of Research in Crime and Delinquency* 32, no. 2 (1995): 191–213.

Savage, David G. "Justices Uphold Limit on Death Penalty Pleas." *Los Angeles Times,* June 29, 1996.

Schlesinger, Arthur M., Jr., ed. *The Almanac of American History.* New York: Barnes & Noble, 1993.

Schmalleger, Frank. *Trial of the Century: People of the State of California vs. Orenthal James Simpson.* Upper Saddle River, N.J.: Prentice-Hall, 1996.

Schneider, Victoria, and John Ortiz Smykla. "A Summary Analysis of Executions in the United States, 1608–1987: The Espy File." In Roger M. Bohm, ed., *The Death Penalty in America: Current Research.* Cincinnati: Anderson Publishing Co., 1991.

Schwed, Roger E. *Abolition and Capital Punishment.* New York: AMS Press, 1983.

Sellin, Thorsten. *The Death Penalty.* Philadelphia: The American Law Institute, 1959. In Hugo Adam Bedau, *The Death Penalty in America.* Chicago: Aldine, 1964.

———, ed. *Capital Punishment.* New York: Harper and Row, 1967.

———. *The Penalty of Death.* Beverly Hills, Calif.: Sage, 1980.

Smith, Morton, and R. Joseph Hoffmann, eds. *What the Bible Really Says.* Buffalo, N.Y.: Prometheus Books, 1989.

Spear, Charles. *Essays on the Punishment of Death.* Boston: Charles Spear, 1844. [Littleton, Colo.: Fred B. Rothman, 1994.]

Staunton, Marie, and Sally Fenn, eds. *Amnesty International Handbook.* London: Macdonald Optima, 1990.

Stephan, James, and Tracy L. Snell. *Capital Punishment 1994* (NCJ-158023). Washington, D.C.: U.S. Government Printing Office, February 1996.

Sterritt, David. " 'Last Dance' Follows Other Capital Punishment Movies: Some May Call it 'Dead Woman Walking,' but Its Message Is Earnest." *Christian Science Monitor,* May 10, 1996: 12.

Streib, Victor L. *Death Penalty for Juveniles.* Bloomington: Indiana University Press, 1987.

Strong, Nathan. *The Reasons and Design of Public Punishments.* Hartford, Conn.: Ebenezer Watson, 1777. [Early American Imprints; New York: Readex Microprint, 1985.]

Tushnet, Mark. *The Death Penalty: Constitutional Issues.* New York: Facts on File, 1994.

Upham, Thomas C. *The Manual of Peace.* New York: Leavitt, Lord; Brunswick, Me.: Joseph Griffin, 1836.

U.S. Bureau of the Census. *Historical Statistics of the United States: Colonial Times to 1970.* Washington, D.C.: U.S. Government Printing Office, 1975.

*U.S. News & World Report* 109, no. 12 (September 24, 1990). "Death in the States."

van den Haag, Ernest. *Punishing Criminals.* New York: Basic Books, 1975. [Lanham, Md.: University Press of America, 1991.]

———. Book Review. *American Political Science Review* 74 (June 1980).

———. Book Review. *Contemporary Issues Criticism* 1 (1982): 40.

———. "Why Capital Punishment?" *Albany Law Review* 54 (1990).

van den Haag, Ernest, and John P. Conrad. *The Death Penalty: A Debate.* New York: Plenum Press, 1983.

Vito, Gennaro F. "The Penalty of Death in the Next Century." In John Klofas and Stan Stojkovic, eds., *Crime and Justice in the Year 2010.* Belmont, Calif.: Wadsworth, 1995.

Wade, Richard C. "Expanding Resources 1901–1945." In Arthur M. Schlesinger, Jr., ed., *The Almanac of American History.* New York: Barnes & Noble, 1993.

*Washington Post,* July 1, 1996. "Preserving Habeas."

Weaver, Warren, Jr. "President Asks Law to Restore Death Penalty: Gives Drug Plan." *New York Times,* March 11, 1973.

Weinbaum, Paul O. *Mobs and Demagogues: The New York Response to Collective Violence in the Early Nineteenth Century.* Ann Arbor, Mich.: UMI Research Press, 1978.

Weisberg, R. "Deregulating Death." In P. B. Kurland, G. Casper, and D. J. Hutchinson, *The Supreme Court Review.* Chicago: University of Illinois Press, 1984.

White, Welsh S. *Life in the Balance: Procedural Safeguards in Capital Cases.* Ann Arbor: University of Michigan Press, 1984.

———. *The Death Penalty in the Eighties: An Examination of the Modern System of Capital Punishment.* Ann Arbor: University of Michigan Press, 1987.

———. *The Death Penalty in the Nineties: An Examination of the Modern System of Capital Punishment.* Ann Arbor: University of Michigan Press, 1991.

Whitlock, Brand. *The Turn of the Balance.* Indianapolis: Bobbs-Merrill, 1907. [Lexington: The University Press of Kentucky, 1970.]

Wilbanks, William. *The Myth of a Racist Criminal Justice System.* Monterey, Calif.: Brooks/Cole, 1987.

Wilson, James Q. *Thinking About Crime.* New York: Basic Books, 1975. [New York: Vintage Books, 1985.]

———. "What to Do about Crime." *Commentary* (September 1994): 25–34.

Wolfgang, Marvin E., and Marc Riedel. "Race, Judicial Discretion, and the Death Penalty." *Annals of the American Academy of Political and Social Science* 407 (May 1973).

Wolpin, Kenneth. "Capital Punishment and Homicide in England: A Summary of Results." *American Economic Review* 68 (May 1978): 422–427.

Wright, Julian H., Jr. "Life-Without-Parole: An Alternative to Death or Not Much of a Life at All?" *Vanderbilt Law Review* 43 (March 1990).

Zimring, Franklin E., and Gordon Hawkins. *Capital Punishment and the American Agenda.* Cambridge: Cambridge University Press, 1986.

## BIOGRAPHICAL REFERENCES

*The Annual Obituary 1982*. New York: St. Martin's Press, 1982.

Bryfonski, Dedria, ed. *Contemporary Issues Criticism*. Detroit: Gale Research Co., 1982.

*Contemporary Biography Yearbook*. New York: The H. W. Wilson Co., 1983.

*Encyclopedia Americana*. New York: Americana Corp., 1993.

Hamilton, Luther, ed. *Memoirs, Speeches and Writings of Robert Rantoul, Jr.* Boston: John P. Jewett, 1854.

Johnson, Allen, and Dumas Malone. *Dictionary of American Biography*. New York: Charles Scribner's Sons, 1934.

Mackey, Philip English, ed. *Voices Against Death*. New York: Burt Franklin, 1976.

*The National Cyclopaedia of American Biography*. New York: James T. White, 1939, 1942.

*The New York Times Biographical Edition*. May 1972.

Trosky, Susan M., ed. *Contemporary Authors*. Detroit: Gale Research Inc., 1969, 1992, 1994.

*Webster's Biographical Dictionary*. Springfield, Mass.: G. & C. Merriam, 1972.

*Who Was Who in America*. Chicago: Marquis, 1963.

Wilson, James Grant, and John Fiske, eds. *Appleton's Cyclopaedia of American Biography*, 1888.

# Index

## About the Editors

BRYAN VILA is Associate Professor of Criminology, Law & Society in the School of Social Ecology at the University of California, Irvine, and Director of the School's Focused Research Group on Orange County Street Gangs. His research specialties include criminology theory, crime control policy, the police, and human ecology. Prior to becoming an academic, Dr. Vila spent seventeen years in local, national, and international law enforcement.

CYNTHIA MORRIS is a freelance writer based in Irvine, California. From 1985 to 1995, she was a research and science writer at the University of California, Irvine. She currently is working (with Dr. Vila) on a second book in Greenwood's Documentary History Series, titled *The Role of Police in American Society: A Documentary History*, and on a novel, *Micronesian Blues*.